THE GLOBAL ECONOMY

BY THE SAME AUTHOR

Beyond Capitalist Planning *(ed.)*
Capital versus the Regions
The Market Economy (volume 1 of
   Towards a New Political Economy)
Out of Crisis *(ed.)*
The Regional Problem
The Socialist Challenge
The State as Entrepreneur *(ed.)*
Uncommon Market

THE GLOBAL ECONOMY

From Meso to Macroeconomics

Stuart Holland

WEIDENFELD AND NICOLSON
LONDON

To Becky

First published in Great Britain by
George Weidenfeld and Nicolson Ltd
91 Clapham High Street, London SW4 7TA

ISBN 0 297 788 40X (cased)
ISBN 0 297 788 418 (paperback)

Filmset by Deltatype, Ellesmere Port
Printed by Butler & Tanner Ltd
Frome and London.

Contents

Acknowledgements   xi
Introduction   xiii

1 The Global Framework   1

1.1 From Reconstruction to Crisis   2
Historic Trends – The Postwar Boom – Modern Capitalism – Recession and Crisis – OPEC and After – The Less and Least Developed – The Pre-OPEC Decline – Beggar-my-Neighbour Deflation

1.2 Ideas and Institutions   11
Investment Push: Marshall Aid – Demand Pull: GATT – The IMF and the World Bank – Keynes versus White – Dollar Dominance and Decline – Devaluation and Deflation – The Fund and the Slump – Top Countries and Top Companies

1.3 The Macroeconomic Framework   21
The Keynesian Challenge – Interest and Inequality – Socialisation – Maximal and Minimal – Beyond Victorian Morality – Keynes versus the Keynesians? – Neo and Post-Keynesian Economics – Keynes and Friedman – Keynes-Plus: The Mixed Economy – Demand and Supply Side – Draining versus Sustaining – Crowding In or Crowding Out? – A US Federal Deficit?

1.4 From Meso to Macroeconomics   360
Marx, Kalecki and Keynes – The Role of the Mesoeconomy – International and Multinational – Macro and Micro Implications – Enterprise and Institutions – Conventions in Question – National and International – The Multinational Model

1.5 Summary   46

2 Demand and Supply   48

2.1 Spending and Savings   48
Ex Ante and *Ex Post* – The Consumption Function – Public and Private Spending – Empirical Testing – Spatial and Social Shifts – The Ratchet Effect

2.2 Income and Distribution   52
The Friedman Hypothesis – Lifetime Consumption? – Unequal Income – Status and Spending – Social, Structural and Spatial Distribution – Redistribution and Demand

2.3 Meso and Macro Dimensions   57
Keynes and Investment Supply – Eichner's Corporate Levy – From Micro to
Meso – Corporate Structure and Self-Finance – Stocks, Shares and Self-Finance
– Meso and Macro Implications – Surplus Generation and Disposal – National
Expansion – Multinational Expansion – Surplus and Unequal Competition –
The Public Presence

2.4 The Modified Multiplier   69
Basic Multipliers – Dynamic Effects – Public and Private Multipliers – Mutual
Demand Generation – Micro Multipliers – Meso Multipliers – International
Multipliers – Multinational Multipliers – Inflows and Outflows – Cost and
Benefits

2.5 Investment and Supply   83
Keynes' Investment Demand Schedule – The Accelerator and Disequilibrium –
The Equilibrated Accelerator – Keynes versus the Accelerator – Kalecki and
After – Micro and Meso 'Accelerators' – Shorter and Longer Term – Planning
and the Planning System – Planning for Life – Practical Limits – Disjointed
Demand and Supply – Dislocated Budgets – Expectations

2.6 Summary   94

3 Growth and Cycles   **97**

3.1 Comparisons and Contrasts   97
The Harrod Model – The Domar Model – Harrod plus Domar – The Role of
the Capital-Output Ratio – Harrod versus Domar – Equilibrium and Dis-
equilibrium – Warranted Growth – Further Questions on Acceleration –
Autonomous and Induced Investment – Capital Stock Adjustment – Marx and
Economic Growth – Quantitative and Qualitative

3.2 Stability and Instability   107
Keynes and the Keynesians – Upswings and Downswings – Harrod's Knife
Edge – Harrod, Robinson and Hobson – Hicks after Harrod – The Role of
Long-Term Investment – Long-Term Expenditure in the Mixed Economy

3.3 The Upper Limits   114
The Innovation Frontier – Trade Constraints – Overheating – Active and
Reserve Labour – The Raised Full-Employment Ceiling – Sustained Accumu-
lation

3.4 Super-Growth and Hyper-Growth   121
Europe and Japan – Profits, Expectations and Growth – Offensive Investment –
Marx and Harrod – Labour Supply and Limits to Growth – Limits to Kaldor –
National and Multinational

3.5 The Lower Limits   128
The Role of Wages – Frictional Unemployment – Declining Wages and Falling
Demand – The First Line of Defence – Public Spending and Effective Demand –
Long-Term Investment and Public Spending – Sustaining versus Draining –

Meso and Micro Dimensions – The Second Line of Defence – Growth and the
Mixed Economy

3.6 Summary   140

4 Investment and Trade   **142**

4.1 Advantage and Disadvantage   142
International and Multinational – Paradox and Practice – Beyond Ricardo –
Absolute Disadvantage – Ricardian Geography – Ricardo's Multinationals –
Opportunity Costs – Costs and Trade

4.2 Proportions and Disproportions   150
Hecksher and Ohlin – The Leontief Paradox – Explanations – Unequal Capital,
Unequal Costs – Dynamisation – The Japanese Challenge

4.3 Global Investment and Trade   155
Global Factor Flows – The Newly Industrialised Countries – Investment versus
Trade – International Evidence – Maximisers and Minimisers – Multinationals
and Absolute Advantage – Low-Cost Labour – High Tech Plus Low Wages –
Beyond the Sweatshop Syndrome – High Tech, High Wages, High Skills

4.4 Investment and Tariffs   167
Paradox and Protection – Tariffs and Industrialisation – National Infants and
Adults – The Mature and Multinational Economy – List: National Economy
and *Zollverein* – Tariffs, Welfare and Interests – Educative or Prohibitive? –
Hilferding on List

4.5 Meso and Macro Dimensions   175
Price-Making Power – Multinational Implications – Import Substitution and
Effective Demand – Potential Dynamic Effects – Multinationals and Protection
– Offensive versus Defensive Trade – The Japanese Challenge – France and
Germany – Spread and Backwash Effects – Qualified Accelerator Theory –
Planning 'Warranted' Growth

4.6 Summary   187

5 Exchange and Payments   **190**

5.1 Paradigms and Paradox   191
US Evidence – UK Evidence – The Limits of Conventional Theory – Towards
Oligopoly Analysis – International and Multinational

5.2 Devaluation and International Trade   197
Active and Passive Responses – Price and Demand Effects – Cost and Supply
Effects – Export Winners – Devaluation and Deflation – The 1967 Sterling
Devaluation

5.3 Multinational Trade and Devaluation   206
Reverse Trade? – Perverse Trade? – From Perfect to Imperfect Competition –
From Imperfect Competition to Oligopoly – Asymmetric Effects

5.4 Revaluation and International Trade   212
Scale and Specialisation – The Quality Effect – Price Effects – Structural Effects
– Specialisation – Penetration Pricing – Price Umbrellas – Successive and
Successful Investment – UK and US: Failure and Decline – Finance Capital –
'Offensive' Export Strategies – The Long-Term View

5.5 Multinational Trade and Revaluation   225
From National to Multinational – Offsetting Revaluation – Capacity Use –
Versus Exchange-Rate Changes

5.6 Summary   230

6 Transfers and Technologies   **232**

6.1 Transfer Payments and Pricing   232
Unrecorded and Under-Recorded – Macroeconomic Effects – National and
Multinational – International Trade – Normal or Cost-Plus Pricing – Transfer
Pricing – Nominal versus Real Prices – Price-Makers and Price-Takers –
Inflation, Trade and Tax – Avoidance versus Evasion – Follow-the-Leader –
Complex Transfers – The Inflation Effect – Cumulative Effects

6.2 Evidence and Evaluation   246
Scope and Scale – The Ford Transit Truck – Pharmaceuticals – Implications –
Electronics – Global Control – Commodity Trade – Switching – The Role of
Tax Havens – Offshore Banking – Global Trends – Transfer Booking –
Transfer Parking – Accounting and Accountability

6.3 Innovation and Technology Transfers   258
National and International – Keynesian Technical Progress – Top Companies
and Top Countries – The Conventional Model – Simple and Complex –
Multinational Transfers – The Modified Product Cycle – Technology Transfers
and Payments – Technologies and Technicians – Global Standards – Global
Sales Strategy

6.4 Technology, Growth and Trade   272
The Keynesian Model – Post-Keynesian Realities – Globalisation – Global
Multipliers, and Divisors – Harrod Plus Multinationals – Dependency and
Dualism – Relative Autonomy

6.5 Summary   279

7 Money and Monetarism   **281**

7.1 The Quantity Theory of Money   282
Hume and After – Ricardo versus Hume – Fisher's Assumptions – Competitive
Assumptions – Marshall, Keynes and Money

7.2 Keynes and the Classics 287
Interest-Responsive Savings – Keynes, Profits and Expectations – Barometers, Stock Markets and Casinos – Liquidity Preference – Liquidity Preference and Disequilibrium – Psychology, Saving and Spending – Hoarding versus Borrowing – Totem and Taboo – Neutral versus Natural – Low Interest Rates

7.3 The Keynesian-Neoclassical Synthesis: *LM/IS* 295
The *IS* Curve – The *LM* Schedule – *LM* Plus *IS* – Price-Making Power – Lower Costs versus Higher Interest Rates – Bigger Business, Lower Interest Rates – Multinational Transfer Pricing – Micro and Meso *IS* Schedules – Interest in Perspective – The Corporate Levy – Planning Supply and Demand

7.4 Friedman and Monetarism 306
Friedman and the Demand for Money – The 'Crowding-Out' Hypothesis – Causation or Mirrors? – Stability in Question – Keynes versus Friedman – Keynes Plus Friedman? – Superficial Synthesis – Qualified Full Employment

7.5 Monetarism in Question 313
Cherchez la Monnaie – Exchange Rates – Which Money Supply? – Hidden or Revealed? – Powers of Prediction? – Monetary Targets – Off Target, Off Course – Abandonment of 'Minimum Lending' – The Purifiers – The Purists – The Pragmatists – 'Monetarism is Dead: Official'

7.6 Summary 328

8 Inflation and Deflation 330

8.1 Money Push and Demand Pull 331
Deflationary and Inflationary Gaps – Budgetary and Fiscal Policy – Monetarist Claims – Cautious and Brazen – Contested Claims: The US and the UK – Cost-Push and Demand-Pull

8.2 Cost-Push: Big Unions 338
The Phillips Curve – Proportionality? – US Evidence – UK Evidence – Wage Costs and Labour Supply – Global Labour Reserves – Dynamic Effects – Over-Consumption and Union Power – Qualifying Factors – The Mesoeconomy – The Microeconomy

8.3 Cost-Push: Big Business 348
Price-Making Power – From Micro to Meso – Mesoeconomic Power – Pricing and the Product Cycle – Prices and Unequal Competition – The Competitive Frontier – Accolades and Ironies – Limits to Competition Policy – Inflation and the 'Price Umbrella' – Multinational Pricing and Inflation

8.4 Stagflation and Deflation 358
Disinflation and Cash Flow – Reflation and Disinflation – Circular and Cumulative Causation – Virtuous and Vicious Circles – Deflation and Cumulative Decline – Social Income and Expenditure

8.5 Prices and Incomes   366
Wage and Price Controls – Proto and Neo Keynesians – The Need for
Disaggregation – Stagflation and Capacity Use – Devaluation and Inflation –
Banks, Bonds and Borrowing – Inflation and Fixed Interest – Commodities and
Inflation – Deficit Financing and Tax Push – Inflexibility and Inflation – Prices
and Incomes in Context – Quantity and Quality – Social Justice

8.6 Summary   376

9 Accumulation and Crisis   **379**

9.1 Marx Plus – Keynes Plus   379
From Marx to Keynes – Keynes after Marx – Under-Consumption and
Deflation – Multiplier Effects – Cumulative Crisis – Capital Intensity and
Over-Investment – The Innovation Frontier – Excess Capacity – Rising
Technical Composition – Disproportion and Imbalance

9.2 Cycles and Crisis   389
Crisis and Restructuring – Innovations and Public Spending – Schumpeter:
'Creative Destruction' – 'Bunched' Innovation – Small Firms and Big Firms –
Four Phases – Scope and Limits – Kondratieff: Long Cycles – Stylisation and
Simplification – Mensch: Towards a Fifth Cycle?

9.3 Compound Crisis   398
Four Theses – 'Fordism', Expansion and Crisis – Fordism in Question – Short
and Long Term – The Role of the State – The Keynesian Case – Fiscal Crisis and
Social Spending – State Intervention and Crisis – State Capitalism – Questions
on Late Capitalism – Social Distribution

9.4 Global Crisis   409
Past, Present and Future – The Debt Crisis – The 'Eurocurrency' Markets –
Lenders and Borrowers – National and Multinational Interest Rates –
Speculation versus Precaution – Expectations and Instability – Real and
Pretend – Beggar-my- Neighbour – Better-my-Neighbour – Global Challenge

9.5 Summary   422

Bibliography   424
Index   435

Acknowledgements

I am grateful to several people who have helped in the commissioning, writing, processing and publishing of the trilogy of which this is the second volume.

They include Robert Baldock, formerly an editor with Weidenfeld and Nicolson and now with Yale University Press, who first commissioned the work; Ben Buchan, still with Weidenfeld, who helped see it through several drafts with understandably varying degrees of patience and desperation; and Heather Sherrat, who drew the diagrams, often from fragmentary sketches.

I am deeply indebted to Bill Bourne, who word-processed the text with sustained and enthusiastic interest, and to Gareth Locksley, who not only read successive drafts but also made a major contribution to both the empirical evidence and the analysis. I am also grateful to Michael Barratt Brown, who made a host of useful suggestions, and to Terry Ward and Paul Ormerod, whose comments and assistance in the earlier chapters of this volume were both helpful and encouraging.

Throughout this text I have been able to draw on the excellent work of former students such as Henry Ergas, Richard Luedde-Neurath, Dan Jones and Edmond Sciberras, all of whom have established reputations for their own analysis of multinational big business. It was Robin Murray who first alerted me, many years ago, to the scale of transfer pricing by multinationals, and much of the empirical support for the models developed in chapter 6 is drawn from work edited by him. Chapter 7 makes extensive use of Meghnad Desai's outstanding work on the testing of monetarism. Christopher Barclay and members of the statistical division of the House of Commons have been helpful in providing information which has been both useful in debate and relevant to specific parts of the argument.

My thanks to Jenny Holland are very much due for encouraging me to complete the work on as wide a canvas as originally envisaged and to keep on with the job. This volume is dedicated to our daughter Rebecca, who through much of her early life asked – with reason – whether I would not stop writing and come and play with her.

Introduction

This is the second volume of a trilogy called *Towards a New Political Economy*. The first volume, *The Market Economy: From Micro to Meso-economics* (1987), covered issues normally described as price theory and the theory of the firm. This volume considers what is normally called macro-economics and the theory of international trade. The third volume, *The Political Economy: From Theory to Practice* (forthcoming), will deal with issues which in much conventional economics teaching are barely covered at all – although it is precisely such issues in which many students are most interested.

This book employs the concept of the global economy in two ways. First, there is the overall or aggregate economy normally examined in the analytical framework of economics. Second, there is the world economy of international trade and payments. French economists have used the term 'global economy' in both senses for many years.

But *The Global Economy* also seeks to advance on conventional macro-economics and trade theory in key respects. For one thing, it argues that the synthesis of so-called Keynesian demand economics with conventional neoclassical analysis of supply in fact gelded the power of many of Keynes' own insights into the working of market economies in the first half of the twentieth century. For another, by analysing the role of public spending and the mixed economy in the context of neo-Keynesian models of economic growth, it shows the superficiality of monetarist claims that such spending drains rather than sustains the modern market economy. Further, it argues that both the Keynesian and monetarist paradigms of the macroeconomy have been compromised by the rise of multinational big business, which has divorced the conventional micro-macro synthesis popularised first by economists such as Samuelson, and more recently by others such as Begg, Fischer and Dornbusch.

Defending Keynes versus Friedman will soon be an exercise for historians of economic thought. But extending Keynes' own insights to the economics of the postwar mixed economy is still a priority for political economists. Modifying conventional models of international trade and payments to account for the rise of multinational capital is imperative if we are to understand how the world has changed both since Keynes and since Ricardo. Understanding the current crisis of the global economy means both recognising the role of the mixed economy and multinational capital, and gaining insight into the end of the long cycle of postwar economic growth which was aided and abetted by dollar dominance and the hegemony of the United States.

Analysis of the modern mesoeconomy and the role of multinational capital is integral to such qualification of conventional macroeconomic theory. This is reflected in the central role which it plays in this volume. Policy prescriptions derived from this analysis are elaborated in the third volume of the trilogy.

If *Towards a New Political Economy* helps to counter unreal teaching of the real world, it will have been worth writing. If it reinforces the case for new national and international policies, that will be a bonus. Some of its arguments have already registered in economics teaching. Others have been adopted by trades unions, political parties and some governments. In the meantime, I trust that the reader will at least feel the effort of following the argument to be worthwhile.

Stuart Holland
House of Commons
April 1987

1 The Global Framework

For some thirty years after the Second World War, economics reigned as the queen of the social sciences and appeared to have gained a global consensus. The revolutionary power behind the throne had been John Maynard Keynes. Ministers who had never read him, and some advisers who had, were proud to call themselves 'Keynesians'. Individual problems remained as a challenge to the intellect and to institutions, not least those of inflation and spreading the gains from growth worldwide. Nonetheless, Keynes appeared to have transformed economics from a dismal science into a means of producing a brighter future.

With hindsight, it is not hard to see why this was so. Keynes' *General Theory* (1936) not only gave a coherent rationale for state intervention in spending and demand: it also left the supply side of the economy largely free for the play of market forces. Thus competition could determine what was produced, in what way and on what scale, as well as 'how the value of the final product would be distributed' (Keynes, 1936, chapter 24). Moreover, the role of the Keynesian state as demand manager, spender, social guardian and umpire of the competitive process offered more than techniques of national or international economic policy. Keynes offered a middle way between the excesses of a wholly planned and a wholly unplanned economy. In doing so, he also appeared to have reconciled political democracy and economic freedoms.

Few people could ask for more. Yet by the mid 1970s the postwar Keynesian consensus was thrown into question by the crisis in the international economy. Keynesian 'fine tuning' of demand, with appropriate fiscal, monetary and exchange-rate policies, was no longer able to command widespread political support following devaluation of the dollar, structural imbalance in global trade, soaring commodity prices and rising unemployment. Economic theorists such as Milton Friedman, upstaged during the Keynesian era, stepped in front of the footlights with simple remedies for global economic crisis: reduce the money supply, cut public spending, restore 'flexibility' in labour markets, float exchange rates and the market would steer us out of crisis. Committed Keynesians gave way to casual or enthusiastic monetarists. They prioritised the fight against inflation, and cut public expenditure and welfare programmes to reduce import deficits. Thereby, they reduced other countries' exports, and contributed to global slump.

Such new economic 'realism' downgrades the postwar Keynesian commitment to full employment, high public spending, managed exchange rates and international credit agencies whose initial aim was to promote and sustain high trade, payments and welfare. It is less neo-Keynesian than monetarist, while monetarism itself is but a new name for an old game of putting 'sound money' and 'sound profits' before people and the public interest, as if either money or profits could be generated without sustained or increased public and private spending.

Meanwhile, multinational big business has established a new global mesoeconomic power between the micro capital of national economies and the global macroeconomy which it now spans like a colossus (Greek: *micros* – small; *macros* – large; *mesos* – intermediate). As analysed in detail in *The Market Economy*, this phenomenon, evident in embryo in the late nineteenth century, and maturing between the wars, has now flourished on such a scale that a few dozen companies dominate the world's output, employment, pricing and trade. By the early 1980s, 200 such multinational companies accounted for a third of global GDP, or one and a half times the production of the world's less developed economies including Latin America, Africa, India and China.

Such multinational capital has profoundly changed the global framework of policies pursued by governments and international agencies. Yet most governments behind the big international institutions, such as the Organisation for Economic Cooperation and Development (OECD) and the International Monetary Fund (IMF), have failed to grasp the international implications of a world economy dominated by multinational big business, whether in agribusiness, industry, services or finance. Virtually no international agency other than the United Nations Conference on Trade and Development (UNCTAD) makes any sustained effort to account for the share of multinational big business in the output, pricing, trade or payments of the global macroeconomy. Such governments and most institutions thus are seeking to build a New International Economic Order (NIEO) while failing to recognise the role in production, distribution or finance of the very firms whose accountability is a keystone to its construction.

1.1 From Reconstruction to Crisis

This was not among the problems faced by the architects of a new international economic order after 1945. But there were other problems and other precedents which gave few grounds for optimism. The cycle of boom, slump, armament and war had rent the world economy twice in the first half of the twentieth century. For policy-makers to assume to overcome it appeared not only bright-eyed, but positively brazen.

Historic Trends

Angus Maddison's analysis of rates of growth among the developed countries since the early nineteenth century, as illustrated in Table 1.1(a), shows that while the growth of gross domestic product averaged more than 2 per cent per year until the onset of the First World War, and just under 2 per cent thereafter, the growth of GDP per head was closer to 1 per cent per year for most of that period, with an exception of 1½ per cent per year from 1870 to 1913. The rate of growth in the capital stock, or capital formation, fell by nearly half from the period before the First World War to the interwar period, while the rate of growth of exports fell fourfold from an estimated 4 per cent a year between 1820 and 1870 to 1 per cent a year between 1913 and 1950.

TABLE 1.1(a)   The Developed Countries

% growth per year	GDP	GDP per head	Capital stock	Exports
1820–1870	2.2	1.0	(n.a.)	4.0
1870–1913	2.5	1.4	2.9	3.9
1913–1950	1.9	1.2	1.7	1.0
1950–1973	4.9	3.8	5.5	8.6
1973–1979	2.5	2.0	4.4	4.8

Source: Maddison (1982).

Little in Maddison's scenario could presage the remarkable rate of growth of GDP of nearly 5 per cent a year and GDP per head of nearly 4 per cent a year from 1950 to 1973, nor the increase in the capital accumulation of over 5 per cent or of export trade of over 8 per cent (more than double the previous historic long-term record) during the same period.

   Likewise, there was little precedent for the remarkable output growth of the less developed countries. In the period from 1952/4 to 1970, as shown in Bairoch's estimates in Table 1.1(b), they more than doubled their annual average rate of growth of GDP, and GDP per head, relative to the interwar period, even if their share of world export trade declined by a third between the interwar period and the decade of the 1960s.

TABLE 1.1(b)   The Less Developed Countries

% growth per year	GDP	GDP per head	World exports share
1900–1913	2.1	1.2	.17
1913–1929	1.9	0.9	.21
1929–1952/4	2.2	0.6	.28
1952/4–1960	4.8	2.4	.23
1960–1970	5.1	2.4	.19

Source: Bairoch (1975).

The Postwar Boom

This unprecedented growth of output in the post World War Two period was reflected, and in large part made possible, by dramatic increases in labour productivity. As shown in Table 1.2, while labour productivity in the United States maintained a steady average increase from 1870 to 1970, in the European economies from 1950 to 1970 it doubled, tripled or near quintupled relative to the 1870–1950 trend. In Japan, the results were even more dramatic, with a fourfold increase in the 1950–60 decade and a sixfold increase in the decade from 1960 to 1970.

TABLE 1.2   The Rise and Fall of Productivity
(GDP per hour worked)

	1870–1913	1913–50	1950–60	1960–70	1970–80	1973–80	1980–84*
France	1.8	1.7	4.3	5.1	3.8	3.7	1.6
W. Germany	1.9	1.2	6.6	5.2	3.6	3.2	1.8
Italy	1.2	1.8	4.3	6.3	2.5	1.7	0.3
Japan	1.8	1.4	5.7	9.6	4.3	2.6	2.8
UK	1.1	1.5	2.3	3.2	2.4	1.6	2.7
USA	2.1	2.5	2.4	2.4	1.5	0.8	1.2

* GDP per person employed
Source: Freeman, Clark and Soete (1982) and OECD.

Table 1.3 shows the results commanding most interest at the time – the abolition of mass unemployment and in some countries its reduction, from the late 1950s until the early 1970s, to effectively 'frictional' levels of people changing jobs.

TABLE 1.3   From Unemployment to Unemployment 1933–85*

	1933	1959–67	1973	1977	1979	1981	1985
Belgium	10.6	2.4	2.9	7.8	8.7	12.9	13.9
Denmark	14.5	1.4	0.7	5.8	5.3	9.5	8.4
France	na	0.7	1.8	4.8	6.0	8.9	8.3
W. Germany	14.8	1.2	1.0	4.0	3.4	6.7	8.0
Ireland	na	4.6	5.6	9.2	7.5	11.5	10.9
Italy	5.9	6.2	4.9	6.4	7.5	9.6	9.8
Japan	na	1.4	1.2	2.0	2.0	2.2	2.6
Netherlands	9.7	0.9	2.3	4.1	4.1	10.2	13.7
UK	13.9	1.8	2.5	5.7	5.8	11.3	12.6
USA	20.5	5.3	4.9	7.0	5.8	8.9	9.5

* Per cent of total labour force unemployed.
Source: Freeman, Clark and Soete (1982), OECD and *Eurostat*.

Modern Capitalism

It is hardly surprising that Maddison should see this postwar period as a 'Golden Age', nor that recovery in countries such as West Germany, France and Italy should have been hailed as economic 'miracles'. Some commentators, such as Andrew Shonfield (1965), asked what was it that converted capitalism from the cataclysmic failure of the 1930s into the great engine of prosperity of the postwar period. He concluded that the change reflected both (i) a new Keynesian-inspired intervention by the state through planning and positive use of the public sector, and (ii) accelerated innovation in a global economy increasingly exposed to market opportunities and competitiveness through international trade. Others, such as Anthony Crosland (1956), argued that the change in both government intervention and public spending was so novel that it was misleading to use the word 'capitalism' to describe the postwar period.

Recession and Crisis

But by the mid 1970s the global postwar boom had bust. Maddison's figures in Table 1.1(a) show that between 1973 and 1979 the rate of growth of exports and GDP per head had fallen by nearly half in the developed countries compared to the period 1950–73, and that capital accumulation was also declining.

The result was that mass unemployment was back on the agenda with a vengeance. As shown in Table 1.3 – apart from the USA, West Germany and Denmark – by 1985 the registered level of unemployment was nearly as high or higher than it had been in the early 1930s. In the UK, registered unemployment in 1985 would have been higher than in 1933 if the government had not changed the statistics in a manner which understated the real unemployment level (partly by obliging workers over the age of 60 to register for benefits at social security rather than unemployment offices, partly by Youth Training Schemes, and by other cosmetic devices).

Meanwhile, as shown in Table 1.2, the registered average annual growth of productivity by the mid 1980s had slumped from its peak growth rates of the 1950s and 1960s in the leading market economies. In France and West Germany it fell by more than two-thirds, in Japan by more than a third and in Italy by more than 90 per cent. In the USA, despite record overall economic growth in the early 1950s, it halved. In the UK it was down by a half from 1973 to 1980, while the registered normal increase from 1980 to 1984 reflected more the closure of less effective plant than an increase in overall efficiency.

OPEC and After

What went wrong? One of the simplest answers which became part of the conventional reasoning in policy circles in the early seventies was the major increase in petroleum prices made by the Organisation of Petroleum Exporting Countries (OPEC) in the autumn of 1983. Certainly, as shown in Figure 1.1, the initial price increase was dramatic, by over 200 per cent from 1973 to 1975 in real terms.

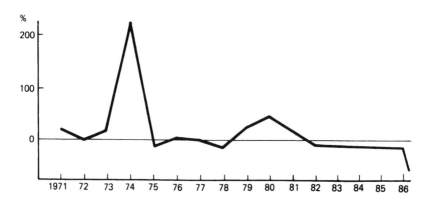

FIG. 1.1 OPEC rates of price change since 1971 (% annual change in petroleum prices) (Source: World Bank and IEA)

However, as shown in Figure 1.2, while inflation rose from an average of 5 per cent to over 12 per cent in the industrial market economies between 1972 and the end of 1974, in large part because of the OPEC price increases, it had fallen again to below 7 per cent by the end of 1978 and, except for a short period in 1979–80 reflecting the 1979 OPEC price increases, it fell again to less than 4 per cent by the end of 1985.

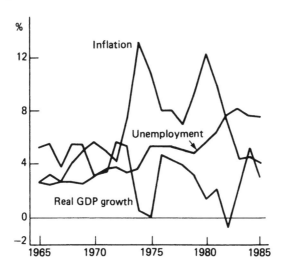

FIG. 1.2   Growth, inflation and unemployment in the seven major industrial countries (Canada, France, Germany, Italy, Japan, the UK and the US) (Source: For GDP growth: World Bank; for inflation and unemployment: OECD.)

In practice, the results of the original OPEC price increases were complex rather than simple. For one thing, several of the OPEC countries which gained major surpluses as a result of the initial price increases from 1973 invested them either directly through shares in companies in Europe or the United States, or – more substantially – on the so-called Eurodollar markets. These in turn were recycled towards middle-income economies which, as illustrated in Table 1.4, reduced their annual rate of growth of GDP in the decade 1973–83, but managed to sustain growth levels which were nearly double those of the industrial market economies. In particular, major petrodollar surpluses were recycled through the private Eurodollar markets and multinational banks to the key Latin American economies which had already come into the 'newly industrialised' category. The debt crisis for such countries in the 1980s, reflecting reduced exports with increased borrowing, was yet to come.

The Less and Least Developed

For the low-income countries other than India and China, as shown in Table

1.4, the picture was dire. Most of them were far more sensitive than the developed countries to an increase in oil prices, both because they lacked alternative energy sources and because oil amounted to a greater share of their total import bill. For many such countries, the problem of higher-cost imports due to the increased price of oil was compounded by falling prices for their commodity exports with the onset of recession.

TABLE 1.4   The Onset of Recession

	Annual GDP growth (%)		Annual GDP growth (%) per head
	1965–73	1973–83	1965–83
1. Industrial Market Economies	4.7	2.4	2.5
2. High-Income Oil Exporters	9.0	5.2	3.8
3. Upper-Middle-Income Economies	7.4	4.9	3.8
4. Middle-Income Economies	7.1	4.7	3.4
Oil Exporters	7.2	4.9	3.3
Oil Importers	7.0	4.5	3.5
5. Low-Income Economies	5.5	5.0	2.7
China and India	6.0	5.4	3.2
Other Low Income	3.7	3.3	0.7
Sub-Saharan Africa	4.2	1.7	−0.2

Source: World Bank, *Development Report*, 1985, Tables 1 and 2.

This was in part due to an exaggerated increase in commodity prices with an undue and unmanaged 'spurt' in global demand in the early 1970s, but also due to deflation or a cut in domestic demand from the mid seventies by the developed countries as they tried to adjust to the higher price of oil imports by reducing their overall import demands. For individual countries such as Zambia – ninety per cent dependent on copper for its export trade – the result was little short of catastrophic. And as shown in Table 1.4, while low-income economies other than India and China experienced a reduction of their average annual rates of growth of GDP of only just over a tenth in the decade 1973–83 compared to the period 1965–73, growth for sub-Saharan Africa fell over the same period from 4.2 to 1.7 per cent, reflecting massive rural poverty and reducing the ability of peasant farmers to withstand the crop and cash loss from drought both in 1974–5 and more especially in 1984–5. Meanwhile, 'miracle' economies of the sixties and seventies such as Brazil were increasingly forced by the IMF to slow their domestic economic growth.

The cumulative result was a major contraction both of North-South and South-South trade in the global economy. For instance, until the early 1970s

Brazil had been exporting some 70 per cent of its manufactures to other developing economies. But these countries were forced to cut back manufacturing imports to pay for higher oil prices, which in turn collapsed Brazilian export sales.

The Pre-OPEC Decline

Clearly, in one sense, the OPEC price increases from 1973 were a turning point in the postwar period. As illustrated in Figure 1.3, the demand-pull effect of an expansion of world trade, which had averaged nearly double the rate of increase of world output for 30 years, gave way to a trade growth much closer to the world's output increase.

Nonetheless, such simple explanations of the oil price increase and contracted trade fail to explain both the underlying causes of crisis in several of the developed countries from the mid 1960s and the reaction or over-reaction of governments to those increases themselves.

TABLE 1.5   Relative Growth and Decline of Export Volume

Average annual growth (%)	1953–59	1959–71	1971–74	1974–84
USA	0.2	6.3	13.6	1.6
West Germany	16.9	9.2	10.3	3.7
Japan	19.0	15.0	11.1	7.7

Source: Armstrong, Glyn and Harrison (1984) and IMF, *Financial Statistics Yearbook*, 1985.

For instance, as shown in Table 1.5, while the United States increased its annual export growth in the 1960s relative to the 1950s, and nearly doubled its export rate in the early 1970s, such export growth slumped in the decade after 1974. The exports growth rate of Japan and West Germany, the two key 'winners' on postwar world markets, declined over the same pre-OPEC period. West Germany's short-term recovery in the early 1970s was short-lived, with the annual rate of growth of exports from 1974 to 1984 less than a quarter of the 1953–59 period. For Japan the decline was also considerable, with export growth rates down by more than a half in the decade from 1974 relative to the peak rates of the 1950s.

The symptoms of declining growth are even more marked from the evidence on the fall in the rate of growth of overall gross capital formation in West Germany from the mid 1950s. As shown in Table 1.6, a rate of growth of total investment (industry, housing, infrastructure, etc) of over 9 per cent a

TABLE 1.6   Declining Capital Formation: West Germany*

1950–54	1955–59	1960–64	1965–69	1970–74
9.2	7.1	6.3	3.0	0.2

* Average annual percentage rates of gross domestic capital formation.
Source: Zinn (1978).

year between 1950 and 1954, had fallen to an average of 3 per cent between 1965 and 1969 and to only one fifth of one per cent from 1970 to 1974. In other words, capital formation in West Germany had virtually ground to a halt before the impact of the OPEC price rises in 1973.

Beggar-My-Neighbour Deflation

On the global demand side, there were in addition the deflationary policies pursued by leading governments. For instance, faced with an oil slick on their growth prospects from the first round of OPEC price increases in 1973, the OECD governments could have touched their demand management steering or changed down a gear in economic growth. In fact most of them slammed the brakes on their domestic economies to reduce non-oil import demand and pay for the higher cost of oil imports. Each government thereby claimed that it was putting its own house in order. But what might have been good sense for some countries at such a time was not sense when all of them deflated together. One country's imports are other countries' exports. As shown in Figure 1.3, mutual contraction of import demand from 1974 reduced the growth of global export trade and with it the trade demand-pull on domestic rates of economic growth. In contrast with the 'better-my-neighbour'

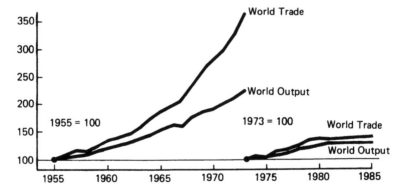

FIG. 1.3   Trade-led Growth – and Decline (Source: *The Economist*, UN and GATT)

expansion of trade throughout the 1960s and early seventies, there was a 'beggar-my-neighbour' deflation of trade from 1975 onwards.

Thus import contraction by the leading world economies in turn damaged their export trade – as well as the commodity export trade of many less developed countries.

1.2 Ideas and Institutions

The cumulative results were devastating for developed and less developed countries alike. For more than a decade, the world economy has suffered from low real growth, a major contraction of trade, record levels of unemployment and soaring debt. By 1986 the total value of world debt was in excess of $3 trillion (three thousand billion), or some half the total gross domestic product of the developing countries (BIS and Bank of England, 1986). The crisis in many ways is worse than the 1930s. This is partly because the globalisation of trade, investment and exchange in the international economy has made countries more interdependent, thereby reducing their capacity for national recovery policies. Also, the optimism concerning public intervention engendered in the mid 1930s by Keynes' *General Theory* was replaced in the 1970s by a new-found pessimism about the effectiveness of public action, due partly to the simplicity of Milton Friedman's claims that Keynesianism had failed and was outdated.

This is not to say that Keynes got everything right and Friedman everything wrong. However, a distinction needs to be made in this context between Keynes' own economics and those of so-called Keynesians. Moreover, Keynes died in 1946 and therefore did not live to see key changes in the postwar global economy which have qualified or undermined some of his main policy prescriptions.

Nonetheless, in contrast with Friedman's claims, it can reasonably be argued that the so-called 'Keynesian era' for a third of a century was an unparalleled economic success, while a decade of monetarism has been a scarcely less qualified disaster. It is therefore relevant to analyse the main features of the postwar period and the nature of some of its Keynesian institutions.

Investment Push – Marshall Aid

For instance, it has become commonplace to claim that those who lost the war – Germany, Japan, Italy and, in one sense, France – thereby won the first economic round of the ensuing peace. Each experienced so-called 'miraculous' recovery in the 1950s and 1960s. Yet the basis of this recovery was less the restoration of market forces, on the lines now recommended by monetarists for the global economy, than massive public transfers by the United States. Part of this was through the Marshall Aid Programme of 1948, named after and promoted by the then Secretary of State and former wartime Chief of Staff George Marshall.

In this context the motives for Marshall Aid – whether altruism or concern by some in the US Congress to stop Communism – are less important than its quantitative global impact.

TABLE 1.7   Postwar American Aid ($ million per year)*

	UK	France	West Germany	Italy	Japan
1946–7	1,722	948	371	474	419
1948–50	857	668	847	378	373

* US non-military grants and government long-term capital.
Source: Armstrong, Glyn and Harrison (1984).

Table 1.7 shows that the launching of the Marshall Aid programme in 1948 followed two years in which already sizeable transfers had been made by the United States through non-military grants and government long-term capital expenditure in favour of the wartime 'losers' West Germany, Italy and Japan, with double to triple the same aid to France and nearly double that again to the United Kingdom. From 1948, with the advent of the Truman administration and the onset of the Cold War, this advantage in favour of the United Kingdom was more than halved, while US aid to West Germany outstripped that to France and more than doubled that to Italy and Japan.

Further, while Marshall Aid may have been meant to support market forces and eschew four-letter words such as 'plan', in practice it did nothing of the sort. This was partly because the US left the main beneficiaries themselves to sort out how they would allocate the money through a committee of the OEEC (Organisation for European Economic Cooperation – forerunner of the later OECD).

In France, the availability of 'counterpart funds' from Marshall Aid assistance enabled the French not only to give a boost to their postwar 'indicative planning' framework by scheduling specific funds towards major public investment projects but also thereby to break through what Jacques Delors has called the 'Malthusianism' and pessimism of a society which under free-market forces had seen no increase in real national product for 35 years.

French GDP only regained its 1913 real level in 1929, then slumped, to regain it once more in 1939, when it was interrupted by the war. By 1948, under the First Plan, it had recovered the 1939 level of output within three years (Delors, in Holland, 1978, chapter 1).

In Italy, Marshall Aid made possible the first ever long-term economic plan (*Programma a lungo termine*) from 1948 to 1953, which the government presented to the organising committee for Marshall Aid in October 1948 and for which it gained approval. This plan was actively supported by Left, Right and Centre in Italy, and introduced under a Conservative Christian Democratic government. It was reckoned such a success that an even longer-term plan, the *Piano Vanoni*, was adopted for the period 1955 to 1964. In turn Marshall Aid funds were used in both these plans for precisely the kinds of activities which the monetarists now abhor – public expenditure on regional development, and modernisation programmes undertaken through public enterprise groups such as the Institute for Industrial Reconstruction (Holland, 1972).

In West Germany, Marshall Aid funds were distributed through a public agency known as the *Kreditanstalt für Wiederaufbau* or Reconstruction Loans Corporation, rather than left to free-market forces. As Shonfield (1965, p. 276) has put it: 'the heroic legend of German reconstruction as a spontaneous upsurge of aggressive private enterprise has been so sedulously fostered that the crucial part played by the public authorities in the process tends to be overlooked. In fact they not only supplied the money, but also exercised a significant influence in selecting the projects on which it was to be spent.' Indeed the famous currency reform of 1948 in West Germany which ended hyper-inflation and restored stability did so in part by limiting for any one individual the number of Reichsmarken which could be translated into the new Deutschmark.

Therefore, in stark contrast to two of Friedman's key tenets, the postwar German recovery was based upon both social redistribution and structural intervention by public authorities – all on the basis of the aid injection through Marshall Aid funds.

Demand Pull – GATT

If the Marshall Aid Programme was designed to give a push to investment reconstruction in the war-strained economies of Western Europe, the postwar US administration was especially concerned to ensure a parallel liberalisation of international trade. Complementing the investment push through Marshall Aid, this could be conceived as seeking to provide demand pull through the expansion of mutual trade and 'virtuous circle' effects, via export multipliers on employment, income and investment. Such concern by the United States reflected its new role in political and military affairs in the Western world, and the desire of many of its industrialists to ensure that if the markets of Western Europe were to be aided and abetted in their recovery through Marshall Aid, then the gains available to the United States from such a programme should be continued through the postwar period by the export access for US goods to European and other markets.

The formal framework for such postwar liberalisation was the General Agreement on Trade and Tariffs (GATT). As Brett (1985, pp. 75ff) has stressed, the actual structure of GATT is itself largely historical accident. It was the by-product of a far more ambitious proposal by Keynes in 1945 to establish an International Trade Organisation. But the US blocked the ITO initiative, and proposals for liberalism in trade encountered strong opposition from India, Australia and other countries, so that the resulting GATT agreement which came into force in January 1948 was envisaged as a temporary compromise. The Indians bluntly called GATT a one-way street for Western goods. Various safeguard clauses could in principle be invoked by countries which ran into serious balance-of-payments difficulties. Nonetheless, the fundamental reasoning of GATT was that the working of the market mechanism through the liberalisation of trade would assure precisely the 'harmony of interests' advocated by Adam Smith and his neoclassical disciples.

But in reality the progress towards liberalisation was relatively slow. It followed rather than caused the high rates of capital accumulation and output growth during postwar reconstruction in economies such as West Germany, Italy or Japan. This was partly because GATT was not the only actor in the international arena. On a more limited basis, certain European countries proceeded with policies both for a Free Trade Area and a Common Market. The decisive series of GATT negotiations were those of the so-called Kennedy Round, whose first round was begun in November 1964 and completed in May 1967. This negotiated reductions of tariffs equivalent to about one-third of the then existing world rates. The agreement was that these should be phased out over a further five-year period, with the last instalment in 1972.

No new major tariff reductions were on GATT's agenda by 1974, by which time the impact of OPEC oil price rises – following a period of major inflation in the price of basic commodities in world trade – had considerably destabilised the balance-of-payments prospects of the oil-importing countries which were GATT signatories.

Thus, GATT certainly played a role in the postwar recovery. But the multinational companies who were the main actors in postwar international trade and payments proved to be less influenced by tariffs the more global their reach became. This was partly because multinationals increasingly invested within other countries and behind tariff barriers, in some cases substituting investment for trade (as analysed in Chapter 4). It was also due to the scope they found for so-called 'transfer pricing' or large-scale under-invoicing of imports and over-invoicing of exports (analysed in Chapter 6), which enabled them to circumvent tariff barriers where these remained high – especially in some of the faster growing developing economies.

The IMF and the World Bank

The establishment of the International Monetary Fund (IMF) and the International Bank for Reconstruction and Development (the World Bank) was influenced by Keynes, but in practice dominated by the United States and its prevailing economic orthodoxies. Both institutions were the outcome of the conference at Bretton Woods in New Hampshire in 1944 to agree on a system of international payments for the postwar period, and which included representatives of the key countries that had taken part in the alliance against Germany, Italy and Japan.

Keynes himself later said that the International Monetary Fund ought to be called a bank and the World Bank should be called a fund. This back-to-front name game was to be reflected in a constrained role for the World Bank in the later postwar period. In terms of the Bretton Woods objectives, the IMF was supposed to deal with short-term foreign-exchange and balance-of-payments problems. The World Bank was scheduled for the more ambitious aim of global development.

On the trade and payments front, Keynes was concerned that the key lessons should be learned from the crises of the 1930s. In his view, a system of floating exchange rates could lead to disaster in international economic affairs. One of the vital roles of the Fund in what might be called the 'partial Keynesian' period of its operation, was to achieve an ordered system for exchange-rate changes. It was anticipated that such changes would be made only in the face of serious and persistent disequilibria in the balance of payments of individual countries, and only after consultations with the IMF. IMF lending to an individual country would be conditional on evaluation of the viability of a particular exchange rate.

By contrast with this short-term interventionist role anticipated for the IMF, the International Bank for Reconstruction and Development, or World Bank, was designed to facilitate long-term capital movements. With funds of its own, the Bank can in principle lend to countries in need for development purposes, but also – like the IMF – its lending gives a 'seal of approval' which legitimates additional private bank spending in such countries.

The marginal role of the World Bank can be illustrated by the fact that in 1985 its total disbursed resources were equivalent to less than two per cent of

FIG. 1.4 IMF quotas as share of world imports (Source: IMF and *The Economist*)

global debt. Meanwhile, as illustrated in Figure 1.4, the IMF quotas which Keynes intended should offset temporary payments deficits and avoid domestic deflation had shrunk from an eighth to a twentieth of world import trade between 1950 and 1984.

Keynes versus White

In practice this meant that Keynes' proposal was not the basis of the new international economic order at Bretton Woods. Sir Roy Harrod (1963) has chronicled Keynes' exchanges with his formal antagonist at the conference – US representative Harry White. But Keynes' real antagonist was the profound conservatism of a US establishment much less convinced than an already ailing President Roosevelt that the Bretton Woods system should establish a global New Deal.

Keynes had been ambitious for the IMF. He wanted it to overcome the preoccupation with available savings to finance investment, and instead provide sufficient finance to meet increased demand with increased investment and output. The issue as to whether one has the money today to finance investment or whether one should borrow to increase investment, jobs and income has been one of the ongoing differences between Keynesians and monetarists through the 1970s and 1980s.

Such analytic differences about the role of public borrowing became subsumed at Bretton Woods into how big the new IMF's lending facilities should be. Keynes envisaged an IMF scheme involving funds some *five times* those advocated by White. In practice the final act of Bretton Woods contained a compromise figure much closer to the White recommendations than to those of Keynes. As Harrod (1963, p. 549) stressed:

Keynes wanted a fund so large as to give governments the confidence necessary to relax unneighbourly restrictions; $25 billion might have achieved that (the Keynes plan); $5 billion (the White plan) certainly would not. Was this Fund really to be the foundation for the building of a better world? Or was it to be merely a modest subscription towards meeting some of the needs of poorer countries? Contemporary and subsequent opinions outside the United States have on the whole agreed in holding that Keynes was right. One could only console oneself by hoping that, should the Americans prove obdurate now, the Fund might be enlarged in the course of its operation.

Allowing for the facility introduced since the late 1970s (whereby central banks can exchange unwanted dollars for Special Drawing Rights or SDRs), Keynes' proposals for IMF quotas, translated into current terms, could have meant a level of official quotas equivalent to between a fifth and a quarter of current trade. As it is, the leading industrial economies at the end of 1984 had reserves excluding gold equal to only the value of some two months' import trade, while the ratio of such reserves to import finance for all the market economies was only some 10 weeks.

Dollar Dominance and Decline

Keynes wanted to see potential world demand matched by an expanding international currency unit which would not need to be fully backed either by gold or national currencies: *Bancor*. But, in reality, international trade and payments in the postwar period up to the early 1970s was dominated by the United States dollar. So long as the dollar was strong and stable, it played a primary global role, while the IMF and World Bank were upstaged minor actors. But within a quarter of a century of the Bretton Woods settlement, with its much weakened version of Keynes' own proposals, the dollar itself was under major pressure.

One of the main reasons was the recovery of two of the key economies defeated during the Second World War. The relative decline of US dominance is illustrated in Table 1.8. Thus while the United States in 1950 had accounted for more than half of the output of what now are the OECD countries, by 1973 this had declined to less than two-fifths.* The US share of world trade including the centrally planned economies had declined from about 17 per cent to 12 per cent over the same period. More strikingly, US gold reserves had fallen from nearly 70 per cent to under 30 per cent of the world total from 1950 to 1973, and to less than a quarter by 1984.

* The increase in the US share of OECD output by 1984 reflected both the sustained expansion of the American economy and the restraint on growth in the other principal OECD economies – analysed in more detail in the context of global crisis in Chapter 9. In contrast with the low share of the US in world total exports in 1984, US imports were 18 per cent of the world total, reflecting the vast trade deficit which accompanied the US 'boom'.

TABLE 1.8   The Relative Decline of the United States

US % share of:	1950	1973	1984
OECD output	54	39	42
World trade*	17	12	11†
World gold reserves‡	68	27	23

* Including centrally planned economies.
† Exports only.
‡ Excluding Soviet Union and Comecon.
Source: *The Economist*, October 1985, OECD, GATT and IMF.

Moreover, the new postwar competitors to the United States – most notably West Germany and Japan – had managed to achieve levels of innovation, productivity and competitiveness which had already pushed the US government onto the trade defensive by the mid 1960s. Throughout the postwar period, as consonant with its new world role, the United States allowed or encouraged the export of capital and direct investment on a global scale. But, as we will see in Chapter 4, this tended to substitute direct foreign production for export trade, and considerably undermined US visible export performance. The emerging US dollar deficit gave rise to a market for dollars mainly managed in Europe, and soon identified as the 'Eurodollar' market, lying outside the control of the US Treasury. Meanwhile, the US trade deficit, aggravated by the Vietnam War, resulted in major pressure on the dollar and its devaluation under the Nixon administration in 1971.

Had Keynes been able to create a genuinely international reserve currency such as Bancor, the devaluation of the dollar might not of itself have resulted in the collapse of the Bretton Woods system. But dollar devaluation meant a significant decrease in the value of (dollar-denominated) revenues for the petroleum-producing countries, which anyway had suffered a decline in the real value of their dollar earnings per barrel of oil in preceding years. They hit back by forming OPEC. In response, as already indicated, the developed countries cut civilian public expenditure.

Such 'beggar-my-neighbour' deflation was aggravated by the re-emergence of the pre-Keynesian orthodoxy of 'sound money supply', validated in the eyes of many treasuries, chancelleries and central banks by the work of Milton Friedman and his associates. Thus, although Keynes had never wanted the dollar to be the key to world monetary stability, the failure of the dollar as a currency of last resort and the linchpin of the international monetary system, combined with inflationary tendencies from the mid 1960s, represented a profound challenge to the viability of so-called Keynesian policies in the international economy.

Devaluation and Deflation

In recent years the International Monetary Fund has contradicted the Keynesian commitment on currency support to maintain full employment. Keynes himself had allowed for the need for a negotiated devaluation of individual currencies if countries encountered serious balance-of-payments problems. In principle, this was supposed to increase the competitiveness of an individual economy through making possible a lower export price of its traded goods abroad without reducing export volume. 'Orderly devaluation' was one of the key principles of the operation of the International Monetary Fund during what could be called the Keynesian era following the war.

Keynes himself never saw devaluation as a universal panacea for payments adjustment. He stressed that in a fully employed economy, devaluation would need to be accompanied by a degree of deflation of domestic demand in order to release resources for export on a sufficient scale to re-establish equilibrium in the balance of payments. But success for some countries with such a formula depended on the maintenance of buoyant demand for their exports in the world economy. By contrast, with the emergence of the monetarist challenge to Keynesian orthodoxy, and policies of domestic deflation followed by a wide range of governments in the developed countries from the early 1970s, there was no guarantee that the level of effective demand abroad would be sufficient to compensate for the deterioration in the terms of trade of that country by increased export volume in foreign sales.

The Fund and the Slump

If the International Monetary Fund in the period following the dollar devaluation and the rise of OPEC had followed the main lines of Keynes' own analysis, it would have placed a major emphasis on the maintenance of a high global level of effective demand to avoid the 'vicious circle' of a contraction of trade in the world economy. Instead, the IMF imposed conditions for its loans to countries in balance-of-payments difficulties which aggravated the problem of crisis and contraction on a global scale. In essentials, the IMF 'formula' amounted to the following: the demand for (1) devaluation of the domestic economy; accompanied by (2) deflation of domestic demand in order to release resources for export; plus (3) cuts in public expenditure designed to release resources for private-sector investment and to reduce the public-sector borrowing requirement.

Much of this was done in the name of 'sound money' and reduction of inflation. Superficially, the prescription may seem sound. Certainly too much money chasing too few goods (and services) can cause inflation if an economy is working at full capacity. But for the world economy as a whole, the formula was fatal. One would not thank a doctor for reducing one's temperature if the result was rigor mortis. Likewise, it is not clear why one should thank the IMF for reducing inflation while decimating demand in the global economy. By imposing devaluation, deflation and denial of the mixed economy in several dozen countries, in both Europe and the Third World, the IMF has been less the promoter of economic health – as in Keynes' original global vision – than the undertaker of global slump.

Top Countries and Top Companies

Further, it is strongly arguable that institutions such as the International Monetary Fund tend to service the interests of top countries, multinational companies and banks rather than the governments, institutions or peoples of the global economy which they were designed to serve.

In one sense, this should not be surprising. It has already been indicated that the postwar international settlement at Bretton Woods included the victors rather than the vanquished of the postwar settlement. Similarly, it excluded the then mainly colonial countries of the Third World which had no initial voice in the postwar global economic settlement.

It was some time after Bretton Woods before the leading industrial countries got together and formed the Group of Ten, which agreed to provide reciprocal credit facilities for each other through the IMF and known as the General Arrangements to Borrow (GAB). This group, which developed the pressure for Special Drawing Rights, was complemented by the Committee of Twenty which in 1972, following the devaluation of the dollar, provided what Brett (1985, p. 127) has called a 'retrospective legitimation for what had been done and to establish a new basis for its work'. In turn, this was replaced from 1974 with the so-called Interim Committee, or a standing committee of the IMF, which has had to deal ad hoc with problems arising since then.

In reality, both the Committee of Twenty and the Group of Ten have been dominated by an inner group of the top five countries comprising the United States, Japan, the United Kingdom, West Germany and France. Strikingly, as illustrated in Table 1.9, these G5 or Group of Five countries dominate the top 200 multinational companies in manufacturing and services (including banking) which themselves now represent the phenomenal total of one third of the market economies' GDP.

As illustrated in Table 1.9, the United States still accounts for one half of the global revenue of multinational companies in the manufacturing sector and nearly one third of those in the service and banking sector. Japan, still essentially an exporter of goods rather than investment, represented less than 10 per cent of the revenue of the top 200 multinational companies in

TABLE 1.9   Top Countries and the Top Companies, 1982*

| | Manufacturing | | Services | | Total | |
	MNCs	%R	MNCs	%R	MNCs	%R
USA	50	49.1	30	32.9	80	42.8
Japan	14	9.2	21	40.9	35	21.3
UK	9	8.9	9	8.4	18	8.7
W. Germany	13	8.8	4	3.8	17	6.8
France	7	4.8	9	7.8	16	6.0
Other countries	25	20.0	9	6.2	34	12.2
Top 200 companies as percentage of World GDP*						32.3

* Excluding socialist countries.
R = % revenue of top 200 companies.
Source: Clairmonte and Cavanagh (1984).

manufacturing in 1982, but a remarkable two-fifths of the revenue of multinational companies in services and banking. The United Kingdom, West Germany and France together represented one half of the global revenue of US multinational companies in the top 200, but only half that of Japan in the multinational revenue of service companies.

The dominance of such multinationals in global GDP has profound implications for the relevance of textbook models of the international economy such as those of Samuelson, Lipsey or Kindleberger which still reason in terms of assumed equal trade on the basis of comparative advantage between different firms in different countries, each of which is supposed to be able to derive some mutual gain from international specialisation. In reality, the world economy is increasingly dominated by a few dozen firms based in less than half a dozen countries whose governments in turn dominate global institutions.

1.3 The Macroeconomic Framework

Keynes warned that practical men, thinking themselves free from any intellectual influence, are normally the slaves of some defunct economist (Keynes, 1936, p. 383). After the Second World War, as already stressed, many of those in authority in fact thought they were following the intellectual principles of Keynes. But in reality they pursued a macroeconomic policy in Keynes' name which neglected many of his own priorities and also the changing nature of the modern capitalist firm and its ability to qualify, offset or undermine many 'Keynesian' policies. Thus, as much or more than OPEC, oil prices and inflation, they opened the way for a resurgence of pre-Keynesian, non-interventionist, market economics, 'born again' as monetarism.

The Keynesian Challenge

So what were the essentials of Keynes' own economics, and how did they differ both from the 'Keynesians' and from the monetarists?

Essentially, Keynes challenged the key prevailing orthodoxies of his time. Before him, governments had largely thought of the economy as a super-firm. This was not especially surprising since many ministers had come straight into government from the boardroom of private companies. They knew that if a firm's budget was in deficit for any period it could only survive by a combination of good luck and sound borrowing. Such hazards to security were unwelcome. Therefore the firm should cut back during a recession.

Keynes' achievement was to show that at the level of the national or international economy, such microeconomics was misplaced. If the national budget was kept in surplus during a recession, this would worsen the recession through a cutback in orders laid, wages paid, and effective demand in the system. In such circumstances, the budgeting principles of the firm should be stood on their head, and the national budget run at a deficit in order to get the firms' budgets back into surplus at some level of full employment.

In simple terms these are the essentials of the Keynesian principle of 'unbalanced' budgets. In his view, fiscal or tax policy should not simply be used to pay for whatever government had in mind at the time (whether a road, a public monument or a war) but employed to manage the overall level of economic demand, and thus the level of supply. Keynes did not so much prefer fiscal policy to monetary policy per se (i.e. raising or lowering taxation rather than changing interest rates), but he believed that there were some jobs which monetary policy simply could not do, where it would fail if tried, and where fiscal policy should have been used in the first place.

Interest and Inequality

Also, Keynes was very much aware of the implications of high interest rates in promoting social inequality. As he put it in his notes on the social philosophy to which his General Theory might lead (1936, chapter 24): 'the outstanding faults of the economic society in which we live are its failure to provide for full employment and its arbitrary and inequitable distribution of wealth and incomes. . . . Interest today rewards no genuine sacrifice, any more than does the rent of land. The owner of capital can obtain interest because capital is scarce, just as the owner of land can obtain rent because land is scarce. . . .'

Deprecating the claims of growth through inequality, he challenged the assumption that recovery from a recession would be assured if only the borrowing cost of capital (rate of interest) and the cost of labour (wages and salaries) was sufficiently low. Stressing that one person or one firm's expenditure is another's income, Keynes took on the 'monetarists' of his own time who believed in minimal intervention by the state in either the demand or the supply side of the economy. In so doing, he argued that the extent of effective saving is determined by the scale of investment and that investment is not promoted by a low rate of interest. He claimed that there was no way in which the market mechanism itself would reverse a downward spiral in the system or its 'hitting the floor'. Arguing for state expenditure to offset the crisis of under-consumption and mass unemployment in the 1930s, he maintained (ibid., chapter 24) that with a much lower rate of interest than had ruled hitherto 'it should be practicable to maintain conditions of more or less continuous full employment – unless, indeed, there is an excessive change in the aggregate propensity to consume (including the state)'.

Keynes compared interest-rate policy with 'pushing on a piece of string'. If the level of effective demand and consumption was less than that necessary to achieve a full employment of resources, lowered interest rates would not pull the economy out of underemployment or slump. Again, the market alone could not guarantee a full-employment equilibrium: 'the state will have to exercise a guiding influence on the propensity to consume partly through its scheme of taxation, partly by fixing the rate of interest, and partly, perhaps, in other ways' (ibid., chapter 24). The implications for a lowering of the floor to which the private sector can sink – through public-spending cuts – will be analysed extensively in relation to the Keynesian theory of economic growth in Chapter 3.

Socialisation

Keynes was well aware of the political implications of his *General Theory*, and claimed 'that a somewhat comprehensive socialisation of investment will prove the only means of securing an approximation to full employment, though this need not exclude all manner of compromises and devices by which public authority will cooperate with private initiative.'

While such policies were anathema to monetarists in his own time and also today, Keynes nevertheless saw his own theory as 'moderately conservative in its implications. . . .' Apart from the recommended state intervention just cited from the *General Theory*, he commented that:

beyond this no obvious case is made out for a system of state socialism which would embrace most of the economic life of the community. It is not the ownership of the instruments of production which it is important for the state to assume. If the state is able to determine the aggregate amount of resources devoted to augmenting the instruments, and the basic reward to those who own them, it will have accomplished all that is necessary. Moreover, the necessary measures of socialisation can be introduced gradually and without a break in the general traditions of society [ibid., chapter 24].

Maximal and Minimal

In terms of state intervention, the difference between Keynes and the monetarists is not simply between *maximalists* and *minimalists*. Certainly Friedman and the monetarists have sought the minimum of intervention of the state, deregulation of activities and the privatisation of publicly owned assets. But their assault on the public sector and on public spending is only in part inspired by arguments concerning the role of the money supply and inflation. The pace and passion with which the monetarists have sought to roll back the frontiers of the state clearly implies more of the 'personal view' with which Friedman subtitles his *Free to Choose* (1980) rather than the 'positive economics' of his scientific pretensions.

Certainly Keynes' emphasis was upon permanent demand management and an active role for the public sector in stimulating demand in the market economy. In essence this meant positive public spending rather than simply the fine-tuning of demand through fiscal and monetary policy.

In his economic analysis Keynes was not much concerned about the social distribution of demand. This was not because he lacked concern about the use of public spending. He more than once remarked on the satanic quality of many of Britain's industrial towns and how it should not be beyond the reach of ingenuity to undertake a programme of public expenditure for urban renewal. During the Second World War he proposed a national scheme for the mass production of houses to make good the losses caused by the war, a new road system adapted to the needs of modern transport, and major schemes for electricity and electric power (Harrod, 1963, chapter 9).

Beyond Victorian Morality

But in the exposition of his theory, Keynes did not want to confuse the distribution or structure of public spending with the essentials of his argument on its impact on the overall level of activity in the macroeconomy. He was concerned that the force of his arguments on the generation of demand and full employment should not be lost through a confusion of ends and means. His aim was to show that slump was neither an act of God nor of

Masoch. Recovery would not naturally follow recession as day follows night, nor would it be stimulated by the laceration of yesterday's industry and employment. Lamenting the Victorian morality underlying much of the charitable work in his own time – recently renascent in the avowed values of Margaret Thatcher – Keynes was concerned to avoid a debate on the relative merits of specific public works or social service. This is understandable in terms of his desire to counter the under-employment of resources in the short term. But over the longer term – such as fifty years after *The General Theory* – the structural impact of technological unemployment and the social distribution of demand between different groups and classes becomes more crucial to the feasibility of full-employment policies than Keynes himself was ready to admit.

Keynes versus the Keynesians?

The distinction between Keynes and the Keynesians has been put most forcefully by Axel Leijonhufvud in what is already a classic work – *On Keynesian Economics and the Economics of Keynes* (1968). Leijonhufvud's argument is technical, but his claim for a basic difference between the economics of Keynes and Keynesian economics is plain and forceful. The main similarities and differences, with some simplification – and ranging beyond Leijonhufvud – are shown in Table 1.10.

The distinction between Keynes and the postwar Keynesians in part reflects the difference between the unemployment context of the 1930s in which Keynes himself pioneered his reasoning and the fuller or full-employment postwar period in which – partly under his influence – governments lost their phobia of full-employment policies. Keynes' own views on the relative merits of protection versus free trade varied over time, depending partly on his estimate of the probability of persuading other economies to join Britain and the British Empire in recovery programmes.

But by the 1960s, it was becoming increasingly apparent that there were strains on Keynesian full employment. By the 1970s, with inflation rather than unemployment becoming the target for most policy-makers, many 'Keynesian' economists lost their confidence in the combination of fiscal and monetary adjustments, prices and incomes policies and indicative planning, and became concerned with a more active monetary policy, a reduced role for public spending, the espousal of floating rather than fixed exchange rates, and increased support for wage restraint.

Neo and Post-Keynesian Economics

By contrast, as shown in Table 1.11, from the early 1970s a post-Keynesian

TABLE 1.10   Keynes and the 'Keynesians'

KEYNES	'KEYNESIANS'
Counter-recessionary demand generation	Counter-inflation emphasis
Direct and indirect demand management	Indirect demand management
Active fiscal policy	Fiscal policy plus prices and incomes policy
Low interest rates Low priority monetary policy	Higher and more active interest-rate policy and greater role monetary policy
Direct and active public-spending policy	Indirect or negligible public-spending role in economic management
Full-employment (FE) policy	Modified FE policy (with increased concern for inflation)
High wage emphasis	Income restraint emphasis and pro 'incomes policies'
Fixed exchange rate emphasis	Fixed or floating exchange rates
Liberalisation or protection/import substitution (depending on international conditions)	Free trade emphasis (with some protectionist variants)
Supply-side reliance on perfect and imperfect competition	Supply-side concern for oligopoly pricing and 'prices policy'
Planning: predominantly macroeconomic	Some macro indicative planning plus industrial and regional policy

economics was emerging in programmes of radical economists and the international Left. This asserted the feasibility of full-employment priorities, and emphasised the case for (1) a recovery, restructuring and redistribution of resources; served by (2) an active fiscal and demand-management policy, and a reduction to secondary importance of monetary policy; (3) a renewal of the primary public-spending role stressed by Keynes himself; and (4) specific planning in the big business sector, jointly negotiated by government, management and unions.

This alternative to monetarism and supply-side economics also argued for strategic price controls as a counter to monopoly pricing, greater supervision or control of multinational companies' trade and transfer pricing, and direct

TABLE 1.11   Neo-Keynesians and Post-Keynesians

NEO-KEYNESIANS	POST-KEYNESIANS
Counter-inflation emphasis	Full-employment priorities
Active fiscal policy for demand management	Active fiscal policy for both demand management and social redistribution
Active monetary policy	Secondary monetary policy – primary controls over the banking system
Secondary public spending	Primary public spending and emphasis on structural change and social redistribution
Fixed/floating exchange rates as primary international trade instruments	'Managed' exchange rates plus supervision/control of multinationals' trade/transfer prices
Free trade emphasis	Planned or managed trade emphasis
Limited price controls as counter to cost-push inflation	Strategic price controls to match unit cost reduction with reflation
Wage restraint for counter-inflation	Relate wages to new technology/ productivity structures and distribution
Incentives/subsidies and intervention in industry	Planning/public-sector intervention in the structure of the economy and social and regional distribution

planning and public-sector intervention on the supply side of the economy, rather than indirect incentives and subsidies (Holland, 1978 and 1983, and Brandt and Manley, 1985).

Keynes and Friedman

The basic contrast between Keynes and the most renowned apostle of monetarism – Milton Friedman – is indicated in Table 1.12. The demand-supply polarity should not be overstated, since with his stress on a constant money supply Friedman is also making certain arguments about demand. However, the contrast between Keynes' emphasis on the level and effect of demand, with Friedman and the monetarists' emphasis on the rate of growth of the money supply, is very clear.

Monetarism is a new name for an old game. Stressing stable money, it also means putting profits and market forces in command, with state intervention playing a minor or secondary role. The market 'supply-siders' and monetarists of Keynes' time had similarly argued that market forces plus a steady money supply would assure an adjustment of supply and demand and the clearing of markets.

TABLE 1.12 Keynes and Friedman

KEYNES	FRIEDMAN
Effective Demand – main policy emphasis	*Money Supply* – main policy emphasis
Monetary Policy – insignificant: pro low interest rates	*Monetary Policy* – crucial: pro constant rate of growth of supply and real interest rates
Fiscal & Budgetary Policy – anti monetary policy as primary instrument – pro discriminatory/unbalanced budgets	*Fiscal & Budgetary Policy* – anti deficit fiscal and budgetary policy – pro neutral/balanced budgets
Managed Employment Level	*'Natural' Unemployment Level*
Wage Restraint – if inflationary gap	*Wage Level* – determined by supply and demand
Market Mechanism – assumed instability/disequilibrium and inequality	*Market Mechanism* – assumed long-term stability/ equilibrium and equality of opportunity
State Intervention – permanent demand management – state supply-side 'compromises and devices'	*State Intervention* – minimal and reducing 'interference'
Public Sector – active demand role – reduced spending with inflation	*Public Sector* – reduce and if possible 'roll back' by privatising public spending and public enterprise
Exchange Rates – managed and adjustable	*Exchange Rates* – floating

Keynes is famous for stating that 'in the long run we are all dead'. He meant that we might have to wait for ever for markets to adjust global demand to lower supply-side costs. Crisis, slump and the collapse of the civil economy has also meant pressures in the 1930s and 1980s for armaments expenditure as enterprise seeks to offset profit decline through state military spending.

The emphasis on monetary policy in Friedman and fiscal and budgetary policy in Keynes is also very clear. Keynes not only gave no particular priority to monetary policy. He tried to get interest rates 'out of the way' by his argument that they should be low during either recession or recovery (to avoid deepening the former or restraining the latter). In terms of unbalanced budgets, Keynes was also arguing for deficit or surplus financing to cope with problems of deflation or inflation, respectively. In other words, in contrast with the long-run stability and self-adjustment of the market assumed by Friedman and the monetarists, Keynes assumed a basic instability in the market mechanism.

Therefore, rather than fine-tuning the engine on occasion, Keynes assumed that governments would need to steer the economy most of the time to keep it on the road to full employment. Fiscal policy was crucial for this purpose, on the basic principle that tax reduction would stimulate demand and tax increase would restrain demand.

Keynes-Plus: The Mixed Economy

The striking contrast between Keynes' economics and the economics of Friedman is Keynes' own emphasis on the role of the mixed economy. If Keynesians, as already suggested, have tended to neglect this, the reason in part lies with Keynes' own exposition in *The General Theory*, whose implications for public spending and public intervention are spelled out only in chapter 24 or the 'Concluding notes on the social philosophy towards which the General Theory might lead' (Keynes, 1936, pp. 372ff). Both Keynesians and monetarists have tended to overlook such implications, despite the fact that Keynes spent much of his professional life and certainly much of his correspondence on such issues.

As illustrated in Figure 1.5, the conventional model of income and expenditure even in so-called Keynesian texts of the macroeconomy (such as Lipsey, 1979, p. 474) focuses on expenditure by households and a reverse flow of income from firms through wages and salaries to 'households' (an economism meaning individual people and deriving from the era when home-owning heads of households were the main taxpayers). Although Lipsey later modifies this framework, his figure (Lipsey, 1979, p. 489) introduces taxation and government purchases as factors extrinsic to the basic circularity of income and expenditure in the mixed economy.

But in reality, as illustrated in Figure 1.6, not only taxation but also government spending is intrinsic to the circularity of income and expenditure in the modern mixed economy. Thus (1) expenditure by households on the output of firms, and income to households in wages paid by firms, is also matched by (2) corporation tax paid by firms to government and government

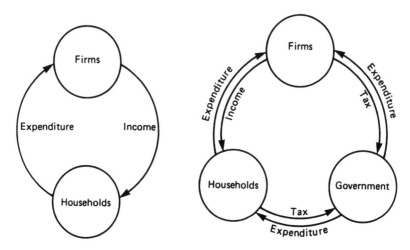

FIG. 1.5 Income and expenditure: the private market model

FIG. 1.6 Income and expenditure: the mixed economy model

expenditure on the output of firms, as well as (3) tax paid by households to government and expenditure by government on households such as social security, pensions, education, health services etc.

Such public spending is now crucial to the process of demand generation in the developed countries. During the 'Keynesian' era, public expenditure in the main European countries rose from between a quarter and a third of total spending in 1950 to between a half and two-thirds in 1975. Lesser but still pronounced increases were registered in the United States and Japan (see Chapter 3, Figure 3.14).

The implication that this trend had risen, was rising and would rise still further concerned many policy-makers in the 1970s and opened the way for the influence of monetarist theorists who claimed that such spending 'crowded out' private spending and initiative. Most Keynesian economists had neglected the actual role of such public spending, and were ill-prepared for the monetarist counter-offensive. Meanwhile the monetarists focused their analysis on competition for investible funds rather than on the demand generated by public spending for the output and sale of private-sector goods and services.

Demand and Supply Side

Figure 1.7 illustrates a key relationship between the demand and supply sides of the postwar mixed economy. As typical of several of the West European economies, it represents demand as divided equally between public and private spending, while public enterprise constitutes only a tenth of the supply of goods and services. On the demand side, as shown in Table 1.13, public spending in the UK economy from the mid 1970s to the mid 1980s ranged between 42 and 46 per cent of total spending. But on the supply side, as shown in Table 1.14, the share of UK public enterprise in total output has fallen to below 10 per cent, in part because of the 'privatisation' or selling of public enterprise by the Conservative government since 1979.

TABLE 1.13   The Mixed Economy and Public Spending*

	Including transfer payments	Excluding transfer payments	Direct absorption by government
1976–77	46.0	25.5	21.5
1977–78	42.0	25.5	18.5
1978–79	43.0	22.5	19.5
1979–80	43.5	22.5	21.0
1980–81	46.0	24.0	22.0
1981–82	46.5	23.5	23.0
1982–83	46.5	23.5	23.0
1983–84	46.0	23.5	23.0
1984–85	45.5	23.5	22.0
1985–86†	44.5	23.0	21.5

* Public expenditure as a % of GDP.
† Estimated outturn.
Source: Parliamentary Question, Treasury, 17 February 1986.

TABLE 1.14   The Mixed Economy and Public Enterprise

Public corporations as a % of UK value added								
1976	1977	1978	1979	1980	1981	1982	1983	1984
11.7	11.6	11.5	11.3	11.3	10.1	10.0	10.6	9.3

Source: UK National Accounts, 1985.

It should be evident from Figure 1.7 and Tables 1.13 and 1.14 that there is a very unequal mix between the share of the public sector in the demand and supply sides of the economy. This unequal mix has been masked by the common but inappropriate measurement of public spending as a share of gross domestic product, since public spending includes so-called transfer payments such as pensions, social security and unemployment benefits which are not counted in GDP itself. In the UK in recent years, as indicated in Table 1.13, such transfer payments have been as high as a quarter of GDP. Therefore the widespread impression has been given that public spending (expressed as a share of GDP) has approached (and indeed for a time exceeded) half of total supply in the UK economy. In the mid 1970s this caused former Chancellor of the Exchequer Roy Jenkins to declare that if public spending carried on rising, the mixed economy, a viable private sector and 'all our democratic freedoms' would be at risk. In reality, as shown in the right-hand column of Table 1.13, only just over a fifth of the nation's resources were directly absorbed by government when he made his apocalyptic prediction.

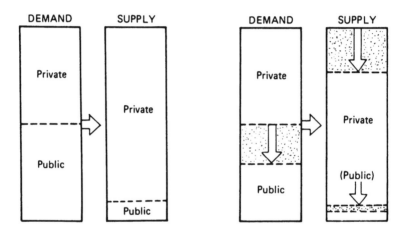

FIG. 1.7 Unequal mix: public spending and public enterprise

FIG. 1.8 Unequal effects: impact on private demand of public spending cuts

Draining versus Sustaining

Such ill-informed reactions from the highly-placed aided the claims of the monetarists that public spending was draining the private sector. But in fact such spending sustains the private sector by generating demand for its goods and services. Figure 1.8 represents such an unequal or asymmetric effect of public-spending cuts, which are far greater on the private sector because of its overwhelming dominance of the supply of goods and services in the mixed economy.

This theoretical example is illustrated in Table 1.15 from the public or council housing market in the UK. All demand for council housing is public, generated by orders made by local authorities and financed both from local tax (rates) and from central taxation (through the Housing Investment

TABLE 1.15   The Mixed Economy and Construction

	Local authority housebuilding by type of contract (percentage of dwellings approved)			
	1974–76	1977–79	1980–82	1983–84
England & Wales*				
Public direct-labour schemes	7.3	7.1	6.0	5.0
Private contractors' schemes	92.7	92.9	94.0	95.0
Scotland				
Public direct-labour schemes	0.5	2.2	0.1	1.5
Private contractors' schemes	99.5	97.8	99.9	98.5

* Excluding Greater London Council housebuilding.
Source: Parliamentary Questions 28 July 1980, 11 July 1983 and 13 February 1986.

Programme or HIP). But Table 1.15 shows that from 1974 to 1984 in England and Wales, private contractors built and supplied well over ninety per cent of the council houses generated by such public demand, and in Scotland very nearly 100 per cent, with the rest being undertaken by the Direct Labour Organisations owned and managed by local authorities themselves.

It could reasonably be argued that public services such as health, education and social services are also part of GDP output, and that in a country such as the UK, with minor exceptions in the private or voluntary sector, they all constitute the public sector. However, each of these sectors replicates the main pattern of demand and supply already indicated in Figures 1.7 and 1.8 and as evidenced in detail for the construction industry. Thus buildings for hospitals and health clinics, polytechnics and schools are overwhelmingly built by private-sector companies (and, in the main, major private companies). Similarly, their furnishings, fittings and equipment are supplied almost without exception by private companies. Likewise British publishers found to their dismay that the cuts in the 1980s in grants for libraries in higher and secondary education collapsed their textbook sales.

The demand generated by wages and salaries paid in the public health, education or social services shares the same overall pattern as the personal income paid by private companies to their employees. In the public and private sectors alike, a similar flow of savings from income is channelled through private financial intermediaries into mortgages for private house purchase, into private insurance schemes, into private pensions and private charge on credit cards. On average no more is spent by public employees on gas, electricity and other public utilities than by private employees. Nor is there evidence that more of them travel on public transport, or buy more cars from public enterprise producers than those in the private sector.

Crowding In or Crowding Out?

These points outline a key argument which will be elaborated through Chapters 2 and 3 in the context of a wider analysis of the mixed economy, in terms of the flows of income and expenditure and their role in economic growth. But the main point is important in relation to the monetarist assault on public spending. For instance, in striking contrast with the monetarist claim of the so-called 'crowding-out' of private by public expenditure, Figure 1.8 illustrates that the monetarist prescription of restricting the money supply to counter inflation in practice cuts public expenditure and therefore public demand. In turn, because of the greater share of private rather than public supply of goods, this disproportionately deflates the private sector of the economy.

A further illustration can be given from the case of UK council-house building, where public spending was reduced by more than two-thirds between 1979 and 1985 (*The Economist*, October 1985). The result, plainly following from the ratios given in Table 1.15, was that over nine-tenths of the contraction in public demand collapsed supply in the private house building sector, with up to two thousand failures of private contractors per year by 1984 (Parliamentary Question, Trade and Industry, 13 February 1986) and hundreds of thousands of construction workers unemployed. A recovered public-spending programme on construction would less 'crowd out' such contractors and employees, than bring them in from the cold of the current crisis in the industry.

A US Federal Deficit?

Part of the problem of misguided theory and policy concerning public spending lies less in giving technically wrong answers to the questions as posed than asking the wrong questions in the first place. As Robert Eisner (1984 and 1986) has recently shown, this has certainly been the case with the question of how to cut the US Federal deficit, since it is very much open to question whether there recently has been such a deficit – and certainly a deficit of the magnitude commonly supposed.

The essence of Eisner's argument is the failure of public accounting procedures in the US government to follow the basic principles of accounting prevailing in private business practice. He maintains that a measure of the real actual surplus or deficit in the US can be viewed in terms of three key components: (1) the nominal surplus or deficit as currently measured; (2) an adjustment for changes in the market value of government financial assets or liabilities, due to changing market rates of interest; and (3) changes in the real value of net debt due to inflation. The same criteria are relevant for adjusting estimates of the federal government's budget surplus or deficit.

Recalculating US data by these criteria, Eisner found that higher interest rates lowering the market value of debt, along with higher prices of gold increasing the value of gold as a government asset and in particular general inflation, combined to cut the real market value of the net debt virtually in half since the end of World War Two, with a long-term decline in net debt since 1946. On the same basis, the US Federal budget turns out not to have been in deficit in recent years, as usually supposed, but in considerable surplus (Eisner and Pieper, 1984).

The issue is not simply technical. As Eisner comments: 'the false perception of a real deficit led to restrictive monetary *and* fiscal policies and the worst recession since the Great Depression of the 1930s. Misunderstanding the facts, we have foolishly courted and deepened recession. We have confused economic and financial analysis. We have encouraged economic theorists off on a tangent to our central concerns.' Not least, there has been the spectacle of the Senate of the United States, without hearings, adopting by an overwhelming 73 to 21 vote a deficit elimination bill which would revolutionise the fiscal process (Eisner, 1986, pp. 176–7). Further, cutting the US deficit, as ritually demanded by European central bankers and many politicians, not only could deflate the US economy to no purpose granted the questionable nature of the deficit in the first place. It also would impose major deflation on the rest of the world economy by reducing the US trade deficit and with it the exports of other countries.

There is an analogy between false perception of the US federal deficit and an equally false perception of the factors underlying the US trade deficit. Conventionally, this is explained by claims of loss of competitiveness by US firms on world markets, combined with the implication of excessive imports to the United States. Yet, as will be shown later in Chapter 4, while US manufacturing exports declined by 40 per cent from the late 1950s to the late 1970s – a trend underlying the already cited declining share of US exports in total export trade – this did not reflect a loss of competitiveness by US companies in their operations world wide. US manufactured exports had declined by 1977 to less than 15 per cent of the total world share. But US multinational companies at global level – exporting both from the United States and from locations elsewhere in the world economy – had sustained a share of manufactured exports nearer to 25 per cent of the world total (Lipsey and Kravis, 1985). The example shows the importance of integrating the role of the modern multinational enterprise into an analysis of the global economy.

1.4 From Meso to Macroeconomics

Relatively few twentieth-century economists have translated the theory of the firm, or what is conventionally called microeconomics, into implications for the macroeconomy. One such an economist was Bertil Ohlin (1933), whose analysis of international investment and trade is considered and developed in Chapter 4. Other notable exceptions include François Perroux (1964 and 1965), Paolo Sylos-Labini (1962), Paolo Leon (1967) and – in the United States – Eisner (1963) and Eichner (1976), whose contributions will be examined in Chapter 2 of this volume. There are also a range of economists who have followed the present author in developing the concept of mesoeconomics or the mesoeconomy, including Peters (1981) and Preston (1983). However, the most notable of all was the Polish economist Michael Kalecki, who has the additional and not inconsiderable distinction of being credited with the invention of Keynesian economics before Keynes himself.

Marx, Kalecki and Keynes

Kalecki was trained initially as an engineer. He therefore came to economics in the 1920s unencumbered by the straitjacket either of the Austrian neoclassical marginal revolution or of that version of it which – replete with qualifications – was established as the main student text in the Anglo-Saxon world at the time, Marshall's *Principles*. He was also more influenced by his first experience of economics in the real world, as a credit controller in a company, than by the texts of the founding fathers or specialist commentators. It is now widely recognised that, in key articles published between 1933 and 1936, Kalecki anticipated by some three years the arguments which were to receive so much more acclaim when published in 1936 in Keynes' *General Theory of Employment, Interest and Money*.

The parallel between Kalecki and Keynes was not readily acknowledged in the first instance by the economics profession, although by 1951 Lawrence Klein (1951, pp. 447–8) was writing that: 'After having re-examined Kalecki's theory of the business cycle I have decided that he actually created a system that contained everything of importance in the Keynesian system, in addition to other contributions . . . it is explicitly dynamic; it takes income distribution as well as level into account, and it makes the important distinction between investment orders and investment outlays.'

Not least, Kalecki's theory differed from and in a real sense transcended that of Keynes by its inclusion of the impact of the enterprise on the macroeconomy. Joan Robinson (1972) made the point unequivocally when she wrote that 'Keynes himself was not very much interested in the theory of value and distribution. Michael Kalecki produced a more coherent version of *The General Theory* which brought imperfect competition into the analysis and emphasised the influence of investment on the share of profits. Kalecki's version was in some ways more truly a general theory than Keynes'.'

As Asimakopoulos (1977, p. 334) has put it: 'A Kaleckian approach to the interrelations between profits and (macro) investment is based on the recognition of the firm (entrepreneur) as the key decision-making unit in the process.'

Thus Kalecki developed an argument which both was more dynamic than that of Keynes and explicitly integrated the role of the enterprise which had conventionally been divorced by its microeconomic terms of reference from reasoning on the macroeconomy. In so doing it might well be argued that he was developing a Marxist line of argument. Certainly he explicitly related his own microeconomic theory to Marx.

Relatively few contemporary economists would classify Kalecki as a Marxist. Yet one also hesitates to categorise as a Keynesian a man who himself anticipated and in key respects transcended Keynes' own analysis. In fact such issues concerning the impact of big business on the macroeconomy cannot be settled simply by reference to Marx or Keynes alone. This is one reason, among others, for developing the concept of the mesoeconomy.

The Role of the Mesoeconomy

The mesoeconomy has profoundly qualified – and in key respects under-mined – conventional macroeconomic theory and policy. Its significance lies in the fact that it not only represents a new power structure of monopolistic and multinational business, but also that intermediate mesoeconomic economic power impacts on both the micro and macroeconomy, and in large part divorces the macro-micro synthesis of Keynesians and monetarists.

One of the main qualifications of conventional macroeconomic theory on prices and inflation arises from the price-making power of mesoeconomic big business. As we will see in Chapter 8, this has major implications for the analysis of 'cost-push' inflation in the macroeconomy.

Monetary policy entails interest-rate changes or more direct changes in the money supply through restriction or expansion of the level of public spending. But in an open multinational economy, such a national monetary policy may be counter-productive if pursued within a conventional macroeconomic framework (whether monetarist or Keynesian). In other words, if frustrated in a given national market by a restrictive macroeconomic monetary policy imposed by a government concerned to restrain the rate of expansion, a multinational company in the mesoeconomic sector may well raise finance abroad for investment in a project in the country concerned which is merited according to its own corporate strategy.

Deflationary policy may be designed to reduce pressure on resources or claims for funds in order to ease balance-of-payments difficulties. But a mesoeconomic company with price-making power on the domestic market may be able to increase its rate of self-financing and thus decrease its dependence on external borrowing by virtue of its dominant position in the market. Also, while deflationary policy may reduce the earnings, self-finance and market rating of a national or micro enterprise, a foreign multinational company pursuing an 'offensive' investment strategy may increase its penetration of the domestic market through investment financed either by foreign borrowing or by income earned elsewhere in the global economy, thus indirectly frustrating national deflation as a policy objective.

Reflationary policy, based on the old-style Keynesian concept of the marginal efficiency of capital or profit expectations within one country, now may well be frustrated by the global market expansion and profit expectations of an individual multinational company in the mesoeconomic sector. In such terms, as we will see in Chapters 2 and 3, the 'accelerator', 'capital stock adjustment' and 'multiplier' principles of standard macroeconomic theory now tend to be profoundly qualified by multinational companies producing components in different countries for final production and sale either in those countries or elsewhere.

Fiscal policy also tends to be undermined by mesoeconomic companies. Direct fiscal controls aimed at increasing investment and production within one country, by raising the fiscal allowances (tax allowances) or incentives to an individual firm, tend to prove ineffective in the big business sector. This appears partly to be due to the scale of self-financing without the inconvenience of negotiating with governments which such companies can achieve through their price-making power, and substantially to the scale of their multinational operation where gains in production costs through the exploitation of labour in less developed or intermediate countries are such as to massively offset the incentives available from governments in more developed countries.

Income and expenditure analysis by households and government also needs to be qualified by the rise of the mesoeconomic sector and the scale of self-financing by big business. As shown in Chapter 2, when big business commands so large a share of the macroeconomy, its role as not only investor but also spender plays a dominant role in macroeconomic outcomes. Any macroeconomic policy designed either to sustain economic growth or offset cyclical depression and crisis will be qualified or undermined if it reasons only in terms of the conventional macro-micro synthesis and misses the principal actors in the economic drama – global big business.

International and Multinational

Both Keynesian and monetarist macroeconomists throughout the postwar period refused to recognise the transformation of global investment, payments and trade by the rise of multinational companies. Virtually all conventional macroeconomic tests still reason in terms of trade in product 1 and product 2 between country A and country B, neglecting the extent to which for more than a quarter of a century international trade between different firms in different countries has been overtaken by multinational trade between the same firms in different countries.

Yet the value of total production by multinational companies worldwide has exceeded the total value of world trade for more than 15 years. In individual economies such as the United States, the value of foreign production by US companies for the same period has been some four times the total volume of US visible export trade (and double such trade for the United Kingdom). Trade conducted directly by multinationals, or indirectly between their subsidiaries, accounts for between 80 and 85 per cent US and UK visible exports. Not least, as we will see in Chapter 7, global finance and debt is overwhelmingly the responsibility of a handful of multinational banks whose activities are outside both the conventional paradigm of international finance and the effective control of governments.

Further, the country A and country B paradigm of the conventional model neglects the role of dominant countries in the world economy, whether the dominance is hegemonic overall, as for the United States in the quarter century following the Second World War, or within individual export markets, as has been the case with Japan over the last 20 years. Such failures of both the Keynesian and monetarist macroeconomic model to recognise the new postwar realities would be less damaging were they confined simply to private language games between professional economists. In reality, however, the paradigms obstruct perception of new policy alternatives which go beyond both Keynes and Friedman.

Macro and Micro Implications

If the mesoeconomic and multinational sector is a key to the new global economy, it has neither displaced the role of macroeconomics, nor ended the role of the continuing microeconomic sector of smaller scale national capital.

But the behaviour of multinational big business and its relations to government are different – both quantitatively and qualitatively – from that of smaller national capital in the microeconomic sector.

Conventional exchange-rate theory is compromised by the rise of multinational big business. The fact that multinational companies now in many cases produce abroad rather than export to other countries has resulted in a situation where they have increasingly become their own global competitors. Therefore if they follow the devaluation of a national currency by lower prices on foreign markets where they are already direct producers, they would in effect be undercutting themselves. It is beyond not only self-interest, but also economic logic in terms of revenue maximisation and efficient use of capacity in different countries for them to do so.

Comparative advantage theory is also qualified by multinational enterprise which – on a global scale – can allocate capital to sectors and regions of the world economy which are in growth when other sectors and regions are in decline. Its power to combine modern technology with low or least-cost labour worldwide, profoundly undermines the principles of Ricardian comparative advantage on which not only international trade theory but also key international policy institutions are based, such as the IMF.

Subsidy and incentives have also been qualified by multinational capital. In contrast with Keynesian theory, it is arguable that big business is no longer influenced significantly by the 'compromises and devices' on which Keynes assumed governments in developed countries could rely in order to adjust the supply side of the economy to managed demand. Money supply and monetary policy, so favoured by the monetarists, is undermined by the access of multinational capital to independent finance worldwide and its internal scheduling of funds through transfers between its own subsidiaries in different countries.

Enterprise and Institutions

The question might well be raised why, if mesoeconomics is defined as intermediate between the microeconomic firm and the macroeconomy, the individual sector of economic activity should itself not meet the necessary conditions to justify the application of the term. Essentially mesoeconomics – like microeconomics – applies to the operations of the enterprise within the economy, rather than to the description of statistical categories such as a sector in national economic accounting. The mesoeconomic enterprise exists and operates in the real world; the sector exists on paper as a collection of otherwise unrelated and unintegrated data. This distinction is not so arbitrary as it might appear, inasmuch as microeconomics in conventional usage refers in the main to enterprise rather than to industry. Although orthodox microeconomics may well carry the subtitle 'firm and industry', it is on the behaviour of enterprise itself rather than the abstraction of the sector which the analysis focuses, with good reason.

Alternatively, it might be claimed that state institutions operating at the level of individual sectors, such as the modernisation commissions in postwar France or the National Economic Development Councils in Britain, meet the requirements of mesoeconomics as hitherto defined in relating the concept of 'intermediacy' to actual institutions operating in the real world. But such institutions do not allocate capital in the manner of actual enterprise. They rarely if ever decide what shall be done, why, when, how or where in the manner of enterprise itself. Besides which, while the abstract concept of the sector world wide (e.g. the world motor industry, or the world steel industry) may be international in character, it is companies in the mesoeconomic sector rather than abstract sectoral categories which allocate resources on a global scale and thereby change the shape of the world economy.

Similarly, while some public institutions between the individual firm and the level of the macroeconomy may under certain circumstances allocate resources, there are few government institutions at the international level which allocate resources on a global scale in the manner of multinational companies in the mesoeconomic sector.

The closest approximation to a multinational company among international agencies is to be found in those institutions such as the Common Agricultural Fund of the EEC, the International Monetary Fund or the World Bank which in effect schedule and allocate finance and capital resources in individual sectors in different countries – or in and between sectors in different countries – on a global scale. To this extent, such public bodies cross the frontier between *advisory* and *allocative* agencies. In fact, this has been one of the strongest criticisms made of the IMF and the World Bank by many smaller countries and of the EEC's agricultural policy by smaller farmers.

Conventions in Question

At the very least, such arguments suggest the need for a review of conventional distinctions between micro and macro economic theory and policy. Yet the striking feature of conventional textbook analysis is the dominance of the assumption of perfect competition and the price-competitive process on the microeconomic side of the economy. This clearly has major implications for the plausibility of the macroeconomic analysis in conventional theory and the policy implications – Keynesian or monetarist – drawn from it.

Indeed, most professional macroeconomists in their student days spent a week or two on the theory of oligopoly or the dominance of individual markets by a very few firms. Yet their macroeconomics is not based on such oligopolistic assumptions. Almost without exception, it assumes that the supply side of the economy is composed of a large number of perfectly competitive firms. It is as if a kind of dyslexia gripped such professionals when they viewed the real world economy from the august heights of macroeconomic theory. They know that the supply side of the economy is not really divided between many small firms which have no influence on macroeconomic outcomes. But, partly through respect for convention and partly because, as Wittgenstein (1922) would say, they are trapped by their own rules of the game, they continue to claim that it is so.

Figure 1.9 represents this analytic dyslexia or shift in emphasis made in macroeconomic reasoning of the kind which assumes an essentially competitive microeconomic structure. Thus on the left-hand side of the diagram, the microeconomic structure is assumed to be some three-quarters competitive, with imperfections, oligopoly and monopoly reduced to a minor and by implication subordinate role. Macroeconomic variables, represented on the right-hand side of the Figure, such as savings, investment, employment, prices etc., are implicitly assumed to be determined by the workings of a more or less perfectly competitive microeconomic structure. The normally implicit assumptions in such reasoning are made explicit by the double-headed arrow relating micro supply structures to macro demand aggregates.

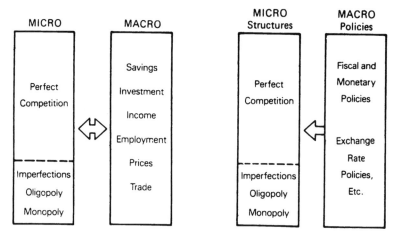

FIG. 1.9 Micro foundations of macro-economic theory

FIG. 1.10 Micro assumptions of macro-economic policy

The same assumed dominance of competitive structures on the micro-economic or supply side of the economy underlines conventional theories of the effectiveness of macroeconomic demand-management policies, whether these have a monetarist emphasis on the role of money supply in relation to prices, or a Keynesian emphasis on exchange-rate changes and fiscal and monetary intervention.

This assumption, represented in Figure 1.10, is in no sense arbitrary. As we will see in Chapter 2, the condition of 'price-making' power by big business, or its ability to finance a major part of its investment needs through internally generated funds, qualifies conventional macroeconomic analysis of both savings and consumption, and expenditure and multiplier effects in the modern market economy.

National and International

Indicated in Figure 1.11 – and synthesising extensive evidence in *The Market Economy* (Holland, 1987) – the trend to concentration and the rise of big business now represents a new intermediate or mesoeconomic structure between the assumed competitive enterprise of the microeconomic model and macroeconomic aggregates. Such enterprise 'becomes the "bridge" between micro- and macroeconomics' (Paolo Leon, 1967). Similarly, public expenditure on the demand-generating side of the macroeconomy now constitutes half or more of total spending in the main Western European economies.

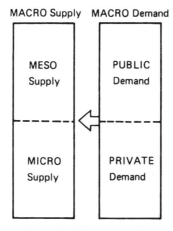

FIG. 1.11   Meso-micro supply and public-private demand

In practice, the scale and share of mesoeconomic big business in this supply structure now represents between a half and two-thirds of the supply of goods and services in the economy as a whole. Apart from this direct receipt of public funds, or those expenditures which may still be induced by conventional Keynesian policies such as tax cuts and interest reductions on

personal expenditure, mesoeconomic enterprise also tends to dominate the
microeconomic sector of the economy on the supply side through its crucial
role as dominant buyer and subcontractor of goods from microeconomic
companies.

Multinational enterprise also qualifies conventional micro and macro
theory. As suggested earlier, but now made explicit in Figure 1.12, the
conventional theory of international trade tends to argue in terms of product
1 and product 2 being traded between country A and country B as if the
countries were macroeconomic and the *companies* were microeconomic in
character.

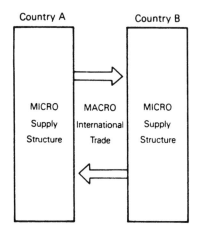

FIG. 1.12 International trade: the
micro-macro model

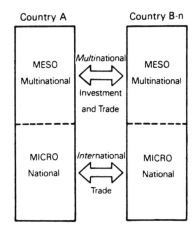

FIG. 1.13 Multinational trade: meso and
micro dimensions

Thus Richard Lipsey (1975, p. 636) argues that the basic fact is 'that, in
capitalist economies, foreign trade, just like domestic trade, is determined
mainly by thousands of independent decisions taken by firms and households
and co-ordinated – more or less effectively – by the price system'. Lipsey
claims that 'the major difference between foreign trade and domestic trade
results from the fact that the domestic trade of different countries makes use
of different monies.'

Having analysed some of the principal mechanisms in the conventional
theory of international trade, Lipsey does admit that 'the theory is based on
an assumption of competition that ensures that relative prices will reflect real
opportunity costs,' adding that 'if the degree of competition differs among
different industries, relative prices may not reflect comparative costs'. Lipsey
also argues that in those cases where relative prices do not reflect real
opportunity costs, trade between countries will reduce world output (ibid.,
p. 673).

What he does not admit is the existence of the multinational division of capital between the *same* companies in different countries, rather than the international division of labour between different countries and different companies on the lines of the competitive model. In fact, in their introductory texts, neither Lipsey nor Samuelson admit the existence of multinational or transnational firms at all, despite the fact that their combined output for more than a decade has been greater than the total volume of world trade.

It is perhaps not surprising that one cannot find in either Lipsey or Samuelson a reference to the techniques of transfer pricing or to the ability of multinational companies to set prices or schedule goods in trade between subsidiary companies in such a way as to suit their global strategies of tax minimisation and profit maximisation.

Such a technique in reality very much ensures that 'relative prices may not reflect comparative costs,' quite apart from the fact that by combining the highest available world technology with some of the world's lowest cost labour, multinational companies profoundly qualify the neoclassical principle of comparative advantage.

The Multinational Model

Again, the form or representation of this new reality is important to understanding the mechanics of big business competition worldwide. Thus in Figure 1.13, the distinction between meso and micro-economic enterprise on the supply side of the economy is paralleled by a distinction between multinational and national capital. This is not to suggest that all multinational companies are large. Some are small in relation to other companies operating in the same country, or to the global economy as a whole. But relatively few microeconomic companies are multinational in character, whereas virtually all private mesoeconomic companies tend also to be multinational.

Figure 1.13 seriously modifies the comparative-advantage framework of the neoclassical international trade model described in Figure 1.12. For one thing, rather than trade between companies in country A being undertaken exclusively in the form of a final product with a given country B, trade between subsidiaries of the same multinational company in different countries tends to be divided between more than one country (i.e. countries B to n). Moreover, as represented by the upper arrow in Figure 1.13, multinational capital typical of the mesoeconomic sector by definition undertakes investment in different countries as well as trade between them.

By contrast, as represented by the lower arrow in Figure 1.13, microeconomic capital is mainly concerned with international trade between countries rather than direct investment and production in them. Such mesoeconomic and multinational power profoundly qualifies both the Keynesian and monetarist macroeconomic paradigm of international trade and payments.

1.5 Summary

(1) The unprecedented combination of high growth and full employment after World War Two coincided with the 'Keynesian era'. Although monetarists and supply-siders have stressed its 'failures', after a decade of global monetarism many politicians and economists would now be prepared to trade the so-called shortcomings of the Keynesian era for the so-called 'successes' of monetarism and neo-liberal market forces.

(2) 'Better-my-neighbour' increases in mutual output and trade sustained the recovery of the postwar economy. However, the demand-pull from GATT followed the investment-push from Marshall Aid and policies of state intervention pursued by the economies which achieved allegedly 'miracle' growth rates in the quarter century after the war.

(3) The Keynesian 'revolution' set the framework for the postwar international economy, including both the framework of national and international accounting, and the Bretton Woods settlement. Nonetheless, Keynes' vision of a genuinely international economic order was defeated at Bretton Woods by more orthodox American interests, with the dependence of the so-called Keynesian order on dollar hegemony.

(4) Dollar devaluation in 1971 followed a relative decline of the US in the world market economy as those countries which lost the war thereafter won the peace through economic recovery (in particular Germany and Japan). Dollar devaluation was the symptom of declining US dominance in the postwar international economic order.

(5) Dollar depreciation prompted the OPEC oil price 'shocks' of 1973 and 1979, and were compounded by 'beggar-my-neighbour' deflation of spending and trade, as leading governments sought to reduce their imports to pay for the higher price of oil.

(6) Previous postwar confidence in the 'Keynesian revolution' collapsed with post-OPEC inflation. Keynesians and monetarists alike shared an analysis of the 'inflationary gap' as too much money chasing too few goods. This was the exposed flank of the Keynesian revolution which the previous advocates of full employment and welfare spending could not close against the monetarist counter-revolution.

(7) The combination of inflation and unemployment in the 1970s

legitimised the preference of the International Monetary Fund for deflation, devaluation and deregulation of the world's economy. But in pursuing such policies the IMF thereby contributed substantially to the ensuing global slump.

(8) The conceptual framework or paradigm of the original Keynesian revolution was weakened by the concern of neo-Keynesian analysts with macroeconomic reasoning on inflation and unemployment, and their failure to match a Keynesian economics of demand management with an analysis of the supply side of the economy which recognised the trend to multinational global big business.

(9) The neo-Keynesians thereby failed to develop a model or paradigm of the new mix between the public and private sectors of the postwar market economies, or to challenge the claims of Milton Friedman and the monetarists that public spending drained rather than sustained the private sector of the economy.

(10) While Kalecki, before Keynes, had developed a model relating oligopolistic models of supply (or the dominance of supply by a few firms) to government intervention in demand (shortly before Keynes' *General Theory* of 1936), most postwar Keynesians relied on Keynes' own assumption that provided the state could manage aggregate demand through a combination of fiscal, monetary and exchange-rate policies, the economics of perfect or imperfect competition would ensure a viable supply-side economy.

(11) In reality, the trend to big business within national economies has established a new mesoeconomic sector between the micro and macroeconomies, which in turn has qualified major policy implications of both the Keynesian and monetarist models or paradigms of the global economy.

(12) Multinational big business in the mesoeconomic sector now dominates the regional, national and international economy in a manner which is not widely recognised by the Keynesians or monetarists, and which has major implications for the transformation of the current crisis in the global economy.

2 Demand and Supply

2.1 Spending and Savings

When Keynes resuscitated a hitherto obscure French economist called George Baptiste Say (1767–1832) as a main target for his argument in *The General Theory*, he was not playing games as an economic historian. Say epitomised precisely the confidence in automatic adjustment of supply and demand through market forces which Keynes held responsible for the interwar slump. Indeed Ricardo, over a century before, had likewise targetted Say as a counterpoint to his own argument (Ricardo, 1816).

Say's so-called law is usually summarised as the argument that 'supply creates its own demand'. Essentially, Say claimed that the very act of production by producer x constitutes a demand for the goods of other producers y-n, in the sense that the producer x will exchange a surplus over and above his own consumption for the products of others. Therefore, an implication of Say's is that any increment in output will generate an equivalent increase in income and also in *spending*. So far so good. Say maintained that if the cost structure of supply was appropriate, additional production generating further demand would continue until full employment was reached. More simply, Say claimed that, in the long run, supply would create its own demand.

Ex Ante and Ex Post

It was this aspect of Say which Keynes criticised in *The General Theory*. Keynes' main claim was that only demand management by government could ensure sufficient supply to achieve full employment. Keynes focused his argument on the relation between savings and investment. He also made much use of the distinction between *ex ante* and *ex post* savings and investment, or savings before being invested – when they might be put under the bed, put in the bank, or taken off the public-sector borrowing requirement – and savings after investment (which he assumed meant actual investment in plant or equipment). For national income accounting purposes, largely under Keynes' own influence, it is a convention that savings and investment will be equal. Certainly they will be equal by definition *ex post*, when investment has actually taken place, since the investment itself implies embodied saving.

But Keynes was concerned with more than definition. He criticised those economic models which assumed that – in the long run – an equality of savings and investment would provide full-employment equilibrium. In this sense he was arguing for a behavioural theory of savings, investment and output, rather than simply working with identities. In particular, he was concerned to show that savings could exceed investment not simply in the short run but also over longer periods. In other words, savings might not be embodied in actual investment. *Ex ante* potential might not match *ex post* reality, with the result that available savings, placed in banks or other financial institutions, could earn monetary interest but fail to match investment to potential employment.

The Consumption Function

Keynes was the first economist to give a full and clear statement of the idea that consumption is a relatively stable function of income. Aggregate relations between consumption and income were not something with which pre-Keynesian economists were very much concerned. Like contemporary monetarists, they reckoned that flexible interest rates and flexible wage rates would align real income with the productive power of the economy. If a divergence occurred, it resulted either from imperfectly working markets or the intractability of workers.

Keynes basically assumed a simple proportional relation between consumption and savings, such that four-fifths of disposable income is consumed and one-fifth saved whatever the level of income. This is one of the key hypotheses in the so-called 'consumption function'. Algebraically this can be represented as $C = 0.8Y$ (or consumption equals four-fifths of disposable income), and on the income side as $Y = C + I$, where Y again represents disposable income, C is real consumption expenditure and I is investment.

The slope of the consumption function in Figure 2.1 is 0.8. In other words, for every increase of 10 units in income (on the horizontal axis) consumption rises (on the vertical axis) by 8 units. It was this function which Keynes called 'the marginal propensity to consume'. The 'marginal propensity to save' is the inverse of the consumption function, and in the simple numerical example which Keynes himself gave it is 0.2, or a fifth of disposable income.

Public and Private Spending

Economists since Keynes have had a good deal to say both for and against his hypotheses on consumption and saving, not least since the outcome has

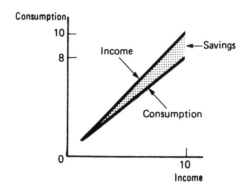

FIG. 2.1   The Keynesian consumption function

significant implications for the achievement of full employment, and the economic effects of income distribution.

For instance, can the proportion of consumption to income be expected to decline in the long run as income rises? In other words, do poorer people save proportionately less than those who are better off and – if so – does this affect aggregate changes in demand, income and savings? Also, is there a non-proportional relationship by which we save more as we grow older, or a proportional relationship in which the marginal or current propensity to consume will equal the average propensity to consume?

A key practical question for government is to know whether increasing the productive power of an economy will automatically ensure that savings will increase in the same proportion as income. If the consumption (or savings) function is proportional, other sources of aggregate demand (investment and government expenditure) need only expand at the same rate in order to maintain full employment. If the consumption function is non-proportional – if consumer demand expands less than increases in savings – maintenance of full employment will require that other sources of demand should rise in greater proportion than income. This implies either an expansion of public expenditure, or an additional stimulus to overall private spending, or both.

Empirical Testing

Keynes' own observations on the consumption function were intuitive and impressionistic. The first significant empirical evidence from which economists could test his theory was made available by Simon Kuznets (1946a and 1946b), when he published estimates of national income and product for the United States – by overlapping decades – from 1869 to 1939. This showed that the average propensity to consume stayed relatively stable (between 0.84

and 0.89) over a very large growth of both total and per capita income. This was close enough to Keynes' consumption function of 0.8. It rose above 0.89 only when per capita income fell between the wars, when people were spending a greater proportion of a lower income to maintain their real consumption level.

However, as Ackley comments, 'we can see that any view that the consumption function is both linear and nonproportional produces ridiculous implications when such a function is assumed stable over long periods of time'. For example, as he illustrates the point, had the relationship, derived from data for the 1930s, prevailed in the 1870s, per capita consumption in the US in the earlier period would have been almost twice as large as per capita national income. Perhaps there existed a 'long-run' consumption function involving a proportional relationship and a 'short-run' function involving a marginal propensity to consume less than the average propensity. But how exactly were the two to be related? And what were their implications for government policy? (Ackley, 1961, pp. 238–40.)

Spatial and Social Shifts

One of the first attempts at reconciliation was provided by Arthur Smithies (1945). Smithies argued that the consumption function could have been shifting up over the decades as average income had grown in real terms. He suggested three main reasons for the upward drift in consumption, to which we shall return later. First, the inter-regional and inter-sectoral shift of American population from rural agriculture to urban industrial and service employment from the late 1860s to the 1940s. Certainly the data shows that, at any given personal income level, farmers consume less and save more than urban workers. Therefore, the shift to the city and into industry and services could be expected to raise consumption relative to savings. Second, Smithies argued that consumption had also been stimulated by the constant introduction of new commodities 'creating' new consumer needs. Along with this aspiration of social groups – and especially the working class – to a new consumer society, was a third factor, namely that the proportion of unearned income was increasing and personal consumption decreasing as a larger share of the population lived longer, and drew retirement pensions rather than earned income for a greater share of their lives.

The Ratchet Effect

James Duesenberry (1949) was dissatisfied with Smithies' argument. He argued that neither changing occupation from rural to urban environments, nor innovation of consumer commodities nor increasing average age could be expected to produce the long-term upward shift in the consumption function. He believed that the claim that the savings ratio would have risen had it not been for the response of consumers to the appearance of new products 'tells us nothing about the effects of the new products on the propensity to save'. Thus, according to Duesenberry, advertising and the 'brand attachment' beloved of imperfect competition theory had little or nothing to do with aggregate levels of consumption – or savings.

Duesenberry recognised that if income grew steadily over time, consumption could grow in the same proportion. But, he stressed, income growth is neither steady or regular. In the short run it may fluctuate, and fluctuate considerably. Consumption responds to this fluctuation, but during a depression tends to fall less than income as people try to protect their previous standard of living.

Duesenberry argued that the reason why consumption falls less than income when income falls, is that consumers adjust their consumption not only to their current income, but also to their previous income. During the decline they are trying to protect their consumption standards relative to previous income and they reduce consumption very little, while reducing saving significantly. But if income rises again with a recovery period for the economy as a whole, much of the increase will restore the savings rate rather than add proportionately to spending to sustain the recovery. In effect, because consumers find it easier to increase spending than to reduce it, there is an aggregate 'ratchet effect'. Consumption goes forward and up more easily than it goes backwards and down.

2.2 Income and Distribution

Milton Friedman has proved to be the key antagonist of Keynes so far this century. It therefore is of more than passing interest that he claims that his counter-attack on Keynesian economics stemmed from his dissatisfaction with Keynes' analysis of the consumption function. Ironically, in his early work Friedman (1957) largely corroborated Keynes' own intuition, arguing that the consumption function was proportional to income. But Friedman distinguished between what he called 'permanent' and 'transitory' components of the measured income for an individual or economy for any period.

The Friedman Hypothesis

In practice there were key differences in Friedman's path to initially

Keynesian conclusions. For Friedman it was 'permanent' consumption which was proportional to 'permanent' income. More specifically consumption – for a family or for the economy – is 'x' times 'permanent' income. But for Friedman 'x' (and therefore the ratio of consumption to permanent income) is independent of the level of permanent income and is a function of (i) the ratio of assets to permanent income, (ii) tastes, age and family composition, and (iii) the rate of interest. Thus the cost of money – banished by Keynes – crept back onto the mainstage macroeconomic argument.

Friedman also dismissed income inequality or income distribution from explanations of the central relations between income, saving and investment. He allowed that many low-income families will include victims of temporary bad luck just as high-income families include many with temporary good fortune. Thus in maintaining that savings do not rise with income, Friedman claimed that a 'basic' and permanent consumption function equates the average propensity to consume to the marginal propensity to consume – irrespective of income distribution.

Lifetime Consumption?

A similar theory was developed by Modigliani and Brumberg (1954). They saw the proportion of income saved as dependent on average *lifetime* income and the length of earning life, as well as the retirement span and age distribution of the population.

Modigliani and Brumberg thereby reinforced Friedman's argument. They built a simple model of rational consumption or saving behaviour by assuming that a basic reason for saving in any period is to smooth out consumption and income over a personal planning period which is longer than the conventional annual accounting period of firms. The result of their assumption is that top income groups save the same proportion of their average, expected or permanent income as lower income groups. By implication, therefore, relative income inequality was good for aggregate savings. The privileged income groups saved rather than squandered their income, and thus preserved investment for future generations. Indirectly, they provided a rationale against public intervention to avoid disequilibrium between personal savings and corporate investment.

Unequal Income

Friend and Kravis (1957) developed several objections to the Friedman and Modigliani-Brumberg theses, claiming that 'there are circumstances which create a presumption in favour of the hypothesis that the preference for future goods – and therefore the income-saving ratio – rises as the real income of the consumer rises.' Simply stated, their contention is that consumers with unequal income are subject to different pressures and motivation, and that these operate to keep the savings of low-income earners low and the savings of high income recipients high relative to their incomes. They claimed that a family with low income will be subject to physical, psychological and social pressures to maintain a spending level which is high relative to income, with a reverse relation for the rich.

Status and Spending

Friend and Kravis argued that 'a permanently small income . . . increases the want for immediate consumption even more than it increases the want for future income'. They stressed the fact that uncertainty – treated in cavalier fashion by both Friedman and Modigliani-Brumberg – pressures low-income families to spend today rather than wait till tomorrow for future goods in the manner of high-income families. They also argued that managers, whether or not they own their enterprises, are less likely to show a consumption function or lifestyle similar to that of their employees. They recognised that entrepreneurs may save rather than spend, and that some people are successful in business because they enjoy other pleasures than consumption: 'For some the making of money becomes such an enjoyable and time consuming process that it competes effectively with the spending of it . . . [indeed] entrepreneurial saving has long been high relative both to entrepreneurial income and to total personal saving.'

Such social phenomena are not explained by the macro Modigliani-Brumberg theories of aggregate saving. They can be explained by the Friedman hypothesis only by assuming that the high saving can be attributed exclusively to greater year-on-year income for entrepreneurs, or higher cumulative rates of return on invested capital. From extensive empirical evidence covering current income, constant income and family income, Friend and Kravis concluded that Friedman's permanent-income hypothesis has little to offer over current income or social class in explaining consumption patterns.

Social, Structural and Spatial Distribution

Such findings considerably qualified the consumption and savings arguments of both Keynes and Friedman. By adding the social dimension, Friend and Kravis indicated that inequality counted for more than either Keynes or Friedman allowed in macroeconomic outcomes. Smithies meanwhile had shown that both structural shifts (from agriculture into industry and services) and spatial migration (from country to town and city) were significant in explaining changes in the relations between consumption and savings over a long period.

This three-dimensional, or '3S', relationship between structural, social and spatial factors proves significant not only in explaining relations between consumption and saving, but also the process of accumulation and growth, and cycles in the global economy (examined further in Chapters 3 and 9). Thus an apparently technical argument about the correlation between consumption and savings in fact implied a radical critique of structural economic change and its social and spatial distribution.

The significance of social distribution to consumption is illustrated indirectly by the widened social base of demand in the long boom after the Second World War. Product-demand saturation and the product cycle also play a role in this process. Put simply, while automobiles and refrigerators in prewar continental Europe (or Japan) were an upper-middle-income market, their demand was extended postwar through most middle and many lower-income groups. Yet the rate of growth of consumption slowed as many families gained a car, a refrigerator and a deep freeze, a television, a tape deck and a video.

One of each was a real welfare gain. For some households two cars, or two televisions, were useful (whether in the latter case to watch programmes upstairs and downstairs, or to keep the kids quiet, was immaterial). But virtually no household needed three cars, four refrigerators, five televisions and half a dozen tape decks. In other words, even at prevailing and unequal levels of income distribution, the rate of consumption of new products would tend to slow down or tail off, and savings tend to rise.

In turn this has structural effects which become important to understanding the changed effectiveness of Keynesian demand management (or the failure of monetarist policies to promote a sustained upturn in demand) at the end of a long boom period such as that between 1950 and 1975. While specific factors such as oil price increases may have seemed to government at the time to have been the critical check on their growth prospects, the long-term output prospects of their economies were already being limited by slowing rates of investment in the growth industries which supplied the previous decades of consumer boom (not least steel and chemical-based plastics).

Redistribution and Demand

One of the key social shifts in consumption therefore may be widened markets for existing goods generated by higher wages. But as growth slackens, a redistribution of social demand through non-market or government forces may be necessary to sustain growth. Moreover such a shift may need to be less towards new goods (where demand may be relatively saturated at prevailing levels of income inequality) than into services such as education, health care, increased assistance for the elderly in an ageing population, pollution restraint and environmental preservation, or raising the quality of telecommunications and televised entertainment versus improved images for unimproved programmes etc. All of which may imply public intervention rather than market forces.

Alternatively, consumption growth may be sustained by a spatial shift in demand, either through market forces (on the lines of the shift from country to town stressed by Smithies) or as a conscious act of public policy. Thus a declining region (whether through over-concentration of traditional industry, or a dependence on diminishing natural resources such as coal or oil) will contribute to declining national demand unless this is offset by an active regional policy – using incentives or, more effectively, direct public spending on infrastructure and direct public investment (Holland, 1976a and b). Such interregional dimensions to effective demand and sustained income, consumption and savings are also matched by the dimension of international demand, where the combination of a debt burden in some cases exceeding total export earnings, plus declining terms of trade and spending cuts imposes beggar-my-neighbour deflation on both the South and the North of the global economy (Brandt and Manley, 1985).

These arguments clearly indicate that consumption and savings are not a stable and simple function of income, and that both analysis and policy needs to advance beyond the simplicity of the intuitive judgement expressed by Keynes in *The General Theory*. It is not so much that Keynes was simply right or simply wrong, as that he implied answers to only some aspects of the overall consumption and demand argument. For the short run, aiming to provide an analysis which indicated the possibility of under-consumption unreversed by market forces, Keynes was right enough. For the longer run, the consumption function did not provide an adequate framework for analysis of dynamic change in a market economy.

Moreover, Keynes himself stressed the level of aggregate demand in the economy rather than its distribution. But dynamising a multidimensional structural, social and spatial model over the longer term means that redistribution comes into its own as a factor which may offset declining economic growth or promote recovery. Thus the product saturation implied by falling rates of growth of sales towards the end of a long boom in turn implies falling rates of growth of demand at prevailing levels of income distribution. Redistribution of demand may be able to offset decline or promote recovery. Whether such redistribution is structural (between the main sectors of the economy, or between the private and the public sectors), social (between different income groups and classes) or spatial (between regions of the national or international economy) implies a wider analysis of the nature of growth and cycles of the kind undertaken in Chapters 3, 9 and 10. But it also implies a further three-dimensional perspective on the structure of supply and demand, as outlined in the following section of this chapter.

2.3 Meso and Macro Dimensions

Milton Friedman achieved the demise of Keynesianism in most of the world's treasuries and finance ministries in the mid 1970s on the basis of his claims for the 'permanent income' hypothesis. Friedman also claimed that there was a strict correlation between inflation and the rate of growth of the money supply – of which M3, or cash plus certain deposits, was for some years the favoured measure. At the same time, Keynesianism was weakly defended in the mid 1970s. This was not only because it shared with monetarism the basic assumption that inflation arose from too much money chasing too few goods and services. It was also because Keynesian demand management appeared incapable of ensuring the sustained long-term growth of investment and supply.

Keynes and Investment Supply

Keynes was not so much concerned with those situations in which savings equalled investment *ex post*, but those in which *ex ante* there could be a divergence between savings and investment, and in particular an under-utilisation of available savings in investment plans, or anticipated investment. He reckoned that investment plans would reflect the reaction of entre-preneurs or managers to the overall rate of growth in the level of income or demand. However, as some contemporary critics of Keynes stressed in the 1930s, account also has to be taken of structural differences in demand at the firm and industry level. Thus savings and investment will be influenced by the structure and size of the firms concerned. And in turn their size and structure will produce different macroeconomic outcomes.

For instance, in assuming that the process of 'perfect and imperfect competition' would by and large take care of the supply side of the economy (Keynes, 1936, chapter 24) Keynes implied what later became known as the macro-micro synthesis: i.e. that demand management would have relatively uniform effects on firms and industries. Thus it would not of itself favour big versus small business or generate abnormal versus normal profits. This was different from the assumptions of 'Keynesians' in postwar France or Japan who sought to promote bigger, more globally competitive business through long-term investment planning *within* rather than *through* a Keynesian macroeconomic framework of fiscal, monetary and exchange-rate policy.

Keynes also shared another assumption of the neoclassical economists whose macro theory he sought to demolish: i.e. that no individual firm or group of firms was able through their action to significantly affect macro-economic performance. Again, this was contested by the French and the Japanese who saw the role of big business 'sector leaders' as crucial in determining the outcome of entire sectors of economic activity, whether in industry or services. Further, Keynes tended to downgrade monetary or interest-rate policy on the counter-recessionary grounds that high interest rates would inhibit recovery from slump, and also choke off a boom. But thereby, with most of his generation, he neglected the extent to which the rise of big business in what we have called the mesoeconomic sector implied increased self-financing of investment needs and a reduction of the significance of interest-financed external borrowing.

Eichner's Corporate Levy

Alfred Eichner (1976) has emphasised this point in arguing that the level of investment in the big business sector – in his terminology the 'mega-corporation' – will not be constrained by conventional finance limits because big business with price and profit-making power can command a 'corporate levy' to finance the level of desired investment irrespective of marginal interest-rate changes in the cost of external borrowing.

As Eichner puts it: 'assuming that the restraints on pricing discretion are not so great as to preclude any further increase in prices, the availability of funds or liquidity will not set a limit on the amount of investment expenditures undertaken.' He argues that the past trend of corporate sales will be the basis for the expected rate of future industry sales and will be taken as the best proxy for future investment. An increase in prices will increase revenue and thus feasible savings not only for the large corporation but also – to the extent that big business is dominant in an industry – for the industry as a whole.

From Micro to Meso

Thus big business plans its future investment as a function of both *ex post and* projected *ex ante* savings. The feasibility of such planning reflects its market power as a price-maker rather than price-taker. It also reflects its higher potential for self-financing – or internally generated funds – compared to that available to smaller firms in the microeconomic sector. This is illustrated in

Figures 2.2(a) and 2.2(b). Figure 2.2(a) simply applies the standard theory of imperfect or monopolistic competition dating from Joan Robinson (1933) and Edward Chamberlin (1933), and analysed in detail elsewhere (Holland, 1987a, chapter 4). In other words, while the LAC or long-run average cost curve for two firms may be identical, product differentiation or brand attachment can mean that the 'imperfectly competitive' or monopolistic firm can charge price p^1 while the more perfectly competitive firm can only charge price p^2. The imperfectly competitive firm therefore gains a surplus represented by the shaded area *abcd* relative to the perfectly competitive firm. Allowing for the fact that the height of the (broken) vertical axis does not necessarily represent the scale of the price differential on total costs, it is nonetheless clear that there are important long-run differences in the cash flow accruing to the two firms. Through such differences the scope and scale of potential retained earnings for future rounds of investment are increased for the higher price firm. Meanwhile the imperfectly competitive firm can finance advertising or other expenditures from its higher profits, which can in turn reinforce or increase its unequal competitive advantage.

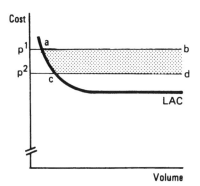

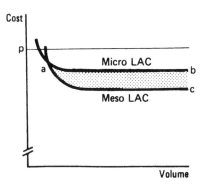

FIG. 2.2(a) Imperfect competition: equal costs and unequal profits

FIG. 2.2(b) Unequal competition: different costs and profits

It is not necessary for the argument that the firm charging the higher price p^1 in Figure 2.2(a) should be large or dominant in its market. Not all imperfectly competitive firms are members of the big league sector rather than small or medium sized. But those firms consistently able to charge higher prices over the long run tend to be big and typical of the mesoeconomic sector rather than small and microeconomic. There are various reasons. For instance, small firms may only be able to charge higher prices representing abnormal or super-normal profits early in a product cycle, i.e. when they are early entrants into a new product market and can 'profit cream' until new entrants pull prices down (Sciberras, 1977, chapter 5). Not least, as is accepted in the standard theory of oligopoly or dominance of markets by a few firms, bigger business can and does exert market power to its own advantage, whether it has gained this in the first instance through (i) effective product differentiation and consumer brand attachment, (ii) successful transition in the product cycle from small-cycle innovation to the economies of scale and low costs possible from high production, or (iii) tactics to block entry or eliminate other firms, or a combination of all three (see further Holland, 1987, chapters 5 and 6).

In other words, some firms also can gain higher profits, and with them the ability to achieve a higher self-financing ratio, through lower costs rather than higher prices. Again, these will tend to be mesoeconomic and especially multinational companies. This result is represented in Figure 2.2(b), where for the assumed prevailing price level p, the LAC or long-run average cost curve of the meso enterprise is lower than the LAC of the micro firm. The abnormal or super-normal profit accruing to the meso enterprise is represented by the shaded area abc.

The reasons for the lower meso cost schedule can include not only (i) straightforward economies of scale through large volume production, but also (ii) oligopsonistic power over suppliers resulting in lower cost inputs, (iii) productivity-raising and cost-lowering innovation in production processes and techniques, and (iv) access to lower-cost labour through multinational investment not available to smaller national companies (Holland, ibid., chapters 5, 6, and 7, and later this volume).

Clearly the higher profit for bigger versus smaller business need not arise exclusively either from lower costs or higher prices. In practice it is likely to represent both. Nonetheless, this results in a situation where self-financed savings from retained earnings in the mesoeconomic sector will tend to be higher than for microeconomic enterprise. Thus for different kinds of firm, as for different social classes of consumer, the savings ratio (or inversely the consumption function) will itself tend to be different. In other words, the consumption or savings ratio of not only households but also of firms is crucial for macroeconomic behaviour.

Corporate Structure and Self-Finance

Such higher self-financing feasible for bigger business not only reduces its dependence on external sources of finance for investment; it also reflects change in the organisational structure of large enterprise with the evolution of the market economy.

For instance, one of the marked features of the rise of the so-called 'managerial capitalist enterprise', as opposed to the old-style 'owner-entrepreneurial enterprise', was its increased demand for external finance and its related dependence on external funds for savings and investment. Marx in *Capital* (Vol. 1, chapter 15) noted the extent to which the early nineteenth-century firm was giving way increasingly to enterprise which was more dependent on external finance for investment – essentially via the stock market. In analysing the increasing divorce between ownership and control in the United States economy in the early twentieth century, Berle and Means (1932) had focused on the structure of ownership rather than the ratio of internal to external finance. But while share ownership may have diluted the control of the owner-entrepreneur of the nineteenth-century model, external finance still represented only a minor share of total corporate finance.

By the mid twentieth century, both managerial control and also finance was increasingly internalised through retained earnings. This amounted to a third phase in the savings-investment relationship. For the first-generation owner-entrepreneur of the late eighteenth and early nineteenth centuries, capital derived mainly from retained earnings. For nineteenth-century firms, with the rise of joint-stock companies, external finance through shares was critical. But for the third-generation giant enterprise, there has been a reversion to retained earnings and where necessary bank borrowing (rather than stocks and shares) to finance investment (Holland, 1987a, chapter 8).

Stocks, Shares and Self-Finance

This phenomenon – suggested especially by UK and US data – has implications both for the role and function of stock markets, and for the savings-investment process in the modern market economy. Keynes himself never exaggerated the role of stock markets in financing savings for industrial investment. Castigating the London market as a casino, he regarded it as a means whereby 'investors' were concerned to make money from money rather than to make money from investment.

As shown in Table 2.1, by the late 1970s and early 1980s the London stock market was providing an insignificant share of funding for UK industrial and commercial companies of less than 5 per cent. Similarly insignificant shares for equity funding were evident from the mid 1970s to mid 1980s in the United States, West Germany and Japan, with the difference between internally generated funds and external share issues represented by a combination of corporate bonds (roughly equivalent in volume to equity), government loans or (in Japan) loans from financial institutions backed by government (*The Economist*, 7 June 1986).

Earlier in the twentieth century Hilferding had observed that in Germany stock-market finance provided a very low level of industrial investment. Similarly, in Italy, throughout the twentieth century, the stock market has been peripheral to the scheduling of savings into investment. In both Italy and

TABLE 2.1   Source of Funds in British Industrial and Commercial Companies (%)

Year	Total internal funds	Issue of ordinary shares for cash
1978	78	4
1979	75	3
1980	65	3
1981	64	5
1982	63	3
1983	78	5
1984*	89	3

* January/September.
Source: UK Financial Statistics and Parliamentary Question, 22 January 1985.

France, state credit agencies since the 1920s and 1930s have provided the bulk of the external finance for growth which neither the stock market nor internally generated funds could ensure. As indicated in Table 2.2, overall self-financing has ranged from 80 to 85 per cent for US companies, and around 70 per cent for European companies, from the early 1970s to early 1980s.

TABLE 2.2   Self-Financing as a Share of Fixed Investment (%)*

	1973	1980
USA	80.0	85.1
Europe	68.8	72.3
Japan	57.8	53.0

* New financial companies. Source: OECD National Accounts 1981, Vol. 1, Table 13, cit. Armstrong, Glyn and Harrison (1984).

Japan has been the exception for two main reasons: first, reliance on state-backed credit institutions which have taken a long-term view of future investment; second, the limited feasibility of financing 'hyper-growth' investment which was double, triple or quadruple the UK and US level from current corporate income.

Meso and Macro Implications

As indicated by such Japanese hyper-growth investment financing, it is clear that the rate of self-financing will tend to vary in relation to (i) the overall rate of growth of the economy, (ii) growth of individual markets, and (iii) the growth of individual enterprise. A higher rate of growth will generate a higher volume of profits, in turn making possible higher self-financing ratios for a given rate of growth. But increased investment growth will tend to reduce feasible self-financing from current revenue. A lower rate of growth will generate lower volume profits. This may be reflected in lower self-financing ratios. Alternatively firms may reduce their forward investment plans and therefore schedule a higher share of a lower profit volume for the self-financing of future investment. For instance, decreased dependence of mesoeconomic enterprise on external finance in turn decreases the extent to which the overall investment schedule of enterprise in an economy will depend on the savings ratio of individuals or households of the conventional model. Such individual or household savings in fact have increased as a proportion of total shareholding in countries such as Britain, through the rise of pension and insurance funds (Holland, 1987a, chapter 9). But the savings schedule itself has increasingly been internalised within meso-economic firms, with major implications for the dynamics of macroeconomic growth.

However, there are three dimensions to the process which need to be considered by policy-makers. First, macroeconomic growth itself will affect not only management expectations, but also feasible self-financing within enterprise. This has implications for monetary policy in the non-monetarist sense of the need to make sufficient finance available for those firms prepared to undertake longer-term investment but unable to finance it adequately from retained earnings. Second, such macroeconomic growth will register different effects on the forward investment planning of meso and microeconomic enterprise, to the extent that they differ in relative market power and can or cannot count on what Eichner has called the 'corporate levy' to appropriate a given share of that macro growth for corporate revenue. Third, the simple income and expenditure model of 'firms' and 'households' reproduced in conventional tests needs to be modified to take account both of the role of government and public credit, and of the role of self-finance in the new big business sector.

There are also implications for monetary policy in the form of government-determined interest-rate changes. Put simply, setting a higher interest level through the rate which the Federal Reserve or Treasury is prepared to pay on bonds, or through a government-determined minimum lending rate, will certainly affect the international flow of savings between countries under a liberal exchange system. Similarly, with a high pound or high dollar, capital inflow can be expected. But whether such an interest rate is appropriate to increasing savings in relation to feasible economic growth is another matter. On the evidence that the external financial needs of leading companies in recent years have been as low as 10 per cent, the cost of raising the macroeconomic interest rate to increase finance for less than a tenth of companies is both astronomic for borrowing in the economy as a whole, and punitive for those smaller microeconomic enterprises which cannot avail themselves of Eichner's 'corporate levy', and may simply find that their higher bank charges put them out of business.

Surplus Generation and Disposal

Inversely, allowing for lower cost borrowing for meso rather than micro-economic companies (Chapter 7), big business will be better able to ride out higher interest rates than smaller firms. Also, with the transformation of the savings function from individual households to institutional investors, it is rare to find a trust or pension fund which is prepared to prefer a minor versus a major company for more than a risk venture fraction of its overall investment portfolio.

Moreover, if there is merit to Keynes' case that household savings increase with higher income, there are grounds from the evidence on corporate self-financing that one should expect the same for business. In other words, bigger business, having achieved a dominant position in a given market in a particular country, may generate a savings surplus in excess of investment needs. Thus the earnings from retained corporate income in the big business sector may tend to exceed investment in individual markets. The higher corporate revenue obtainable either from diminishing costs over the long run or from price-making power tend to increase the internally generated funds, and thus the internal savings ratio of such an enterprise. This is suggested by the rising share of internal self-financing versus external finance in the US and Japan from 1970 to 1985 (*The Economist*, 7 June 1986).

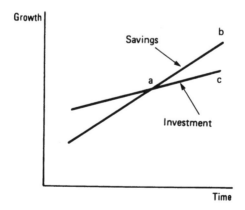

FIG. 2.3 Savings-investment asymmetry

The argument can be made more specific by reference to Figure 2.3, which is adapted from Eichner (1976, p. 207) and derived in turn from Joan Robinson (1962). This indicates the manner in which the rate of growth of savings, ab, will tend to exceed the rate of growth of investment, ac. Eichner rightly stresses that a particular factor in the investment-savings or the consumption ratio of the large corporation refers to the manner in which it evaluates future investment planning in relation to projected sales. Thus, as he says, 'this gives an investment-savings adjustment process that is inherent in combining an investment demand function based on the trend of past sales – as a proxy for the expected future growth of the industry – with a savings function highly sensitive to current sales alone'.

National Expansion

But what does big business in the mesoeconomy then do with the increased savings? Essentially it can follow one of four main strategies.

(1) It can turn its attention to increasing its share of the market through expenditure to improve the quality of its products or services, or other measures – including advertising – to maximise revenues or profits.
(2) It may spread its activities through multiproduct or multisectoral diversification.
(3) It may take over another enterprise in the same or another sector.
(4) It can invest the surplus abroad through multinational expansion.

Such options can be illustrated as follows. First, in sector x in Figure 2.4 mesoeconomic enterprise may command an increasing share of the expansion of output (or the value of services), as indicated by ab and the area corresponding to them. This amounts to market concentration. Second, in sector y mesoeconomic firms may increase their market share through the takeover or elimination of microeconomic enterprise in the market area corresponding to cd. This amounts to the centralisation of markets.

Alternatively, as indicated in Figure 2.5, the mesoeconomic enterprise in sector x may seek to diversify by penetrating sector y either through takeover of a microeconomic enterprise in that sector as indicated by the line ab, or by the more hazardous task of the takeover of the mesoeconomic enterprise in sector y on the line ac, thereby fulfilling the third main option for savings disposal. Since direct takeover between equals is more difficult than takeover of smaller firms by bigger firms, the line ab may be more probable.

Penetration of sector y from a base in sector x may be undertaken by a path similar to ab or ac through the direct establishment and setting up of major mesoeconomic or minor micro operations, rather than takeover. It also, of course, is open to microeconomic enterprise to diversify into other sectors of activity. If they do so, it is likely that they will either take over other micro

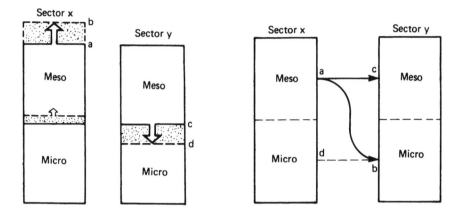

FIG. 2.4   Concentration and centralisation: surplus and increased market share

FIG. 2.5   Surplus and multi-sectoral expansion

firms or establish direct operations in sector y on the broken line db in Figure 2.5, rather than challenging established mesoeconomic enterprise.

Multinational Expansion

The fourth main option for surplus disposal, through multinational investment abroad, is represented in Figure 2.6. In form this corresponds with the process of expansion represented in Figure 2.5, with the difference that the diversification is multinational rather than multisectoral, with countries x and y in Figure 2.6 replacing sectors x and y in Figure 2.5. But the same mechanisms are involved. The mesoeconomic firms in country x may expand their activity in country y either through takeover of microeconomic firms on the line ab, or a joint venture negotiated with mesoeconomic firms in country y on the line ac. Alternatively, as already argued in the context of multisectoral expansion, the mesoeconomic enterprise may simply seek to establish itself through a subsidiary corporation in the mesoeconomic sector of country y, or in a smaller subsidiary enterprise in its microeconomic sector. It is also in principle open to microeconomic enterprises to undertake multinational investment of surplus in country y on the broken line db. However, as with multisectoral diversification, it is unlikely that micro firms will challenge established meso enterprise abroad.

Surplus and Unequal Competition

The process by which big business can expand or diversify its activity on a multisectoral multinational basis is not automatic, pre-determined or

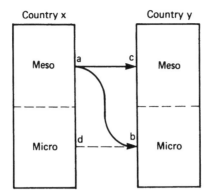

FIG. 2.6   Surplus and multinational expansion

effortless. In practice it reflects the struggle of equal and unequal competition, in which the outcome of specific contests may be unpredictable. However, it modifies the conventional market model in the sense that equal competition tends to be within the meso and microeconomic sectors of a dual market economy, and unequal competition between meso and microeconomic enterprise.

In seeking to increase its share of an expanding market such as sector x in Figure 2.4, the meso enterprise may need either to maintain a relatively low price or restrain the rate of price increase. Similarly, in seeking to increase its relative share of a static market as in sector y in Figure 2.4, the mesoeconomic firm may need to restrain prices under inflationary conditions, or reduce price to the average or variable short-term cost levels of microeconomic competitors in order either to prevent their expansion or alternatively to ensure their takeover or elimination.

Likewise, in aiming to diversify into another sector, on the lines of Figure 2.5, the mesoeconomic enterprise may need to maintain a relatively low price level in order to penetrate the markets concerned through an entirely new subsidiary investment project, whether in the micro or meso sector. Likewise, the same price-competitive conditions may be necessary for the successful establishment of multinational investment in another country on the lines of Figure 2.6.

However, such multisectoral, multiregional or multinational diversification does not necessarily reduce surplus profits or invisible surplus over the medium to long term provided that the markets in the sectors or countries themselves are still expanding. In particular, joint ventures or mergers in one or more economies may increase the price-making power of the mesoeconomic sector by increasing the degree of concentration or share of markets dominated by big business. If this is offset by relatively equal competition between big business on the global market, it nonetheless is a profit game in which minor players from the microeconomic sector rarely survive and most frequently quit the field. Individual markets tell their own tale. In the 1950s there were over two hundred microeconomic motorcycle manufacturers in Japan. By the mid 1980s there were only four mesoeconomic giants – Honda, Yamaha, Kawasaki and Suzuki – each dominant also over international competition (Ohmae, 1985, p. 35).

The Public Presence

A key question is whether the rise of increasingly global big business reflects the art of innovative entrepreneurship, the accident of 'mistakes' by entrepreneurs, or a conscious act of policy in the boardrooms of big business and in government. Schumpeter (1934, pp. 223–36) suggests the first; Friedman (1962, p. 150) claims the second. In practice real winners in the postwar global economy – such as Japan – have combined the skill and muscle of well-managed big business with an intelligent readiness by government to back 'national champions' by forward finance and investment assistance (Vernon, 1974).

Yet not all bigger business is backed by the state. The centralisation of market power in the hands of fewer firms in postwar Britain was only partly aided by government. In services, the firms commanding the upper half of British retailing between 1950 and 1984 shrank from some 4,750 to just over 100 without any government intervention. In manufacturing industry, the top 100 companies increased their share of output from around a fifth to nearly two-fifths in the same period (Holland, 1987, chapter 8). Moreover, coherent state intervention may lack political consensus. Institutions such as the Industrial Reorganisation Corporation in the 1960s and National Enterprise Board in the 1970s – designed to achieve more effective channelling of savings into investment – led to interesting results. But they certainly did not achieve the main aim of their respective architects (including the late Lord Balogh and this author), who had intended that they should directly harness the big business power towards given macroeconomic policy ends such as investment promotion, import substitution or the promotion of a broad wave of innovative new technology. Moreover they were scrapped by the incoming Conservative governments of 1970 and 1979.

By contrast, postwar Japan has achieved a very successful and sustained liaison between big business and the state, with a conscious forward planning of surplus savings into investment. This is not to say that such intervention supplanted the market. But it sought to 'back winners' by extended credit facilities, reinforcing and promoting market success and 'sack losers' by refusing to underwrite or indefinitely subsidise market failure. Of course, such a public policy was facilitated by sustained macroeconomic growth and super-growth. It is easier to be sanguine about winners and brutal about losers if the winners increase employment prospects for those made redundant in flagging or failing enterprise.

In other economies such as France, the state itself has contributed to this centralisation of capital. Andrew Shonfield (1965) has stressed the extent to which the French planners in the 1950s actually sought to achieve a situation in which some 80 per cent of the output of a given sector was produced by 20 per cent of its enterprise. This government strategy less reflected an uncritical assumption that 'big is beautiful' than what Vernon (1974, chapter 3) has identified as concern by French planners to build up 'national champions' among their own enterprise able to compete both in domestic and foreign markets with the larger firms typical of German, British and American competition.

In each case, with government aid or assistance, the result has been a sizeable increase in the share of mesoeconomic at the cost of microeconomic enterprise. Essentially it has been possible through the savings and investment function of big versus small business. A major disposable surplus can be commanded by big business whether the ratio of savings to corporate income is constant or increasing. Simply through its greater scale, larger turnover and more sizeable surplus, big business is in a position to follow any of the main intra-sectoral, multi-sectoral or multinational investment options specified in the foregoing argument. To the extent that big business tends to be able to achieve a higher savings ratio over a greater volume of sales than small enterprise, such trends are significantly increased. They also register a major impact on the performance of the macroeconomy.

2.4 The Modified Multiplier

Through the idea of the multiplier, pioneered by his Cambridge colleague Richard Kahn (1931), Keynes developed the key concept for understanding the process of income generation in the modern capitalist economy.

The concept of the multiplier in its basic income-generation form is derived from the marginal propensity to save (MPS). For instance, we have seen earlier in this chapter that Keynes assumed a consumption function of 0.8, and thus a savings ratio of 0.2. Supposing the MPS to be 0.2 (and inversely the marginal propensity to consume, or MPC, to be 0.8), then four-fifths of £100 million will go to consumption on the first round of expenditure, and four-fifths of four-fifths on the second round, and so on. Such a sequence is spelled out in Table 2.3. At this stage, the essential analytical point to grasp is that the multiplier is the reciprocal of the MPS or marginal propensity to save. Therefore, if the MPS is 0.2, the multiplier is 5 (i.e. $1/0.2 = 5$).

In fact, allowance has to be made for part of the extra income generated to be spent on imports, and also on indirect taxes. Taking total leakage into account, the postwar marginal propensity to consume in Britain has been closer to 0.6 than to 0.8, and the marginal propensity to save therefore 0.4 rather than 0.2. As a result, a 'standard multiplier' can be derived of 2.5, i.e. half that following from Keynes' 'intuitive' assumptions. Nonetheless, the concept of the multiplier is clearly important. You may or may not 'double your money' for any given injection of income into the economy. If you are the government, and are charging an effective rate of both indirect tax and direct tax on companies and individuals, you can also get a large part of your income back through the tax due on successive rounds of the income generated.

For many years after the war the concept of the multiplier was un-controversial, and played a key role in economic planning or programming. Yet under the monetarist pall, the multiplier baby was thrown out by some policy-makers with the Keynesian bathwater. When the present author asked, in a written parliamentary question in 1983, what estimates had been made of the private income generated by public expenditure since 1979, Chancellor of the Exchequer Nigel Lawson simply replied that 'estimates of this kind are not made' (Parliamentary Question, 13 July 1983).

For reasons shown later in this chapter, such anti-Keynesian obtuseness would be dismissed as at best idiosyncratic by the managers of those economies such as Japan which have decimated Britain's shipbuilding and motorcycle industries, taken over a large share of its passenger motor vehicles, and ensured that the UK, with the highest consumption of video recorders per household in the world, imports such videos or produces them from imported kits.

Basic Multipliers

One reason is the implications of the multiplier for public spending in the economy. This can be explained from the simple mathematical model set out in Table 2.3. This assumes that £100 million is added to the economy. As already indicated, if the marginal propensity to save is 0.2, then the multiplier is its reciprocal, i.e. 5. Keynes had assumed that the multiplier would be more or less proportional. Therefore a given injection of £100 would result in the kind of sequence represented in Table 2.3.

Thus a given injection of income will generate increased demand for sectors *a* to *n*, which in turn results in firms in those sectors taking on more labour to

TABLE 2.3   The Basic Income Multiplier

| | Response to injection of £100m | | |
	Consumption (£m)	Savings (£m)	Total (£m)
1st round	80	20	100
2nd round	64	16	80
3rd round	51	13	64
4th round	40	11	51
nth round	0	0	0
Total	400	100	500

meet the demand concerned. Table 2.4 gives a hypothetical exposition of the additional employment generated – or multiplied – through the economy as a result of an addition to expenditure on house building of £100 millions.

TABLE 2.4   The Basic Employment Multiplier

| | Year 1 | | Year 2 | | Year n |
| | (£m) | (000s) | (£m) | (000s) | |
	Y	E	Y	E	Etc
Housing demand	100	10	110	11	Etc
Construction companies	40	4	44	4.4	
Construction materials	30	3	33	3.3	Etc
Other materials	20	2	22	2.2	
House furnishings	10	1	11	1.1	Etc

(where Y = value added, and E is employment.)

TABLE 2.5   The Basic Matrix Multiplier

| | | Period 1 | | | | | Period 2 | | | | |
		a	b	c	...n	Total	a	b	c	...n	Total
Final demand		10	5	15	10	100	12	6	18	12	120
Intermediate demand	p	5	2	5	3	40	6	2.4	6	3.6	48
	q	3	2	4	5	35	3.6	2.4	4.8	6	42
	r	2	1	6	2	25	2.4	1.2	7.2	2.4	30

Just as the income multiplier implies an employment multiplier, so this in turn also implies inter-industry or inter-sectoral effects known as a matrix multiplier. Set out in Table 2.5, this simply means conceptualising or representing the income or investment multiplier in another way which focuses on inter-sectoral effects between firms.

Thus as shown in Table 2.5, an increase in aggregate consumption from 100 to 120 first generates an equivalent demand for the output of sectors *a* to *n* (whether for goods or services, or both), which in turn generates indirect demand for additional output from sectors *p* to *r*.

Dynamic Effects

A combination of the income, employment and matrix multipliers makes possible an analysis of the dynamic effects of additions to expenditure in the economy. Figure 2.7(a) reformulates the identities of the basic Keynesian model of the circularity of income and expenditure. The left-hand side of the diagram shows the transmission of savings (S) into investment (I), and of consumption (C) into employment (E). This sequence represents demand generation, as does the right-hand side of the Figure, where MD represents the matrix or inter-sectoral demand for additional investment generated by firms expanding investment, and WD represents the wages demand generated by additional employment. The resulting additional expenditure produces a higher level of income in the economy as a whole.

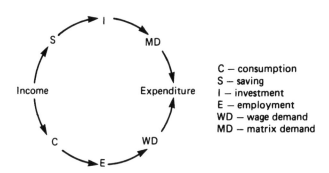

FIG. 2.7(a)   Keynesian circularity of income and expenditure

Figure 2.7(a) implies both theoretical concepts and causal effects. For instance, S and C represent effectively the savings and consumption functions analysed earlier in this chapter. The sequence S-I does not necessarily imply that all savings are embodied in actual investment; only than that some savings are. The sequence C-E and sequence S-I are complementary, implying both that additional consumption creates demand for greater output and that this is met by higher investment which generates additional employment. The matrix demand (MD) on the right-hand side of Figure 2.7(a) includes demand for investment goods generated by firms undertaking new investment expenditures, but it also represents demand for components, raw materials, energy and services in other firms in the economy. The wages demand (WD) implies an increase in waged (or salaried) expenditure from the higher level of employment represented by E, and does not necessarily imply (although it may mean) higher real wage levels.

The consequential effects of an initial increase in income are represented in Figure 2.7(b). This makes explicit some of the main relationships implied by the first, second and third rounds of the multiplier process. Thus, simply extrapolating from the basic sequence of Figure 2.7(a), the first investment and employment effects I^1 and E^1 generate matrix and wage-demand effects MD^1 and WD^1 and imply first-round total expenditure effects Exp^1. In turn, the second investment and employment rounds I^2 and E^2 imply secondary matrix and wage-demand generation MD^2 and WD^2 and secondary total expenditure effects Exp^2, with repeated (and diminishing) investment, employment and other consequential effects I^3, E^3 etc.

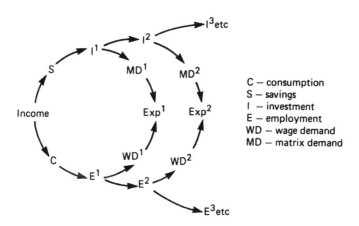

FIG. 2.7(b)   Multiplier effects of income and expenditure

Public and Private Multipliers

So far, the exposition of multiplier effects has not distinguished between private and public income and expenditure. However, as already outlined in Chapter 1, public income and expenditure typically represent between a third and a half (and in some cases up to two-thirds) of total spending in the advanced capitalist countries. **Figure 2.8** illustrates this parallel and complementary sequence of private and public income and expenditure. The sequence in the upper part of the diagram simply rearranges the various functions of savings, investment, consumption, employment, wage demand and matrix demand already outlined in Figure 2.7(a). The lower sequence of Figure 2.8 is essentially the same. The key difference is that the savings function performed in the upper sequence by private financial intermediaries is undertaken in the lower sequence through either taxation or public borrowing which finances the process of public spending and investment. This does not mean that public corporations (whether in mining, industry or services) do not themselves save. In practice they do so with retained earnings on the lines already examined in this chapter, thereby reflecting their respective savings and consumption functions. Further, the multiplier from public spending creates new taxable income or a new tax base in both the public and private sectors, thereby financing some of the initial expenditure.

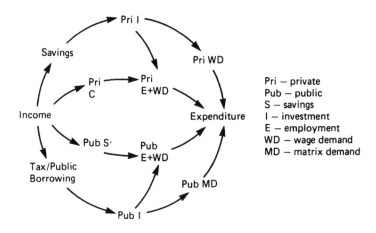

FIG. 2.8   Multipliers in the mixed economy

Mutual Demand Generation

Extending the analysis of Chapter 1 on mutual demand and supply relations in the mixed economy, Figure 2.8 implies that demand generated by (i) private consumption and public spending, and (ii) private investment and public investment, will necessarily generate income for both the private and public sectors of the economy. For instance, public investment in power stations where these are within the public sector generates demand for the output of private-sector companies (such as GEC in the United Kingdom and GE in the United States), which in turn may promote private-sector investment by such a company. Similarly, public housing or hospitals in the UK economy is overwhelmingly constructed by private enterprise so that the housing and hospital spending budgets generate consumption, and in turn investment, for the private sector. Similarly, as represented by the centre-vertical arrows in Figure 2.8, private employment wage demand generates demand for public services in many of the mixed economies, for instance in utilities such as gas and electricity, and public services such as transport, health and education. In turn, public-sector employment and wage demand generates or sustains employment and income in the private sector through consumption of the broad range of private-sector goods and services.

As Michael Barratt Brown (1970, p. 183) has rightly stressed, such multiplier effects are an example of the central economic principle of cumulative causation – a principle applied extensively in the context of regional and development economics by Gunnar Myrdal (1957 and 1968). This is especially important because, as we shall see in Chapter 3, the multiplier can as easily work in reverse as it can in forward gear. Thus positive multipliers can become negative, reversing a 'virtuous' circle of expansion into a 'vicious' circle of decline.

It should be noted that the mutual multiplier generation of demand and supply between the private and the public sectors as indicated in Figure 2.8 registers only the primary or first-round multiplier effects. Second- and third-round effects on the lines of Figure 2.7(b) clearly apply for both the public and the private sectors.

Micro Multipliers

Conventional multiplier theory tends to assume that the matrix or inter-sectoral effects of any given increase in aggregate expenditure will be neutral between firms. This follows partly from the hold of the paradigm of the 'representative' firm in a 'representative' industry. It is also partly a consequence of the theoretical 'dyslexia' noted in Chapter 1, by which some economists who have in their time studied the theory of oligopoly nonetheless assume that the behaviour of individual microeconomic firms is not significant in affecting macroeconomic outcomes.

Some exceptions have been made for the social effects of external diseconomies such as pollution. For instance, Samuelson (1976, p. 477) allows that 'wherever there are externalities, a strong case can be made for supplanting complete individualism by some kind of group action'. But this potentially powerful admission has not been followed through by admitting that the role of the matrix multiplier, when combined with internal and external economies, will register significantly different effects for different kinds of firm in the economy.

For instance, the conventional microeconomic model of external economies can be represented in the form of Figure 2.9(a). In this perception, or *gestalt*, a firm which manufactures product *x* but which either chooses or is not able to produce a range of its own components or supplies, will purchase them from firms *a* to *e*. Figure 2.9(b) shows that if the firm doubled its output from *x* to 2*x* while buying its supplies on the same ratio from other firms, its increased output would raise the production of its external suppliers to 2*a*, 2*b*, 2*c*, etc.

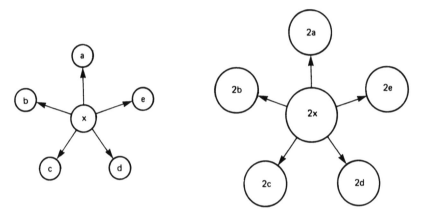

FIG. 2.9(a)   External suppliers and external economies

FIG. 2.9(b)   Expansion and external economies: the conventional model

Even if all the firms concerned were very small, such a doubling of their output would register some effect on the macroeconomy. Moreover, the doubling of output for the six firms registers only the first-round matrix multiplier effects. These in turn will give rise to second- and third-round effects on those companies and sectors from which firms *a* to *e* buy their own inputs, and will generate demand from those services and utilities, as well as consequential employment, wage and income multipliers.

Meso Multipliers

Moreover, if conventional theory explains its relative silence on such matters on the grounds that the effects are very small, the same cannot be said for oligopolistic sectors typical of the mesoeconomy, where three, four or five firms often represent between two-thirds and 95 per cent of output.

For instance, Figure 2.9(c) reproduces the actual supply and output structure of the Toyota car company. Toyota accounts for a quarter of the Japanese automobile industry, and increased its output 3.5 times from the mid 1970s to the mid 1980s (Ohmae, 1985, p. 4). Unlike the 'externalised' model of demand and supply in conventional theory, Toyota both has internalised much of its main components production and also has direct links with subsidiary and affiliate companies accounting for 60 per cent of its domestic sales through 250 exclusive retail companies representing 2,850 retail outlets.

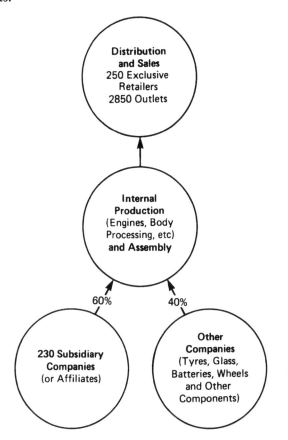

FIG. 2.9(c) Toyota's internalised economies

The result of Toyota's long-term expansion has not only been a significant addition to macroeconomic output in the Japanese economy, and a dynamic *inter*-sectoral matrix multiplier on the lines of the conventional model. It has also meant major *intra*-sectoral concentration of production in the hands of a few firms. Japan used to have 32 separate motor-vehicle manufacturers. It now has eleven, of which two are truck firms. Of the rest Toyota, Nissan and to a lesser extent Honda dominate both domestic industry and – increasingly – the international economy.

International Multipliers

The export multiplier operates in essentially the same way as an investment or employment multiplier. In other words, as illustrated in Figure 2.10(a), increased demand for exports generates demand in both what is commonly termed the export sector of the economy, and secondary demand for domestic inputs supplied to exporting firms (in other words those activities in the economy which are not directly exported). The export multiplier plays a key role in explaining the process of sustained growth, super-growth and in some cases the hyper-growth of so-called 'miracle' economies, as analysed in some detail in the following and later chapters.

The export multiplier does not of itself imply that all inputs for production of exports come from the domestic economy, rather than also generating import demand. The most successful of the postwar economies – Japan – ensured a specific liaison between the private sector and public institutions such as the Ministry of International Trade and Industry (MITI) to maximise the domestic economy inputs and minimise imported inputs for investment and production in the export sector. Nonetheless, the export multiplier implies a relatively clear distinction between different firms in different

FIG. 2.10(a) The national export multiplier

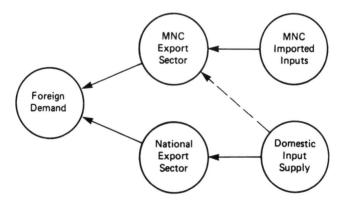

FIG. 2.10(b) The multinational export multiplier

countries. It essentially assumes that exports promote beneficial multiplier effects for domestic industry.

Multinational Multipliers

By contrast, as indicated in Figure 2.10(b), both the export and domestic multipliers assumed in conventional theory are profoundly qualified by the role of multinational companies which typically supply a significant share of component inputs for production in any one country from subsidiary plant in other countries. Table 2.6 (already cited in *The Market Economy*, Chapter 7, in the analysis of vertical integration) reproduces the range of subsidiary plant in different countries which the Ford Motor Company has employed to produce components for its Fiesta model.

TABLE 2.6   Multinational Component Production for the Ford Fiesta

Part	Source
Suspension components	Wulfrath, West Germany
Fuel tank	Saarlouis, West Germany
Window winder	Croydon, UK
Distributor	Belfast, Northern Ireland
Transmission	Bordeaux, France
Road wheels	Genk, Belgium
Engine	Valencia, Spain
Bumper plating	Cologne, West Germany
Spark plugs	Enfield, UK
Windshield glass	Tulsa, Okla. USA
Carburettor	Belfast, Northern Ireland
Engine components	Leamington and Basildon, UK
	Cologne, West Germany
Final assembly	Valencia, Spain
	Saarlouis, West Germany
	Dagenham, UK

Two implications in this context are, first, that demand expansion induced by fiscal policy in one country does not necessarily register matrix multiplier effects on its domestic industry; the second, that export demand for the final product will not register the conventional export multiplier sequence of Figure 2.10(a). In fact, as illustrated in Figure 2.11, a recent empirical study by Dan Jones (1985) has shown that while the imported components of Austin-Rover amounted to only some 10 per cent of the final value of UK production in 1984, those of Ford and Citroen-Peugot-Talbot (formerly

Chrysler UK and previously Rootes UK) averaged some 20 per cent, while those of Vauxhall (owned by General Motors) constituted about half of the final value of UK production (and nearly 100 per cent of total bought-in components).

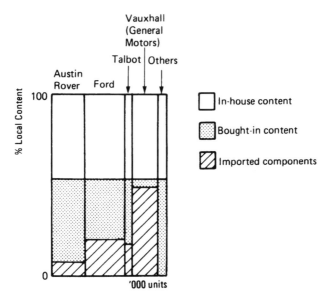

FIG. 2.11   Multinational sourcing of components to the UK in the passenger vehicle industry (Source: Jones, 1985)

There is a third implication which is important for the theory of international trade and payments. Conventional multiplier theory has always allowed for a reduction of the domestic income multiplier due to imports from abroad. However, within a paradigm of international trade between different firms in different countries, it has hitherto been assumed that a government can offset such imports (and also increase export competitiveness) be devaluing its currency. Within the conventional paradigm of international trade, such a devaluation would increase the domestic currency price of imports and thus tend, under price-competitive assumptions, to reduce import volume and thereby improve the balance of payments. But, as illustrated by the examples of Ford and General Motors/Vauxhall, the integrated structure of components supply on a multinational scale within the mesoeconomic sector inhibits such devaluation and price effects. Thereby it profoundly qualifies some of the most basic assumptions of international trade and payments theory (as elaborated further in Chapter 5).

An irony of this process is that such substantial sourcing of components from outside the UK by multinational companies is registered in conventional national accounting as UK manufacture. In other words, the external foreign multiplier effect of such imported inputs is registered on the trade account as an import, but on the domestic production account is registered in terms of the final value of the vehicle in which a major share of the value in fact is imported. This failure of conventional accounting procedures to register the real matrix effects of the inputs and outputs of multinational companies is compounded by the extent to which production abroad by foreign-based multinational companies has increasingly been financed in the 1980s by savings outflow from the UK (following the abolition of exchange controls by the post-1979 Conservative government).

Inflows and Outflows

The analytic sequence is illustrated in Figure 2.12, where for argument it is assumed that the economy with savings outflow and imported final goods or components is either the UK or the US. Thus savings (S) from income registered in the UK or US has outflowed to investment either in other countries (I^{ioc}) or investment by UK and US based multinational companies abroad (I^{mnc}). While this may generate demand for imports from the UK or US economies (either between different companies in different countries or through the subsidiaries of a multinational company), it also generates matrix demand in other countries and in other subsidiaries, outside the UK or US, of the same multinational company $(MD^{ioc/mnc})$.

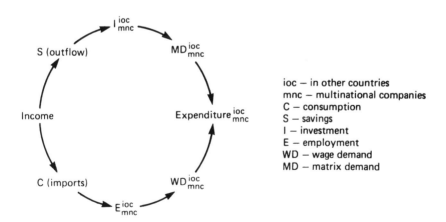

ioc — in other countries
mnc — multinational companies
C — consumption
S — savings
I — investment
E — employment
WD — wage demand
MD — matrix demand

FIG. 2.12   Multinational investment, employment and multiplier effects

Therefore, while such foreign investment and matrix demand may generate some exports from the UK or US, as represented in Figure 2.12, it will also generate substantial expenditure in other countries for foreign subsidiaries of the UK or US multinational company (Expenditure$^{ioc/mnc}$). Similarly, the consumption (C) from income in the UK or US results in imports which generate employment in other countries or in the subsidiaries of British or American multinational companies abroad ($E^{ioc/mnc}$). This in turn generates wage demand on the same basis outside the UK or US ($WD^{ioc/mnc}$) and therefore expenditure abroad rather than in the domestic economy.

The argument does not imply a presumption against gains from international trade. One country's imports are other countries' exports. It is crucial for recovery of the global economy, deeply in crisis for more than a decade since the early 1970s, that the current beggar-my-neighbour deflation of trade and payments should be reversed through a better-my-neighbour recovery of global spending, trade and payments.

The key point is that multinational multipliers profoundly qualify the national multipliers of conventional post-Keynesian theory. In the conventional sequence there is an increase in domestic demand either through autonomous market forces or as a result of government demand-management policy. The latter may take the form of a tax-reducing fiscal policy or monetary policy which lowers the interest-rate cost of credit and purchase finance. But such aggregate demand changes in an economy with a highly multinational trade structure may generate as much or more demand abroad (e.g. for automobile components) as it does at home. Therefore, rather than promoting a process of industrial regeneration it may simply worsen the balance of payments. Such 'multiplier leakage' is especially important for economies such as those of the US or UK, where the value of foreign production by US and UK multinationals abroad has since the early 1970s been more than double those countries' visible export trade (UN, 1973).

The argument is only partly modified by the fact that many multinationals operating abroad tend to finance a high proportion of their investment needs through retained local earnings rather than savings outflow from the parent company or home country. A major share of the foreign investment outflow from the United Kingdom economy following the abolition of exchange controls by the 1979–83 Conservative government has been in property and financial investments abroad. This total capital outflow has on an annual basis equalled or exceeded total UK manufacturing investment and illustrates a profound asymmetry or imbalance in the structure of UK trade and capital flows.

Costs and Benefits

Clearly the government of any economy experiencing a major savings and investment outflow, such as that of the UK, should be advised to analyse the net gain or loss from such foreign investment in terms of remitted profits from abroad versus net savings or capital outflow. But remitted profits to the UK economy from foreign investments represent a minor fraction both of the profits earned abroad – a high share of which are recycled through tax havens – and of the cumulative savings outflow from the UK. From 1980 to 1985 (*Economic Trends*, HMSO, July 1985, p. 49) interest, profits and dividends remitted to the UK were almost exactly offset by transfers of capital abroad. Further, the argument made by Mrs Thatcher that there is no disadvantage from major investment outflow abroad, since Britons would be able to live on the income remitted from it, overlooks precisely the investment, employment and income generated in other countries by capital outflows from the United Kingdom. By investing British savings, such countries are able to undertake successive rounds of productivity-raising new investment and thus make possible an increase in their own income, tax and welfare levels which are unavailable to a disinvesting or de-industrialising UK economy.

Moreover, if an alternative government in the United Kingdom were to aim to channel a higher proportion of savings from national income into domestic investment it would need to be able to ensure a domestic supply structure adequate to meet a higher proportion of domestic demand. Thus while an alternative government might well be advised to reintroduce exchange controls to reduce the disproportionate scale of savings outflow, it would also need to pursue an industrial policy aiming to increase the share of the investment, matrix, employment and income multiplier effects within the UK.

If such a government seeks to fulfil this objective simply by operating at the abstract level of sectors of activity through Sector Working Parties or National Economic Development Committees, it will fail to identify the main potential actors in the dynamics of investment generation and modernisation in the economy, and in particular large-scale and mainly multinational enterprise versus smaller-scale national capital. Thus it is important for any industrial policy worthy of the name to be able to identify whether multiplier effects benefit multinational rather than national, and large rather than small, enterprise.

2.5 Investment and Supply

One of the most striking differences between Keynes and the Keynesians was in their respective analysis of the supply of investment.

Keynes' Investment Demand Schedule

Keynes knew very well that no manager hoping to survive in business would invest without expectation of a profitable rate of return. At the same time, as already stressed in Chapter 1, he realised that managers or entrepreneurs would not invest simply if the cost of investment was low (or if interest rates were also low) but would be crucially influenced by their expectations of the likely rate of the growth of demand. This underlay his concept of the 'marginal efficiency of capital', which he defined in terms of the expectation of the yield and of the current supply price of capital assets. As he put it, the marginal efficiency of capital 'depends on the rate of return expected to be obtained on money if it were invested in a newly produced asset; not on the historical result of what an investment has yielded on its original cost if we look on its record after its life is over' (Keynes, 1936, p. 136). Thus Keynes emphasised that for investment to occur what had happened *ex post*, or in the past, was less important than the rate of return which it would gain *ex ante*, or in the future. Such a rate of return would need to subtract or discount the prevailing or anticipated annual rate of interest.

In this sense, Keynes was seeking an analytic counterpart for the marginal propensity to save in terms of the marginal propensity to invest. In other words, he was seeking to identify main elements of *an investment demand schedule*.

However, in stressing psychological factors in the concept of the marginal efficiency of capital, and thus the social psychology of an investment decision-making class, Keynes was sceptical about the rationality of those expectations later given such cardinal importance by some monetarist economists. Thus he wrote in *The General Theory* (ibid., p. 149): 'There are not two separate factors affecting the rate of investment, namely the schedule of the marginal efficiency of capital and the state of confidence. The state of confidence is relevant because it is one of the major factors determining the former, which is the same thing as the investment demand schedule.' Yet it could not be assumed that such expectations would be rational. They could be influenced by a range of factors, including not least the political predisposition or prejudice of managers depressed, as he put it, by the prospect of a Democratic 'New Deal' in the United States or the advent of a Labour government in Britain. Keynes did not mean by this that the marginal efficiency of capital or the investment demand schedule was entirely irrational. As he put it: 'we are merely reminding ourselves that human decisions affecting the future, whether personal, political or economic, cannot depend on strictly mathematical expectations, since the basis for making such calculations does not exist' (ibid., pp. 145–7 and 162–3).

The Accelerator and Disequilibrium

In contrast with the concept of the multiplier, which only entered the arena in the early 1930s with the publication of Richard Kahn's article on the relation of investment to unemployment (Kahn, 1931), the concept of the *accelerator* dates back at least to the First World War with an article by J. B. Clark (1917, pp. 217ff).

Clark realised that relatively small changes in demand could lead to quite large changes in investment. The basic reasoning was simple enough. While demand is continuous, investment is not. But investment, even if it means adding an assembly line rather than an entirely new plant, may be necessary to meet any increase in demand if existing plant is near full capacity. Managers may need to invest now to meet expected future demand.

In this sense the economic concept of the accelerator is different from the mechanical principle of acceleration in a motorcar. The former assumes a disproportionate response from investment to demand. The latter assumes a proportionate response from the motor to putting one's foot on the accelerator pedal.

This point has been well put by Stonier and Hague (1957, pp. 428–9) in the following terms. Assume in a hypothetical economy that there are 1,000 machines making consumer goods. If the life of each machine is 10 years, then the output of the investment goods industry will be 100 machines per year. If the demand for consumer goods rises by 10 per cent, the industry will need not only another 100 machines to meet the additional demand, but also the 100 new machines which on an annual basis it installs to meet replacement demand. Thus a 10 per cent increase in demand in any one year will mean an enormous rise of 100 per cent in the demand for machines (from 100 to 200). If the machines last longer than 10 years, the proportionate effect on the machine-making industry will be even greater. Thus, especially when combined with the cumulative effects of multipliers, accelerator theory provides a key insight into disequilibrium in the market economy.

The Equilibriated Accelerator

The imbalancing effects of the accelerator and its role in fluctuations of national income and expenditure are admitted by Lipsey (1979, p. 527), but Lipsey does not follow through this admission in the illustration of the accelerator theory which he then gives in his text (ibid., Table 36.1). As he puts it himself, the arithmetic example in his own illustration shows that 'the amount of net investment is *proportional* to the change in sales' (our emphasis). Or, as he again states it, 'for net investment to remain constant, sales must rise by a constant amount per year'. The point is not that Lipsey is fiddling the figures so much as that his representation of the argument accents the conditions for equilibrium rather than admitting the disproportionate impact of the accelerator on investment.

The same tendency (or bias) follows from the best known exposition of the accelerator principle by Samuelson (1939). Following a suggestion by Alvin Hansen, Samuelson sought to derive the principle of acceleration from Keynes' multiplier analysis. In essentials, this amounted to the application of 'difference equations' to models of a business cycle with a lagged consumption function in which – in technical terms – the period for analysis was defined as having the same length as the consumption lag. The result was an assertion that investment would occur in the period concerned at a level sufficient to supply the added capital goods required to produce the increment of consumer goods output which had occurred since the last period.

As with Lipsey, Samuelson does not deny possible disequilibrium effects of multipliers and accelerators but he downgrades destabilisation by specifying the conditions under which equilibrium could occur. The same is true with Ackley, one of the foremost Keynesian analysts of the consumption function, who is concerned in his own analysis of multiplier and accelerator models to specify the conditions for a path to restored equilibrium (Ackley, 1961, p. 489).

Keynes versus the Accelerator

Moreover, such equilibrium application of the accelerator principle implies a rationality in the decision-making of entrepreneurs or management which Keynes himself maintained was not feasible. In other words, it assumes away those factors of social psychology which Keynes argued could not be reduced to simple mathematical formulations.

Indeed, in contrast with the general assumptions that the accelerator is a Keynesian principle, Keynes entirely ignored it in writing the *General Theory*, despite the fact that it had been widely recognised since Clark's original article in 1917. He not only did not mention the technical principle of the accelerator, but stressed instead both the multiplier and the marginal efficiency of capital – both of which are essentially psychological concepts. For Keynes, the multiplier depends ultimately on a psychological propensity to save rather than to consume, which in turn is determined by consumption tastes and habits as against the propensity to thrift.

By contrast, in its allegedly Keynesian (or neo-Keynesian) applications, the accelerator principle depends on highly technical assumptions. As Ackley himself admits (Ackley, 1961, p. 492), 'one trouble, perhaps, is that the accelerator relationship is given too fixed and rigid a form. The acceleration principle is sometimes presented as a technological or engineering relationship: more output requires more machinery, and more output is therefore impossible until more machines have been produced.' Following Samuelson and other Keynesian economists, Ackley implied that the difficulty with such a technological formulation could be overcome by the introduction of lags in the relationship. But for many years, accelerator models met with only a mixed reception under empirical testing.

Kalecki and After

During the postwar period, several economists sought to improve on these mixed results for accelerator models by assessing the capital stock adjustment principle analysed in more detail in Chapter 3. However, neither the accelerator nor capital stock adjustment provided the apparent stability found in the first empirical testing of Keynes' own concept of the consumption function.

Part of the problem, reflecting the analysis on paradigms and perceptions in Chapter 1 of *The Market Economy* (Holland, 1987), lay less in giving wrong answers to the right question than asking the wrong question in the first place. The obvious question to ask in any analysis of the accelerator which assumed investment responses by firms to changes in demand would be to analyse and evaluate what firms themselves actually do. Kalecki (1954) did this by specifying an investment demand function for the business or corporate sector. But Kalecki's arguments stayed in the footnotes of mainstream postwar economic theory, appreciated only by a few cognoscenti.

It was several years later that Robert Eisner in the United States advanced the argument by introducing an accelerator model which was different from previous formulations in two important respects. First he argued, with empirical support, that a properly specified investment demand function would depend on changes in aggregate demand, not only in the previous year, as implied by some of the previous lagged models, but over several previous years. Second, he claimed, again with empirical support, that changes in investment were related less to changes in aggregate demand, than to changes in the demand experienced by individual industries, with these changes being reflected in past sales figures (Eisner, 1963).

Eisner's analysis related changes in the demand for investment by individual industries, to changes in sales over the previous seven-year period, with his aggregate investment demand function amounting to the sum of individual industry demand schedules.

Such disaggregation was bringing accelerator analysis nearer to the main actors in investment decision-making, i.e. leading companies. Alfred

Eichner (1976, ch. 6) advanced on Eisner by claiming that bigger business invests in terms of (i) an accelerator-type 'investment demand function' related to sales trends and (ii) the 'corporate levy' through which it can assure sustained self-finance by its oligopolistic pricing.

Micro and Meso 'Accelerators'

If we focus on the investment decision-making of enterprise over the kind of seven-year period to which Eisner has drawn attention, we can identify two factors which are significant in updating the relevance of the acceleration principle.

The first factor is the trend to big business or the change in the size and structure of enterprise over the period in which accelerator models had themselves been developed, i.e. since the 1930s. This may well account for some of the success which Eisner encountered in testing accelerator models over such a time-period. In other words, by the early 1960s, when he was writing, big business of the kind we have identified as mesoeconomic in character had come to dominate specific industries, and in the case of the United States had become typical of the economy as a whole.

The second related factor is that only relatively large enterprises are in a position to plan investment for a period of, for example, the seven years over which Eisner found significant results for the accelerator principle. In other words, only the mesoeconomy has sufficient command over the market to be able to plan for a period such as seven years with relative impunity.

This is partly due to the character of big business as price-makers rather than price-takers. Such price-making is especially relevant when they are faced with a recession in demand for products, since it increases the extent to which they can compensate themselves for lower sales by raising prices (as we will see further in Chapter 8). Broadly speaking, microeconomic enterprise, reflecting its role as a price-taker, tends to be *passive* in relation to the rate of growth of demand, whereas mesoeconomic enterprise can afford to be more *active*, reflecting its role as a price-maker. This does not mean to say that mesoeconomic enterprise is in a sufficiently powerful position to create its own demand – though it may influence it by advertising. But it does mean that it can afford to take a longer-term view of markets than can smaller firms.

Shorter and Longer Term

The point at issue can be illustrated by practical examples from the automobile industry over the period from the 1930s to the 1960s and 1970s. For instance, as illustrated in phase I of Figure 2.13, in the United Kingdom in the 1930s the Morris Motor Corporation was introducing a large number of new models over the short term. With an average of one new model every two or three years, it on one occasion introduced as many as three new models in one year. This is illustrated in the diagram by the rising step-like pattern of its investment, which – for simplicity of exposition – has been represented as an increment to investment in each of three successive years. The rate of growth of demand relating to this investment decision, which in conventional analysis would imply an accelerator relationship, is indicated by the rising demand curve d^1d^2.

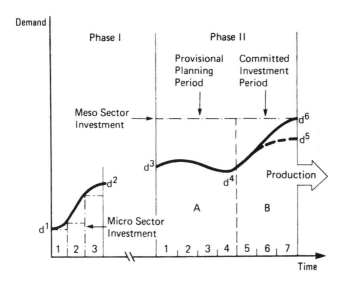

FIG 2.13   The investment supply schedule

If, however, we move to the 1960s, as indicated by phase II of Figure 2.13, we find a quite different type of investment schedule in the mesoeconomic motor-vehicle sector. For instance, when the Ford Motor Company in the United Kingdom introduced its Escort model in the UK, it took some seven years for the vehicle to advance from the stage in which it was a gleam in its designer's eye to unveiling for the first time at a motor show. The investment schedule of Morris's owner-entrepreneurship, in which he could dash from design ideas into immediate production, supervising the process in his own workshops, has been replaced in the big business sector by careful long-term planning of research, development, product profile and pricing, not only in relation to other companies' products and their likely reaction but also in relation to the existing product range or mix of the investing company itself.

Planning and the Planning System

In other words, the relatively simple accelerator principle of Keynes' economics is now part of the more complex forward planning in the big business sector which Galbraith (1974, part 3), with reason, has called *The Planning System*.

In today's big league markets, the pre-market research and other factors involved in the forward planning of such a product may take at least three to four years. Such a provisional planning period is indicated by phase A in Figure 2.13. The investment planning period itself – including the very important consideration of which companies would provide which inputs, on what specification and according to what quality, i.e. the matrix multiplier effect of the investment where this was external to the enterprise – may take a further three to four years, represented by phase B of Figure 2.13.

In this forward-planning period, the demand for vehicles may or may not rise consistently. There may in fact be a downturn in demand similar to the line $d^3 d^4$ in Figure 2.13. Nonetheless, to maintain market share, i.e. for reasons pertaining more to competition from other big businesses than to the overall rate of growth of income in the economy, or even the rate of growth of sales in the industry as a whole, the big business may consider it necessary to pursue the investment despite an interim fall in the rate of growth of demand.

The specifics of such provisional planning and the investment scheduling itself are less important than the general picture. An enterprise considering globally competitive investment today needs to do so on a large scale, which implies a longer period of forward planning and investment decision-making than in the 1930s when the Keynesian macro-micro synthesis of the accelerator concept was established. However, the force of the argument does not depend simply upon the previous rate of growth of demand in the industry, or the previous rate of growth for the model in the firm concerned. It also depends very much on what Keynes rightly called a psychological as well as a more strictly economic judgement. And this includes the judgement of the long-term growth of the industry irrespective of short-term demand changes of the kind stressed by accelerator and capital-stock adjustment models.

Planning for Life

Thus what happens to current demand does not necessarily determine the investment decision of enterprise in relation to projected demand. In contrast with accelerator models, investment may be committed by big business irrespective of the variation of actual demand between d^5 and d^6 in Figure 2.13. For one thing, to survive, the modern corporation must grow in its own markets, and knows it. It therefore has to plan for growth by aiming to sustain or increase its market share, whether or not this is justified by current demand.

Thus while Morris may have planned for three years ahead in response either to actual demand changes or a projected anticipation of increased demand, the provisional planning period for committed investment in the modern motor-vehicle industry – as already indicated in Figure 2.13 – may well amount to seven years. Adding a minimum seven to eight year production period, a period of up to 15 years may therefore be necessary to achieve real prospects of investment pay-off. For an industry such as steel, the planning, investment and production time-period necessary for a fully economic pay-off of investment is considerably longer, and indeed may act as a disincentive to private producers (Holland, 1972, chapter 1).

Precisely because of these long-term supply schedules, it is possible that a major investment project will not be brought fully on-stream in the earlier part of its life-cycle. Certainly it is clear that even if capacity exactly fulfils the rate of growth of demand for the product over the period of its planning cycle, management cannot be influenced by short-term changes in the rate of growth of demand if it is to undertake the investment necessary to achieve technically feasible economies of scale.

Practical Limits

This is realistic to the extent that it is possible for a motor-vehicle producer to lay down an additional assembly line to take account of increased demand, and for a steel producer to increase capacity. But in the real world there are limits to which such increases in investment capacity can be undertaken in response to short-term demand changes. A new production line cannot be introduced without considerable forward planning both for direct pro-duction and for the indirect provision of its inputs. In a very high assembly industry such as motor-vehicles, the assurance of a supply on an appropriate scale at the appropriate time is of critical importance for the enterprise.

Similarly, in the case of steel, it is not feasible to add capacity unless such increases had been anticipated in the overall planning of the plant in the first place. In practice, for very long-term investments such as steel, this will involve the scheduling of major overhead costs, such as the selection of a site of sufficient size and the basic infrastructure necessary for later expansion of capacity in integrated production. It should be clear, at the very least, that it is almost exclusively large enterprise which is in a position to be able to envisage such long-term investment planning. Likewise, such enterprise cannot be influenced in its investment planning simply by short-run changes either in the overall level of demand in the economy as a whole or for its own product range.

Disjointed Demand and Supply

This is not to say that there is no long-term 'accelerator' mechanism for large-scale mesoeconomic enterprise. Nor is it to suggest that the investment decision-making typical of the mesoeconomic sector is irrational, or based simply on intuition of future demand. In practice, Eisner's seven-year lag in the accelerator makes good sense in terms of the analysis which we have introduced. For highly capital-intensive industries with very long-term pay-off, such as steel or heavy chemicals, companies such as ICI in the United Kingdom have revealed that they take a very long-term judgement of the overall rate of growth of demand for their products. In the case of ICI, as indicated personally to the present author, this involves looking at the rate of growth of demand over a period of decades and judging viable capacity expansion in terms of the long-term past trends rather than the short-term demand changes.

Clearly such a long time-period for an accelerator effect can promote major divergences between the anticipated and the actual rate of growth of demand. The size of investment increases both through the rising technical composition of capital and through the simple fact that bigger business tends to undertake larger investment with a longer pay-off. This gives rise to very considerable potential divergences between actual and feasible economic growth.

Dislocated Budgets

Not least, when big business dominates so large a share of capital formation, output and employment, the decisions of a few big firms to invest or disinvest can prove critical not only to the future of an industry, or a national economy, but also, in the case of the global demand by multinational companies, to the world economy as a whole. A fuller appreciation of this process depends on analysis of the dynamics of economic growth outlined in Chapter 3, and also of the trade, investment, location and capacity use by multinational big business worldwide, examined in Chapters 4, 5 and 6.

However, it should already be clear that a basic asymmetry has now emerged between the short-term demand management implied in government budgetary policy and the longer-term investment supply schedules of big business (whether national or multinational) in individual economies. Whereas the investment horizon for big business under modern production conditions may range from seven to twenty years, it is conventional for governments to introduce *annual* budgets adjusting fiscal or monetary policy. While such annual budget changes may have suited Morris and his improvised investment and production sequence in the 1930s, there is no way in which they can individually determine the longer-term investment planning of big business in the modern market economy.

This is not to say that fiscal policy through annual budgets can have no influence on investment supply. In any fully employed economy, where investment was correspondingly fully employed, an expansionary budget would tend to influence decisions to undertake additional investment by some firms.

But in some economies such as the United Kingdom there has typically been a 'stop-go' budget cycle, in which periods of 'go' or demand expansion – whether stimulated by fiscal policy and tax reductions, or increases in public spending – have been followed by periods of 'stop', in which indirect taxation in particular has been raised (as was typical in the 1950s) or public expenditure has been cut (as was typical since the major deflationary package of July 1966). The result has been that, in their own interest and with considerable rationality for their own longer-term investment planning, big business may discount the expansionary or deflationary intentions of short-term macro budget changes.

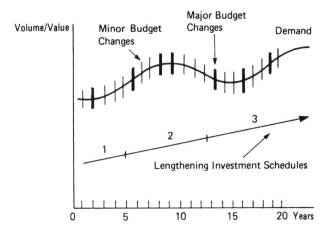

FIG. 2.14   Short- and medium-term Budgets: long-term investment

As indicated in Figure 2.14, this has increasingly been reflected in a dislocation of demand-side government budget changes and supply-side investment planning. Whereas governments may seek to promote a 'climate of expansion' or alternatively a 'climate of stability' through fiscal or monetary policy, a lengthening time-period for the amortization of investment, represented by phases 1 to 3 on the supply side of the economy in Figure 2.14, tends to counter or discount either major or minor budget demand adjustment by government.

Expectations

Monetary policy alone cannot offset with such an asymmetry between short-term demand changes and the lengthening investment schedule of companies. Monetarists have tried to bridge the increasing divorce between demand management and the supply side of the economy by developing the theory of 'rational expectations'. This is based on the principle that if governments show a sufficient political will to commit themselves to a constant increase in the year-on-year money supply, as recommended by Friedman, and if this is combined with restraint of public expenditure to avoid the Keynesian 'inflationary gap', then rational management (and unions) will respond in their investment planning (and wage restraint) as inflation falls. However, the monetarists face the same problem as the Keynesians in terms of the 'credibility gap' between the demand-management intentions of governments and the supply-side imperatives of big business which increasingly needs to undertake larger-scale and longer-term investment in order not only to compete but also to survive.

As elaborated in later chapters of this volume, the problem is compounded for the monetarists by the extent to which liberalisation of capital flows means that firms are encouraged to relate their investment decisions to demand changes on a global scale, through multinational operations, rather than to the more 'stable' climate expected in any one country through a regular increase in the money supply. Also, for governments pursuing Keynesian demand-management policies, the multinational trend of savings and investment tends to qualify the simple accelerator or decelerator effects intended by governments pursuing expansion or contraction in the domestic economy.

Caught in the perception or paradigm of the conventional macro-micro synthesis, and neglecting the dominance on macroeconomic outcomes of big business in the multinational sector, governments in the advanced capitalist countries have been reluctant to admit the imperative of gaining more effective accounting and accountability over the investment planning intentions of big business as a prerequisite for ensuring a closer alignment between their own demand forecasts and domestic supply.

2.6 Summary

(1) Like Ricardo, Keynes chose to elect the economics of Jean Baptiste Say as the target for his own economic theory. Essentially Say had asserted that, left to its own devices, the market would ensure that supply created its own demand.

(2) Keynes challenged this by claiming that supply would not automatically create its own demand, and that the state needed to intervene to ensure adequate demand to keep resources at full employment.

(3) A key concept in Keynes' original exposition was the consumption function or the share of income consumed (rather than saved) by individuals in society. This by and large assumed that individuals would save a constant share of their income.

(4) Milton Friedman developed his attack on Keynesian macroeconomics from his dissatisfaction with consumption function theory. But in fact such theory can be criticised on non-monetarist grounds. Several economists after Keynes criticised his neglect of structural change in the supply side of the economy and the impact on macroeconomic policy of unequal social and spatial income distribution within society.

(5) Such limits of Keynes' macroeconomic paradigm are matched by other limits in the neo-Keynesian model of the macroeconomy. In particular, it is now evident that the consumption-investment functions of leading firms in the big business multinational sector (the mesoeconomy) dominate the macroeconomic performance of individual economies.

(6) Such big business is not dependent on monetary policy (or interest-rate changes) in its corporate investment strategy. In particular, self-financing through price-making power in the big business sector enables it to increase retained earnings (savings) in such a way as to finance desired investment expenditure in a manner neglected by both Keynesian and monetarist theorists.

(7) In contrast with conventional models of the multiplication of income, employment and inter-industry demand in the market economy (the income, employment and matrix multipliers), big business has tended to internalise the supply of commodities and components in its own production process and has extended this on a multinational basis throughout the world economy.

(8) Such multinational multipliers profoundly qualify conventional Keynesian or neo-Keynesian theory. The investment decision-making of multinational big business is now determined by its market strategies worldwide rather than simply responding to changes in income in any given national economy (on the lines hitherto assumed by Keynesian accelerator or capital stock adjustment theory).

(9) Broadly speaking, small-scale national enterprise conforming with the conventional microeconomic model tends to be passive and reactive in relation to the rate of growth of demand (the Keynesian accelerator), whereas bigger mesoeconomic multinational enterprise pursues an active investment strategy worldwide in relation to its prospects and potential in global markets.

(10) The supply-side planning of global big business to meet such market potential often means commitment of investment which needs to be covered over a period of 10–15 years or more. Such investment planning spans periods longer than the lifetimes of several governments, and certainly longer than the tenure of most national finance ministers.

(11) As a result, a disharmony has emerged between short-to-medium-term 'fine tuning' of national budgets by Keynesian finance ministers (or short-term adjustment to money supply by monetarist ministers), and investment planning by big business.

(12) This disharmony is compounded by the multinational range and spread of big business decision-making.

3 Growth and Cycles

Although Keynes claimed to have written a general theory of employment, interest and money, he was preoccupied with the challenge to how to increase employment in the short run. He made no more than passing observations on the theory of long-run economic growth or development. This is under-standable granted the battle he had to wage with the 'monetarists' of his time, who assumed that short-run unemployment would be remedied in the long run by the readjustment of costs and prices through the free working of the market.

Keynes countered this view with his famous aphorism that 'in the long run, we are all dead'. Or, in other words, we might have to wait for ever before the market readjusted demand and supply at full employment. He was especially concerned that a downwards spiral of demand and supply could reach a level of unemployment equilibrium, or a stalemate of market forces which could not be broken without active government intervention to reverse the spiral and promote recovery of supply through increasing demand. Nonetheless, he provided no systematic theoretical framework for the application of his own concepts of demand management to the long-run working of the market economy.

3.1 Comparisons and Contrasts

It is arguable that if the Keynesians after Keynes had been better able to wed his own insights with those of Kalecki (1954) on the role of the firm, the result could have been a theory of the dynamics of economic growth which bore a better relation to postwar reality. But in practice the first-generation Keynesians sought to develop long-run models of economic growth which stayed firmly within the new macroeconomic paradigm which Keynes himself had helped to establish. In so doing, they addressed themselves to two main questions. First, if the economy was below full employment, under what conditions would entrepreneurs or managers invest so as to realise growth potential? Second, granted the multiplier effect of an expansion of demand, what was to prevent the economy from an 'explosive' upswing in activity leading to excess demand over feasible supply, inflation, increased imports and a balance-of-payments crisis?

The Harrod Model

The basic insight which established 'Keynesian' growth theory was Harrod's formula (Harrod, 1939 and 1948) that the rate of growth of an economy would depend on three or four main factors: how much it saved and invested, the efficiency with which it used this investment, and the way in which actual growth affected the confidence or investment expectations of entrepreneurs. From the start, such a formulation had its critics. Thus David McCord Wright (1949) ended a review of Harrod's *Towards a Dynamic Economics* by stating that:

> The author will have to broaden his methodology greatly if he is really to develop a true theory of dynamic growth and its consequences. Partial equilibrium problems of *regional* and *industrial* relocation, the resulting pressure group obstructions, the instinct of workmanship and insecurity, *cultural* rates of change in innovation and formulation of desires, basic shifts in *social* outlook induced by change, all these must be considered. One looks forward to an eventual theory in which the econometric and the sociological may be harmoniously merged. [italics added]

It is striking that nearly forty years after the publication of this review, and nearly half a century after Harrod's pioneering article of 1939, very few of the factors stressed by Wright have been generally incorporated into the mainstream of Anglo-American growth theory. For many years, rather than seeking to include structural, social or spatial dimensions of growth and change, neo-Keynesian theory evolved models of economic growth which in large part exorcised the very process of change itself.

The Domar Model

Ironically, this was only in part due to the original Keynesian growth model of Harrod. To a considerable extent it derived from the model of economic growth devised at about the same time by Evesey Domar (1946).* On the other hand Domar was trying to go 'beyond Keynes' in a very crucial sense, stressing the importance of what in later years has become known as the 'supply side' of the economics of growth, as opposed to the 'demand side' of the management of output and employment.†

---

* An allowance which he made himself, for while claiming that his approach was 'superior to that of Keynes', he added that it should not be looked on as 'a final solution'.

† 'Supply side' in this context means literally what it says, rather than implying the monetarist theory which in the 1970s was to come to dominate the popular use of the same words, but which amounted in practice to a restatement of the business case for tax reduction.

The reason was simple enough, for as Domar himself wrote: 'Because investment in the Keynesian system is merely an instrument for generating income, the system does not take into account the elementary fact that investment also increases productive capacity.'

Domar added, that 'clearly a full employment level of income five years ago would create considerable unemployment today,' and stressed that 'the standard Keynesian system does not provide the tools for deriving the equilibrium rate of growth. Growth is entirely absent from it because it is not concerned with changes in productive capacity. This approach permits the assumption that employment is a function of national income (and the wage unit), an assumption which can be justified for short periods of time, but which will result in serious errors.'

Domar did not deny the importance of the Keynesian emphasis on the level of income but assumed instead that 'employment is a function of the ratio of national income to productive capacity'.

Harrod plus Domar

Conventionally, the Harrod and Domar formulations or growth models have been considered to be not only similar but identical. In fact there are vital differences between them. But to facilitate first comparison and – later – their contrast, Domar's model is here expressed in symbols similar to Harrod's.

Both models start from the Keynesian *ex post* identity of savings and investment. In other words, they assume that savings actually are invested, rather than resulting in an uninvested surplus. They also assume a stable savings relation, in which the propensity to save – or savings function, s – is a constant proportion of national income. The capital-output ratio, c, represents the ratio of an increase in output to the capital necessary to produce it. Thus $G = s/c$, where G is the rate of growth of output, s is the marginal propensity to save and c is the capital-output ratio.

The formulation stresses two factors in economic growth. First, the savings ratio s, and second the capital-output ratio c. Logically, either an increase in s, i.e. the ratio of embodied savings to income, or a decrease in c, i.e. the capital necessary for a given increase in output, can increase the rate of economic growth.

The point can be put simply in numerical terms. If the ratio of national income saved and invested is 15 per cent and the capital-output ratio is 5, then the rate of growth of the economy will be 3 per cent ($^{15}/_5 = 3$). With a savings ratio of 25 per cent and the same capital-output ratio, the rate of growth would be 5 per cent. Conversely, with a savings ratio of 15 per cent and a capital-output ratio of 3, the rate of growth would be 5 per cent; and with a savings ratio of 25 per cent and the same capital-output ratio of 3, it would be 8.33 per cent.

Such differences are not purely hypothetical. For much of the postwar period, savings in the British economy amounted to some 15 per cent of national income, but the annual rate of growth of total output (GDP) amounted to some 3 per cent per annum, indicating an average capital-output ratio of just under 5. By contrast, the Italian economy throughout the 1950s achieved a rate of growth of over 5 per cent a year in GDP, with an average savings ratio of some 22 per cent of national income. Thus in Italy savings were higher than in Britain, but the capital-output ratio was slightly lower (around 4). In West Germany for much of the 1950s savings were high (around 24 per cent) and the capital-output ratio low (around 3), with an annual rate of growth of GDP of some 8 per cent.

The Role of the Capital-Output Ratio

The relation between capital and output represented by the concept of the capital-output ratio can be measured in physical units or value terms. It can also measure either the average or the marginal relation between capital and output. Thus the average capital-output ratio for an economy is the stock of capital divided by the annual flow of output, while the marginal or incremental ratio (ICOR) measures the relation between increments in the capital stock and increments in output.

As Thirlwall has stressed, with fluctuations in income the average capital-output ratio may differ substantially from the ICOR. In periods of recession the average ratio will tend to be higher than its 'normal' value, since output will be depressed in relation to the size of the existing capital stock. At the start of an upturn in activity, the ICOR will appear low relative to the average. Thus the value of the ICOR depends very much on the stage of the business cycle (Thirlwall, 1978, pp. 112–13).

There is also a relation between the *structure* of the economy and the value and significance of capital-output ratios. A high savings ratio or savings function for an economy as a whole is the inverse of its consumption ratio or consumption function. As already stressed, various factors can contribute to such high savings, including not only the savings of households and government credit but also the retained earnings of firms. In turn, the rate of saving by firms will depend on the rate of profit, including the basic difference between revenue (sales) and costs (including wages). This will determine the ratio of self-financing to external borrowing, which in turn will influence the feasible ratio of capital invested in the economy as a whole. When a few companies can dominate the investment structure of key sectors of modern industry – as is typical of the mesoeconomy – such *corporate* capital-output ratios can register not only a significant effect on the macroeconomic investment growth rate, but also thereby on the success or failure of recovery or development programmes.

Thus the aggregate capital-output ratio has both the scope and limits of a purely macroeconomic concept. It does not of itself explain the process of economic growth, its rate, structure or spread. As Kuznets (1966) has stressed, such a process demands both disaggregation and interpretation. Moreover, given the extent to which modern technology in the late twentieth century can substitute or displace labour rather than create new jobs, raising capital accumulation does not necessarily raise employment.

Nonetheless, at the analytic level, it is clear that lowering the capital-output ratio can raise the aggregate rate of growth of an economy or sustain profits (depending on the rate of growth of costs) and thereby enlarge the capacity both for self-financing and for credit.

Thus the gains from lowering the capital-output ratio are considerable. Higher rates of growth or development become possible both with the same savings ratio and also – under certain conditions – with a lowered ratio of savings to national income. Thus an economy which initially was growing with a savings ratio of 15 per cent and a capital-output ratio of 5, giving a growth rate of 3 per cent per annum, could in principle gain a higher growth rate of 4 per cent per annum by lowering its savings-investment ratio to 12 per cent provided that it also managed to lower its capital-output ratio from 5 to 3. A variety of factors would be involved in such a lowering of capital-output ratio, including (1) gains from size and economies of scale; (2) what has become known as 'X' efficiency, or the role of managerial efficiency; (3) technical progress and productivity-raising innovation in enterprise; (4) structural change from traditional sectors to modern sectors of activity; and (5) improved labour utilisation.

Harrod versus Domar

It has already been suggested that the conventional identification of the Harrod and Domar growth models is mistaken. But the differences have not been made explicit. Their basic formulation, in Harrod's terminology, is literally an identity and should in effect be written as $G = s/c$.

The reason for this can be seen by translating the individual terms into their Keynesian context. Thus G is the growth of output, which could therefore be expressed as O. Savings are assumed to equal capital investment, and the savings therefore amounts to capital, c. The capital-output ratio or capital coefficient in turn could be written in fuller form as c/o rather than c. Which in turn gives the identity $O = s/c/o$.

This identity formulation of the basic Harrod and Domar equation does not render it meaningless. For the reasons already given, it focuses attention on both the potential for raising growth by raising investment, and the potential of raising output per unit of capital through technical progress (lowering the capital-output ratio). But the significance of the equation lies very much in which factor, i.e. higher savings and investment or a lowered capital-output ratio, plays the more important role in promoting economic growth.

For instance, constrasting conclusions were drawn from the basic Harrod and Domar equations by economists in Britain and France after the war. In Britain much attention was drawn to the lower share of savings and investment in the 1950s than in continental European countries. In France, which started the decade with a similar savings and investment ratio, far more attention was paid to the qualitative rather than quantitative aspects of the Harrod-Domar basic formulation, i.e. to lowering the capital-output ratio and thereby increasing productivity through innovation. This was especially the case with the work of François Perroux, who stressed the importance of productivity-raising innovation in the economy as a whole and particularly in 'entirely new' industries in 'growth poles' or development centres attracting new activity (Perroux, 1963 and 1965). Thus Perroux allocated a central role to the industrial and regional dimensions of growth which McCord Wright had criticised Harrod for neglecting. His emphasis had a considerable influence on the course of French postwar planning and the emergence of a modern French economy.

Equilibrium and Disequilibrium

The differences between the Harrod and Domar models do not lie simply in their respective emphasis on the role of savings or technical progress, permitting a lowered capital-output ratio. Domar stresses the *capacity* of an economy under growth, and the need to ensure sustained investment to achieve an equilibrium of supply, demand and employment. Harrod, in a more strictly Keynesian sense, introduces entrepreneurship into his model, and in particular the reaction of entrepreneurs or managers to changes in the rate of growth of national income. He thus evolves what amounts to a behavioural model of economic growth. Also, more in line with Keynes' economics, and certainly the Keynes stressed by Leijonhufvud (1968), Harrod concerns himself as much or more with departures from equilibrium, or disequilibrium growth, than with those conditions which may be necessary to achieve an equilibrium growth path in the economy.

Part of the contrast between the fuller version of the Harrod model and the basic Domar equation lies in Harrod's use of the 'accelerator' concept. For while c in Harrod's basic equation simply means a capital-output ratio, he transforms this in the fuller version of his model into Cr, or the Keynesian accelerator.

The other new component in the fuller Harrod model is Gw, the 'warranted rate of growth'. Rewritten, the fuller Harrod equation thus becomes $GwCr = s$, where Cr is the accelerator. Harrod distinguishes the concept of 'actual' growth (G or Ga in his notation), i.e. that growth which actually occurs, from what he calls the 'natural' growth rate (Gn). Gn means the maximum potential growth of the system as limited only by physical, financial and labour constraints.

Warranted Growth

Yet it is Gw, the 'warranted' rate of growth in Harrod's model, rather than simply the accelerator Cr, which takes it beyond the basic Domar formulation of economic growth. In essence, Gw means the growth rate which entrepreneurs consider to be justified or 'warranted'. The concept is important, and has survived initial criticism. Nonetheless, it has been claimed that Harrod gives at least six independent qualifications of the Gw concept:

> Gw progressively becomes the rate which (1) leaves each entrepreneur satisfied with what he has done; (2) allows for some individual disappointments but keeps entrepreneurs as a group, on balance, satisfied; (3) keeps them doing the same thing; (4) equates *ex ante* savings and investment; (5) concerns only the part of investment directly linked to consumption; (6) somehow differs from the 'proper' warranted rate 'which would obtain in conditions of full employment' [Wright, 1949].

The criticism may be over severe, since Harrod himself applies his concept of Gw in different contexts. In itself the warranted growth concept had the considerable merit of introducing the reactions of entrepreneurs or management into what otherwise in the Domar formulation, despite his concern to introduce a 'supply side' to Keynes, remains essentially a demand-side drama without supply-side actors – a criticism of so-called Keynesian economics later to be made by the new conservative economics in the United States in the 1970s and 1980s to considerable effect.

In fact, one of the most telling criticisms of Harrod's concept of Gw lies precisely in its assumption that firms behave in the same way, responding like some kind of chorus line, to given demand changes. Harrod did not distinguish, as Kalecki did, the performance of oligopolistic firms dominating whole sectors of activity – or what could be called 'sector leaders' – from smaller and in the main dominated firms, or 'sector followers'. Also, though with more reason granted the predominantly national structure of production in his time, Harrod did not distinguish between national and multinational companies, or meso and microeconomic enterprise. And criticism can be made of Harrod's somewhat unquestioning use of the accelerator concept. This is crucial not only in the sense that (in the form of

Cr) it is central to his $GwCr = s$ formulation, but also in his own description of his model as 'a marriage of Keynes' "acceleration principle" with his "multiplier" theory'.

Further Questions on Acceleration

The limits of the accelerator principle have already been criticised in Chapter 2 on the grounds that it failed to take account of changes in the structure of the supply side of the economy. In reality, as Perroux (1965) has stressed, neither firms nor sectors of activity have (a) the same structure or size, (b) the same level of activity, (c) the same speed of reaction or adaptation, nor (d) the same growth potential. Such criticism is especially important in relation to the difference between traditional and modern sectors of the economy, where the scope for expansion is determined not only by the overall rate of change of income in the system but also the rate of growth of specific markets – a distinction well grasped by the Japanese Ministry of International Trade and Industry but almost entirely neglected by the British Treasury since 1945. In short, any theory of economic growth which is to be useful in explaining change, needs to disaggregate the accelerator concept below the macro-economic level – as has already been done in part in Chapter 2 by specifying different reactions by meso and micro companies to income or revenue changes.

But even at the level of macroeconomic aggregates, the accelerator principle has been subjected to extensive criticism. By concentrating on net investment it sidesteps the issue of replacement investment, which may well change in such a way as to offset the changes in net investment. Also, more basic versions of the theory, such as Harrod's initial formulation, under-estimate the issue of stock adjustment, or the extent to which firms will tend to build up stocks of inputs and raw materials during periods of high growth in order not to be 'caught short', while running down stocks (which imply a cost in purchased but unused materials) during periods of slacker demand.

Autonomous and Induced Investment

There is also a problem for the accelerator principle of relating so-called 'autonomous' and 'induced' investment. The accelerator is assumed to 'induce' investment in the short term through the response of management to changes in the rate of growth of demand. But much of the investment undertaken in the real world economy is not simply 'induced' by demand changes in this short-term reactive manner. Quite apart from the lengthening time-period for 'pay off' in many large-scale investment projects, there is the whole area of economic and social infrastructure in contemporary economies, such as motorway construction, electrification schemes, oil and gas networks, or hospitals, schoois and housing, which are not 'induced' by short-term income changes.

Various efforts have been made to overcome such deficiencies in the macroeconomic accelerator concept. For instance, Matthews (1959) has commented that:

> The basic idea underlying the acceleration principle – that the desired stock of capital will depend on the level of output – is a sound one, and has great importance for the theory of the cycle and the theory of long-run growth. But the particular formulation of it involved by the acceleration principle, that investment is a function of the rate of growth of output, depends on too many special assumptions to be acceptable.

For instance, the stock of capital at the start of an investment period is not necessarily that appropriate to the level of income in either the current or preceding period; there may already be excess capacity or – alternatively – unfilled areas of investment potential. Moreover, the investment committed during the current period will not necessarily adjust the capital stock to the level appropriate to match the actual change of income in the current period. Hence the level of investment during any given period is not satisfactorily expressed as a function of the rate of change of income as implied by the basic accelerator concept.

Capital Stock Adjustment

However – following others – Matthews argued that most of these difficulties can be overcome by modifying the basic accelerator mechanism through the *capital stock adjustment* (CSA) principle. This means that investment decisions will vary directly with the level of national income and inversely with the stock of capital in existence. It is consistent with the basic idea of the acceleration principle, but claims that investment will be directed towards bringing the stock of capital into alignment with changes in the level of income (Matthews, 1959, p. 41).

The CSA principle has received more favourable statistical analysis than the simple accelerator mechanism.* Nonetheless, in advocating it, Matthews stresses that what is relevant to investment decisions in a particular sector of the economy is the stock of capital in that sector, not the stock of capital in the whole economy. He argues that the CSA equation for an economy as a whole should therefore be properly understood as that which is obtained by summing the CSA equations for individual sectors (Matthews, 1959, p. 42).

* In particular the work of Jan Tinbergen (1938), Klein and Goldberger (1955) and Hollis Chenery (1952).

Perroux also warns against over-aggregation, with more force, arguing that if we express all 'induced investment' (whether in accelerator or CSA models) by a single aggregate coefficient, 'we give up all sectoral analysis and omit the fact that economic activity is unequally active and passive. . . . In any actual situation unutilised resources (labour, raw materials, unused capacity) are not equally distributed among industries and regions but concentrated and polarised' (Perroux, 1965, p. 87).

Perroux is also highly critical of the distinction between autonomous and induced investment, claiming that it 'does not bear very serious examination'. Criticising the marriage of accelerator and multiplier models of the Keynesian kind explicitly avowed by Harrod, he claims (ibid., p. 101) that:

> Quite apart from their questionable behaviour assumptions . . . the family of models born of these parents, despite the undoubted rigour of their presentation, remains highly unsatisfactory because of the insufficient disaggregation. Where has one ever met entrepreneurs who purely and simply make investment decisions in terms of the level of income of yesterday and the day before? These creatures endowed with memory but deprived of every other sense would be a poor argument for capitalism. Fortunately for the system, however, they are less common in life than in economic literature.

Marx and Economic Growth

Marx's argument on what later became known as the theory of economic growth is wider-reaching than most neo-Keynesian formulations. It encompasses not only (a) the quantity and type of capital employed and (b) the productivity of labour, but also (c) the role of labour reserves in permitting restraint of wages (in his terminology, the role of the 'reserve army' of labour) and (d) the centralisation and concentration of capital in the hands of big business.

Marx stresses the relation between the quantitative and qualitative aspects of capital. In his own terminology, a rise in the *organic* (quantitative) ratio of capital to labour also tends to be associated with a rise in its *technical* (qualitative) composition.

For much of his exposition in volume 1 of *Capital* Marx describes accumulation or growth as a quantitative rise in the mass of the means of production (or, in his terms, constant capital). As he puts it, 'if the extension is only quantitative, then for a greater or smaller [proportion of] capital in the same branch of business the profits are as the magnitudes of the capitals advanced' (Marx, 1887, vol. 1, p. 629). Such an exposition is comparable with the emphasis on savings in the basic Harrod and Domar expositions of Keynesian growth theory, where it is assumed that savings are embodied in investment and thus form capital. Less capital will mean less output and lower profits, and vice versa.

Quantitative and Qualitative

However, Marx also stresses that with the increased use of machinery in modern industry, there is not only an increase in the mass of constant or fixed capital, but also an increase in its productivity. Thus in his own words, 'the means of production play a double part'. The growing mass of the means of production, or a rising organic composition of capital, also imply a change in its technical composition. 'This change in the technical composition of capital, this growth in the means of production . . . is reflected . . . by the increase in the constant constituent of capital at the expense of its variable component', i.e. labour and wages. (Marx, ibid., p. 622).

Marx argues that the accumulation of capital, though originally appearing only quantitative, is in fact qualitative (ibid., pp. 628–9). He illustrates this by contrasting the spinning industry in Britain in the mid nineteenth century with its more primitive condition at the beginning of the eighteenth. Expressing the contrast in contemporary non-marxist terms, the difference was between a capital-labour ratio of 1:1 in the early 1800s and a capital-labour ratio of some 7:1 half a century later – a difference which we have seen replicated for various sectors of 'modern industry' in economies such as Japan since the Second World War, where labour costs have fallen to less than a twentieth of total costs in some industries such as automobiles (Ohmae, 1985, p. 4). Marx realised that this meant a relative displacement of labour by machinery, but not necessarily an absolute decline in the labour employed in the industry concerned: 'if the progress of accumulation lessens the relative magnitude of the variable part of capital [labour costs], it by no means in doing this excludes the possibility of a rise in its absolute magnitude' (Marx, ibid., p. 623).

In effect, Marx was stressing the rise in what today is usually expressed as an increase in the capital-labour ratio and with it an increase in output per unit of capital employed: i.e. a rise in output, implying a falling capital-output ratio. He was well aware of the critical nature of these relationships to what he called the 'vast transformation' of the process of production with capitalist accumulation, and the force of his insight clearly impressed itself on Evesey Domar, who acknowledges Marx in the statement of his own argument.

3.2 Stability and Instability

Keynes and the Keynesians

It has been stressed in earlier chapters that Keynes' demand economics of disequilibrium have been wedded by so-called Keynesians with equilibrium models of supply. The search for equilibrium conditions thereafter dominated many allegedly Keynesian models of the macroeconomy.

Harrod's analysis, however, is very much within the tradition of both Keynes and – perhaps unconsciously – Marx in *hypothesizing* equilibrium conditions but stressing the instability of the system. Moreover, this stress is crucial to the relevance of Harrod's model of economic growth to real world conditions. As a macroeconomic view it is open to the criticisms already outlined. But it also contributes to our understanding of the divergence between the 'balance' of theoretical models and the 'imbalance' of reality. Also, as correctly emphasised by Hicks (1949), Harrod's theory of economic growth provides a very useful framework for an analysis of the trade or business cycle in capitalist economies.

Upswings and Downswings

The basic reason for the instability of economic growth in the Harrod model lies in the nature of the accelerator-multiplier relationship of Keynes. The multiplier mechanism increases (or decreases) the cumulative value of any given injection (or contraction) of income into the economy. Therefore a given initial expansion of the system will be amplified in a manner probably unforeseen by those whose individual investment and spending decisions contribute to it.

Harrod (1939) expresses this in terms of his own warranted growth concept as follows:

> Suppose that G exceeds Gw. The consequence will be that C, the actual increase in capital goods per unit increment of output, falls below Cr, that which is desired. There will be an undue depletion of stock, or shortage of equipment, and the system will be stimulated to further expansion. G, instead of returning to Gw, will move further from it in an upward direction, and the farther it diverges, the greater the stimulus to expansion will be. Similarly, if G falls below Gw, there will be a redundance of capital goods, and a depressing influence will be exerted; this will cause a further divergence and a still stronger depressing influence, and so on.

Harrod's Knife Edge

The system is unstable. Any so-called equilibrium position in fact represents a 'knife edge' between expansion and contraction. The situation can be expressed diagrammatically as follows. In phase 1 of Figure 3.1 actual growth, G^1, exceeds warranted growth, Gw^1. Due to multiplier effects, in phase II it continues to diverge (G^2) from that growth path which management in phase I would have considered likely to be warranted in the latter period. But management reacts to the higher-than-anticipated expansion and adjusts its warranted growth expectations accordingly, from Gw^1 to Gw^2.

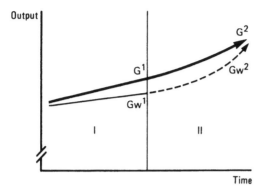

FIG. 3.1   Harrod instability: the upswing

Conversely, in phase I of Figure 3.2 actual growth, G^1, is lower than anticipated warranted growth, Gw^1, and due to 'negative multiplier' effects sinks further, to G^2, in phase II. Management again reacts – this time to the lower-than-anticipated path of the economy, and expectations are revised downwards, from Gw^1 to Gw^2.

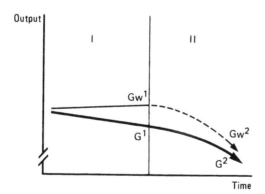

FIG. 3.2   Harrod instability: the downswing

According to Harrod, if the actual rate of growth is higher than the warranted rate, there is a deficit of capital. The attempt to make this up acts through the accelerator and produces an even greater rate of growth. The same holds in reverse in the downwards direction.

Harrod's analysis of the likely impact on growth expectations of a divergence of *G* and *Gw* can be expressed in terms of what Keynes succinctly called the 'animal spirits' of entrepreneurs, i.e. their profit expectations or the marginal efficiency of capital. Thus a greater expansion (or contraction) of the system than expected will in turn increase (or decrease) profit expectations and with it the instability of the system.

Harrod, Robinson and Hobson

In an early review of Harrod, Joan Robinson (1949) admits that Harrod's theory amounts to a projection into the long-period of the central thesis of Keynes' *General Theory*, but makes the criticism that the accelerator principle, by stressing the relation of investment to changes in income, neglects surplus capacity and redundant stocks of the kind which could have been left behind by 'the last boom'. Nonetheless, she allows that 'if all equipment were very short lived Harrod's method would not be very far wrong'.

In addition, however, Joan Robinson claims that Harrod's formulation not only goes beyond Keynes but also provides 'the missing link' between Keynes and Hobson (1902) – the British liberal economist who, with Hilferding and Bukharin, most influenced Lenin in his theory of the monopoly stage of capitalism. As she stresses, Hobson had maintained that excess savings may cause a crisis if there is no outlet in consumer demand for the goods which new capital equipment produces. By contrast, if the population is increasing with deficient thrift and savings – so that Harrod's 'natural growth' (*Gn*) cannot be fulfilled – the stock of capital will be growing more slowly than available labour, with a progressive increase in unemployment. But this is not susceptible to Keynesian remedies, since if the level of effective demand were boosted without an appropriate supply response it only would result in inflation.

Joan Robinson argues that the reverse of the Hobson situation is that there may not be enough labour to work the new equipment as it comes into being. In this case there would be an over-production of capital. This would deter further investment and precipitate a slump. As a result, labour becomes unemployed, investment would fall, and there would not be enough effective demand even to keep the existing capital stock in use. The relative share of labour in national income is falling and the share of profits rising. Thrift increases and the Hobsonesque limit on accumulation comes into play. As she puts it, such an excursion from Harrod's own text 'gives an idea of the vistas which his analysis opens up'.

Hicks After Harrod

Joan Robinson was an exception among exponents of Keynesian economics for her knowledge of Marx. Like Hobson and Rosa Luxemburg, she considered the problem of under-consumption in a wider context of the compound problems of the accumulation of capital. However, some of the most profound insights into the implications of Keynes' employment theory of economic growth – in direct parallel with some of Marx's most basic insights into the process of capital accumulation – have come from John Hicks, the economist who (with Paul Samuelson) is most notable among those who have sought to overcome Keynes' own effort to divorce himself from what he called the 'classicals' or those who now are known as neoclassical economists.

Hicks acknowledges his own indebtedness to Harrod, stating that 'it was not until I had read Mr Harrod's book that I realised what it was that I had overlooked. Then everything began to fall into place' (Hicks, 1949). In particular, Hicks contributes to explaining both upper and lower limits to the disequilibrium process in Harrod's 'explosive' system. He does so in part through a focus on the differences between short and long term, or 'induced' and 'autonomous' investment.

Hicks evolved a graphic model derived from Harrod which gave plausible reasons why if the expansion of the system could 'hit the ceiling' on upper limits, it tended to upswing well before it 'hit the floor'. His diagram, with his own notation, is reproduced in Figure 3.3. As he puts it himself:

> Time is on the horizontal axis. . . . On the vertical, is the logarithm of output (or investment). Steady progress is therefore represented by a straight line which slopes

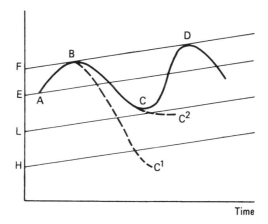

FIG. 3.3   Upper and lower limits: the basic Hicksian model.

upwards, and steady progress at the 'natural rate of growth' by a straight line of a given slope. There are four such lines. . . . First there is the Full Employment equilibrium line F. Second, there is the 'upper equilibrium' line E; and thirdly there is the 'lower equilibrium' line L. Finally, there is the 'long-range' investment line H, *the upward slope of which is responsible for the upward slopes of E and L* [italics added].

The Role of Long-Term Investment

Thus, in Hicks' exposition, (1) the full-employment line, F, is equivalent to what Harrod means by 'natural' or potential growth of the system, and (2) the upswing of the system before its collapse is due to the reaction of 'induced' short-term investment (Keynesian accelerator, or Harrod's warranted growth) to 'autonomous' long-term investment.

Hicks argues (i) that the full-employment line F may slope upwards on account of the upward trend in productivity, even if population is constant, because output is measured in real terms; (ii) that L must lie above H because of the multiplier effect; (iii) that E must lie above L, because E includes the multiplier effect of induced investment as well as the multiplier effect of H; and he assumes (iv) that E lies below F.

It should be clear that a key role in the analysis is played by the multiplier effects registered from longer-term investment. This includes investment which, unlike that effected by accelerator or capital stock adjustment mechanisms, is not influenced by short-term changes in income and output. As Hicks says, the downward path BC^1 in Figure 3.3 (with output falling) is 'too pessimistic'. He stresses that both lines E and L (the upper and lower

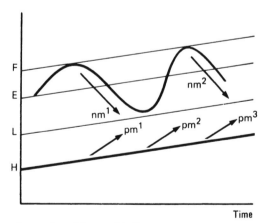

FIG. 3.4   Negative and positive multipliers

equilibrium lines between the ceiling of the economy and its floor) are upward-sloping – implying expansion of the system – because of the upward slope of H, i.e. his 'long-range' investment line.

It is the multiplier effects of such long-range investment – stressed by the downwards and upwards arrows in Figure 3.4 – which prevent the system 'hitting the floor', although at point C in Figure 3.3 – i.e. above C^2 and the lower depths of C^1, 'the accelerator also comes back into gear' (Hicks, ibid.). In Figure 3.4, nm^1 and nm^2 represent the negative multipliers from downward short-term or 'induced' investment, while the positive multipliers pm^1–pm^3 represent the income generated from the upward trend of long-term investment expenditure.

Long-Term Expenditure in the Mixed Economy

It is striking that few postwar macroeconomic theorists followed up the implications of Hicks' analysis of rising long-term investment expenditure for the mixed economy. Hicks' subsequent writing on the trade cycle (1950) attracted more attention for its development of 'the monetary factor' and what was later to be known as LM and IS analysis (liquidity/ money and investment/savings), analysed in more detail in Chapter 7.

Yet in his *Contribution to the Theory of the Trade Cycle* (1950) Hicks devoted his main attention to development of the model of growth and fluctuations which has just been considered, and whose analysis is extended through the rest of this chapter. It is only in the eleventh of twelve chapters in that volume that he analysed 'the monetary factor' and the outlines of LM/IS analysis. Indeed he opened chapter 10 of that volume by stressing that: 'regarded as a constructional enterprise ... the main building has now been completed; what remains to be done is tidying up and the strengthening of weak points' (Hicks, 1950, p. 124). Such tidying up included introduction of the role of money relative to the Keynesian 'real' economy which he had already analysed.

Posterity may judge whether the major contribution of Hicks' theory of growth and the trade cycle lies in his analysis of long-term trends in the real economy or in its contribution to monetary theory. But there is no doubt that the emphasis which he placed himself in that contribution was on the instability of equilibrium (Hicks, 1950, pp. 65ff). Moreover, his stress on the importance of rising long-term investment in offsetting a recession in short-term spending and investment had very considerable relevance to what happened in following years. Not least, his observation that 'the cycles produced by a single shock will be explosive' (ibid., p. 91) was prescient indeed for the consequences of the major shock to the postwar economy in the form of the OPEC oil price rises in October 1973.

The significance of Hicks' long-term or long-range investment line for restraint of recession should not be underestimated. In the postwar market economies, such long-range investment expenditure was typically represented by the rise of public spending on housing, health, education, social services and on social and economic infrastructure. It also accompanied a period of relatively full employment, relative price stability and unparalleled productivity increases. The Hicks model therefore anticipated, and can in large part explain, the postwar welfare boom.

3.3 The Upper Limits

This is not to claim that Hicks fully anticipated all change in the postwar mixed economy. Putting on one side the differences between the accelerator and capital stock adjustment mechanisms, the basic Hicks model was constrained by some of the same factors which inhibit wider application of the Harrod model. These constraints included the assumption of a uniform, aggregate reaction by micro entrepreneurs to macro demand changes. Harrod was later to try to confront these issues in his concept of the 'representative' entrepreneur, which is analysed later.

The Innovation Frontier

The Hicks and Harrod models were also less than wholly explicit on the role of technical progress and innovation, with their varying implications for short- and longer-term (or induced and autonomous) investment. Kaldor and others later focused attention on technical progress in macroeconomic models. But few Anglo-American economists at the time disaggregated technical progress to identify structural change in the manner stressed as important by Schumpeter, Perroux and others.

In fact, the upper limits of expansion in any given economy will very much depend on its capacity to innovate or respond effectively to innovation. If it lacks such capacity, as in postwar Britain or Belgium, it will fail to reach the theoretical upper limit of that expansion which the application of technical progress – or Harrod's 'natural' growth rate – should permit. In terms of a lack of modern manufacturing capacity, many less developed countries clearly come into this 'shortfall' position below the theoretical full capacity which would be implied by their potential full-employment ceiling. They have an abundance of labour but lack the capital, economic structures or personnel to employ it efficiently and approach a full-employment ceiling. By such standards Bangladesh cannot compare with Brazil, nor Brazil with Japan.

Trade Constraints

A further clear upper limit on the achievement of full employment is the trade constraint. This can be expressed in various different ways. One of the most basic is illustrated in Figure 3.5. Actual output growth rises above Hicks' upper equilibrium line E and hits what he has called the full-employment line F (the 'full-employment ceiling' FEC) at point B. In basic Harrod terms the system at this point would no longer expand because of labour shortages and the loss of international competitiveness. By implication, the expansion of income through the multiplier – which previously had brought the system to full employment – would fall away, while entrepreneurs would react to the upper limit to expansion by curtailing investment programmes. The joint effect, as Harrod has stressed, would be unstable. Output growth would not conveniently coincide with the full-employment ceiling FEC, but would result instead in a downturn in a cumulative spiral.

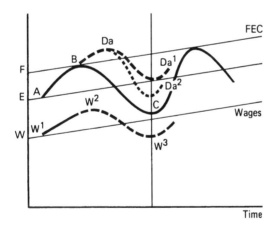

FIG. 3.5   Upper limits: trade and cost constraints

However, multiplier effects do not diminish as an economy reaches full employment. They continue as long as it continues to expand (and at a faster or slower rate depending on the rate at which full employment is approached). Thus actual demand including imports (in our terms Da), as opposed to the growth of domestic output (Harrod's Ga), will tend to increase above the full-employment ceiling FEC. The rate and scale of this excess of total demand over domestic supply will be determined in part by lags in the system. Import orders could be cancelled by firms curtailing their expansion plans and as Da begins a downswing to C. But some imports will not be cancelled in this way since they are necessary for the maintainence of current production.

Overheating

Moreover, consumer demand will not automatically be choked off as the economy approaches its full-employment ceiling. It may well increase during the period of the growth path AB as firms, growing relatively short of labour, either agree to higher wages to retain workers or bid wages up to attract them. Thus wages may well rise from W^1 and peak at W^2 as the economy hits its full-employment ceiling. Such a rising wage cost would tend to result in a loss of international competitiveness.

In the above terms, and in a vocabulary much favoured in the postwar period, the economy will tend to 'overheat' as it approaches the upper limit of the full-employment ceiling. Excluding government intervention and borrowing, a combination of factors would tend to result in a downturn of activity, and reinforce negative multiplier effects. Scarcity of inputs and raw materials during the upswing AB in Figure 3.5 would aggravate inflation from higher-cost labour. The loss of international competitiveness would mean a loss of foreign exchange and thus finance for imports. Even the cushioning effects from private or public credit facilities would be unlikely to offset a weakening export performance.

The path of the fall in actual demand, Da, in the downturn from the full-employment ceiling will vary according to circumstances. It might fall to Da^1, to Da^2 or even lower still, though it is not necessary for actual demand to fall below the level of domestic output (i.e. output on the domestic market and excluding exports) for an upswing or recovery to occur. Similarly, wages in Figure 3.5 having risen from W^1 and peaked at W^2 could well fall to W^3. The reasons for the upturn – in Hicksian terms – have already been given. In Figure 3.5 our wages line W coincides with the Hicksian lower equilibrium line L. If wages had continued on their upwards trend line equivalent to Hicks' line L in Figures 3.3 and 3.4 rather than sunk below it, their multiplier effect (income multiplier) would tend to swing sales and output up again before point C in Figure 3.5.

Active and Reserve Labour

We have already seen that Harrod's concept of a full-employment growth path or the potential growth path of an economy (in his terms Gn) assumes a natural rate of growth of the labour force (implicit in his stress on the natural rate of growth of the population). But in reality, upswings in an economic activity are not necessarily constrained by natural population growth. Marx was more perceptive on this than the neoclassical theorists of economic growth since Keynes. As he puts it, capitalist production 'can by no means content itself with the quantity of disposable labour power which the natural increase in population yields. It requires for its free play an industrial reserve army independent of these natural limits. . . . Surplus population becomes . . . the lever of capitalist accumulation (Marx, 1887, vol. 1, p. 635).

There are several aspects to this process of bringing reserve labour into the active labour force during a period of sustained accumulation and economic growth. They have various implications for the structural, spatial and social dynamics of growth and distribution cycles.

Thus, at the *structural* level, labour can be drawn from declining into growing sectors of the economy during an overall period of macroeconomic growth. This was very much the case in even the relatively slowly growing British economy in the 1950s, when more than a million jobs were lost by modernisation and the displacement of labour by capital embodying innovation in coal, steel, shipbuilding and textiles. Nominally, this process might well be considered simply as a transfer of labour from one 'active' labour force (in declining sectors) into another (in growing sectors). Alternatively, it could well be viewed as a more active or fuller employment of labour which was relatively under-employed in the traditional or declining sectors of the economy. This phenomenon of under-employment (in 'disguised' form) is well recognised as a feature of those economies where productivity in agriculture has not attained the levels of productivity obtaining in industry or services.

At the *spatial* level, the expansion of output and employment in economic growth will tend to be concentrated in certain localities. This point has been well stressed by Perroux in a key article on the regional distribution of economic growth published in 1955, which influenced a generation of regional theorists and policy-makers. As Perroux says:

> Growth does not appear everywhere at the same time: it shows itself in growth points or growth poles, with varying intensities.

Or, as Marx put it earlier:

> The foundation of every division of labour . . . is the separation between town and country. . . . Just as a certain number of simultaneously employed labourers are the material prerequisites for division of labour in manufacture, so are the number and density of the population . . . a necessary condition for the division of labour in society [1887, vol. 1, p. 352].

Closer therefore to Wright's criticism of Harrod, both Marx in the mid nineteenth century, and Perroux in the mid twentieth, stressed the key role of modern industry in innovating and sustaining growth promotion, and the regional and urban implications of such growth.

At the *social* level, there are several dimensions to the drawing of 'reserve' labour into active or 'front line' employment. One of the most important in the postwar period has been the increasing employment of women. Previously consigned by convention to the home, or to what many feminists designate as unpaid labour, the needs of the war economy in countries such as Britain and the United States drew many women for the first time into the active and paid labour force. While most returned to domestic and unpaid labour thereafter, the threshold on employment of women had been lowered, and their increasing employment in not only support roles such as secretarial work but also in production in specific industries (such as textiles and later electronics) changed the social shape of the active labour force.

In Marx's time, the taboos against employment of women were greater than today. But he was well aware of the range of relatively deprived social categories which could be and were called from the reserves into the active labour force by the accumulation and growth of capital in nineteenth-century Britain. Among them he included (1) a 'floating' urban surplus population, comparable with some definitions of 'frictional' unemployment; (2) 'latent' labour, comparable directly with the modern concept of 'disguised' unemployment; (3) 'stagnant' labour in irregular service employment; (4) 'pauper' labour, including those unable to work; and (5) 'nomadic' labour, directly comparable with the modern category of migrant labour (Marx, 1887, vol. 1, pp. 642–63, and also Holland, 1976a, chapter 2).

The Raised Full-Employment Ceiling

It is tempting to suggest that it was precisely because of his awareness of the social or class implications of accumulation in capitalist societies that Marx was able to perceive the implications of the change from 'reserve' to 'active' labour for the dynamic expansion of capitalist economies.

Marx stresses that accumulation is the independent rather than the dependent variable, i.e. it is employment and wages which depend on accumulation rather than vice versa (Marx, 1887, vol. 1, p. 620). Accumulation occurs both through the profit motive in a society with unequal distribution of income and wealth, and also through the exploitation of new technologies and the rise of new industries. Marx also stresses that capitalist accumulation essentially creates the labour force which it needs. In other words, it pulls labour from less productive into more productive sectors and regions of the economy, and at the same time pushes them out of those activities where accumulation itself makes them redundant or surplus to needs:

As soon as capitalist production takes possession of agriculture, and in proportion to the extent that it does so, the demand for an agricultural labouring population falls absolutely. . . . Part of the agricultural population is therefore constantly on the point of passing over into an urban or manufacturing proletariat, and on the look out for circumstances favourable to the transformation [Marx, 1887, p. 642].

Thus mechanisation in agriculture in the nineteenth century (like enclosure of the common land in the fifteenth and sixteenth centuries) pushed labour off the land and into the towns. Similarly, in nineteenth-century Britain and in the mid twentieth century in continental Europe and Japan, industrial demand pulled labour into the factories of the city and the metropolis. These mechanisms amount to a compound of structural, social and spatial change. During periods of sustained accumulation they register crucial consequences on the process of accumulation itself. In our own terms, extending the Harrod and Hicks terms of reference, they raise the full-employment ceiling of the economy over and above that which would be possible with a natural increase in population and thus of the labour force.

The process is illustrated in Figure 3.6. Maintaining the general framework of the Hicks model, and the full-employment ceiling FEC^1, it can be seen that the structural shift of labour (arrow A), the spatial migration of labour (arrow B) and the social change in the composition of the labour force (arrow C) contribute in phase II of a period of accumulation to increasing the active labour force in the more productive sectors of the economy and thus raising the initial full-employment ceiling FEC^1 to the new and higher ceiling FEC^2.

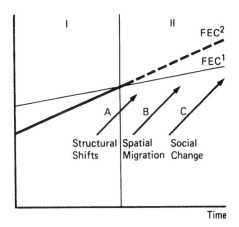

FIG. 3.6   Raising the full-employment ceiling

Sustained Accumulation

Such a change in the height of the full-employment ceiling has major consequences both for the extent of accumulation, and for the business or trade cycle. For instance, adopting Harrod's concepts of actual and warranted growth, and applying them to the framework of the Hicks model, it can be seen from Figure 3.7 that if the process of actual growth, G^1, in phase 1 of expansion 'hits its head' on the full-employment ceiling *FEC*, actual growth will tend to turn down and decline, from G^1 to G^2, as a result of the various mechanisms analysed earlier in relation to Figure 3.5. Warranted growth, having lagged behind the actual expansion in phase 1, will then follow the actual downturn of G^2 in phase II (from Gw^1 to Gw^2). One might have misgivings about Harrod's location of his Gw path in the upswing (i.e. below rather than above the growth of G), granted that in any sustained boom, management confidence (or what Keynes called the 'animal spirits' of entrepreneurs) would tend to be high and possibly overestimate rather than underestimate the growth of the system. But the essential constraint to growth through the upper limit of a full-employment ceiling remains clear.

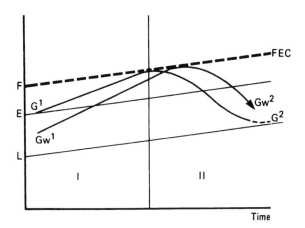

FIG. 3.7 Hitting the full-employment ceiling

By contrast, as shown in Figure 3.8, with the raised full-employment ceiling made possible by structural, social and spatial shifts in the labour force, the system can expand beyond what otherwise might be considered 'normal' limits to economic growth and achieve a super-normal or super-growth path. Entrepreneurs or managers, instead of finding themselves short of labour in the approach to a full-employment ceiling at point *A*, with the resultant downturn of actual and warranted growth on the lines of G^2 and Gw^2, would find that their expansion had attracted sufficient (or abundant) labour from slower growing or declining sectors, less developed regions or less fully employed social groups and classes. Animal spirits and profit expectations would also remain high, with warranted growth in Harrod's terms at Gw^3 and the system expanding beyond the assumed 'natural' limits of FEC^1 to a growth path of G^3.

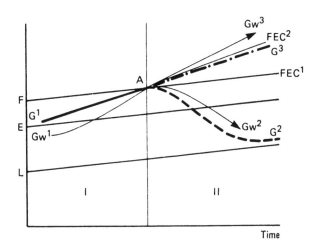

FIG. 3.8 The raised ceiling and 'super-growth'

3.4 Super-Growth and Hyper-Growth

In principle, at least for a period of time, the growth path G^3 in Figure 3.8 could keep just under the full-employment ceiling FEC^2 rather than 'bumping against' or going through it. Allowing for the instability inherent in the Keynes-Harrod application of the accelerator-multiplier mechanisms (or in capital stock adjustment-multiplier combinations), a further and third phase of expansion can occur in which the system moves from growth to 'super-growth' or 'hyper-growth'. For instance, the West German economy during its '*Wirtschaftswunder*' recovery in the early and mid 1950s expanded at some 8–9 per cent a year in GDP terms. In the 1960s the French economy reached 4.5–5 per cent annual growth of GDP and the Italian economy for a time reached 6 per cent annual GDP expansion. Japan outstripped everyone, with annual rates of GDP growth in the 1950s of over 8 per cent, rising in the early 1960s to nearly 10 per cent and in 1965–70 to over 13 per cent. The fact that Japanese annual GDP growth thereafter fell to an average of 4.5 per cent through the 1970s and early 1980s does not detract from this phenomenal growth achievement.*

Allowing for the arbitrariness of 'super' and 'hyper' growth distinctions, it is striking that all of the economies in either category experienced both a very high rate of capital accumulation *and* major shifts in the composition of the labour force which in effect raised their 'full-employment ceilings' above the natural increase in population.

As already indicated in a comment on Domar's passing recognition that Marx had preceded him in analysing the growth potential of economic systems, the insight of Marx on the role of labour reserves as the pivot of capital accumulation was recognised by Arthur Lewis (1954) in his analysis of the phenomenon of growth with unlimited supplies of labour. In turn, Charles Kindleberger (1967), beginning from Lewis's model of growth with unlimited labour, applied similar arguments on the importance of labour availability in the high growth achieved by several of the postwar European continental economies.

Europe and Japan

In West Germany, a key role in raising the full-employment ceiling was played by the massive inflow of labour from East to West Germany in the 1940s and 1950s before the building of the Berlin Wall. It has been estimated that this added some 7 million (already educated and in the main already skilled) workers to the West German labour force, especially in the period from 1948 to 1955 when the West German economy achieved what we have called 'super growth' rates of GDP (Kindleberger, 1967). In a sense, granted the prewar integration of East and West Germany in one country, the spatial East-West flow of labour could be considered interregional rather than strictly international. Nonetheless, West Germany also benefited during the 1950s and 1960s from the international migration of labour from (first) Italy and (later) Yugoslavia, Greece and Turkey on a significant scale (Lee and Ogden, 1976, chapter 1).

In Italy itself, the agricultural labour force of the South fell by three-quarters, and that of the Centre-North by 60 per cent, from 1951 to 1980. This included a net outflow from agriculture in the South of 1.7 million

---

* See further Edward F. Denison (assisted by Jean-Pierre Poullier), *Why Growth Rates Differ* (Brookings Institution, Washington DC, 1967). Denison does not employ the categories of super and hyper growth used above. He also rightly considers a wider variety of factors in economic growth than those analysed in the above argument, including the contributions of technical progress, skill, training and education to the growth process, even if the argument is rendered somewhat less than wholly plausible by specification of largely arbitrary components in growth to several decimal points.

migrants, and in the Centre-North of 3.6 million people, many of them gaining urban employment in the so-called 'golden triangle' between Genoa, Milan and Turin. This was less than the 7 million addition to the West German labour force through migration from East Germany during the period of the *Wirtschaftswunder* in the 1950s. It is also clear that the lower growth rate of the Italian economy during the 1950s was due in large part to limits on the adaptive capacity of enterprise and constraints on the adjustment capacity of the system. Nonetheless, on the basis of higher-than-normal growth in the 1950s, the Italian economy achieved – as already indicated – annual rates of growth of GDP in the 1976s of some 6 per cent per annum (Saraceno, 1983).

Kindleberger considered France an exception to the role of the labour availability factor in high economic growth. Yet this in part reflects his neglect of the inter-sectoral and inter-regional shifts of labour in the postwar French economy. In 1950 more than a quarter of the labour force in the French economy was employed in agriculture. By the end of the 1970s this was reduced to less than a tenth. Such a shift in the working population out of agriculture was equivalent to nearly 4 million people of working age. It was not so much a matter of laying down their scythes and becoming computer programmers, as the offspring of agricultural workers not going into farming but moving off the land into manual work in industry and also to skilled work in services (in social terms to higher grades of employment in the secondary and tertiary sectors).

Similarly, in Japan (not considered by Kindleberger) the main source of that labour which raised the full-employment ceiling to 'hyper growth' potential was inter-regional and inter-sectoral migration. In 1950 there were nearly 16 million farmers in Japan, amounting to over 44 per cent of the total working population. By 1960 the number was down to 13 million, or under 30 per cent of the total, and by 1980 only 5 million, or under 10 per cent of the workforce. Ohmae (1985, p. 86) claims that 'no modern government has been so successful at shifting its working population so dramatically from primary industries (agriculture, fisheries and forestry) to secondary (industrial) and tertiary (service) industries in such a short time.' But in fact, as already indicated, the structural and social shifts of Japanese labour were exceptional only in degree. Comparable shifts occurred on a dramatic scale in the main continental European economies after the Second World War.

The increase in labour costs in the period of super and hyper growth in economies such as Japan, West Germany, Italy (to a lesser extent) and France tended to be below the rate of growth of productivity or output per worker. Such a wage-productivity relationship was crucial to sustaining growth and hyper-growth. Analytically it means that if entrepreneurs or shareholders do not consume all of the profits made possible by the excess of productivity over wage increases, retained earnings will be available to finance a 'virtuous circle' of successive rounds of capacity-increasing investment. Inversely, if wage increases exceed productivity and profits, a 'vicious circle' downturn may ensue.

Profits, Expectations and Growth

Such virtuous and vicious circle effects (for the expansion of the system) are illustrated in Figure 3.9. This shows that in phase I the rate of growth of wages is consistently lower than the rate of growth of productivity. Such a relationship obtained for a fifteen-year sustained boom in the Italian economy from the late 1940s up to 1963 (Forte, 1965). It not only contributed to high 'animal spirits' for entrepreneurs/managers (represented in Figure 3.9 by a high and initially rising Gw or warranted growth rate through the main part of phase I), but meant in turn high self-financing for successive rounds of investment. Similar phenomena are observable for other super-growth economies of the 1950s and 1960s, as well as for the hyper-growth economy of Japan.

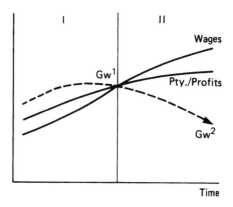

FIG. 3.9   Wages, profits and expectations

Inversely, as represented by phase II of Figure 3.9, a rate of increase of wages higher than the rate of increase of productivity will tend to reduce profits (or eliminate them, depending on the initial level of the profit rate and the rate of productivity increase). This in turn, for obvious reasons, will have a depressive effect on expectations, with a decline in the warranted growth rate (Gw^2 in phase II of the Figure) causing at least an 'upper limit' check to accumulation, or a crisis proper.

Offensive Investment

On the capital side (whether finance or real investment), 'virtuous circle' effects from expansion (and especially the expansion of productivity and profits over wage and other costs) raise the growth potential of the economy itself in a manner not fully appreciated by Harrod's Gn or 'natural' growth concept. In other words, especially in conditions where the rise in the full-employment ceiling means 'super' or 'hyper' growth, both enterprise itself and finance and credit institutions respond to rapid accumulation by further rapid expansions of capacity and credit. The mechanism has been described as 'offensive' investment in contrast with 'defensive' investment under low-growth conditions (Holland, 1987, Chapter 6). In reality it means a relationship between income, wage and profit changes which goes beyond the accelerator and concerns the response of different firms and their management to different growth prospects.

The increased self-financing ratio for companies during a period of sustained growth does not in itself mean that such firms will lower their ratio of external to internal finance as a whole (their gearing ratio). In practice the popular adage that success breeds success translates directly to the economy. High and sustained profits obtainable when productivity expands at a rate consistently above wage increases, in turn promotes confidence among financial institutions. This obtains whether these are mainly private, as in the case of West Germany, or public, as in the case of the *Caisse des Depôts et Consignations* in France, the public Credit Institutes such as IMI (Instituto Immobilaire) and the 'big three' publicly owned banks in Italy (Banco Commerciale, Banco di Roma and Credito Italiano), or an interface between public and private finance such as is constituted by the Ministry of International Trade and Industry (MITI) and the main banks or financial institutions in Japan (Guillain, 1970, p. 74). Reference has already been made in Chapter 1 to the key role played by the public *Kreditanstalt für Wiederaufbau*, or Reconstruction Loans Corporation, in the period of super-growth in the postwar West German economy. Thus a primary role has been played by public rather than private finance mechanisms – or a combination of public and private finance – in all the developed economies achieving super-normal or hyper growth in the postwar period (see elsewhere this text, and Andrew Shonfield (1965)).

Marx and Harrod

In Marx's terms the formula representing the basic sequence of accumulation is M-C-M', where M means money, C means commodity or product, and M' means that increase in money (i.e. profit) to the entrepreneur which ensues from his successful production and sale (realisation) of the value of his product (Marx, 1887, vol. II, Part I). The difference from the inverse sequence of C-M-C', or commodity (product), money (in exchange) and increased commodity production (C'), is partly a matter of perception or *gestalt*. It reflects the difference between the post-Keynesian emphasis of Harrod and others on an increase in actual growth of output (G–G') which implies the intermediation of finance and money, and the prime motive factor in the system as appreciated by Marx, M-M', i.e. profit. But the fact remains that G-G' implies M-M'. In other words, an increase in the growth of sales, assuming that profits during the period of accumulation are not diminished or eliminated by a rise in labour or other costs, implies an increase in the money (profit) accumulating to entrepreneurs (capital). Such an increase in M makes possible the increase in savings and investment (or savings plus credit into investment), which increases s, the savings ratio, and thus investment and the capital ratio in Harrod's basic formula.

Such factors complement the lowering of the capital-output ratio, c in Harrod's formulation. So does technical progress which – as seen from earlier arithmetic examples – plays such an important part in making possible high or hyper-growth for a given capital-output ratio. The importance of high savings translated into actual investment, in explaining the high growth of the European and Japanese economies in the 1950s and 1960s has already been noted.

Labour Supply and Limits to Growth

A reverse argument on the role of labour availability and economic growth has been put forward in the British case for the 1950s and 1960s by Kaldor (1966). Following and stressing Verdoorn (1949), who had already analysed in some depth correlations of growth rates and labour supply, Kaldor maintained that the key factor in the relatively slow growth rate of the UK economy since the war had been the lack of labour availability.

Kaldor's argument is interesting because of its admission of the importance of the structural distribution of employment between the three main sectors of agriculture, industry and services, with the argument that too much labour had been misdirected into service employment in postwar Britain. As economic advisor to the Chancellor of the Exchequer from 1964, Kaldor was critically influential in the introduction of the Selective Employment Tax (SET). This was designed to shift labour from services (where it was levied) and into manufacturing industry (where it was rebated), and thus uncork the assumed labour bottleneck in postwar British growth.

One of the stiking contrasts between the structural composition of labour in the postwar British economy and that in continental Europe or Japan was the very low proportion of the working population in agriculture. By the beginning of the twentieth century, this was around 12 per cent of the total in Britain, and by 1980 had fallen to less than 3 per cent of the working population. By contrast, in 1950, the average working population in agriculture in the EEC countries (the original six member states) was still one in four, or 25 per cent of total working population, falling below 12 per cent in the 1970s and below 10 per cent in the 1980s.

It is therefore arguable that Kaldor had a strong case in maintaining that labour availability was a significant constraint on the growth of the UK economy in the 1950s and 1960s, at a time when some of Britain's key competitors were able to draw major reserves of labour from agriculture into industry (and from industry into services) on the 'generational' basis of the upwardly mobile young shifting their employment. Put simply, Britain showed all the symptoms of an economy caught in a stop-go syndrome, 'banging her head' on a full-employment ceiling, with regular choking-off of periods of expansion and regular downturns in the manner illustrated in Figures 3.3 and 3.5.

Limits to Kaldor

On the other hand, as an overall explanation of the 'upper limits' to growth, Kaldor's stress on labour supply was subject to substantial criticism. In particular Postan (1964) maintained that far more than labour availability was involved in the rapid rates of accumulation of capital, output and employment in continental Europe after the war. He identified various self-reinforcing components in the high-growth formula of such countries including, in particular, *innovation* and the rise of entirely new techniques of production – a point paralleling both Schumpeter (1934) and Perroux (1965) – and also the *organisation* of specific firms and industries, plus the structure of production itself.

Not least, Postan argued that the structure and composition of capital was itself a key determinant of the high rates of accumulation in the continental European economies. He also argued that the rate of growth of capital – rather than labour availability or labour costs – was the independent variable in high rates of economic growth. In his later work Harrod came to the same conclusion, underlining the role of G and Gn (actual and potential growth) and with them the role of savings (s) translated into actual investment, rather than his former stress on Gw, or the 'warranted' rate of growth. Similarly, Kindleberger, while giving his work on *Europe's Postwar Growth* the subtitle 'the Role of Labour Supply', was careful to stress that labour availability was a necessary but not sufficient factor for high rates of growth and accumulation. The point is relevant to the global economy as a whole. Otherwise, Egypt or the Sudan, with some of the highest surplus population (relative to employment) in the world, would be among the world's fastest growing economies. Similarly, Britain in the mid 1980s has some of the highest unemployment among the developed countries without approaching super-growth or hyper-growth.

National and Multinational

In Kaldor's defence, he would not deny the role of factors such as innovation, and has stressed their importance in other work. Nor would he deny the necessary/sufficient distinction made by Kindleberger. He has also been known to observe that his Selective Employment Tax was introduced too late to have much impact in Britain. Introduced in the mid 1960s and abolished by the Conservatives after 1970, it might have had more effect if it had been introduced fifteen or twenty years earlier.

But there are other basic limitations to the Kaldor model, which had major policy implications. Essentially, it was based on the assumption that shifting more labour into manufacturing would relax the labour-supply constraint on visible exports, therefore making possible increased export volume at lower wage cost. But in practice, as already indicated in Chapter 2 and as will be elaborated in Chapters 4 and 5, some 85 per cent of UK visible export trade by the early 1970s was dominated by multinational rather than national companies. If they wanted lower-cost labour, such companies could get it by investing in Southern Europe, South Africa or South East Asia at a fraction of the cost of UK labour. Also, since they were frequently their 'own competitors' abroad with production subsidiaries in foreign markets, they did not reduce price to exploit the potential foreign competitiveness made possible by measures such as the November 1967 devaluation of sterling, which Kaldor's Selective Employment Tax was designed to aid and assist. Thus major measures affecting both a new employment tax and devaluation were advanced by Kaldor in a 'Keynes plus' package, but the package still did not disaggregate the manufacturing sector sufficiently to identify the multinational companies whose investment and trade response would determine its failure or success.

3.5 The Lower Limits

It has already been seen that one of the most interesting questions posed by Harrod in his initial formulation of his growth model ran as follows. Why, granted the instability implicit in combinations of the accelerator and multiplier mechanisms, does the real world economy not either soar to the ceiling in an upswing, or inversely, in a downswing, fall to the floor? Reasons have already been given, going beyond Hicks, for the 'raised ceiling' effect by which reserve labour is drawn into the active labour force, i.e. the mechanism of structural, spatial and social shifts in employment. However, since the 1970s, the factors offsetting the downswing in the modern capitalist economy are just as important in policy terms as were those affecting the upswing of the 1950s and 1960s.

John Hicks put his finger on the mechanism by distinguishing short-term 'induced' investment of the accelerator kind (compatible with capital stock adjustment theory), from longer-term investment which is not so induced. On the other hand, as already noted, Hicks does not give a developed argument on the nature of longer-term investment. He defines it essentially by what it is not: i.e. it is not short term and is not induced in the manner of accelerator (or capital-stock adjustment) decision-making. In his own terminology and that of much of the subsequent literature on unstable growth, such longer-term investment is 'autonomous'. Yet both the role of wages and salaries and of public spending and investment are crucial to understanding the role of such 'autonomous' investment in the modern mixed economy.

The Role of Wages

Most analysis of wages tends to consider them as a cost pure and simple. This is understandable enough. Viewed by the individual entrepreneur or management team, wages are simply costs. The aim of the individual enterprise is to restrain and if possible reduce the share of wages in overall costs. The reason, again, is simple inasmuch as wages constitute by far the highest single component of costs in most manufacturing enterprise and the highest share (with few exceptions) in services. In manufacturing in the UK or the US it was not uncommon for much of the postwar period for wages to constitute a third, two-fifths or even a half of total costs, compared to a cost of investment of between a quarter and 15 per cent. In services, the share of wages has typically reached some half to two-thirds of the cost total.

However, the managerial or microeconomic view of wages, when translated to the macroeconomic level, is critically misplaced. Wages are not simply micro production costs for firms. At the macro level they constitute a main component of effective demand and thus, indirectly, a main factor of sales. As already indicated in Chapter 2, they do so not simply through some abstract category 'final demand' but also as active elements of the dynamics of economic growth through combined employment, wages demand and income multipliers.

Moreover, for today's global industrial leaders, as in Japan, wage costs have shrunk to a minor fraction of those familiar to many macroeconomists when they last studied the theory of the firm. For instance, in two of Japan's leading steel mills (Nippon Steel and Nippon Kokan KK) labour costs are only one tenth of total costs. Similar or even lower labour-cost shares are now prevalent in other continuous processing industries such as chemicals or textiles. In automobiles, the cost of labour at Nissan in the mid 1980s was under 7 per cent of total costs, and was less than 6 per cent at Toyota. In Japanese electronics, direct labour costs are down to an average of 5 per cent of total costs (Ohmae, 1985, p. 4).

Such lower labour costs as a proportion of total costs have helped give Japanese automobile manufacturers as much or more than a two-to-one advantage over European and American competitors. But they are not simply the result of docile labour or the lifetime employment guaranteed by the major Japanese companies. They are the result both of the higher capital ratios employed by Japanese companies and of the technical progress and innovation which has gone into reducing the capital-output ratio, including automation, numerical controls and other techniques in which the Japanese led and others wondered whether to follow. In Japan, the reduction of labour content has been gained neither by lowering wage rates, nor at the cost of forced redundancies and major unemployment. In fact much of the redeployment of labour achieved by Japanese big business has been either within their own companies or through their own affiliates, aided and abetted by government.

This dynamic can only be outlined in terms of the Harrod-Domar framework, i.e. higher savings (s) embodied in higher actual investment with a lowered capital-output ratio (c) produces both capital widening and capital deepening. To see what has really been happening in postwar Japan means lifting the lid from the Harrod-Domar macroeconomic aggregates and getting a sight of individual firms and industries.

Frictional Unemployment

During most of the postwar period when policies of Keynesian demand management were pursued, relatively full employment was achieved in several of the developed capitalist countries. Thus unemployment fluctuated between 2.5 per cent and 5 per cent but averaged only slightly more than what was defined as 'frictional unemployment', i.e. that unemployment caused by the 'friction' of people dropping temporarily out of work or changing jobs. The unemployment level in the United States was higher, but not dramatically so, and in both Europe and the US the average levels of unemployment in the period from 1950 to the early 1970s were insignificant in comparison with the mid 1980s, when some 35 million people are registered as unemployed in the OECD countries, and when it is estimated that real unemployment is considerably higher due to various social categories of former-workers (especially married women) not registering themselves as unemployed due to their ineligibility for unemployment benefit so long as another member of the family is earning.

During the halcyon postwar years of low frictional unemployment it was perhaps natural that professional economists should focus on the problems for wages and costs caused by 'full employment' conditions. Attention has already been drawn, in the argument relating to Figure 3.5, to the role which rising wage costs can in principle cause in the loss of international competitiveness and a downturn in economic activity. Keynes himself had warned of the problems which would be caused in terms of wage demands and inflation from the pursuit of his own full-employment policies of high public spending, and Kalecki had elaborated the argument before the end of the war in a typically perceptive manner, stressing a 'political' trade cycle by which he anticipated that governments after the war would restrain demand after elections, but boost it before them. Attention is paid in Chapter 8 to the Phillips argument that equilibrium full employment could not be achieved if the economy was run at less than some 3.5 per cent unemployment, i.e. an argument specifying in practice what Hicks had described as his 'upper equilibrium' line of growth (line E in Figure 3.3).

Declining Wages and Falling Demand

However, this concentration on the 'cost-push' element in wages and inflation for some thirty years after Keynes' *General Theory* neglected other roles played by wages and their rising share in national income in key postwar economies. It also ignored other observations made by Keynes about the role of wages in effective demand in the downturn of an economy. At a critical period for the relations between capital and labour in Britain between the wars, at the time of the General Strike of 1926, Keynes was highly critical of government policy, which sought both to revalue sterling and to achieve a real cut in wages. The reason, again, is simple. In a downturn of the system, a cut in aggregate wages will reduce effective demand and further worsen the 'vicious circle' of contraction.

The argument can be made plain by considering the lower limits to growth implicit in the Hicks model of fluctuations. Figure 3.10 includes the essentials of Hicks' analysis of the lower equilibrium line of the economy. The same proportions are maintained for the full-employment ceiling FEC and his lower equilibrium line L as in Hicks' own exposition (our Figure 3.3).

It has been noted that Hicks argued that the actual growth path of the economy – having risen from an under-employment of capital and labour at

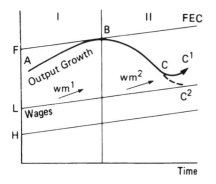

FIG. 3.10 Wages growth and demand upturn

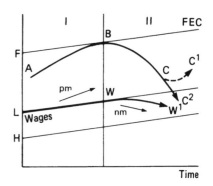

FIG. 3.11 Wage cuts and cumulative demand downturn

point A to the full-employment level at B – is unlikely to sink to C^2 rather than turn up at C to C^1, because at this point the multiplier effects from longer-range investment are registered and 'the accelerator also comes back into gear'. The multiplier effects which Hicks appears to have in mind are those from his long-range investment line H, which in his terms is lower than his lower equilibrium line L. But for the reasons indicated earlier in this chapter, one of the most realistic interpretations of Hicks' lower equilibrium line L is in fact as the trend line of wages in the economy. In this sense, in Figure 3.10 we have simply identified the trend growth of wages and the wages multiplier effects (wm^1, wm^2) within the framework of the basic Hicks model of growth and cycles.

The First Line of Defence

Thus wage income and expenditure in the modern capitalist economy constitute in a real sense the 'first line of defence' against the economy sinking in a downturn of output in such a way as to 'hit the floor'. But inversely, as illustrated in Figure 3.11, if management or government undertake a cut in wages below the trend line L when output in the system is declining from B, the positive wages or income multiplier (pm) of phase I becomes negative (nm) in phase II of the cycle. Therefore there is no mechanism (other than indirect effects of longer-range investment and spending, H) to ensure that actual growth (G) rises at C and proceeds in an upturn to C^1. Also, if the trend line of wages drops from W to W^1, actual growth could fall from C to C^2.

Clearly it is important in this context to distinguish the macroeconomic role of wages in effective demand from their role at the level of the firm in international competitiveness. A high wage level sustains the growth of the domestic economy. A high rate of aggregate wage demand may help promote sustained economic growth. But, at the macroeconomic level, the effects on the economy will be determined essentially by the rate of growth of imports relative to exports. This in turn will relate to the volume and value of imports and exports respectively.

In conventional economic terms, these ratios have been assumed to depend on either strictly macroeconomic phenomena such as the exchange rate or on an assumed macroeconomic index of competitiveness such as aggregate wage costs. But, as suggested by the previously cited evidence on the cost structures of the most successful exporting firms and sectors in the world – in Japan – it is no longer relevant to argue simply in terms of such macroeconomic phenomena in assessing national competitiveness. In other words, wage rates in the Japanese mesoeconomic leaders in global export markets are high. It is the share of wages, or labour content in relation to total costs, which is low. Moreover, the dramatically high productivity of such leading Japanese firms makes it possible for Japan to achieve an export surplus which sustains the import demand from high-wage employees in the non-export sector such as services, as well as offset low export competitiveness from other firms in the microeconomic sector (or less technically advanced sectors) in the economy.

The essential point is that to target aggregate wages for cuts is counter-productive for growth without a consideration of the actual wage content in export industries. Also, it is a mistake to seek to remedy high wage rates through income cuts without seeking to offset such rates by increasing investment, capital-labour ratios, and innovation.

Public Spending and Effective Demand

For many monetarist economists following Milton Friedman, public spending both constitutes a main reason for increases in the money supply and is a prime cause of inflation. But, public spending in the modern capitalist economy is one of the main components of effective demand. As illustrated later in this chapter, its rise in total spending has been dramatic in the postwar period, especially in the European economies and including those such as West Germany, France and Italy which have achieved the highest rates of output growth and capital accumulation in the postwar period.

The role of public spending in the maintenance of effective demand can again be expressed diagrammatically with cross-reference to the Hicksian model of growth and cycles. Thus Hicks in his original exposition (our Figure 3.3) has stressed that the economy does not 'hit the floor' through a combination of accelerator and multiplier effects in the manner posed in Harrod's paradox because of the role of longer-term 'autonomous' investment.

Long-Term Investment and Public Spending

In our earlier exposition of the Hicks model we drew attention to the kind of investment which might constitute such longer-term expenditure, uninfluenced by the shorter-range accelerator (or capital stock adjustment) mechanisms. We gave two main examples. First, the investment planning of big business, which can range up to several years. Second, we cited expenditure on economic infrastructure, e.g. motorway programmes, electrification schemes, oil, gas and telecommunications networks, railway/railroad modernisation, etc. There are also examples of long-term expenditure on social infrastructure including spending on schools, universities, hospitals and health schemes, and public housing. All of these involve long-term investment programmes financed mainly, in Europe, by public rather than private expenditure. To them one might add classic public-spending areas on both sides of the Atlantic including police, defence, fire services, public libraries and urban transportation systems (both buses and traffic control).

As already indicated in Chapters 1 and 2, in most of the continental European economies such public spending generates both capital expenditure on investment in housing, health, education, social services, industry, energy, transport and communications, and also household or personal expenditure from wages and salaries paid to teachers, doctors, nurses and ancillary staff in the public health sector; welfare workers, and public or civil servants and local government employees from designers, supervisors and technicians through to refuse collectors, as well as service personnel, the police and the fire, water, gas, electricity, telephone and other services.

Sustaining versus Draining

In contrast with the simplisms of monetarist theory, such public spending sustains rather than drains spending in the private sector. The mechanisms were illustrated in basic terms in Chapter 1. In Chapter 2, emphasis was placed on the multiplier effects of public spending in the private sector of the economy. The compound picture emerging from them and this chapter should be clear enough. The key factor in Hicks' otherwise unspecified 'longer range' investment and expenditure is *public* rather than private spending, which is not directly affected in the short run by the accelerator/decelerator or capital stock adjustment principles which affect private-sector investment and employment.

This is not to say that actual public expenditure has been conceived or managed in such a way as consciously to complement or offset fluctuations in the private sector of the modern mixed economy. In some cases, and to a certain extent, this has been so. This has been the case to varying degrees in postwar Japan and also in some Western European economies. For instance, from the late 1960s the Italian government consciously pursued public-expenditure programmes in the south of Italy through its state holding companies (and especially the major industrial reorganisation institute IRI), both to promote the development of the *Mezzogiorno*, and to offset the crisis in private capital accumulation which had followed the 'hot summer' of wage demands in 1968 (Holland, 1972). Similarly, the French and Belgian governments in the same period sought and achieved agreement from their major public-sector enterprises to undertake long-term investment programmes, as in steel, telecommunications and infrastructure, which could have a stabilising effect on long-term investment supply, through a 'planning agreements' procedure. In the field of social expenditure, public spending increased during the 1970s with a counter-cyclical effect as unemployment rose and increased aggregate benefits were paid by government. Nonetheless, the conscious counter-cyclical or long-term public investment policies pursued in countries such as Belgium and France, and the readiness to offset increased unemployment by higher social security payments, was first challenged and then defeated by the crisis of the mid 1970s. Thus the potential for publicly managed counter-cyclical policies pursued by some governments in some countries was swamped by the scale of the international crisis, with its vicious circle of 'beggar-my-neighbour' deflation.

Meso and Micro Dimensions

The conventional macroeconomic argument should also be qualified by the distinction between mesoeconomic and microeconomic enterprise. It has already been argued in Chapter 2 that the investment-planning period of big business in the mesoeconomic sector is longer than the lifetime of many governments and therefore much longer than the annual budgets of such public authorities. Such a meso-micro economic distinction should not be underestimated in any model which differentiates shorter- from longer-range investment in the manner of Hicks.

On the other hand, while big business in the mesoeconomic sector simply cannot afford to initiate or cancel an investment project spanning seven to ten years or more on the basis of one annual budget (or one year's change in income), big business is not immune over the longer term to changes in the trend of income.

Thus a multinational company may well read the writing in successive budgets in, for instance, the UK economy, make its own evaluation of the long-term growth potential of the system (i.e. in principle Harrod's Gn) and simply decide to disinvest there rather than elsewhere among the developed economies. But what government does in terms of the trend of growth of public expenditure will itself be crucial to the forward investment planning of mesoeconomic enterprise, not least since big business, with the largest share of given markets, is itself the main beneficiary of such public-spending programmes.

The Second Line of Defence

The implications of the above argument may be made clear by cross-reference to the main diagrams employed to describe the lower limits of contraction in an unstable market system. Thus in terms of Figure 3.12, it has been assumed for the above reasons that the main component of the lower limit of long-range investment in the system (Hicks' line H) is public spending. In terms of the ratio of public spending to private spending in the West European economies, his lower line H is realistic for the resources directly absorbed by government, i.e. the share of public spending in GDP excluding transfer payments on social security, pensions, etc. Including transfer payments, it would be closer to Hicks' L line.

In Figure 3.12 the 'first line' defence of the system from collapse is constituted by rising wage demand and its positive income multiplier effects (wm^1–wm^3) from the trend lines of incomes, L (Hicks' lower equilibrium line). But for Hicks it is essentially the multiplier effects from H (in our terms, the role of public spending) which prevent the economy from hitting the floor in the manner of the Harrod paradox. In our own terms again, both the direct public spending from the long-range investment and expenditure line H and its indirect public-spending multiplier effects (psm^1–psm^3) constitute the 'second line' of defence of the system from collapse.

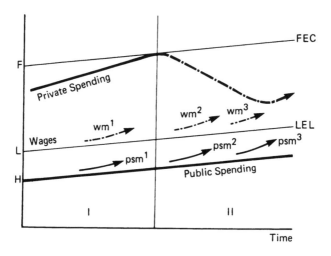

FIG. 3.12 Sustained public spending and cyclical upturn

Such a dramatic hypothesis of collapse is illustrated in Figure 3.13. This simply extends the scenario of the basic Hicks model to a situation in which the public-spending component of the H line is cut (on monetarist or other grounds) from the trend line PS^1–PS^2 to the downward line PS^3. If public spending is cut, it implies that wage demand falls, both directly in the public sector (either lower wage rates or unemployment, or both) and also indirectly in the private sector if public-sector wage restraint is used as a surrogate general incomes policy.

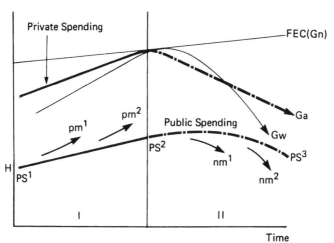

FIG. 3.13   Public spending cuts and cyclical downturn

In turn, the fall in direct spending and wages in the public sector change the positive multiplier effects pm^1–pm^2 in phase I of Figure 3.4 into the negative multiplier effects nm^1–nm^2 of phase II. This further registers negative multiplier effects on private incomes and on the matrix or inter- industry and services multiplier in the private sector. In turn, again, and in contrast with the rational expectations theory on costs and prices argued inter alia by Minford and Peel (1980), this downturn in actual growth, Ga, prompts a decline in Harrod's 'warranted' growth Gw, with the economy entering 'free fall' rather than rising from the floor of Hicks' long-range investment line H, which has itself been cut away.

Growth and the Mixed Economy

Some of the limits of the monetarist case have already been outlined in this chapter. Others are examined in Chapters 7 and 8. But a key limit to either the monetarist or the supply-side case against Keynesian economics is precisely that they fail to address Keynesian or post-Keynesian analysis of growth and cycles in economic activity. It is one thing for some leading politicians to dismiss Keynes without having understood or, in some cases, ever read him. It is another for professional economists not to address, far less refute, some of the main propositions of Keynesian and post-Keynesian theory of the dynamics of a market economy. One of the key claims of Milton Friedman (1962) is to fulfil the criteria of so-called 'positive' economics. But this involves the testing of hypotheses of disequilibrium models of economic growth which he has simply neglected.

Analysis of the role of public spending in the circularity of income and expenditure has already been outlined in Chapter 1, and is further elaborated both in Chapter 8 and in detail in *The Political Economy* (Holland, forthcoming). This chapter has paid more attention to the role of public spending in sustaining and stabilising private income and investment within the framework of post-Keynesian and post-Marxian models of economic growth.

Figures 3.14(a) and (b) reveal an interesting contrast in this respect between the so-called 'Keynesian' and 'monetarist' phases of the postwar era. While bearing in mind that Hicks did not apply his own application of Harrod's model to the role of public expenditure, the most striking feature of Figure 3.14(a) is the coincidence between the upward slope of long-term public expenditure in Germany, France, Italy and the UK from the mid 1950s to the early 1970s with Hicks' *L* or 'lower equilibrium' line. During this period, public spending increased on a major scale as a share of national expenditure in the countries concerned. Relative to its initial level in the mid 1950s, this meant an increase of a third for West Germany and around a quarter for France, Italy and the UK over the next thirty years.

Of itself, such a rising share of public in total spending does not imply a rationale for 'super-growth'. The limited growth of the UK economy during the period (averaging half that of the other three countries) is evidence of this. But when combined with the previous analysis in this chapter of the structural, social and spatial shifts of labour from traditional and low-paid employment to higher productivity sectors in more developed regions of the German, French and Italian economies, the rising share of public in total spending clearly played a key role. For instance, the mid 1950s represented a relative recession in postwar economic recovery, following the first cycle of activity based on reconstruction after World War Two. It was not until the later 1950s, with the 'surprise' of many professional economists at the sustained nature of expansion, that talk became widespread among both policy-makers and the public at large of the 'miracle' nature of postwar economic growth.

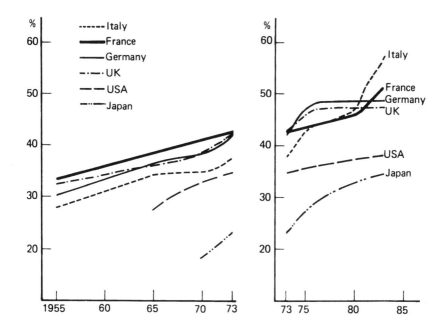

FIG. 3.14(a) Sustained public spending increase: the 'Keynesian' era (Including transfer payments)

FIG. 3.14(b) Stabilisation and slowdown in key economies: the 'monetarist' era

Such variants on the *Wirtschaftswunder, le miracle* or *il miracolo* were matched in the Japanese case by a recovery which has lasted not only for thirty years, but thereafter into the 1980s. In this context, the rise in the share of public in total spending in the postwar Japanese economy is of especial interest, granted that the Japanese government sanctioned a dramatic increase in public expenditure – from less than a quarter to more than a third of GDP – from the time of the first OPEC 'oil shock' through to the mid 1980s, in other words at precisely the time when West Germany and the UK overreacted to oil price increases and applied the brakes to public spending. Italy, for the remainder of the 1970s, did the same, but thereafter recovered public spending and – with it – sustained rates of growth of output which nearly topped the league among the OECD countries. In the US the increase in public spending from just over a quarter to a third of GDP was unchecked by the nominal espousal of monetarist and supply-side economics by the incoming first Reagen administration, where a presumed budget deficit was maintained under the sedulous pressure of the military-industrial complex.

Put simply, during the 'Keynesian' era of sustained and increased public spending the market economies enjoyed rates of growth of output and employment such as they had never previously known. In the period of the monetarist counter-revolution, those following Friedmanite or supply-side dictates curtailed their economic growth and – as shown in Chapter 1 – equalled or surpassed levels of unemployment unknown since the slump of the 1930s.

3.6 Summary

(1) The Harrod and Domar models are both similar and different in their application of 'Keynesian' economic dynamics. Both models stress the share of income saved and embodied in actual investment, and the role of technical progress in lowering the capital-output ratio. But the Harrod model also embodies the Keynesian theory of expectations and the accelerator concept.

(2) While Domar expressed equilibrium conditions for balanced economic growth, Harrod claimed that the combination of multiplier and accelerator effects would give rise to over- and under-reaction by entrepreneurs through their estimates of warranted growth. If the economy were in equilibrium for any time it would therefore be on a 'knife edge' between boom and slump, rather than on a balanced growth path.

(3) The accelerator concept has been supplemented by capital stock adjustment theory, allowing for the dampening effect on trade cycles of the lagged demand for stocks of commodities and equipment.

(4) Neither Harrod-Domar models nor those of capital stock adjustment allow for differences in the response of individual firms or sectors to changes in the rate of macroeconomic growth and income (Kalecki, 1954 and Perroux, 1965). When multinational big business now dominates the rate of growth of investment or output in the national or international economy, the role of such mesoeconomic enterprises becomes central to the dynamics of growth and cycles.

(5) In distinguishing long-term 'autonomous' investment from short-term 'induced' investment, Hicks provided a framework which explained how negative multipliers from a short-term downswing in activity could be offset by the positive multipliers from rising longer-term investment expenditure.

(6) Marx's model of the reserve army of labour and the pulling of labour from declining employment sectors (such as agriculture) into expanding areas of the economy (such as modern industry and services)

explains how Hicks' Full Employment Ceiling can be raised through structural and regional shifts in the labour force during periods of sustained economic growth.

(7) A combination of the Harrod, Hicks and Marx models (compatible with those of Lewis and Kindleberger) explains some of the key dynamics of sustained super-growth in the postwar continental European economies, and hyper-growth in the economy of postwar Japan.

(8) The long-term rise in real wages in the postwar period and wage 'inflexibility' explains, within the Hicksian model, how short-term downturns in economic activity can be offset and reversed by rising long-term real wage expenditure.

(9) Within the same framework, however, it was the long-term rise of public expenditure as a share of total spending which raised and sustained long-term economic growth in the postwar market economies, as well as ensuring a redistribution of investment spending and income between different social groups and classes. Partly due to its major share of markets, and also its more effective bargaining power with government, multinational big business in the meso-economy has been the main private-sector beneficiary of such increased public spending.

(10) Such factors in post-Keynesian and post-Marxian analysis of the dynamics and growth of the modern mixed economy are entirely neglected by monetarist and so-called supply-side theorists, who thereby also neglect the fact that cuts in public spending (or wages) to adjust expenditure (and income) in the short to medium term will register cumulative depressive effects on the rate of economic growth.

4 Investment and Trade

4.1 Advantage and Disadvantage

Orthodox trade theory assumes that capital and labour are immobile between countries, and that trade is essentially between different companies in different countries. But in reality, capital and investment are highly mobile between countries, while trade is increasingly by and between the same multinational companies world wide.

This has major implications not only for the relevance of conventional theory, but also for the effectiveness of economic policies and for international trade and payment arrangements. It helps explain not only some of the outstanding 'paradoxes' in international trade theory but also the apparently poor trade performance of leading world exporters such as the United States and the United Kingdom, which in turn has affected their role as reserve currencies and the breakdown of the postwar Bretton Woods system.

International and Multinational

The dominance by multinationals of global commodity trade is given in Table 4.1. This shows that in contrast with the textbook perception that such trade occurs simply between countries, from two-thirds to 95 per cent of the commodities exported from developing countries is controlled by less than half a dozen multinational companies. This dominance by multinationals has implications for global policies for commodity prices stabilisation and the feasibility of gaining agreement by both countries and companies on price stabilisation and on measures within individual commodity markets to stabilise export earnings.

Table 4.2 shows that multinationals were responsible for over 80 per cent of UK visible exports in the 1970s and early 1980s.

Table 4.3 shows that this UK visible export trade was highly concentrated in the hands of a few firms typical of the mesoeconomic sector. Thus, over the period up to 1981 when the Conservative government decided to stop collating the data for the company share of trade, it was evident that an average of less than ninety firms accounted for half of UK visible exports and an average of 275 firms for two-thirds of this export trade.

TABLE 4.1   Corporate Control of Global Trade, 1980 ($m)

Commodity	Exports from developing countries	% marketed by the 3–6 largest multinationals
Food		
Wheat	16,556	85-90
Sugar	14,367	60
Coffee	12,585	85-90
Corn	11,852	85-90
Rice	4,978	70
Cocoa	3,004	85
Tea	1,905	80
Bananas	1,260	70-75
Pineapples	440	90
Agricultural raw materials		
Forest products	54,477	90
Cotton	7,886	85-90
Natural rubber	4,393	70-75
Tobacco	3,859	85-90
Hides and skins	2,743	25
Jute	203	85-90
Ores, minerals and materials		
Crude petroleum	306,000	75
Copper	10,650	80-85
Iron ore	6,930	90-95
Tin	3,599	75-80
Phosphates	1,585	50-60
Bauxite	991	80-85

Source: UNCTAD.

TABLE 4.2   The Multinational Domination of UK Export Trade

	Percentage of total exports, excluding diamonds, on an Overseas Trade Statistics basis					
	1971	*1973*	*1975*	*1977*	*1979*	*1981*
Multinational Companies	84	86	85	85	83	81
Represented by:						
United States controlled enterprises	18	18	20	18	19	17
Other foreign-controlled enterprises	6	7	7	10	10	10
UK associates of foreign enterprises	5	5	4	4	4	4
UK enterprises with overseas affiliates	55	56	54	53	50	51
National Companies	16	14	15	15	17	19
Total	100	100	100	100	100	100

Source: *British Business.*

TABLE 4.3 Number of Companies Accounting for Half and Two-Thirds of UK Exports

As recorded in Overseas Trade Statistics (including oil, excluding diamonds)						
	1976	1977	1978	1979	1980	1981
1/2 UK exports	77	90	108	94	95	72
2/3 UK exports	196	262	337	287	317	254*

* The 254 companies in 1981 relate only to enterprises making returns to the overseas transactions inquiry. No allowance is made for companies with exports between £5m and £50m in 1980 which did not publish the value of their exports in 1981.
Source: *British Business.*

A comparable dominance of the US visible export trade by multinational companies is illustrated in Table 4.4. This shows that in 1977, the share of US trade associated with American multinationals amounted to as much as 84 per cent of total US exports and nearly 60 per cent of US imports, with the export share of multinationals in 1983 still nearly 77 per cent, and the import share over 46 per cent.

TABLE 4.4 The Multinational Domination of US Visible Trade (%)*

	1977	1982	1983
Total US Exports represented by	100.0	100.0	100.0
US multinational companies	84.0	77.0	76.8
Other companies**	16.0	23.0	23.2
Total US Imports represented by	100.0	100.0	100.0
US multinational companies	57.7	49.5	46.3
Other companies†	42.3	50.5	53.7

* Non-bank multinationals – annual average compound rate of growth.
† US trade not associated with US multinationals.
Source: Barker (1986).

Noting the relative decline of the share of US multinational companies in US export and import trade for the period concerned, Barker (1986) observes that the recession in the world economy probably played a role, while commenting also, in a manner relevant to the product-cycle analysis stressed in *The Market Economy* (Holland, 1987) and elsewhere in this volume, that:

The slow growth in exports to foreign affiliates may also have reflected a pattern of maturation frequently observed among affiliates of US MNCs. According to that pattern, affiliates are first established primarily to sell their parents' products. Later, they process or assemble their parents' products abroad and, finally, they develop and produce their own products to sell locally, to third countries, or even to the United States. Thus, as these affiliates mature, products exported from the United States become a smaller component and the affiliates' own products a larger component of their total sales.

A similar explanation stressing both the product-cycle model over the long term, and the slowdown of global economic growth in the late 1970s and early 1980s, is given by Jane Sneddon Little (1986) in an analysis of the growth of intra-firm trade between subsidiaries of multinational companies in the *New England Economic Review*.

Paradox and Practice

As already suggested, the multinational structure of global investment, production and export trade by US and UK multinationals helps to explain why American and British visible export trade has performed so unimpressively since the war.

For instance, as Robert Lipsey and Irving Kravis (1985) have shown:

> While exports from the United States had declined by 1977 to less than 15 per cent of world exports of manufactures, exports from all locations by US multinational firms accounted for more than a fifth of the world total, and exports by all US firms accounted for more than a quarter. . . . While the share of US firms in world exports declined, the share of US-owned multinational enterprises remained constant or increased slightly. . . . Another way of putting this development is that there was a large shift in the geographical origins of exports by US firms.

The fall in the share of US world exports of manufactures from 1957 to 1977 had in fact been dramatic, by more than 40 per cent. Its repercussions, with that of the poor export performance of the UK, were wide-reaching. Sterling, as the second reserve currency of the global economy, had been devalued in 1967 for the first time in 20 years. By 1971 the dollar had suffered the same fate. Within two years, oil-producing countries, which thereby had suffered loss of revenue on their dollar earnings, had retaliated by forming OPEC. In reacting to the 'oil shock' and slamming the brakes on domestic demand to reduce oil imports, the leading OECD countries provoked the twentieth century's second major slump.

Beyond Ricardo

Commenting on the fact that the global exports of US multinationals in manufacturing still amounted to more than a quarter of world trade in 1977, against a registered US visible export share in manufactures of only 15 per cent, Lipsey and Kravis observe that the competitiveness and comparative advantage of US firms world wide shows little erosion of their managerial or technological abilities. These just happen to be focused in operations outside rather than inside the United States (Lipsey and Kravis, 1985, chapter 2).

Yet in reality, the scope and scale of multinational enterprise, and the extent to which world trade is now dominated by the same companies operating in different countries, demands a fundamental review of Ricardo's theory of comparative advantage and its assumption of trade between different companies in different countries.

Ricardo's theory of comparative advantage, beloved by authors of conventional texts on international trade, and faithfully endorsed by policy-makers unexposed to its qualification by multinational capital, is very simple. Assuming two countries and two commodities, Ricardo argues that each country can produce one good cheaper than the other. Therefore each country will have a comparative advantage in the production of one commodity and a comparative disadvantage in the production of the other. It benefits each country to export the commodity in which it has a comparative advantage and to import the commodity in which it has a comparative disadvantage.

In Ricardo's exposition, the most frequently cited and familiar example is trade between English exporters of cloth and Portuguese exporters of wine.* The basic framework for such a division of trade is represented in Figure 4.1, which stresses the national character of capital and labour and their immobility between countries, as assumed by Ricardo.

FIG. 4.1   The Ricardian model

Ricardo assumed that wine can be more cheaply produced in Portugal and cloth more cheaply in England. Portugal will export wine and import cloth from England, while England will trade on the reverse basis. The trade for both products, in the simple numerical example of Table 4.5, is at the rate of 4:1 for wine and cloth respectively.

* Ricardo in fact allows that 'wine shall be made in France and Portugal, that corn shall be grown in America and Poland, and that hardware and other goods shall be manufactured in England' (Ricardo, 1816, p. 134). In terms of the ensuing argument, it is worth noting that two of his three product examples are agricultural.

TABLE 4.5   Ricardian Absolute Advantage

| | Production per worker per week | |
	In Portugal	In England
Wine	60 litres	15 litres
Cloth	15 yards	60 yards

Absolute Disadvantage

But what if the labour content of both wine and cloth is less for Portugal than in England, and that instead of only 15 yards of cloth per week, a worker in Portugal may produce 90 yards?

TABLE 4.6   Ricardian Comparative Advantage

| | Production per worker per week | |
	In Portugal	In England
Wine	60 litres	15 litres
Cloth	90 yards	60 yards

In this situation, represented in Table 4.6, labour is more efficient at producing both wine and cloth in Portugal than in England. Portugal would have an absolute advantage over England in both products.

However, Ricardo argued that while one country may have an absolute advantage in both products, it would be likely to have a greater advantage in one of the two products concerned. He argued that the country would export the product in which it had the greater or comparative advantage, and import the product in which it had the lesser advantage, i.e. a comparative disadvantage. In our example in Table 4.6, since Portugal's comparative advantage in wine amounts to 4:1 against a comparative advantage in cloth of only 3:2, it would tend to specialise in the production and export of wine rather than of cloth.

Ricardian Geography

Ricardo's much-cited example of the principle of comparative advantage depended on specific assumptions which should be external to any general model, and overlooked factors which, for observation alone, he should have been able to include in his own time. For one thing, the absolute advantage of Portugal over England in the production of wine depends on climate and geography rather than cost or labour content. England may be blessed with many advantages, but sustained summer sun is not among them. Conversely, water power from the abundant English rainfall was one of the special advantages conferred on British cloth makers during the early pre-steam-power phase of the industrial revolution.

There is a parallel here with another classic of conventional reasoning in economic theory – the so-called technological external economies, where in a generally cited example Tibor Scitovsky was not able to find any external economies which were strictly technological as such, and instead gave the example of beekeepers benefiting from the proximity of a nearby orchard and private mineowners benefiting from the joint pumping and drainage of a coalfield by other companies (Scitovsky, 1954, and Holland 1976a, chapter 7). In both these cases, as with Portugal's absolute advantage in the production of wine, the basis of the advantage is geographical rather than strictly economic. This is quite apart from the fact that Ricardo never considered what would be the consequences for Anglo-Portuguese trade if the income generated by such comparative advantage were unequally distributed between them over the long run.

Ricardo's Multinationals

We also need to modify Ricardo's assumption of factor immobility – the lack of movement between countries of labour and capital. In his own time – the early nineteenth century – while labour may have been immobile between Portugal and England, English or British capital was certainly not immobile relative to Portugal. In fact, in the period following the Napoleonic wars, the wine trade from Portugal to Britain was significantly developed by British capital in Portugal itself. This was through direct investment in vineyards and the production, sea transport and British distribution of that wine for which Portugal is most famous – Port. Familiar brand names for Port are not simply British importers' labels on Portuguese exports, but are stamped on the ground of Portugal itself through the ownership of areas of that country by British companies. In other words, Ricardo assumed that he was giving a clear example of the international division of labour and trade. Inadvertently he was illustrating the multinational division of capital between two countries.

Opportunity Costs

Ricardo's exposition of absolute and comparative advantage was based on the labour theory of value, commonly shared by both the classical economists and Marx. But the labour theory of value is rejected by the neoclassical analysis of the international division of labour and trade predominant both in international agencies and contemporary government policy in the developed capitalist countries. Also, in post-Ricardian neoclassical theory, the stress on comparative labour cost in Ricardo gave way to a theory of opportunity cost in trade.

Opportunity-cost theory has been formulated by various economists, but amounts essentially to saying that the cost of producing rather than importing product A in one country is how much of products B to n (i.e. other products or commodities) have to be forgone to produce, or gain additional units of, product A itself. According to the theory it makes little difference whether the factors released by not producing A are all suited to the output of products B to n. The question is simply how much of one commodity must be given up to get more of another. In this respect, in contrast with the assumption of complete *immobility* of factors in international trade, the theory assumes a complete *mobility* of factors of production within the national market economy.

Costs and Trade

Formal expositions of the theory of opportunity cost have been presented with differing degrees of elegance to successive generations of students. There is real force to the principle given certain assumptions. For instance, it is arguable that the opportunity cost today for some countries of medium size in undertaking the production of computer hardware, such as mainframe computers, is very high, and that they should import such a product and concentrate their own activities on the related computer software. However, the argument does not readily obtain for the broad range of industrial products unless, in effect, one is to argue that an economy traditionally based on industrialisation such as the United Kingdom should forgo it in favour of becoming a services-orientated economic system. While in simple opportunity-cost terms in the short run this might make sense to some people, it nonetheless has further indirect effects such as assuming that the services revenue generated by the economy as a whole will be sufficient to finance industrial imports indefinitely. Such an argument in the United Kingdom context is certainly questionable, just as the financing of industrial imports through the export of oil could in the medium term lead to a major deindustrialisation of the country, and a dependent relationship with the rest of the world.

4.2 Proportions and Disproportions

Ricardian comparative advantage theory assumes that all will be for the best in a free-trading world. But gains and losses are not evenly distributed in the global economy. For decades Germany and Japan have built massive structural surpluses of a kind which would have been even greater if genuinely free trade had in fact prevailed.

Hecksher and Ohlin

A significant and important advance on the Ricardian principle of the international division of labour arose from the following questions. If international trade is based on differences in comparative costs, what accounts for the differences in such costs themselves? This advance was made respectively by Eli Hecksher and Bertil Ohlin in the 1930s. This is the *factor proportions* basis for the theory of international trade (Hecksher, 1958; Ohlin, 1933).

The formulation runs as follows. Different goods require different factor inputs, and different countries have different factor endowments. Arguing in terms of what is popularly known as the Cobb-Douglas production function, whereby production itself is a function of the combination of capital and labour plus residual factors, Ohlin argued that countries would tend to specialise in exports in whose production factors they had a comparative or relative factor abundance.

The essentials of this theory are illustrated in our own terms in Figure 4.2. In this example, it is assumed that the United States and the United Kingdom have a relative capital abundance *vis-à-vis* the 'rest of the world'. The ratio of their capital to labour is 2K to 1L, versus a capital/labour ratio in the rest of the world of 1K to 2L. Therefore it is assumed that the United States and the United Kingdom would tend to specialise in the export of capital-intensive goods, whereas the rest of the world will specialise in labour-intensive exports.

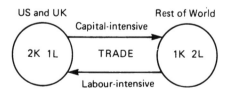

FIG. 4.2   The Hecksher-Ohlin model

The Leontief Paradox

Most students who have encountered this theory will be aware of its challenge by the 'Leontief paradox'. Essentially, Wassily Leontief found that the United States in fact specialised more in the export of agricultural products rather than in the industrial goods in which it might be assumed *a priori* to have an advantage (Leontief, 1951).

The Leontief paradox may have unduly perplexed international trade theorists. For one thing, the emphasis in the Hecksher-Ohlin model on capital and labour to the neglect of land (a factor certainly not neglected by Ricardo) oversimplifies reality and thereby biases the emphasis on capital and labour as factors of production.

If capital, labour and land are taken into account as three joint factors, it becomes clearer why the United States has an advantage in agriculture. First, this is due to the very high land/labour ratios in the United States compared with most other countries, including Western Europe, where there is less land per worker due to small-scale tenant or peasant farming. Secondly, a greater capital intensity is more easily achieved in agricultural production in the United States (partly due to the greater land/labour ratio). Thirdly, more intensive use of productivity-raising chemicals and fertilizers. Fourthly, a more efficient forward linkage from production through to large-scale sales outlets (from agribusiness through to hypermarkets). Fifthly, extensive state intervention and support, plus road building, eletrification and water resource projects since the Roosevelt New Deal in the 1930s.

Therefore it could be argued that the advantage of the United States in agricultural exports confirms what could be called an extended Hecksher-Ohlin theory of factor proportions in international trade. However, the fifth cause – state intervention – was crucial in making possible the second and third key conditions of higher capital intensity and fertilisation. Left to market forces, the US farmer in the 1930s either was stuck in an undrained Tennessee Valley or staring distractedly at the dustbowls of the unirrigated Mid West states.

Explanations

There are further explanations of the Leontief paradox. Foreign trade is a relatively small proportion of the national income of the United States. For most of the past half century it has been 10 per cent or less, as opposed to a quarter or a third of national income for many other leading economies. The US economy is continental rather than simply national. In this respect, the United States might be regarded as atypical of advanced capitalist economies and their trade patterns. Thus the Leontief paradox qualifies rather than displaces the Hecksher-Ohlin paradigm.

More importantly, as already stressed, American capital has massive direct investment abroad where production by multinationals by 1970 was more than four times the US visible export trade. Such foreign production by US companies has been notably capital and technology intensive. Therefore in evaluating the so-called Leontief paradox on US trade it is important to take account of the degree to which US capital abroad may be fulfilling the Hecksher-Ohlin thesis on relative factor intensity, albeit through multi-national investment rather than international trade.

However, one of the main limitations of the factor proportions theory in international trade has been not only the substitution of national by multinational trade but also the assumption that each country has the same technological possibilities of producing a given good, in other words that the production functions – the combinations of labour and capital – are the same in different countries. In practice, technological potential relates to capital potential inasmuch as technology is (1) embodied in capital itself, and (2) tends to be capital-intensive.

Not all countries have equal access to capital either in the liquid form of savings, or the embodied form of investment. This is vividly illustrated by the differences between less developed countries and the United States, Europe and Japan.

Nor do all firms enjoy equal access to capital, or equal potential efficiency. Conventional trade theory neglects the production functions of different kinds of *firm*, assuming an aggregate production function for economies or countries.* In one sense, this should not be surprising in view of the assumption of the macro-micro synthesis in neoclassical theory that firms are relatively similar in their cost, profit and price structure through the working of the market mechanism, and that aggregation at the macroeconomic level is thereby legitimate.

Unequal Capital – Unequal Costs

Introducing the theory of firms, costs and competition to factor proportions analysis of trade can certainly yield significant analytic results. But few economists have translated an oligopolistic theory of unequal cost and distribution structures through to their implications for a theory of unequal trade. Yet, in principle, the one should parallel the other. In practice this is

* Essentially the standard Cobb-Douglas formulation of $P = f(K, L) + r$, where production (P) is a function (f) or capital (K) and labour (L) and r is residual or other factors. It has already been noted that Denison has found the residuals (including technical progress, education and the skill of the labour force) more important than the simple capital/labour ratio (Denison, 1967).

attempted in the meso and microeconomic context, in relation to macro-economic factor proportions theory, in the following analysis.

For example, in Figure 4.3(a), modifying the ratios of Figure 4.2, it is now assumed at a macroeconomic level that US firms on average have more capital per unit of labour than UK companies. Thus the US capital/labour ratio is 2K:1L, against a UK capital/labour ratio of 1K:2L.

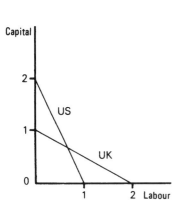

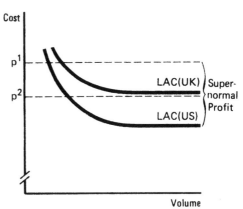

FIG. 4.3(a)   Relative factor
proportions: the US and the UK

FIG. 4.3(b)   Normal and super-normal
profits: UK and US firms

Orthodox theory rarely translates such ratios through to the production and cost schedules of individual firms. But more capital per worker makes possible more technical progress and innovation, higher productivity and lower costs. In Figure 4.3(b), this would be reflected in different long-run average cost or LAC curves for UK and US companies. In principle the US company could charge a price of p^2 for exports to the UK, which could undercut UK companies on the domestic market and eliminate UK domestic production. The dynamics of such 'elimination' pricing have already been analysed in the national economy context in *The Market Economy* (Holland, 1987, chapter 6). But in practice the profit motive may prove more simple. The US firm may simply choose to export to the UK at the prevailing British domestic price level p^1 and thereby gain itself a super-normal or double profit on UK sales.

Dynamisation

Conventional international trade theory assumes, in Kindleberger's words, that 'capital is more mobile within than between countries' (Kindleberger, 1963, p. 7). If this obtains in practice, it can be assumed in a dynamic model that capital in the United Kingdom, under the constraints of the competitive process, will move into those sectors or products in which UK exporters have an advantage. It also can be assumed, in terms of conventional theory, that British producers will shed labour at the same time.

This situation is represented in Figure 4.4(a), where the initial 2:1 capital/labour ratio in favour of the United States and 1:2 ratio to the disadvantage of the United Kingdom (UK^1) has changed to a UK capital/labour ratio of 1.5:1.5 (UK^2). But while this would enable UK companies to lower their average costs on the lines of $LAC(UK)^2$ in Figure 4.4(b) and charge a price permitting a normal profit at p^3 rather than the original UK domestic price p^1, this still enables the US firm to make a higher profit at the same price, or continue to undercut the UK firm at price p^2. Thus the US firm can continue to generate re-investment on the UK market or reallocate its surplus elsewhere at price p^3. It is also possible that if the UK firm can lower its costs to $LAC(UK)^2$, the US firm can do the same with a further round of productivity-raising and cost-lowering investment which would still enable it to eliminate the UK firm even after the latter's second-round investment.

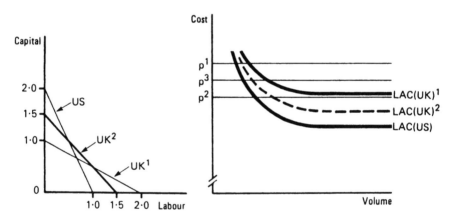

FIG. 4.4(a)   Factor realignment and trade: the US and the UK

FIG. 4.4(b)   Factor realignment and price and profit differentials

Such dynamics are excluded by conventional models of international trade, which focus on static comparison of cost structures for different products in different countries. They do not follow through the cost and competition implications of different factor endowments for trade in the same goods or commodities. Rather than resulting in mutually beneficial specialisation, the relative advantage for lower-cost firms in international markets will extend the dynamics of unequal domestic competition with unequal gains to the global economy as a whole. Such factors are crucial in explaining the penetration by multinational capital of foreign markets, both on the basis of international trade and on the basis of direct investment in other countries.

The Japanese Challenge

In other words, although throughout the figurative examples have compared or contrasted UK and US companies, the reasoning can be extrapolated to competition on a global scale. The nominal nationality of the company with a lower long-run average cost – whether American, Japanese or German – does not affect the analysis.

Moreover, international trade and direct foreign investment are not self-exclusive alternatives. The global multinational corporation, of whatever initial nationality, can gain absolute advantages in both international trade and multinational production over time, with cumulative self-reinforcing effects which can amount to the devastation of production in what are conventionally represented as developed and mature capitalist economies. The most dramatic recent example has been the Japanese penetration of domestic markets in both the United States and the United Kingdom since the 1960s. But on current trends Japanese capital is increasingly extending its operations on a basis of multinational *production* rather than simply international trade. Such a challenge augurs ill for any economy whose policy-makers are still influenced by the conventional textbook theory of comparative advantage in international trade.

4.3 Global Investment and Trade

Successful export companies can further their international advantage through multinational investment and production. But in doing so they may disadvantage the export trade of their 'home country' by substituting foreign production for exports.

This argument was first elaborated by Bertil Ohlin in an analysis which has been largely neglected by theorists of international trade, reared in their student days on second-hand versions of the Hecksher-Ohlin theory of comparative advantage. Ohlin (1933) argued that while trade itself between regions or countries would tend to occur through specialisation on the basis of comparative factor abundance, international trade theory was limited by its assumption of the immobility of factors of production, i.e. capital and labour. In other words, like Gunnar Myrdal (1957), Ohlin was well aware both that capital and labour were mobile between regions and countries and that this factor mobility would profoundly qualify the nature of trade for those countries affected by such factor flows.

For instance, Ohlin laid some stress on the extent to which the agricultural specialisation of Australia and New Zealand arose from their established links with a UK economy which even before the First World War was no longer providing all its own food needs. Thus, despite their location on the other side of the world, in economic terms Australia and New Zealand were for years the farming 'backyard' of the UK economy. Even before such global integration of production, colonial links such as those of the Société Générale of Belgium in Zaire (formerly the Belgian Congo), or even earlier of the East India Company in India, had show the importance of direct investment giving rise to trade.

Global Factor Flows

More recently, the global multinational corporation has invested not only in other developed countries but also in less developed countries where the costs of labour have been a fraction of those 'at home'. This situation, reflecting Ohlin's insights, and in contrast with the international immobility of factors of production assumed in Figures 4.1 and 4.2, is represented in Figure 4.5.

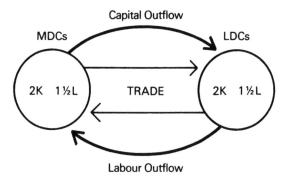

FIG. 4.5 Relaxing the constraints: trade *plus* factor flows.

In terms of the analysis of Figure 4.2, capital has not increased in the MDCs and remains at the level of 2K. However, either through savings outflow or foreign investment by multinational companies, capital has now flowed to the LDCs. Thus, in contrast with the 'rest of the world' in Figure 4.2, the LDCs have increased their share of capital from 1K to 2K, i.e. equivalent to the more developed countries. At the same time, by the process of migration, labour has moved from the LDCs to the MDCs, reducing the 'rest of the world's' labour in terms of Figure 4.2 from 2L to 1.5L, and increasing the

MDC's labour from 1L to 1.5L. This is in contrast to the disparity between capital and labour in different countries assumed by the factor proportions theory of international trade commonly identified with Hecksher and Ohlin, according to which lower wage costs in less developed countries should offset their capital (and technology) disadvantage in trade with developed countries. Yet Ohlin's own original model assumed that migration of factors of production between countries and regions of the world economy can result in an equalisation of relative factor proportions (Ohlin, 1933).

The Newly Industrialised Countries

In real terms, as implied by the partial equalisation assumptions of US-UK factor flows in Figures 4.4(a) and (b), and their accompanying analysis, such a literal equalisation of factors of production (and production functions) between developed and less developed countries is unlikely, although for a while it may have been achieved for some production in South East Asian city states such as Singapore and Hong Kong. As illustrated in Figure 4.6, while multinational capital has flowed to some of the less developed countries on a significant scale since the 1960s, this has mainly been to intermediate or newly industrialised countries (commonly known as NICs). In fact, as shown in Table 4.7, from two-thirds to four-fifths of foreign direct investment by First World companies has been in only a dozen nominally Third World countries, some of whom have a GDP per capita higher than Portugal and approaching that of Greece. Such intermediate economies (or IMCs) with an inflow of foreign capital, backed in some cases by major state intervention, have achieved 'hyper-growth' of investment, GNP and income. They include the South East Asian 'quartet' of Singapore, Hong Kong, South Korea and Taiwan, plus certain regions of countries in the Latin American subcontinent, in particular the Sao Paulo and Rio de Janeiro regions in Brazil and the Greater Mexico City region in Mexico. Such 'megapolitan' urbanisation has resulted in urban pollution (especially in Sao Paulo and Mexico City) and a dramatic dualism between city and country, employed and unemployed, rich and poor. Thus there has been uneven development within some of the major NICs, while by the mid 1980s some of the 'city state' NICs such as Singapore were already experiencing symptoms of negative economic growth, in part due to (i) global recession and in part to (ii) the reduced significance of low wages with rising wage costs and (iii) the increased importance of labour-displacing innovation and technical progress.

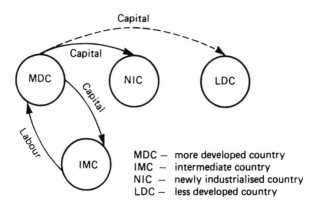

FIG. 4.6   Global factor flows: key relationships

TABLE 4.7   Multinational Investment in Developing Countries: the Focus on NICs

	1969–73	1974–78	1979–83
All non-oil developing countries,			
$ million		28,200	53,300
Total for 27 middle and upper income countries included below	6,674	20,829	48,645
		Percentage of total	
Newly industralising countries	80	74	64[a]
Brazil	37	36	21
Mexico	25	16	16
Singapore	11	14	16
New NICs	17	23	27
Malaysia	8	10	11
Other middle income countries	4	3	9
Area Totals			
Africa	2	7	13
Asia	30	36	38
Latin America	68	57	50

a. Estimate.

Source: IMF, *International Financial Statistics*, IMF, *Foreign Private Investment in Developing Countries*, January 1985, and Overseas Development Institute, June 1985.

Investment versus Trade

In this context we need to distinguish global capital flows between primary, secondary and tertiary sectors. In terms of Figure 4.6, capital flow from MDCs to NICs has been mainly in the secondary or manufacturing sector, whether the more developed countries have been American, European or Japanese. Capital flow in the form of direct investment towards less developed countries has been mainly in primary agricultural and mineral production or basic infrastructure projects. Meanwhile, capital flow in the form of direct investment in intermediate countries (IMCs) such as Mexico, Spain, Portugal, Yugoslavia, Greece and Turkey, was paralleled until the mid 1970s by a flow of labour towards the United States and the European countries. Between developed countries, the most recent capital flows have been in the service sector, including banking and finance (see further *The Market Economy*, chapter 8).

In *International and Inter-Regional Trade* (1933), Ohlin spells out the potential consequences of such factor flows. His essential argument is that *direct investment and production may or will tend to substitute for export trade*. Or, as Kojima (1977, p. 115) has put it in a key analysis of the macroeconomic implications of foreign direct investment (corroborating Ohlin's original insight), international capital movements 'necessarily result in the destruction of commodity trade'. The underlying reasoning is simple, but crucial. In other words, as companies shift capital in the form of direct investment to other countries and regions of the world economy, they substitute production and sales *in* such countries or regions for exports *to* them.

International Evidence

The evidence for this is now considerable. For instance, in a survey of 3,200 subsidiaries of 1,250 parent companies in manufacturing, the Japanese Ministry of International Trade and Industry MITI found that 78 per cent of such subsidiaries abroad manufacture goods to *replace* exports (Kono, 1984, pp. 143–4). It should be allowed that the foreign investment may occur in the first place because direct export trade is blocked or impeded by tariffs. Also, first- or second-round export multiplier effects may be registered in the parent company or home country as the initial investment takes place.

According to Lahera (1985, p. 27), 'the principal interest of multinational companies in Latin America is in the internal market and not in the realisation of exports'. In this respect, for both Japan and Latin America, the Ohlin effect is substantially corroborated.

Clearly, the decline of domestic exports relative to exports from foreign subsidiaries may well be relative rather than absolute. This is indicated in the evidence of Table 4.8, in which Robert Lipsey and Irving Kravis chronicle the relative decline of manufacturing exports from the US by American multinational companies as a share of their global manufacturing exports from subsidiaries world wide.

TABLE 4.8   Exports from the US by US Multinational Firms as % of Their Exports from all Locations, by Industry

	Exports classified by industry of parent			Exports classified by product
			1977	
	1966	1977	1966	1977
All Manufacturing Industries	58.7	47.6	.81	47.9
Foods	48.8	39.5	.81	47.8
Chemicals	64.8	46.1	.71	41.7
Metals	72.0	41.8	.58	41.9
Machinery	60.2	49.7	.83	53.6
Transport Equipment	55.1	50.4	.91	47.9
All Other	54.8	44.8	.82	44.7

Source: Lipsey and Kravis (1985).

As Lipsey and Kravis comment, 'there was a substantial shift away from the United States in the source of US multinational enterprise exports' (Lipsey and Kravis, 1985, p. 19). The relative fall was up to a fifth in all manufacturing industry and in machinery and foods, up to 30 per cent in chemicals, and over two-fifths in metal manufacturing. Multinational firms, according to Lipsey and Kravis, still increased exports from the US more than did non-multinationals. But the effect of relative substitution of domestic exports by foreign production and exports, reflecting the Ohlin hypothesis, is nonetheless very clear.

Maximisers and Minimisers

The rationale of such exports substituting foreign investment has failed to penetrate the expositions on trade and investment of conventional textbook theory. It also perplexes those who cannot escape from the Ricardian paradigm of international trade. An illustration of its significance can be made in relation to the UK economy – the second most multinational in the world, after the US, in terms of ratio of foreign production to visible export trade.* A British export trade research project analysing over 120 leading companies in the early 1970s found that export representation by such firms was absurdly low in comparison with German and Japanese firms (Betro, 1975). As John Carvel commented (*Guardian*, 23 April 1975):

> There is a widespread failure to export. This shows up most clearly in the report's assessment of manpower devoted to export effort. In about 50 per cent of the exporting companies interviewed – which were responsible for about a *quarter* of Britain's total manufactured exports – there was either nobody at all whose specialist function was to promote the firm's exports or, at best, only one such specialist.

Or as the report itself observed, it is at least surprising that Britain hopes to do well in the world export league when 'against a German or Japanese "eleven" we put in the field one man, and sometimes not even one' (Betro, 1975).

Conventional international trade theory is hard put to answer the question why there should be such a dramatic contrast in export representation by British versus German and Japanese companies. Its standard recourse, reflected in the general conclusions of Hague, Oakeshott and Strain (1974) and Holmes (1978), is to claim that British exporters are slackers rather than thrusters, or insensitive to opportunities for profit maximisation in export markets. This amounts to extrapolation of the conventional paradigm of the firm and industry to global trade. Within this paradigm it gives a plausible but wrong answer to what in fact is the wrong question.

In practice, the reason for the absurdly low share of the sampled British export representatives reflects less on their lack of profit-maximising thrust than on the very high ratio of foreign direct investment and production by the same companies in foreign markets. In other words such companies have relatively little inducement to maintain a permanent export sales team in countries in which they are already established as direct investors and producers. British capital maximises foreign investment, but thereby fails to maximise direct exports.

The findings of the study very much reflect the structure of foreign direct investment and production by British companies on the lines of Ohlin's theory, rather than sheer inefficiency or apathy by British exporters. We have already seen, in Table 4.3, the extent of the concentration in the UK visible export trade, which is predominantly in the control of multinational companies operating directly in other countries.

A comparable judgement on US export performance has been made by

---

* If account is taken of the greater ratio of foreign trade to national income in Britain compared to the United States, one could argue that the British economy is the most multinational in the world.

Kojima (1977, p. 102). As he puts it, recognising the exceptional rate of innovation in the US:

> It is true that new products are successively created and new product cycles take place one after another in America. Multinational companies grow larger and maintain monopolistic or oligopolistic gains. But it is also true that the creation of new products does not keep pace with the spread of new technology, which itself is accelerated by foreign investment. Thus the American economy will lose its comparative advantage in new products . . . sooner or later and has already lost it in traditional manufacturing industry. . . . In the long run this creates export difficulties and adversely affects the US balance of payments.

Multinationals and Absolute Advantage

Ohlin's analysis foreshadowed and anticipated the rise of multinational capital on a major scale through direct investment in the postwar period. But, reflecting the historical circumstances of the 1930s during which he wrote, he did not distinguish between the investment and trade characteristics of big and small business, or multinational and national enterprise.

Clearly there are a range of factors which inhibit the alignment of comparative cost curves by different firms in different countries in international trade and production. For Kindleberger (1963, p. 96), 'the failure of specialisation to become complete is due to decreasing returns'. But without entirely arguing the reverse case – i.e. that specialisation tends to become complete because of increasing returns – it is clear that the multinational division of labour and capital by leading firms in different countries enables them to achieve increasing returns on a global scale entirely neglected in conventional international trade theory.

The result is less international comparative advantage than an absolute advantage for multinational companies in global trade. For instance, while it used to be argued in conventional textbook theory that in trade between the US and Brazil, higher US productivity would be offset by Brazil's advantage of low wages, in reality the operation of US multinational companies in both countries transforms Brazil's assumed comparative cost advantage. By locating high-productivity investment in Brazil, US multinationals can pay local wages (or more frequently local wages plus a goodwill mark-up) and thereby not only undercut domestic Brazilian industry but also compete on terms of absolute advantage elsewhere in the world economy.

This contrast between comparative and absolute advantage has been well established for some time in regional economic theory (*inter alia* Holland, 1976a and 1976b) and also argued in the context of multinational trade and payments (Holland, 1975, chapter 3). But it is only after a further decade of penetration by multinational companies of global trade that multinationals' global division of capital and labour has come to be more widely accepted as a qualification of the Ricardian theory of the international division of labour and trade.

Dunning (1985) has pointed out that while all first-year students reading economics are taught the conditions under which trade is beneficial, the well-known principle of comparative advantage holds good only under very restrictive conditions, including: (i) the existence of perfect competition, (ii) full-employment conditions, and (iii) the previously stressed immobility of factor flows. In addition, Dunning stresses that comparative advantage theory is concerned only with efficiency goals, and that it assumes that the economic structures of the trading countries are different from each other. With multinational companies, production often takes place in different countries through the same companies in similar sectors.

Low-Cost Labour

One of the historical factors in this new global division of capital has been the access of multinational companies to labour in less developed countries at a fraction of the real wage cost in their home countries or countries of main operation.

Evidence from a range of leading UK companies in the early 1970s showed that labour in South East Asia, i.e. in countries such as Hong Kong, Taiwan, the Philippines, Indonesia and South Korea, was both available to and exploited by multinational capital at a fifth or even a tenth of its cost in Europe and the United States (House of Commons, 1972). Similarly, very low wage costs could be achieved by multinational capital in areas of Latin America, especially Mexico and Brazil. The dramatic reduction of unit transport costs in the postwar period, with the rise of bulk carriers and container handling techniques, has meant that the distance factor in exploiting such labour, and its component costs, has become negligible to the overall costs of global big business (House of Commons, ibid.).

Figures 4.7(a) and 4.7(b) illustrate the different structure of long-run average costs available in more developed (MDC) and newly industrialising or less developed countries (NIC/LDC) for multinational versus national companies. The argument summarises the reasoning already made in detail elsewhere (Holland, 1987a, chapter 7 and 1976a, chapter 7). Thus in terms of Figure 4.7(a), while an MDC location implies a total average cost of 100, reflecting a total wage cost of 50 (wages cost MDC), a wage cost of 10 in an NIC or LDC will give an NIC/LDC total average cost of 60. Translated through to the structure of long-run average cost curves in Figure 4.7(b), this gives an incomparable cost advantage in international trade to the multi-national company with a subsidiary located in an NIC or LDC on LAC^2,

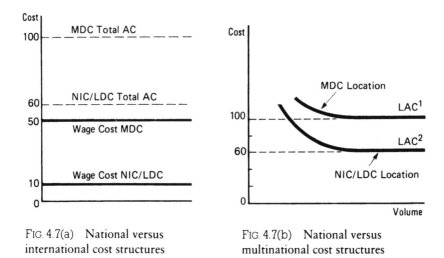

FIG. 4.7(a)   National versus
international cost structures

FIG. 4.7(b)   National versus
multinational cost structures

relative to a national company with an MDC location on LAC^1.

High Tech Plus Low Wages

Such an advantage does not depend exclusively on wage costs. Low wages in less developed countries such as those just cited partly reflect the relative labour abundance (i.e. the depressing influence on wage levels in the active labour force of what in Marxist terms was called the 'reserve army of labour'). But they have also been combined with high rates of capital accumulation and advanced technology, made available either by multi-national capital or state intervention.

The role of the state in promoting such capital accumulation in the South East Asian quartet of Hong Kong, Singapore, South Korea and Taiwan has been documented by White and others (1984). Such countries have not simply relied on low labour costs, but have promoted state intervention to discourage imports (in South Korea and, in key areas, Taiwan) or to promote financial and other services (in Hong Kong and Singapore). But in such countries (partially excepting Hong Kong) welcoming high-technology investment by foreign multinational companies has been combined with a policy of deterring or repressing the organisation of local labour.

Thus in many countries in South East Asia and Latin America trades-union activities which would be considered normal in Western Europe or the United States are banned. Either unions do not exist at all, or they exist in a state-controlled framework where their demands are rigorously limited and controlled. Direct action on the factory or shop floor by workers' representatives to improve conditions can involve the summary arrest and disappearance of trades-union activists. Enquiries into their disappearance, in a number of countries in Latin America and South East Asia, are either not pursued or are disavowed by governments – even when independent observers such as Amnesty International find against the state and police. The lack of a 'free press', or significant limitations on the freedom of the press, inhibit adequate reporting of either working conditions or the repression of trades-union activities. The courts and judiciary in many of these countries are a direct arm of the state apparatus rather than bodies with even relative autonomy. Parliaments or legislative bodies in many cases are either inactive or suspended, or have very limited real powers.

Beyond the Sweatshop Syndrome

Such repression in the labour market clearly does not meet with unanimous approval from all managers of multinational companies. Some lament and regret them. Many have promoted working conditions within their factories abroad which are clearly superior to those prevailing for national capital in the microeconomic sector, i.e. the 'sweatshop syndrome' for which some of these countries are notorious. Nonetheless, whatever occurs in terms of labour relations within the plant of multinational companies in such countries, the prevailing level of wages is determined by the combination of major reserves of labour and relative degrees of repression by the state.

This argument, though it may imply value judgements concerning personal or institutional freedom, is not simply subjective. One of the problems for those aiming to assist high rates of accumulation of social and economic capital in developing countries is precisely the extent to which outstanding economic success in a number of countries has so far been gained at the cost of significant political freedoms. Ricardo's 'harmony of interests' through mutual comparative advantage is peripheral to such realities. Further, to the extent that such exploitation of labour in the newly industrialised countries has been overcome in recent years, this has been through a combination of increased wage costs with the substitution of capital for labour in the global operations of multinational companies, several of which have relocated production in the developed countries.

Hence an irony for the newly industrialised economies of the Asian Quartet, or at least those of the island city state model such as Singapore and Hong Kong. The more that wages and welfare have in fact increased, the less attractive the city states have proved to multinational capital as 'labour havens', and the lower the rate of investment – or the higher the disinvestment – by multinational companies. Hong Kong's situation in the mid 1980s was qualified by the Agreement between the British and Chinese governments on the ceding of sovereignty to China. But the disadvantage for the city state NICs was not merely political. Singapore, with its independence beyond question, experienced a slowing growth rate in the early 1980s, and then a negative rate of growth. Despite the anti-Marxist politics of several South East Asian governments, the Marxist logic of a rising technical composition of capital was returning less labour-intensive investment to the developed countries.

High Tech – High Wages – High Skills

While many multinational companies, including the Japanese, can and do combine high tech with low wages, it is increasingly evident that the core strength of Japanese big business in its home economy lies less in confront-ation with labour to gain low wages than co-operation or co-option of the labour force at high wage and training levels as a key means of achieving greater efficiency in production. Reference has already been made to the massive reduction in the labour content in production made possible in Japanese companies in a range of sectors through technical progress (and not least robotics). But to match such technical progress embodied within increased capital investment (a process consistent with Marx's concept of the rising organic and technical composition of capital), Japanese companies commit dramatically higher resources than multinationals in some other countries to the ongoing training and education of the workforce.

TABLE 4.9 Contrasts in Education and Training

	Toyota			Ford of Britain		
	Basic (years)	Prof (years)	Total (years)	Basic (years)	Prof (years)	Total (years)
Hourly employees						
General assembly worker	4	3	7	2	0	2
Skilled M/C operator	4	5	9	2	3	5
Average Hourly Type	4	4	8	2	1	2.5
Salaried Type Employees						
Production Supervision	4	6	10	2	0	2
Manufa. & Plant Eng.	4	6	10	3	4	7
Other Staff Functions	4	7	11	3	4	7
Average Salary Type	4	6	10	2.5	2	4.5
Average All Employees	4	5	9	2	1	3

Source: GLC (1986).

As shown in Table 4.9, Toyota believes that it needs less management to co-ordinate workers than Ford because their workers are three times more educated. The Japanese worker in general is educated up to the age of 18, and then receives three to five years' vocational training, either in sandwich or part-time courses. As the GLC (1986) report on Ford puts it: 'while Ford neglects training, the Japanese prioritise it'. As a result, Japanese companies, unlike US multinationals such as Ford, can draw on educated workers for problem solving or improving job design, and successfully exploit the growing number of workplace computers. The contrast for salaried employees between Toyota and Ford of Britain is dramatic, with production supervisors receiving the equivalent of ten years' training in Toyota versus two years in Ford.

Clearly such training and retraining of the labour and management force in Japanese companies does not occur within a social vacuum. In practice, key Japanese companies typical of the *keiretsu* or mesoeconomic sector guarantee lifetime employment rather than using the intermittent threat of the dole as a sanction against organised labour. On the other hand, this lifetime-employment guarantee does not extend to suppliers or contractors for Japanese companies which (as already seen in the Toyota case) supply some 40 per cent of Toyota's input. Nor does such a lifetime-job guarantee apply in the foreign operations of Japanese companies in either other developed or developing countries. In this sense leading Japanese companies can combine the best of both worlds in the global labour market: highly skilled and secure labour in core production at home, with less secure and less skilled labour in peripheral production abroad.

4.4 Investment and Tariffs

In the neoclassical paradigm, free trade is a totem and tariffs are taboo. But such reasoning is ahistorical. It denies the major role played by tariffs in promoting the initial industrial growth of the most successful of the market economies, neglects the fact that such economies are now pursuing liberalisation from positions of dominance in the global economy, and discounts the need for weaker less developed countries to employ tariffs to protect infant and adolescent industries. Conventional tariff theory is also stuck in the paradigm of international trade between different companies in different countries, when global trade is today dominated by multinational companies investing and producing worldwide.

Paradox and Protection

An example of the puzzle or paradox posed by multinational trade for conventional tariff policy is given by Jane Sneddon Little (1986) in relation to US congressional demands for protection against import penetration of the US economy. Little claims that at least 35 to 40 per cent of US imports and exports move between members of the same firm (i.e. inter-subsidiary trade by multinationals, complementing the higher figures on the share of total trade by multinationals in Table 4.4).

As evidence of the trend to such imports to the United States from their foreign subsidiaries by US multinationals, Little cites (i) the in-bond *Maquiladora* programme by which US firms have located more than 700 plant employing more than 200,000 workers in specific development areas in northern Mexico, thereby gaining labour at one seventh to one eighth of US labour costs, and exporting the bulk of the output to the United States; (ii) the fact that US firms employ more than half of the 73,000 people working for electronics firms in Malaysia, which has helped make that country the leading exporter of integrated circuits to the US; (iii) the joint-venture arrangements for foreign production by leading US car companies, including a joint venture between General Motors and the Daewoo Group to produce 167,000 cars in South Korea by 1987; as well as (iv) the advantage taken by many US firms of a provision in the US tariff schedule which allows companies to cut fabric in the United States, assemble the goods in the Caribbean countries, and reimport the final product to the US while paying duty only on the labour and not on the domestic materials (Little, 1986, pp. 43–4).

Citing the fact that the US trade deficit in the mid 1980s was approaching $150 billion a year, and that within one year members of Congress introduced over 300 items of protectionist legislation, Little allows that intra-firm trade by multinationals 'is indeed significant for many industries where import competition is causing concern', but observes that: 'It is unlikely that the US public will or should react to requests for import relief with equal urgency when a significant part of the "injurious" imports are known to represent the output of US firms abroad' (ibid., pp. 43 and 48).

Tariffs and Industrialisation

If the US public were this rational, either they – or their leaders and opinion formers – might also take account of the fact that none of the developed countries in the twentieth-century economy – other than the UK – industrialised in the first place through *laissez faire* or a free-for-all liberalisation of trade and payments.

The United Kingdom industrialised at a time when the rest of the world had not achieved an industrial revolution, and therefore for a period of time had in effect no competitors in world trade. Otherwise the leading developed capitalist economies in the world today achieved their own strength in international trade and payments behind tariffs which in most cases were, and were designed to be, prohibitive of imports from other countries.

The United States developed behind such tariffs in the late eighteenth and early nineteenth centuries – as is admitted fully by Samuelson (1976), who illustrates (Figure 35–1, p. 702) the fact that US tariff rates averaged between 40 and 50 per cent of dutiable imports between 1820 and 1833, 1861 and 1909, and 1930–34. The most extensive period of high protection, from 1861 to 1909, was precisely the 'breakthrough' period for American industry. The same was the case for Germany and Japan in the later nineteenth century. In the Japanese case, the Meiji dynasty achieved the basic modernisation of Japan through tariffs which were designed to prevent the penetration of the domestic Japanese market by US or British goods. The fundamental impact on the psychology of Japanese policy-makers and leading entrepreneurs of this 'Meiji revolution' continues today.

Germany, in the early nineteenth century a country of peasants, artisans and clock-makers similar to the popular (and false) image of Switzerland today, was transformed into one of the major industrial powers in the world through the introduction of prohibitive external tariffs in 1878/9 by Chancellor Bismarck. Bismarck's introduction of this tariff was dictated by internal political reasons, including his desire to 'dish the liberals' by changing an alliance between them and the Junker landed aristocracy to an alliance between the Junkers and the nascent industrial middle class. But the effect was to exclude British and American industrial goods from the German market, and thereby to create the conditions for the accumulation of German capital, laying the basis of not only the second but also the third Reich.

France also achieved her industrialisation behind tariffs designed to exclude British goods. In France, as with the Meiji dynasty in Japan, the prevailing ideology and rationale for such protection dates deep into the country's psychological past – in fact it predated the Meiji dynasty by two or three centuries. The tradition of Colbertism in France, which has resulted in the widespread synonym of that word for intervention, dates from the time of Louis XIV and the golden age of French state intervention in public works. Today, despite nominally liberal trading institutions, the EEC pursues a protectionism virtually unparalleled for agricultural products. Its industrial protection, as with Japan, although to a lesser degree, operates mainly through informal non-tariff barriers to trade which are exerted by public purchasing and planning, or a refusal to allow in the imported goods on the grounds of their failure to conform to domestic safety and other criteria.

National Infants and Adults

Such evidence can be generalised in economic terms by identifying successive stages of protection and liberalisation. In Figure 4.8(a) three main stages are assumed, represented overall by the S-shaped curve *AB*. The higher the curve (towards *A*), the greater the degree of protection and the lower (towards *B*) vice versa. In stage I, 'infant' industries are protected on what amounts to a prohibitive basis. In other words, to enable national infants to survive, a domestic market environment is guaranteed for them by tariffs designed to prohibit imports from more developed countries. This was the case with the early industrialisation of the United States, Germany, France, Italy and Japan.

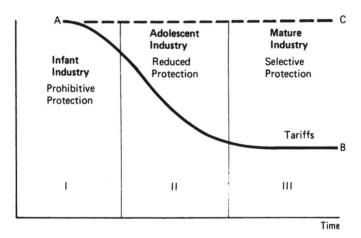

FIG. 4.8(a)   From infant to mature protection

In stage II, with what we have described as 'adolescent' industry, governments have been more prepared to reduce the level of nominal and effective protection. This is not necessarily due to conversion to a neoclassical model of international trade. It may reflect an awareness of the advantages of gaining lower-cost imports as inputs for intermediate production, as the country progresses to more sophisticated forms of capital accumulation.

In stage III, of 'mature industry', the country may employ more selective forms of protection, either by sector or by individual firm, rather than the reduced overall macro or sectoral levels of protection in stage II. This is very much the contemporary situation of protection in countries such as France and the United States, and can be expressed in meso and microeconomic terms.

In other words, by stage III of Figure 4.8(a) the governments of capitalist economies with mature industries are less concerned to protect already well-established companies in the large-scale mesoeconomic sector. These meso-economic firms may well have sought and gained markets abroad which could be put at risk by continued high protection in the 'home' country. Nonetheless, the government may be very much concerned to protect more weakly based microeconomic enterprise in general. They also seek to ensure the protection of individual sectors, typically structured on a microeconomic basis with a large number of small firms, such as textiles, furniture, footwear or agriculture.

Undoubtedly Figure 4.8(a) oversimplifies reality. In practice a country such as Japan has retained a level of protection more similar to the broken line AC in Figure 4.8(a) rather than the reduced protection, by tariffs or non-tariff barriers, represented by the line AB. Nonetheless, it has considerable parallels in the real world economy. It is also striking that much of the pressure in favour of free trade has been undertaken by business in countries which have successfully undertaken the transition from stage I to stage III. Such countries have liberalised as adults rather than infants or adolescents, from strength rather than weakness, and after establishing a powerful mesoeconomy capable of sustaining global competition.

The Mature and Multinational Economy

An irony – if not double standard – of free-trade advocacy by governments such as those of the United States and West Germany is the extent to which, having achieved the mature industry of stage III in Figure 4.8(a) by the turn of the century behind prohibitive tariff barriers, they now seek to impose the reduction of tariffs by less developed countries as a means of expanding their own export trade, or of facilitating their own direct foreign investment.

In reality, the phase of the mature national economy represented by stage III of Figure 4.8(a) is supplemented by the rise of the multinational economy. Translating this situation through to Figure 4.8(b), the mature national economy in stage IV gives way to the nascent multinational economy of stage V, as the now dominant companies within the national economy seek to maintain their rate of growth of profit by direct investment abroad. This is succeeded by what we have described as the mature multinational economy in stage VI of Figure 4.8(b), typical of the United States and the United Kingdom today, in which multinational enterprise is already dominant within the domestic system, visible export trade and foreign operations.

Thus the fall in national protection with the transition from infant to mature industry complements the transition from national to multinational production. Such a perception qualifies the textbook presumption of liberalisation as a process which should be taken by all countries irrespective of the structure and stage of development of their economies.

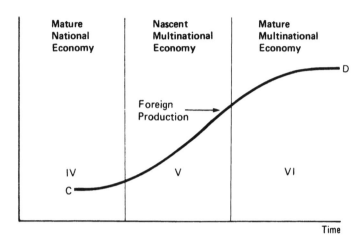

FIG. 4.8(b)   From national to multinational production

List: National Economy and *Zollverein*

In the first half of the nineteenth century, in a German economy completely divided by restrictive tariffs imposed in order to raise revenue by local aristocrats, landlords and magnates, Friedrich List developed a coherent case for the protection of what would now be called 'infant industries'. He did so on the grounds that unless the government of a given economy is able to assure a domestic market for the production of goods, the incentive for domestic entrepreneurs to invest and produce will be lacking. List developed his arguments for national political economy in reaction to the arguments against tariffs of Adam Smith.

Smith in turn was himself reacting to the same phenomenon of taxes and other charges imposed by feudal or neofeudal aristocrats on nascent entrepreneurs and capitalist trade. Certainly, in the transition from feudalism to capitalism, tariffs were in general an obstacle to trade, specialisation in production, economies of scale, and – in a more microeconomic and price-competitive framework – consumer welfare through the alignment of cost, normal profits, earned incomes and prices.

When Adam Smith was arguing the case for free trade in the eighteenth century, and List was putting the case for a *Zollverein* or free trade area within Germany, feudal aristocrats literally constructed chains across the river Rhine in order to restrict the flow of vessels and trade, unless a 'tariff', in practice a toll or tax, was paid to them. Clearly such tariffs represented an imposition on both traders and consumers, amounting to a transfer of surplus in revenue from both the bourgeoisie and working class to the feudal aristocracy.

Unfortunately, as happens only too often not only in the realm of economics but also of other social sciences, a justified criticism and reaction to imposition by a dominant class has been elevated to a metaphysical or 'metaeconomic' principle by those born, studying and teaching in later epochs.

Tariffs, Welfare and Interests

However, with the rise of the modern capitalist state the role of tariffs has been transformed. From the basic principle of revenue raising, governments have increasingly used tariffs to prohibit or restrict imports as a mechanism for economic development. Such tariffs have been imposed by many less developed countries. They have been designed to prevent import dependence and make possible the growth of a domestic economy on lines paralleling those developed countries which have managed the transition from infant to mature industry on the lines of Figure 4.8(a).

The governments of such developing countries are not in themselves retrograde in the manner of the eighteenth-century German aristocrats who put chains across the Rhine. They may be seeking, inter alia, (1) to avoid the undermining of their domestic industry; (2) to avoid an increase in imports and possibly a chronic balance-of-payments deficit through dependence on external supply; (3) a guaranteed market for domestic producers of a critical minimum necessary to achieve economies of scale; (4) internalisation of the indirect multiplier effects on investment, jobs and income which otherwise would leak or flow abroad.

List's theory – in contrast with that of Ricardo and later neoclassical analysis of a 'harmony of interest' through international trade – was based on a powerful intuition that free trade between the American colonies and England in the mid eighteenth century, or between the German states and England in the early nineteenth century, reflected a process of unequal competition between smaller and weaker industry which had 'started late' in relation to the English industrial revolution, and English or British based enterprise which had in fact already achieved a dominance of US and German markets for industrial products.

Educative or Prohibitive?

In this respect, List's theory pioneered the case for economic integration through a customs union or common market as the precondition for a more optimal distribution of resources through free trade.

List stressed the difference between what he called 'educational' tariffs and permanently 'prohibitive' tariffs. In later terminology, and especially that of the theory of development economics, his arguments were expressed in terms of tariffs for 'infant industries', with the implication that as enterprise in the protected area was assured sufficient markets to enable it to grow through protection, it would be able to achieve the transition from infancy to adulthood, at which stage tariffs should be lowered to avoid negative effects arising from tariff-induced monopoly advantages.

However, monopoly problems are not due to tariff protection alone. The dynamics of unequal competition between early and late starters, large and small firms, hold over buyers and sellers, and preferential access to bank and other finance tend to give increased gains from size to early established firms. These in turn come to constitute a dominant mesoeconomic sector, to the disadvantage of smaller enterprises conforming more closely with the microeconomic neoclassical model of competition.

Hilferding on List

Hilferding (1910, p. 304) has stressed that: 'List's system is not a refutation of the theory of free trade as it was formulated, for instance, by Ricardo. It propounds an economic policy which would really make the free trade system feasible, by facilitating the development of a national industry for which that system would be appropriate.'

Similarly, the role of the tariff itself changes with the emergence of dominant big business within an individual economy. Hilferding appreciated this very clearly, contrasting the 'educational' protective tariff of List's analysis with a different structure of capitalist enterprise in the early twentieth century. As he put it, whereas List's protective tariff 'was intended to be both moderate and temporary, simply to help an infant industry overcome its initial difficulties, matters are different in the age of capitalist monopolies. Today it is the most powerful industries, with a high export potential, whose competitiveness on the world market is beyond doubt and which, according to the old theory, should have no further interest in protective tariffs, which support high tariffs.'

Presciently anticipating the way in which the US, and Europe through the EEC, would seek to protect their economic strength against Third World imports, Hilferding (ibid., pp. 307–8) also observed that:

> The protective tariff for industry was one of the most effective means of promoting cartels, first by making foreign competition more difficult, and second, because cartels provide an opportunity to take advantage of the tariff margin even when industry had become capable of exporting. Cartelised industry has therefore a direct and supreme interest in the level of the protective tariff. The higher the tariff,

the more the domestic price can be raised above the price on the world market, and so the 'educational' tariff has evolved into a high protective tariff.

4.5 Meso and Macro Dimensions

The conventional theory of trade and tariffs has been well exposed by Kindleberger. As he puts it in terms of Figure 4.9 (Kindleberger, 1963, Figure 12.1, p. 218), $Q_3 - Q$ represents imports at the price p before the imposition of a tariff. The tariff $p^1 - p$ is assumed to have no effect on the sale or offer price of the exporting country. The protective effect is shown by the increase in domestic production from Q to Q_1. The consumption effect results in a reduction of total consumption from Q_3 to Q_2. The minimum tariff which will keep out all imports is p^2.

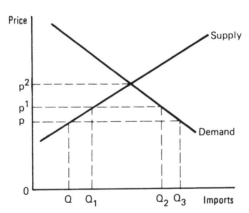

FIG. 4.9   The conventional tariff model.

Kindleberger is among the most creative and realistic of the theorists of modern international trade. Nonetheless, his model of the effect of tariffs assumes (1) micro rather than mesoeconomic enterprise and, with this, (2) national rather than multinational companies. In addition, following the implications of microeconomic theory, it is also assumed (3) that firms are 'price-takers' rather than 'price-makers' and (4) that there is price elasticity of demand at the level of final consumption. Also (5) conventional tariff theory does not normally analyse implications from increased economies of scale in production over the long term, not least since (6) its analysis tends to be static rather than dynamic.

Price-Making Power

The price-making power of mesoeconomic companies and the multinational integration of their global operations profoundly qualify the conventional analysis of tariff changes and their effect. Figure 4.10 represents price schedules in two countries A and B. The prevailing price level p^1 is represented by the broken horizontal line. For balance-of-payments reasons or on account of related problems in industrial structure, the authorities in country B may decide to impose a tariff from a to b.

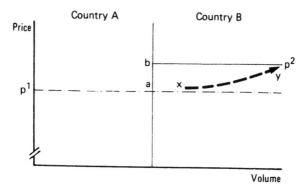

FIG. 4.10   Tariff offset by multinational company

It is stressed in conventional tariff theory that this could enable domestic producers in country B to raise price from p^1 to p^2 on the lines of the arrow xy. Certainly the imposition of a tariff on the lines of ab in Figure 4.10 is likely to allow enterprises in country B to charge higher prices, whether they are competitive firms or monopolistic companies. The conventional argument assumes that enterprise in country B would not have been sufficiently large or dominant in the first instance to have raised prices in such a way without the tariff. But mesoeconomic big business within a national market may well increase price from p^1 to p^2 for a variety of reasons, ranging from simple abuse of a dominant position, or 'profit creaming' early in a new product cycle, through to raising price to compensate for falling rates of growth of sales, thereby offsetting a tariff increase with its price-making power.

Moreover, unlike the conventional model, with mesoeconomic and multinational structures of investment, production and trade it cannot any longer be assumed that a tariff increase will automatically deter imports from other countries. By virtue both of its dominant position within country B and its range of foreign production in other countries, mesoeconomic enterprise may well be able to import a final good from another country which is the focal assembly point abroad for components produced in a range of other countries. This 'transfer pricing' technique will be analysed in some detail in Chapter 6.

Multinational Implications

For such reasons the multinational enterprise may well be able to 'follow the lead' of other firms in country B in Figure 4.10 which have raised price on the line *xy* following the tariff increase from *a* to *b*. The extent to which this will occur depends on a variety of other factors neglected in the conventional model of tariffs. They include (1) the changing comparative cost structures of enterprise under dynamic conditions, and (2) the extent to which dominance of the domestic market is shared by a narrow or wide range of multinational companies in different countries. In Japan big business has gained both major protection of their domestic market from foreign imports and the crucial further condition of government intervention through non-tariff barriers to prevent the location of foreign multinational direct investment in their country. In these respects the prewar Japanese *zaibatsu* and postwar *keiretsu* have mainly acted as national firms.

However, such conditions are exceptional among developed capitalist countries. They are not typical of the United States and the United Kingdom, nor of the continental European countries. We can illustrate this another way in Figure 4.11. On the assumption that the imposition of a tariff in country B enables its enterprise to raise price to p^2 against an external price in country A (or a prevailing world price) of p^1, conventional theory on tariffs might lead one to assume that enterprise in country B would be able to gain the additional revenue and sales/consumption represented by the area *abcd*.

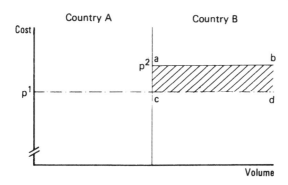

FIG. 4.11 Revenue-substitution effect of tariffs

But under conditions of multinational production and sales in different countries, country B's increase in price level to p^2 would not necessarily mean a prohibitive barrier to imports. It may well mean a sharing of the increased revenue and sales represented by *abcd* between national firms and multinational firms with price-making power, whether these are producing in the domestic market or importing final goods or components from lower-cost sources abroad which can compensate for the tariff increase.

Import Substitution and Effective Demand

This qualifies one of the basic rationales for the imposition of tariffs by any country: to protect the domestic market rather than to raise domestic price levels. On the other hand, depending on the degree of multinationalisation of the import trade of the country concerned, which may well be less than that of export trade, this does not necessarily mean an undermining of the objective of increasing domestic demand. Governments may introduce protection combined with a range of policies including price controls which are designed to prohibit or reduce imports, whilst also prohibiting or at least restraining domestic price increases. As indicated earlier, such policies have been pursued with considerable success by some of the South East Asian NICs, notably South Korea (Luedde Neurath, 1984).

Keynes argued this case on a short-run basis at various times, with the aim of countering the 'vicious circle' effects of deflation and depression in Britain between the wars. He stressed the creation of effective demand made possible in the country adopting protection, and with it the series of employment and income multiplier effects which would ensue as protected firms supplied a greater share of sales in the domestic market.

Over the longer term, following the basic principles of Keynesian theory of economic growth, it could be assumed that a combination of accelerator and capital stock adjustment mechanisms would sufficiently raise profit expectations, or the marginal efficiency of capital, to promote what Harrod has called an increase in Gw, i.e. an increase in the rate of growth of investment which entrepreneurs consider to be warranted.

Potential Dynamic Effects

Figure 4.12 applies such Keynesian effects and their potential impact on industry and enterprise costs within a Ricardian framework, i.e. assuming international trade between different firms in different countries. In country A long-run average costs at LAC^1 are lower than the initial cost level LAC^2 in country B. To offset imports, country B establishes a tariff equivalent to the price level p^2. But the higher domestic sales made possible by protection in country B also make possible a lower industry long-run average cost curve on the lines of LAC^3 from a new round of innovating and productivity-raising investment.

The dynamic implications of tariffs become clear in the following context. It is assumed in Figure 4.12 that long-run average costs in country B are initially higher than in country A. Thus in country A (which might be either intermediate or more developed) the long-run average cost schedule LAC^1 is lower than the schedule LAC^2 in country B. Assuming the embodiment of technical progress and/or more capital per worker with an additional round of investment in new plant and equipment in country B, it is feasible in principle for the firm or firms in that country by such investment to lower their long-run average cost schedule to the level of LAC^3.

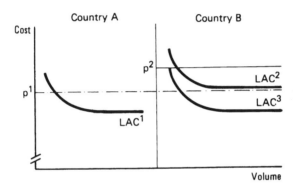

FIG. 4.12   Dynamic cost implications of tariffs

Moreover, in Figure 4.12, whereas the initial price level p^2 in country B would have been necessary to enable firms on LAC^2 to achieve normal profit rates, conventional micro theory would assume that under competitive conditions on the domestic market in country B firms over time would compete for a larger share of the market and a higher utilisation of their capacity, thereby possibly reducing prices. Alternatively, if the initial protection making possible a rise in the domestic price in country B from p^1 to p^2 were successful in promoting a round of efficiency-raising and cost-reducing investment equivalent to an average LAC^3, then the government could well reduce or abolish the tariff in such a way as to ensure a reduction of the domestic price level from p^2 to p^1.

Potentially, this remains one of the key dynamic gains from the application of protection and the creation of effective demand for enterprises in a country whose domestic cost levels have risen out of line with those of foreign competitors and which as a result have been subject to import penetration, with a fall in employment and revenue caused directly by the loss of domestic markets and indirectly by the employment and income multiplier on supplying firms.

Multinationals and Protection

But such reasoning also needs to be modified by the behaviour of multinational companies. The weaknesses of such a Keynesian case for the beneficial dynamic effects of protection lie in (1) the assumptions of national rather than multinational capital and (2) what Harrod has assumed to be 'representative firms' in his later reasoning on Keynesian macroeconomic growth theory (Harrod, 1964).

In reality – especially where they can gain from protection – firms in the mesoeconomic sector tend to be price-makers rather than price-takers. As a result, as represented in Figure 4.13, a firm which is dominant on the domestic market of country B, or which is in a situation of joint dominance with other firms, may simply raise price from p^1 to p^2 following the imposition of a tariff. Thus it may undertake no further investment in country B of the efficiency-raising or cost-lowering kind which could have permitted a reduction of its long-run average costs from LAC^2 to the hypothetical LAC^3. This classic effect of price increase following protection is more rather than less likely because of the multinational trend in the global economy. Indeed, again in terms of Figure 4.13, a multinational company with price-making power in country B may well use the excuse of an imposed tariff to increase price way beyond normal profits, from level p^2 to p^3.

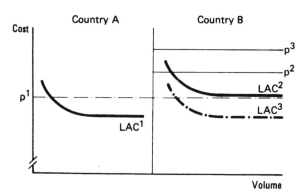

FIG. 4.13 Meso/multinational price increase versus increased production and employment

There are various reasons. One is the opaque nature of transfer pricing and the difficulties for either consumers or government of gaining sufficient 'transparency' on the operations of multinational companies to determine what is a 'true cost' or a 'fair price'. This process is analysed in some detail in Chapter 6. Another is the underestimated 'capacity effect' for multinational companies producing the same product in various different countries. In other words, one of the main priorities for multinational companies in their global investment planning is the fullest possible use of capacity in different countries. New technology tends to imply larger-scale production for minimally efficient plant size. Therefore an increase in investment, reducing costs in country B to LAC^3, could conflict with full utilisation by the multinational company of existing capacity in subsidiaries in other countries.

This is apart from the question whether the net investment hypothesised in country B – even with productivity increases from innovation – would offset the wage advantage open to a multinational company from locating investment in a less developed or newly industrialised country. As illustrated in Figure 4.14, it is perfectly feasible, due to the advantage of lower costs in an LDC or NIC country A, for a multinational company to produce there on a long-run average cost schedule equivalent to LAC^4. In such circumstances, neither the investment, employment nor income multiplier effects in country B assumed in the Keynesian case for tariff protection could be guaranteed to occur.

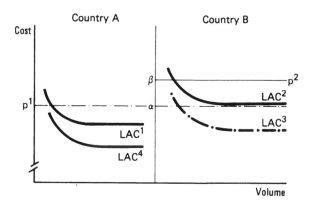

FIG. 4.14   Multinational cost advantages versus protection

Alternatively, it could well be that any investment considered 'warranted' in Harrod's terms by the management of a multinational company operating in a developed country would involve capital/labour ratios and innovation which displace rather than create employment. This has been the case with the recent introduction of robotics in a wide range of manufacturing industry.

As already evidenced by the direct foreign investment of Japanese multinational companies in the United States and UK, the technical progress and innovation made possible for them by major investment programmes in their country of origin (backed by national governments and a range of paragovernmental institutions) may mean that their comparative cost advantage within the multinational circuits of their own subsidiaries enables them to penetrate a tariff-protected country. They can do this simply because their lower cost schedules through successive rounds of innovating investment – when other countries start late or lag behind – are sufficient to offset even very sizeable external tariffs or non-tariff barriers.

Offensive versus Defensive Trade

Such a mechanism can be illustrated by transferring the left-hand side of Figure 4.14 from the previous context of developing countries to the international cost competitiveness of leading Japanese companies, with the right-hand side representing the cost schedules of companies in the country imposing protection. If country B were to impose a tariff equivalent to the difference between alpha and beta and if the long-run average cost curve for the Japanese company were LAC^1, the tariff costs of exporting to country B would be equivalent to the profit represented by the difference between LAC^2 and the previous price level p^1.

However, the Japanese mesoeconomic company may be able to reduce its compound long-run average cost curve on its operations to the equivalent of LAC^4. It may do so either through productivity-raising 'innovation investment' in Japan, or through a combination of such investment plus low-cost labour in subsidiary operations in South East Asia or elsewhere. In terms of the previously cited evidence on Toyota, Nissan, Matsushita or other Japanese companies, it could do so by a greater margin than that of Figure 4.14. Its cost advantage would then offset – or more than offset – the alpha to beta increase in the tariff in country B. Matsushita was able to reduce its labour costs in an air-conditioner plant in Malaysia to one tenth of its equivalent level in Japan (Ohmae, 1985), confirming the previously cited evidence from leading UK firms to the House of Commons Expenditure Committee (Ohmae, 1985, p. 154, and House of Commons, 1972).

The Japanese Challenge

Such go-getting foreign investment and trade policies pursued by the Japanese companies are not an accident of nature. Nor are they simply a reflection of higher 'animal spirits' or psychology of entrepreneurship in Japan rather than elsewhere. They reflect specific characteristics of the structure of Japanese big business and the very close relationship between it and the Japanese government and state. In striking contrast with the claims made by Milton Friedman that Japan is a 'free market' economy, the Japanese in the nineteenth century at the time of the Meiji Dynasty made a conscious decision to protect their domestic markets as the precondition for industrial-isation, modernisation and what Ray Vernon (1974, chapter 1) has appropriately called 'national champions'. To a major degree, in contrast with the highly liberal governments of the US and the UK, foreign operations by Japanese companies have only been endorsed by senior management (and backed by the Ministry of International Trade and Industry MITI) when it is evident that they support the home base of the parent company, or provide direct access to foreign markets behind protective import barriers.

The original phase of Japanese industrialisation benefited, as in other developed capitalist countries over a longer period of time, from relatively low wage costs in the domestic market, where wages were restrained by labour reserves (or in Marxist terms by a reserve army of labour) in a then predominantly agricultural economy with Asian cost and wage levels. Policy-makers and ruling elites in Japan were not handicapped by a devotion to market forces. Judging by results, List rather than Adam Smith was their handbook.

Identifying new sectors of activity which would be essential for Japan's effective modernisation, the Japanese consciously went for the reinforcement and promotion of large economic units from the start. The resulting *zaibatsu*, not unlike the German cartels in the first half of the twentieth century, gained a massive impetus from their role as suppliers to the armaments industry. In other words, from the end of the nineteenth century, Japan developed large-scale vertically integrated and by the standards of the time highly efficient industries in steel, engineering, electrical engineering, chemicals and related products through its own version of what has been called elsewhere the 'military-industrial complex'. Indeed, the Japanese Ministry of International Trade and Industry which has shown such formidable powers of promoting the postwar Japanese export offensive, was formerly the Japanese Ministry of Munitions.

From the end of the Second World War, however, with the loss of political independence and for a time an almost complete restriction on foreign economic operations, Japanese big business reconstructed at home with an active integration of investment and foreign trade operations by MITI, which combined the functions of finance and credit, investment co-ordination, technology promotion and support for a large-scale foreign export trade. Such functions were also partly integrated in other postwar economies such as France and Germany.

France and Germany

For instance, in France the so-called Ministry of Finance is in fact the Ministry of Finance *and Economy*, thereby combining functions which in a country such as Britain in the mid-1960s were divided between the Treasury, responsible for finance, and the Department of Economic Affairs, responsible for economic planning. The French Finance and Economy Ministry was serviced by the Planning Commission (Commissariat du Plan) while also closely integrated with the main state credit institution, the Caisse des Dépôts et Consignations – the equivalent of the British National Savings/Post Office accounts – while the French government also owned and controlled three of the main deposit banks even before the nationalisation programme of the incoming Socialist government in 1981. In Germany, a whole series of credit institutions, enabling the banks to channel savings into investment for both the domestic market and foreign trade expansion, were initially promoted by the Reconstruction Loans Corporation (Kreditanstalt für Wiederaufbau), whose operations were closely integrated with the mainstream bank credit mechanisms under the overall supervision of the Deutsche Bank, with the specific allocation of funds working through the Supervisory Boards (Aufsichtsräte) of companies on which the banks as both lenders and shareholders were represented.

These mechanisms resulted in a close relationship between the state, finance capital and industrial capital in countries such as Germany, France and Japan. Such state macro-meso liaison played an important role in the adoption of 'offensive' go-getting investment and foreign trade policies – in contrast with the more 'defensive' policies pursued with such little success by the United Kingdom and the United States. From the later 1960s, the reconstruction of big business in mesoeconomic combines in Germany, France and Japan was achieving an export penetration of other developed capitalist countries which was seriously undermining domestic industrial production in key sectors in the US and the UK.

Spread and Backwash Effects

Such a state capitalist evolution in such countries as Germany, France and Japan has not been static or final. Figures 4.8(a) and (b) have stressed the extent to which such economies were passing by the later 1960s from the stage of mature national economies to nascent multinational economies. By the late 1970s and early 1980s, foreign investment – especially by German and Japanese firms – was beginning to substitute for exports to the US and the UK on a major scale.

Nonetheless, the conscious promotion of large-scale economic units in countries such as Japan and France and the reinforcement of the foreign trade expansion of big business in Germany registered a series of beneficial 'virtuous circle' effects in their respective economies via the export-sector multiplier on investment, jobs and incomes in their home economies. The 'backwash effects' of their successful expansion were registered in the undermining of domestic industrial production in other countries such as the United Kingdom and the United States, where a wide range of sectors including the automobile and motorcycle industries, electrical and electronic goods, including taperecorders, radio, television and videos, were increasingly dominated by Japanese mesoeconomic companies.

Qualified Accelerator Theory

The difference between 'offensive' and 'defensive' investment and trade has major implications in qualifying standard macroeconomic concepts such as the accelerator or capital stock adjustment principle, the marginal efficiency of capital and 'warranted' growth.

The state capitalist interrelation between large-scale industrial and finance capital, the government and its agencies – in both continental Europe and Japan – bears little relation to the accelerator or capital stock adjustment principles still taught as orthodoxy in much Anglo-American economic theory. Adjustment of the stock of capital, and decisions on changes in the rate of growth, are widely taken on a global project and company basis, at the mesoeconomic level, with active evaluation and assistance by government agencies.

Sales and demand strategies were also extended beyond national frontiers to potential sales on a global scale, in particular but not exclusively in the developed capitalist countries. The marginal efficiency of capital has been qualified as both the government and senior managment in mesoeconomic companies act together in such a way as to sustain either low rates of profit or losses in the early phases of 'offensive' investment and trade expansion – in order to be able to profit at a later date from the fuller utilisation of capacity when the rate of growth of sales and demand had increased. In other words, in contrast with the conventional usage of the accelerator concept, government and mesoeconomic companies together were reacting to anticipated future changes in demand and sales, rather than to current or past sales levels.

Research and innovation is assisted by state-aided contracts, or is helped indirectly through the public contract side of the state's military expenditure. In some countries, notably Italy, the state as entrepreneur was obliged to undertake long-term 'offensive' investment which the private sector was not willing to risk. In the petroleum field, through the state hydrocarbons holding company ENI, plus the industrial state holding company IRI, this yielded a range of public-enterprise joint venture deals, especially in developing countries.

Clearly not even MITI nor the giant Japanese combines were able to counter the effects of the recession in key world markets such as those for oil supertankers which followed the OPEC price increases in the early 1970s. There is nothing infallible about state capitalist forecasting. Big companies in the mesoeconomic sector were crucial to 'offensive' large-scale, technology-embodying investment, with beneficial effects on cost and competitiveness through large volume in international sales. But such companies, whether based exclusively in one country or already in the phase of 'nascent' multinationalisation, were not big enough to determine the macroeconomic growth of sales and demand in their final markets. Put differently, in Galbraith's terminology (Galbraith, 1974, part 3), while such companies within a 'Planning System' not only could plan but indeed were planned with effect in countries such as France and Japan, they were not big enough nor assumed that they were able to plan the overall rate of growth of macroeconomic sales and demand on a global scale.

Planning 'Warranted' Growth

However, apart from modifications of the accelerator, capital stock adjustment and marginal efficiency of capital concepts, mesoeconomic companies also qualify the Harrodian macroeconomic concept of 'warranted' growth. In other words, in contrast with the conventional use of this concept in macroeconomic models, the growth of investment and foreign trade expansion deemed to be 'warranted' is increasingly decided in a consciously 'offensive' strategy by both government and mesoeconomic enterprise rather than by individual entrepreneurs in 'representative' firms of the kind assumed by Harrod. Also, this close relationship between big business and the state in countries such as Japan enabled Japanese planners in MITI and elsewhere to react faster and more effectively to the recession and depression of key product markets in the mid 1970s than was the case in other countries such as Great Britain or the United States where the specific role of big business was understated or under-recognised because of the prevailing ideology or conventional wisdom on the macro-micro synthesis – i.e. the assumption that it was the government's job to influence the 'climate of opinion' through managing overall demand, as opposed to directly intervening in the promotion of investment and trade policies at the level of big business itself.

Following the first major OPEC oil price rises in October 1973, and during the period where governments in other OECD countries were deflating demand and decelerating investment activity in order to make room for the increased price of oil imports, the Japanese planners called together the research and development departments of key companies in the meso-economic sector, and asked them to anticipate those products and technologies which would be commanding world markets in the 1980s. One of the key products which thereby gained massive government and bank finance injection for large-scale 'offensive' investment was the area of micro-computers based on the silicone chip. The decision on whether to produce the silicone chip in large quantities in Japan, with an anticipated initial production cost of between one and two billion dollars, was undertaken about this time, while governments elsewhere – as in Britain – delayed the decision until the later 1970s by which time the Japanese were already in production and exporting the chips concerned on a major scale. Another area in which the close relation between big business and the state profited the *keiretsu* in the mesoeconomic sector was in the decision to go for the large-scale introduction of robotics in engineering and particularly in the motor-vehicle industry.

Thus by the later 1970s the Japanese had massively reduced the unit cost of production of a motor vehicle by employing up to seven times as much capital per worker as in car production in an indigenous British firm such as British Leyland. It was only by the early 1980s, with the Metro car, that the British were able to respond by the introduction of robotics on a major scale for an individual model. In the intervening period, Japanese car sales had increased their import penetration to countries such as the United States and the United Kingdom on a major scale. Such were the gains for an offensive entrepreneurship in which both big business and the state grasped and tackled the world economy as a global market, rather than relying on textbook mechanisms of comparative advantage for future growth.

4.6 Summary

(1) The conventional theory of international trade implied in both Keynesian and monetarist paradigms of the international economy still assumes, following Ricardo, that trade is essentially between different firms in different countries. However, contemporary trade between the developed market economies is overwhelmingly by or between the same multinational firms operating through direct investment, production and distribution in different countries.

(2) Multinational companies now represent up to 85 per cent of US and UK visible export trade, with a major share of this constituting intra-firm trade between subsidiaries of the same companies.

(3) The multinational mode of global production, distribution and exchange profoundly qualifies comparative advantage theory of the Ricardian paradigm. Comparative advantage theory depends on conditions of (i) perfect competition and (ii) immobility of factors (capital and labour) between countries. Neither of these conditions now obtains. Multinational companies producing in and exporting from different countries now dominate the global economy.

(4) The modern theory of comparative advantage has relied on the Hecksher-Ohlin theory of factor proportions, and its assumption that countries will tend to specialise in those products in which they have a relative factor abundance. But a neglected and major element in Ohlin's own theory of international trade is that direct investment in other countries will tend to substitute for trade between countries.

(5) This neglected Ohlin effect explains much of the weakness of UK visible export trade, and lies behind the paradox that while US visible manufactured exports represent less than a fifth of world exports, exports by all US firms in all countries still account for more than a quarter of world exports.

(6) There are differences in the multinational structure of production, distribution and exchange in the leading world economies. In terms of the ratio of foreign production to visible exports, the US economy has been eight times (and the UK economy four times) as multinational as leading continental European economies or Japan. However, this pattern is changing (especially for Japan), with an increasing rate of foreign investment and production.

(7) While Ricardian theory and its modern variants assumed that higher technical progress and productivity in developed countries would be offset by lower wages in other (developing) countries, multinational companies can now combine the most advanced or most appropriate global capital investment with significantly lower wages than those obtaining in developed countries. But the search for low-cost labour or the 'sweatshop' syndrome evident in the 1960s and early 1970s is now being eclipsed by the rising technical composition of capital and the lowering of labour content in production. For Japanese firms in motor vehicles, consumer durables and electronics goods as well as heavy industry, the labour content of production is already less than 10 per cent of total costs.

(8) Orthodox economics allows the case for tariffs to protect 'infant industry'. All of the world's leading economies (other than Britain, which at the time had no competitors) industrialised behind prohibitive tariffs designed to exclude imports, while several of the newly industrialised economies in South East Asia plus Japan still operate selective or comprehensive protection.

(9) Pressure to reduce tariffs (e.g. through GATT) is to the advantage of developing countries' agricultural and commodity exports. But the reverse pressure for developing countries to accept manufactured exports from developed countries frequently denies them the possibility of autonomous industrial development.

(10) Ricardian theory of comparative advantage 'legitimates' the case for global liberalisation. But in reality the reduction of tariffs with the transition from infant to mature industry has been matched by the transition from national to multinational production and exchange worldwide. In key respects, multinational companies are the main beneficiaries of global trade liberalisation.

(11) Multinational big business can offset the impact of tariffs through a combination of factors reflecting (i) its price-making power, and (ii) cost-lowering and quality-improving effects from successive rounds of innovating investment. Lowered costs and export prices reduce the relative incidence of tariffs.

(12) Big business and the state have liaised in countries such as Japan, West Germany, Italy and France to promote long-term 'offensive' investment and export programmes. Self-reinforcing export success has eased transition from older to entirely new industries in Japan. Military and other contracts have helped such transition in the United States, Italy and France.

5 Exchange and Payments

The rate at which a currency is exchanged with other currencies is one of the most important macroeconomic variables. This is because it is supposed to determine the prices at which goods and services can be traded between countries. Thus a rise in the value of a currency (revaluation or appreciation) makes it worth more in terms of foreign currencies, and therefore it is assumed that the price of exports will be higher abroad and inversely that of imports lower at home. A decline, depreciation or devaluation of a currency does the reverse. This argument is supposed to obtain whether the revaluation or devaluation is a conscious act of policy by governments seeking to promote a particular rate through intervention in the market, or whether the currency is allowed to float and appreciate or depreciate to find its own level as determined by private international markets.

The so-called 'fixed' exchange rate system was dominated until dollar devaluation in 1971 by the readiness of the US Treasury to exchange dollars for a fixed gold price. It could well be claimed that this was about the only fixed exchange rate proper during the previous quarter century, since other countries changed their exchange rates relative to the dollar (such as Britain in 1949 and 1967) and therefore also in relation to other countries. These 'relatively fixed' exchange rates reflected Keynes' concern to introduce greater stability into exchange rates than had obtained between the wars, when some currencies had fluctuated dramatically, with the result that exporters and importers could not be sure whether a potential profit on trade would be wiped out by a devalued or revalued currency. According to the counter argument, however, currencies should be allowed to 'float' without government intervention and to find their own value as determined by global demand and supply. Through such 'floating' or flexible exchange rates, 'automatic' devaluation and revaluation through market pressures are supposed to 'clear' the exchanges of a particular country, and bring payments into some kind of equilibrium.

5.1 Paradigms and Paradox

The experience of the pound sterling and the dollar since the mid-1960s indicate that the two main reserve currencies of the world have been devalued, floated and – in the early 1980s for the dollar – revalued without the consequences assumed by conventional theory. Table 5.1 illustrates the relative depreciation of sterling against the dollar, and the relative appreciation of the Deutschmark and the Yen from 1950 to 1985, with the most marked relative change between these main currencies occurring since the devaluation of the dollar in the early 1970s.

TABLE 5.1   Exchange-Rate Changes of Key Currencies versus the US Dollar*

	£ Sterling	DM	Yen
1950	0.36	4.2	361.1
1960	0.36	4.2	360.0
1970	0.42	3.65	360.0
1980	0.43	1.82	226.7
1981	0.50	2.26	220.5
1982	0.57	2.43	249.1
1983	0.66	2.55	237.5
1984	0.75	2.85	237.6
1985	0.77	2.94	238.5

* Average of daily rates – units per US dollar.
Source: OECD, *Economic Outlook* December 1985; IMF, *International Financial Statistics*, 1984 and June 1986

The substantial devaluations of sterling and the dollar neither improved long-term visible export performance, nor strengthened underlying export structure. Meanwhile, since the 1960s countries such as Germany and Japan have successfully revalued their currencies yet not suffered the negative effects which according to conventional theory should follow through revaluation making their goods more expensive on foreign markets. In practice, as shown in Table 5.2, the West German trade surplus grew dramatically to 1982 despite Deutschmark revaluation, and by 1984 was still massive, while the Japanese surplus quadrupled between 1981 and 1984 despite an average value of the Yen which was at a record postwar high.

Nor can the paradox be explained by relative rates of inflation or comparative wage increases in the countries concerned. Table 5.3 shows that Japanese inflation in terms of the consumer price increase was substantially

TABLE 5.2 Relative Trade Deficits and Surpluses in Leading World Economies ($m)

	UK	USA	West Germany	Japan
1950	−981	1,296	−720	−154
1960	−2,425	5,705	1,311	−436
1970	−2,440	413	4,281	436
1980	−5,426	−36,198	4,929	−10,712
1981	95	−39,613	12,109	8,728
1982	−2,633	−42,610	20,572	6,979
1983	−8,361	−69,341	16,526	20,276
1984	−11,077	−123,289	18,538	33,640

Source: UN, *International Yearbook of Trade Statistics*, 1954, 1977 and 1983, and UN, *Monthly Bulletin of Statistics*, December 1985.

TABLE 5.3 Consumer Price Index of Inflation in Leading World Economies

	UK	USA	W. Germany	Japan
1950–1960	38.8	22.9	20.4	48.5
1960–1970	48.9	31.2	29.2	74.8
1970–1980	261.0	112.3	63.9	136.4
1980–1981	11.9	9.9	6.3	4.9
1981–1982	8.6	6.4	5.3	2.7
1982–1983	4.6	3.9	3.3	1.8
1983–1984	5.0	3.8	2.4	2.3
1984–1985	6.1	3.5	2.2	2.1

Sources: IMF, *International Financial Statistics 1985*, June 1986; OECD Press Release 13.1.86, 'Latest Trends in Consumer Prices'.

TABLE 5.4 Increase in Average Earnings in Leading World Economies (%)

	UK*	USA†	W. Germany†	Japan*
1950–1960	73.3	57.9	108.0	119.6
1960–1970	81.5	48.2	126.2	189.1
1970–1980	323.7	116.9	114.6	242.5
1980–1981	13.4	9.9	5.6	5.1
1981–1982	11.4	6.4	4.6	5.2
1982–1983	8.6	3.9	3.2	4.0
1983–1984	5.7	3.8	2.4	4.2
1984–1985	11.2	3.7	3.9	4.0

* Monthly earnings. † Hourly earnings.
Source: As for Table 5.3.

higher in the 1970s than in the United States, and only a few percentage points behind the US in the early 1980s. Also, as shown in Table 5.4, Japanese average earnings increased by a rate more than double those of both the US and West Germany in the 1970s and in line with both countries for most of the early 1980s.

Clearly something is wrong with conventional theory, what it seeks to explain, or both. This paradox has been reflected in the relative silence of those who before the major devaluations of the dollar or sterling predicted a dramatic recovery of the export performance of the US or UK economies through a 'downward float'.

In a rational world, such a paradox would give rise to an alternative paradigm. A key factor explicable in terms of conventional theory is the significance of costs per unit of output in the export sectors of the economies concerned. As illustrated later, this is important in understanding the export success of Japan despite revaluation. But as Ohmae (1985) has shown, less than an eighth of the Japanese economy is export-related. This reflects the efficiency achieved through an industrial strategy focused on export competitiveness. Inversely, much of the rest of the Japanese economy is less efficient or inefficient. Yet conventional macroeconomic policies of exchange-rate adjustment stress the need to adjust costs – and especially wage costs – in the economy as a *whole* to gain export efficiency effects. Such policies can also impose deflation on housing, health, education and social services to release resources for exports without (or in place of) a strategy for the export sector. Further, in both import and export trade, multinational companies now qualify conventional exchange-rate models in critical respects.

US Evidence

An analysis of the effects – or non-effectiveness – of exchange-rate changes on multinational business in the US economy has been undertaken by Jane Sneddon Little (1986), whose findings on the role of foreign direct investment by US multinationals have already been outlined in Chapter 4.

Because of the limited evaluation of multinational companies by central government in the US, Little was obliged to research the impact of exchange-rate changes from 1979 to 1983 on a survey of some 475 New England firms which had identified themselves as being active in international trade or which were foreign-owned firms. Just over 100 of the firms concerned responded to her survey. The results nonetheless have been of remarkable interest, and have attracted considerable attention.

Little asked the surveyed firms whether they had ever shifted the location of production because of an exchange-rate change. Of 28 firms responding on the issue, four said 'yes' and another was considering such a move. Three of the positive replies mentioned a shift away from the United States, while two involved changed locations between other countries. In other words, only a tenth of US respondents to the survey in question were willing to move production out of the United States because of dollar appreciation in the early 1980s.

Crucially, Little's survey found that intra-firm trade by multinational companies responded differently to macroeconomic changes compared with trade by non-affiliated firms. As shown in Table 5.5, intra-firm or inter-subsidiary imports and exports by multinational companies grew faster than total US trade weighted according to the industries represented in the survey.

TABLE 5.5   Multinational versus National Trade: US Evidence 1979–83 (%)*

US Imports†	51.4
Respondent Imports from:	
Companies with Major Affiliated Suppliers	55.8
Affiliates	279.1
Affiliates, excluding Start-Ups	150.3
Unaffiliated Suppliers in the Same Countries	−98.7
US Exports†	23.7
Respondent Exports to:	
Companies with Major Affiliated Customers	18.6
Affiliates	34.6
Affiliates, excluding Start-Ups	11.5
Unaffiliated Customers in the Same Countries	−22.5

* New England Survey Respondents' Trade and Comparable US Trade.
† Weighted average of industries represented in respondent group.
Source: Little (1986).

As is notable from Little's survey, against a decline of imports to the US of nearly 100 per cent by unaffiliated or non-multinational companies from 1979 to 1983, imports to the US by affiliates of multinational companies rose almost threefold, despite appreciation of the dollar, and by one and a half times excluding those firms which had recently begun foreign operations outside the United States. By contrast, intra-firm or inter-subsidiary exports by multinational companies grew substantially less than total US exports in the same industries. Overall, multinational companies' trade was less sensitive to dollar appreciation than that of other companies (Little, 1986, p. 47).

UK Evidence

Earlier UK evidence confirms Little's findings for US trade, and in particular the limited response by leading British companies in either price or volume terms to the devaluation and depreciation of sterling from November 1967. One of the earliest studies was by P. J. Hovell (1968). From a limited survey, this found that no British firm raised sterling prices by the full amount of the 1967 devaluation although most raised prices by a limited extent. Two studies done for the IMF for the period 1968 to 1972 (Artus, 1974 and 1975) found that the response of sterling export prices to devaluation was not substantial, and recommended that further empirical studies at the industry level would be necessary to gain a better understanding of the reasons for this.

A major empirical study on these lines was undertaken by Hague, Oakeshott and Strain (1974). This not only went inside industries to look at individual firms, but also analysed specific products rather than simply general price movements. Hague, Oakeshott and Strain had to hypothesise conditions under which a conventional devaluation response might have been said to have occurred for some of the firms analysed, but admitted that firms themselves did not give such explanations of their behaviour. The general conclusion of their study was similar to that of the other major analysis of the effects of the 1967 UK devaluation and the 1972 float by Peter Holmes, namely that 'the most sensible pricing decisions were taken by those firms that made the minimum possible cuts in foreign currency prices' (Holmes, 1978, p. 19).

The Limits of Conventional Theory

Some economists such as Silberston (1970) have argued that there are limits to empirical studies in that businessmen cannot necessarily know what motivates them in their pricing behaviour, and they therefore offer subjective interpretations after the event which are not necessarily a good guide to what happens in reality. Machlup (1946) had drawn a similar conclusion from the contrast between marginal cost pricing as assumed in the theory of the firm and what firms actually did. However, in commenting on such evidence, Holmes observed (italics added) that 'while it is not *paradoxical* to blame the inability of firms to respond as might be hoped' to devaluation, the majority of firms commanding British visible export trade at the time were in oligopolistic markets.

Holmes chose firms from *The Times* 1000 list on the basis that they had exports of over £5 million per year in 1972, placing them among the top 200 exporting firms. His data from Trade and Industry sources for 1973 included the top 230 exporting firms accounting for about two-thirds of UK exports.

Table 5.6 extends Holmes' analysis of concentration in the UK visible export trade from 1975 to 1981 (when, following changes in the Companies Act introduced by the Conservative government, firms were no longer

TABLE 5.6   Concentration of UK Visible Export Trade 1975–81 (%)

	1975	1976	1977	1978	1979	1980	1981
Top 30 exporters	33	36	35	32	35	35	39
Top 75 exporters	46	50	47	44	47	47	51
Top 220 exporters	64	67	64	61	64	62	65

Source: Department of Trade's Annual Overseas Transactions Inquiry, and Parliamentary Questions 28 July 1980 and 11 July 1983.

required to report their contribution to export share). The Table shows that throughout the later 1970s (consistent with Holmes' findings) two and a half dozen firms accounted for between a third and two-fifths of UK visible exports, 75 firms for up to half, and 220 firms for around two-thirds of this trade.

Towards Oligopoly Analysis

Holmes broke his analysis of firm behaviour into three main categories: (1) what he called *non-market*-oriented firms, which priced simply on a 'cost-plus' basis of the kind analysed in detail in *The Market Economy* (Holland, 1987, chapter 4); (2) *non-oligopolistic* market-oriented firms; and (3) *oligopolistic* companies. He admitted that the actual division between market-oriented and non-market-oriented firms had to be subjective, in the sense that all firms are subject to the constraint that at certain prices they will do no business at all. But he argued with some force that competitive and non-competitive behaviour can be distinguished within oligopolistic markets to the extent that a low-cost market leader setting prices independently of other firms could be classed as non-competitive, while other firms constrained to follow these prices will be seen as competitive (Holmes, 1978, chapter 2).

By analysing the limited price sensitivity of oligopolistic leaders in their response to devaluation, Holmes certainly brought the analysis closer to the real actors in international trade and payments. Thus, for example, in analysing 'non-market' behaviour he examined as examples three firms in the machinery sector, two of which had over 50 per cent of the world market for the products concerned, as well as non-oligopolistic firms responding more directly to market pressures. One of his key conclusions is that pricing policy in the context of devaluation is 'obviously affected by the type of competition the firm faces' (Holmes, ibid., chapters 3 and 4 and p. 41). Similar conclusions have been reached by Cowling and Sugden (1984), whose analysis of exchange-rate adjustment and oligopoly pricing is considered later in this chapter.

International and Multinational

While Holmes' analysis 'lifted the lid' on the behaviour of bigger and smaller business, and analysed the price response (or non response) to exchange-rate changes by big business, the model he extended nonetheless stays essentially within the conventional paradigm of international trade between different companies in different countries. In identifying this problem he observed that 'although devaluation can be grafted on to the theory of the firm, there does not exist any properly developed theory of devaluation for less than perfectly competitive firms on which it is possible to draw', and that 'the factual background to export markets as they are today requires a new theoretical approach which as yet does not properly exist' (Holmes, 1978, p. 18). His own analysis gets us at least halfway towards an alternative theory of exchange-rate changes and payments. But it does not follow through with a recognition of the dual nature of big business in international trade as being both oligopolistic and multinational in character.

The contrast between a conventional paradigm of international trade between different companies in different countries, and multinational trade overwhelmingly between subsidiaries of the same companies, is elaborated in the rest of this chapter. The argument seeks to develop a more complete theory of devaluation and revaluation than those available from the textbook models of perfectly competitive firms in different national markets. It also takes account of the extent to which differences in size between bigger and smaller business in the meso and microeconomic sectors reflect different market capabilities for 'offensive' long-term investment and global market penetration, with a range of export strategies and structural effects which further qualify the conventional model of exchange-rate changes.

5.2 Devaluation and International Trade

Figures 5.1(a) and (b) represent the main price and revenue outcomes which are supposed to follow from the devaluation of a national currency. In the example, the countries are the United Kingdom and West Germany, with a hypothetical exchange rate of $£1 = DM5$. In Figure 5.1(a), following the conventional macroeconomic reasoning on trade between different countries, and as indicated by the arrow ac, it is assumed that if sterling depreciates or is devalued by 20 per cent *vis-à-vis* the Deutschmark, it will be possible for a UK export company to reduce price from p^1 to p^2 on the German market, from DM500 to DM400, while receiving the same export revenue as before devaluation in sterling terms, i.e. £100. The domestic price level of the UK producer remains unchanged on the line *ab*, which was equivalent to the export price of the company on the German market (p^1) before devaluation. By penetration of the German market at level *c*, the UK exporting company is assumed to be able to gain a competitive advantage over German firms at price level p^2, rather than the prevailing level, p^1, for German firms.

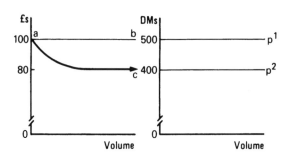

FIG 5.1(a) Devaluation and export trade: lower export price and same domestic revenue

Figure 5.1(b) shows an alternative scenario of conventional exchange-rate theory. Following a 20 per cent devaluation of sterling *vis-à-vis* the Deutschmark, the UK exporting company maintains the previous DM price level p^1 on the German market (in this case DM500), and simply appropriates the higher sterling revenue which follows from devaluation in its continued export sales to Germany. In this case, whereas the previous export price level to the German economy has been on the line *bc*, with sterling receipts of £100, the receipts of the UK exporter following sterling devaluation now rise to £120 on the arrowed line *ac*.

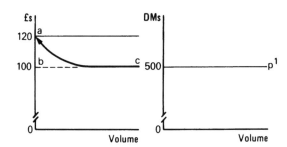

FIG 5.1(b) Devaluation and export trade: same export price and higher domestic revenue

Active and Passive Responses

It is clearly possible in principle that different export firms in the UK economy will react differently to the devaluation of sterling relative to the Deutschmark. This situation, derived from Figures 5.1(a) and 5.1(b), is illustrated in Figure 5.1(c). In this example firm A maintains its DM price at the level p^1, increasing its unit export revenue to £120, while firm B, decreasing its price on the German market to the level p^2 (DM400), retains its unit export earnings in sterling terms at £100. Conventional international trade theory is hard put to explain the different reactions of firms A and B, save on assumptions of alternative views of profit maximisation. Thus firm A takes the windfall profit from devaluation without increasing export volume, while firm B hopes to increase export volume, and thus both profits and export market share, over the longer run. In terms of the theory of the firm already analysed in Chapters 4–6 of *The Market Economy* (Holland, 1987), firm B would represent active and 'offensive' entrepreneurship versus the reactive and defensive management posture of firm A.

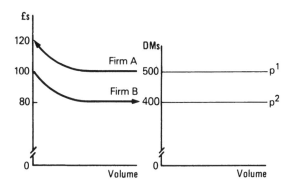

FIG. 5.1(C)   Defensive and offensive export strategies

The different responses of firms A and B are not merely theoretical. They will have significant effects on export volume and revenue.

Price and Demand Effects

Conventional trade theory focuses its explanation of exchange-rate changes and international payments on price and demand effects. Thus 5.2(a) assumes that demand for British exports on the German market is price-responsive or elastic, and assumes also for purposes of exposition that this price elasticity is unitary (so that a 1 per cent decrease in price gives rise to a 1 per cent increase in demand, and vice versa). The example assumes that two

British firms are exporting different products which do not mutually compete on the German market.

According to standard price elasticity of demand, firm A, represented by the dotted line in Figure 5.2(a), will not increase its exports to Germany since it has not altered its DM price, whereas firm B, which has reduced the price of its exported product on the German market from DM500 to DM400, thereby increases its export volume from 100 to 120 units.

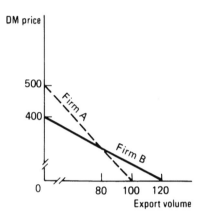

FIG. 5.2(a)   Price-elastic effects of devaluation on export volume

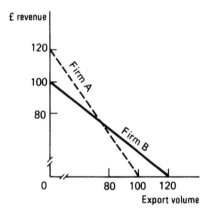

FIG. 5.2(b)   Neutral export revenue effects of price-elastic devaluation

Figure 5.2(b) spells out the implications of this conventional theory in terms of the sterling export revenue of the two companies. Firm A, represented again by the dotted line, receives £120 per unit for its maintained export volume of 100 units to the German market, whereas firm B, represented by the solid line, increases its volume of exports to Germany from 100 to 120 units, while maintaining a sterling export price of £100. Clearly in this situation of a unitary price elasticity of demand, there would need to be some special reason for firm B to reduce its DM price, since its increase in export volume earns it no more sterling revenue than firm A which, without lowering price but without increasing export volume, has not incurred additional costs and inconvenience of production.

A generally assumed condition for a 'follow through' of devaluation by price reduction on a foreign market is a price elasticity of demand greater than unity, i.e. an increase in export demand which is greater per unit than the decrease in the export price. Figure 5.2(c) illustrates such a situation. Firm A stays on the ratio of 100 exported units for a sterling revenue per unit of £120, but firm B increases its export volume on the German market from 120 to 140 units at a sterling revenue per unit of £100.

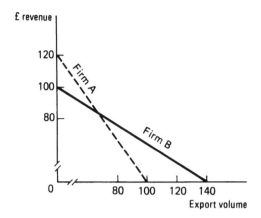

FIG. 5.2(c)   Positive net export revenue effects of devaluation

Cost and Supply Effects

Conventional theory rarely follows such assumed macro price and demand consequences of exchange-rate theory through to the probable consequences for the cost and structure of supply. Such a rationale of the dual effects of devaluation on an increase in export volume and the structure of domestic supply is illustrated in Figures 5.3(a) and (b). These reflect the respective 'defensive' and 'offensive' responses to sterling devaluation of firms A and B in Figure 5.1(c). They also employ a standard analytical framework of U-shaped *sac* or short-run average cost curves, and a declining LAC or long-run average cost curve made possible through (i) greater economies of scale (spreading fixed costs over a greater volume of output) and (ii) productivity-raising technical progress or innovation made possible by a round of entirely new investment.

Figure 5.3(a) assumes that both firms A and B are initially producing on the same short-run cost schedule sac^1. Because firm A does not reduce prices abroad following devaluation, and therefore does not increase export volume, it has no potential to undertake a new round of cost-lowering investment. Firm B, however, which has lowered its export price to DM400 for the same sterling receipts of £100 per unit, can adopt either or both of the following strategies. First, if it had previously been producing at the lowest cost point b on sac^1, it could increase capacity use in its existing plant from b to c. Second, assuming significant price elasticity of demand, it could undertake an entirely new round of investment to meet expanded export demand on the lines of the new sac^2. If firm B achieved volume y at a short-run cost of *e* it would be operating at optimum efficiency. It would be a bonus if, with full capacity working, it increased short-run output to *f*.

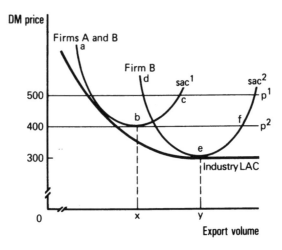

FIG. 5.3(a) Dynamic investment and export price effects of 'offensive' devaluation response

However, Firm B's 'offensive' response to devaluation does not simply register price effects in DM terms on the West German market. As shown in Figure 5.3(b), the new round of cost-lowering investment made possible by a successful export volume response to devaluation means that Firm B can also charge lower prices in sterling terms for production and sales on the domestic UK market. Thus, whereas both firms A and B before devaluation were producing on sac^1 and earning a normal profit at price p^1, firm B now can make a normal profit on its new sac^2 at price p^2.

It is inconsequential for the argument that it has hitherto been assumed that firm B would allocate all of its increased output from sac^2 to exports. In practice this is unlikely, granted the lower ratio of exports to domestic production from most investment in most industries in most countries. The patent result is that firm B could reduce price from p^1 to p^2 for a share of its production from sac^2 and thereby under-price firm A on the domestic market. This would represent an extension, via successful exporting and second-round investment, of the 'elimination pricing' analysed by Sylos-Labini (1962) and examined in some detail in *The Market Economy* (Holland, 1987, chapter 6).

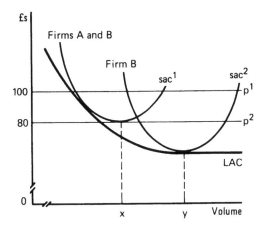

FIG. 5.3(b)   Domestic cost and price effects of 'offensive' devaluation-responsive investment

Export Winners

Therefore export winners do not simply win exports. An indirect dynamic effect of export-led growth is that today's successful exporters are tomorrow's dominant firms on the domestic market. This should not cause undue surprise if we recognise that gains from success include both lowered costs from a new round of investment, and thereby also greater cash flow, and greater volume profits. Thus even assuming a standard rate of profit for 'defensive/reactive' firm A and 'offensive/active' firm B, B will tend to 'win out' over A by being able to achieve lower costs and prices both for foreign sales and for home market sales. It will thus prove more attractive to stock-market investors and (possibly with more importance) be able to obtain preferential or lower rates in its borrowing for yet further investment expansion (Kumar, 1984).

Although the examples have so far been illustrated with reference to the UK and West German economies, such export success has clearly resulted in increased domestic market concentration in the leading exporter of the postwar global economy – Japan. For instance, Japan once had 32 automobile manufacturers. Today it has 11, of which 9 produce passenger vehicles, and of which 7 have been independent exporters. Three, or at most four, are likely to survive as independents into the 1990s. More dramatically, there were over two hundred motorcycle manufacturers in Japan in the 1950s. By 1985 only four had survived, essentially through offensive strategies pursued on global markets (Ohmae, 1985, pp. 47 and 167). Moreover, while all such firms had benefited from an undervalued yen in the

1950s and 1960s, the survivors had achieved such lowered cost schedules by the 1970s and thereafter – when the yen was revalued overall – that they were still able to scoop the global market and demolish other countries' passenger vehicle and motorcycle industries.

Devaluation and Deflation

One of the reasons why conventional devaluation theory neglects such dynamic supply and cost effects has been an undue focus on the short term. This partly reflected the era of relatively fixed or infrequently changed exchange rates – at least for the more developed countries – of the postwar quarter-century before the dollar devaluation in 1971, when it was assumed that if you were going to devalue you should do so decisively, in one announcement and by a sizeable amount, giving a clear message to international money markets that the new level would be supported. Within such a relatively fixed exchange-rate world, it became an additional part of the conventional wisdom that no government should devalue its currency unless it had significant spare capacity either obtaining at the time, or induced through a complementary package which deflated domestic demand and thereby redeployed productive capacity towards exports.

Such a 'Keynesian' conventional wisdom (reflected in the debates preceding the devaluation of sterling in 1967) became transposed into an IMF package for the international economy as a whole, or what could be called the '3D' package of deflate, devalue and diminish the public sector. The diminution of public-sector spending initially followed from the 'Keynesian' perception of the need to deflate domestic demand in a fully employed economy to release capacity and resources for increased exports. From the 1970s, and under the influence of the monetarist assault on public spending via Friedman, the IMF imperative to 'diminish' public spending became transposed into 'deny yourself a mixed economy'. This imperative was to carry special force since private-sector lending from the Eurodollar market or commercial banks was dependent on the IMF's 'seal of approval'. Yet the package was not simply applied to hitherto fully employed developed countries with an adaptable export structure, but to developing and underdeveloped countries with major overt or disguised unemployment, and chronic structural problems of dependence on commodity exports whose value was not price-elastic in the manner assumed by the conventional devaluation model.

Moreoever, to invert the Keynesian aphorism, while in the long run we are all dead, in the medium term most of us are still alive. For economies whose currencies have been devalued either as a deliberate act of public policy, or a consequence of a downward float determined by international money markets, failure to be concerned with the dynamic effects of devaluation on investment ranges from negligent to hazardous. In Britain in the 1960s the Prime Minister's economic adviser Thomas Balogh moved through two phases of policy advice. First, up to the middle of the decade, he advised against devaluation on the short-term 'comparative static' grounds that the accompanying deflation in a fully employed economy would be socially unacceptable and would undermine the expansionary targets of the 1965 National Plan. Thereafter, with the loss of international competitiveness, he joined Nicholas Kaldor (then adviser to Chancellor of the Exchequer James Callaghan) in advising devaluation as the premise to 'export-led' growth as a dynamic condition for fulfilling the kind of targets which the National plan had embodied.

The 1967 Sterling Devaluation

The export-led-growth case for devaluation was flawed by the time it gained prime ministerial acceptance in the UK economy in November 1967. For one thing, in contrast with the subsequent evidence on the effects of the 1967 devaluation from Hague, Oakeshott and Strain (1974) and Peter Holmes (1978), it assumed that UK firms would be price-sensitive in their response to devaluation, and therefore reduce prices on foreign markets. In practice, as already outlined, less than 20 per cent of exporters were price-sensitive (coinciding more or less exactly with the division we have highlighted between national firms and the more than 80 per cent of UK export trade commanded since the late 1960s by multinational companies).

The assumed positive export gains from an 'offensive' response to devaluation have figured as items of primary importance in recent economic history. For example, the Labour Government in Britain in 1964 inherited a balance-of-payments deficit of sizeable dimensions and fought hard for three years, including a major deflationary package in July 1966, to avoid devaluation. This was against the advice of Keynesian policy advisers that a significant devaluation should have been undertaken on coming into government. Finally, in November 1967, the government did undertake a 14 per cent devaluation, rationalising the event on the basis that exporters would now be able to lower prices on foreign markets and increase export volume, with overall macroeconomic benefits to the United Kingdom balance of payments. The UK by 1970 had a balance-of-payments surplus gained through (1) higher unemployment, (2) reduced imports, but especially (3) the discovery of the under-recording of exports on a major scale, to the extent that it has been estimated that Britain may have been in balance-of-payments surplus when pressure on sterling from an alleged deficit in 1967 finally forced devaluation in November of that year.

In reality, in terms of British export performance, it would appear from the overall macroeconomic evidence that many if not most UK firms have been typical of the situation of firm A in our examples, i.e. failing to respond 'offensively' to export opportunities and instead 'defensively' hanging onto markets which they already have. But, as already indicated, there were also other reasons for the inadequate response by multinational big business to devaluation, explaining the paradox of non-response or limited response already evidenced by Hague, Oakshott and Strain (1974), Holmes (1978) and Little (1986).

5.3 Multinational Trade and Devaluation

In practice, as already indicated by the empirical evidence, both US and UK visible export trade is dominated by multinational companies. But multinational companies have little or no incentive to lower price in export markets and increase domestic export volume when they are already producers through direct investment in the foreign market concerned. This situation, which in practice amounts to a major undermining of the conventional international trade theory of devaluation, is illustrated in Figure 5.4(a), where a hypothetical multinational company called General Automobiles produces a vehicle with a brandname Hallvaux in the United Kingdom and a vehicle called the Lepo in West Germany.

Following the general reasoning on devaluation of earlier examples, and in particular Figures 5.1(a) and 5.1(b), if General Automobiles as a multinational company were to fulfil the conditions of devaluation expected in the standard theory of international trade, then a 20 per cent devaluation *vis-à-vis* the Deutschmark, under competitive market conditions, could result in the reduction of the price charged in the West German market by its Hallvaux subsidiary from DM50,000 to DM40,000, reflected in the reduction of the export price curve for Hallvaux (UK) on the line *ab*, still yielding the previous sterling revenue per vehicle of £10,000.

Reverse Trade?

However, General Automobiles is not simply a UK exporter of motor vehicles. It also produces the Lepo range of vehicles on the domestic West German market. While it may well not be the case that its Hallvaux cars are identical in performance and quality to its Lepo vehicles, a price reduction of 20 per cent in the price in the West German market, assuming any consumer rationality on the behalf of West German purchasers, would tend to result in a major switch by them from Lepo to Hallvaux. This could only be countered effectively by the West German subsidiary of General Automobiles through a reduction of the price of Lepo cars on the West German market on the line *cd* in Figure 5.4(a).

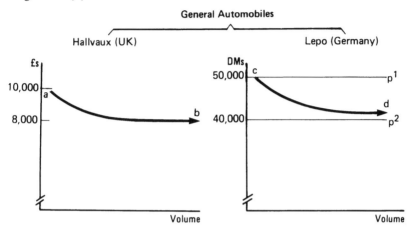

FIG. 5.4(a) Multinational companies' disincentive to lower foreign price following domestic devaluation

It should be evident that General Automobiles is unlikely to allow such a reduction of price from DM50,000 to DM40,000 for its Lepo products. Not least, (1) it would thereby be losing cash flow and revenue in relation to the higher prevailing price p^1; (2) assuming a similarity of real cost schedules in its UK and German subsidiaries, at the lower price p^2 in the West German domestic market it would find its total profit eliminated. Alternatively, (3) it could find itself faced on the German market with the need to undertake an entirely new round of investment in order to offset competition with its own British subsidiary Hallvaux Cars. *Put more simply, if General Automobiles were to follow through the sterling devaluation with a lower DM price on the West German market it would be competing against itself.*

Perverse Trade?

As a result, General Automobiles is not likely to reduce the price of Hallvaux vehicles in the West German market in the simple manner assumed by the macroeconomic theory of international trade following devaluation. As a multinational company, it is likely to be too concerned either with profit or revenue maximisation – or both – to permit such a disruption to its markets. Either it will not follow through the devaluation of sterling in relation to the

Deutschmark by lower prices for its British exports on the West German market, or it will not export at all.

It is notable in this context that General Motors exports virtually no Vauxhall products from its UK subsidiary to West Germany. By contrast, however, General Motors exported a considerable volume of Opel cars to Britain, sold either direct or under GM's Vauxhall brandname and, as shown in Figure 2.10 of Chapter 2, import-sourced the overwhelming share of components for UK production (Jones, 1985).

This again constitutes an unexplained paradox for the conventional exchange-rate theory, granted the very sizeable devaluation of sterling relative to key foreign currencies. For instance, as shown in Table 5.1, between 1970 and 1980 sterling had been devalued relative to the Mark by no less than 50 per cent. Why therefore the export of Opels or other GM components to the United Kingdom throughout this period?

The example demands a systematic analysis of the offsetting of devaluation by multinational companies. Account should be taken of relative costs. As shown in Table 5.3, UK inflation from 1970 to 1980 was more than quadruple that in West Germany. Similarly, Table 5.4 shows that the increase in average earnings in Britain over the same period was nearly triple that of the Federal Republic.

But such factors alone do not explain the paradox of comparative British and West German export performance by multinational companies. First, revaluation itself helps reduce domestic costs for the inputs employed by exporters in West Germany and Japan. Second, by reducing overall import costs, it reduces the pressure for wage increases to protect the value of the real wage. Thus, rather than simply representing a disadvantage through lower export revenue, revaluation may represent an indirect effect countering inflationary policies and sustaining export success. The critical factor will be the extent to which the cost reduction possible through successive rounds of innovating and 'offensive' investment offset the higher cost of exports following revaluation. Both West German and Japanese firms have shown that this 'real' supply-side effect (as opposed to US 'supply-side' economics) can register net gains in terms of export competitiveness.

From Perfect to Imperfect Competition

One simple factor which could explain the export of Opels to the United Kingdom, despite DM appreciation and sterling depreciation, could be the better quality of the Opel in relation to the product of the UK subsidiary of General Motors, i.e. the Vauxhall car. Without much question, the Opel vehicle was on balance considered superior by British consumers to the Vauxhall. This amounted to what in conventional theory of the firm would be called product differentiation, or brand attachment reflecting superior quality. As seen in chapter 4 of *The Market Economy* (Holland, 1987), the theory of costs and prices under imperfect or monopolistic competition enables the product with superior quality or greater brand attachment to charge a higher price. Returning to the hypothetical example of General Automobiles in Figure 5.4(b), Lepos can be exported from Germany to the UK market at the sterling import price of £12,000, reflecting the assumed revaluation of the DM relative to sterling of 20 per cent in real terms. This is despite the prevailing UK domestic price for competing Hallvaux cars, of the UK subsidiary of the same company, of £10,000.

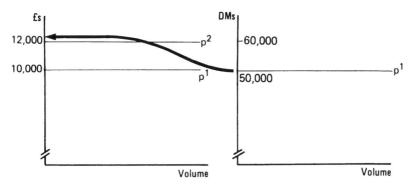

FIG. 5.4(b) Multinational companies' nominal disincentive to import following domestic devaluation

In practice, there have been enormous disparities in the prices of the same cars, net of tax, on sale in the UK and other European countries in recent years. For instance, while disparities in price between continental European countries in the Common Market have varied by some 10 per cent, UK car prices have been up to 50 per cent higher. Ashworth, Kay and Sharpe (1982) seek to explain the difference in terms of strong preferences by British buyers for British products. Such an explanation fits neatly enough within the conventional theory of imperfect competition and the analytic framework of Figure 2.2 in chapter 2 of this volume. In other words, brand attachment of the kind represented by preference for British products makes possible a higher price and profit level for UK products irrespective of differences in quality, which in turn makes it possible for non-British producers to charge higher prices on the same market.

From Imperfect Competition to Oligopoly

However, in analysing the same disparities in UK and continental EEC car prices, Cowling and Sugden (1984) have come to different conclusions.

Analysing the fact that a substantial appreciation of sterling in 1979/80, accompanied by a relative increase in UK production costs, failed to promote a decline in relative price for car imports into the UK, while the relative price of British cars in export markets showed no tendency to increase, they concluded that 'this would seem to be a quite natural consequence of the oligopolistic structure of the market.'

The Cowling and Sugden argument stresses the reaction by oligopolists to the price behaviour of other leading firms, and in particular whether an oligopoly will cut its price when exchange-rate changes cause its costs to fall. Their crucial conclusion is:

> Quite simply, that price may not be cut. . . . That is, firms are aware that they are interrelated and that rivals will respond to their action. This raises the possibility that [the initial firm] does not cut price as to do so would reduce its expected profit – something it wishes to avoid – because rivals fear reduction in their profits. The critical point is this – firms tolerate each others' preferences in the market to the extent of avoiding situations in which each expects to be worse off. In other words, firms collude [Cowling and Sugden, ibid., p. 11].

Such a rationale corroborates the failure of the conventional paradigm of devaluation of orthodox macroeconomic models of international trade. It also supports an alternative model which gives an explanation of the insensitivity of multinational capital to exchange-rate changes.

Exports will not gain price-elasticity effects of the kind assumed in conventional theory, and described in Figures 5.2(a), (b) and (c), under multinational conditions. Nor will they do so if mesoeconomic companies abroad can deter or block entry into foreign markets by no-entry or elimination pricing of the kind analysed in *The Market Economy* (Holland, 1987, chapter 6).

Such dynamics of 'unequal competition' analysed extensively in *The Market Economy* contribute to explaining why many small firms conforming with the conventional 'national' microeconomic model do not follow through devaluation with aggressive lower pricing on foreign markets. If they did so, they could attract the attention of market leaders (whether globally or in the market concerned) who can either lower price to a level which would mean no profit (no-entry pricing) or, if this is not effective, reduce price to below the variable costs or short-term payments such as wages which a firm must meet to survive (elimination pricing).

The gains in terms of economies of scale either from moving down a long-run industry average cost curve, or from undertaking successive rounds of cost-reducing investment, in the manner of Figures 5.3(a) and 5.3(b), certainly makes sense for an offensively exporting company (in our examples firm B, which thereby increases its domestic market share relative to firm A). But this only makes sense at a particular stage of the expansion of the company. In other words, it makes sense for the domestic growth phase (in Vernon's product-cycle model), or the 'national' economy phase of modern capitalist development. As the company increasing its domestic size through an offensive devaluation response at a particular historical phase achieves sufficient scale to undertake direct investment abroad, then in the manner of Ohlin's analysis, such foreign investment will tend to substitute for export trade.

Further, the international division of component production by multi-national companies (illustrated by the example of the Ford Fiesta in Table 2.6) shows that the trading of final products assumed by the Ricardian international trade paradigm has already been superceded by extensive integrated production within the same company in different countries. In this sense the imperative of global division of production, distribution and exchange within the same company becomes more important for such firms than the price, demand and supply relationships between different companies in different countries. Much of this underlies and explains the paradox of the poor response of UK and US multinational companies to exchange-rate changes noted earlier in this chapter (Little, 1986, Holmes, 1978, and others).

Asymmetric Effects

Such qualifications of devaluation have major implications for national government policies. They mean that a national government in an economy with a highly multinational trade structure can no longer count on increased exports through devaluation on the assumption that 'its' exporters will follow through the devaluation with lower prices on 'foreign' markets.

Yet if such governments no longer count on such export volume effects, they can count on the unwelcome consequence that devaluation will increase import prices. This asymmetry in the price effects of devaluation follows essentially from the different structural conditions, at firm and enterprise level, for successful exports versus successful imports.

The reason is basically simple, i.e. that the capacity to export a manu-factured product assumes within it the ability to organise the coordination of factors of production, the embodiment of technology, and the penetration of foreign markets. By contrast, virtually any firm with cash in hand, or able to raise the credit, can import effectively. A minor producer of widgets in Wessex or Wyoming does not need the scale and scope of a major German or Japanese machine-tools exporter to be able to import such machine tools for the production of widgets. In addition, many small companies which advertise themselves as being in the import-export trade are in practice mainly specialist importers. This is one reason import trade tends to be less concentrated than export trade.

As a result, import trade by independent national companies is classically price-taking rather than price-making. Importing companies can exploit their freedom under conditions of global trade liberalisation to import from either the cheapest or cheaper world markets. Such importing companies in general, and in particular such smaller import companies typical of the micro-economic sector, are negatively affected by the devaluation of a currency and its implications in raising overall import costs. Only mesoeconomic majors with significant dominance of particular markets can 'pass on' the import price increase by a higher domestic price.

Thus where multinational big business dominates export trade, de-valuation may register a more clearly negative effect on the trade balance and inflation of developed capitalist countries than any positive effect in increasing export competitiveness and volume.

Devaluation does not necessarily ensure the export response at macro-economic level assumed by conventional trade theory, due to the dominance of export trade by multinational companies. By contrast, it does tend to raise the registered value of imports on a macroeconomic level. Thereby it also contributes to domestic inflation, whether the imported goods are final or intermediate products.

This is apart from (i) the extent to which the transfer-pricing practices of multinational companies, analysed in the next chapter, tend to damage the trade balance of a country through inflating the value of registered imports and deflating the value of exports, and (ii) the degree to which the leading and lagging of payments on intra-firm or inter-subsidiary trade by multinationals can exert upwards or downwards pressure for the revaluation/appreciation or devaluation/depreciation of individual currencies.

5.4 Revaluation and International Trade

Conventional macro theory of trade and payments adjustment following revaluation is based on the assumption that this will result in a reduction of import prices in the revaluing country as a whole, and a parallel reduction of the price competitiveness of exports from that country. The principle, again, is simple enough. In other words, importers in a revaluing economy will pay less in domestic currency terms for each unit of the good or service imported; inversely, exporters from that economy will find that their domestic currency receipts fall if they do not change price on foreign markets, while it is assumed that if they increase the price of exported products abroad in order to protect or preserve their domestic currency receipts, this will represent a loss of foreign sales and foreign market share as a consequence of the loss of price competitiveness.

In essentials, the dynamic effects of revaluation on international trade are assumed to be the reverse of those for devaluation. In other words, with a rise in the value or price of the domestic currency relative to other countries, it is assumed that export revenue will fall overall, reducing both domestic investment and employment through standard accelerator and multiplier effects.

However, as already indicated in Table 5.2, major revaluation or appreciation of key currencies such as the Yen or Deutschmark have hardly contracted Japanese or West German export trade in the manner anticipated in conventional exchange-rate theory. Japanese exports, in particular, seemed unstoppable, with a dynamism which – despite world recession and Yen revaluation – was seen to imperil the domestic industry of both Europe and the United States.

TABLE 5.7 Relative Currency Values and Manufacturing Productivity in UK and Japan

	£ value in Yen	Productivity (1980 = 100) Japan	UK
1970	860	60	90
1985	300	117	125
% change	−65	+95	+38

Source: GLC (1986).

Relative productivity is crucial to the argument. In this respect, as shown in Table 5.7, conventional theory can adequately explain the increased competitiveness of Japanese manufacturing in the UK market over the 1970–85 period. But the key questions concern not only comparative aggregate productivity, or overall productivity in the export sector, but what is happening at the level of leading firms in key export markets.

Scale and Specialisation

According to Ohmae (1985, p. 57), Japan's 'super competitiveness' is limited to only a few industrial sectors, employing only 13 per cent of the working population. The explanation of Japan's export success involves two key factors: (i) scale economies in successive rounds of productivity-raising investment and (ii) export market specialisation.

The investment effect is dramatically illustrated by the fact that the cost of labour at Nissan in the early 1980s was under 7 per cent of total costs and at Toyota less than 6 per cent. A direct comparison with UK or US labour costs is difficult because of the different ratios between internal and external economies (i.e. the difference between the ratio of components manufactured within the company and bought in from other companies). Nonetheless in 1981–2, when comparable data for the US was available, the cost of labour for Ford (with a 45 per cent internal production ratio) was $10 billion, and for General Motors (with a 70 per cent internal production ratio) $18 billion. For Toyota, the cost of labour was only $1 billion.

Such an investment effect diminishes the factor of relative wage cost increases to insignificant proportions. For example, even if Toyota's wage rates matched GM's dollar for dollar, its profit loss would be just over one per cent from its recent 7 to 8 per cent average return on sales. Toyota produces some 3.3 million units a year. But it has reduced the labour component in production in such a way as to maintain its employee level at some 45,000 people from the early 1970s to early 1980s. Meanwhile, with the same labour force, it increased its output 3.5 times. Nissan has taken the same route.

The same trend is apparent in the Japanese electronics industry. Since the later 1970s the workforce required to assemble given consumer electronics has been halved, with direct labour costs in the industry down to an average of 5 per cent of total costs. In two of Japan's leading steel mills – Nippon Steel and Nippon Kokan KK – labour costs are around some 10 per cent of total costs (Ohmae, 1985, pp. 3–4).

The counterpart of such capital-intensive scale economies is export market specialisation. Bearing in mind that Japan accounts for only 2.5 per cent of the world's population, Japanese automobiles now account for 30 per cent of world sales. Japanese merchant shipbuilders have been responsible for about half of the world market for nearly a quarter of a century. Japanese steel has a 20 per cent world market share; semi-conductors 30 per cent and television 40 per cent. In individual markets Japanese companies' share of world export trade is even higher, with hand-held calculators at 60 per cent; motorcycles at 68 per cent; high-fidelity equipment at 70 per cent; single-lens cameras 80 per cent, and video cassette recorders 95 per cent (Ohmae, pp. 58–9).

Such phenomenal export success, in the face of significant revaluation, cannot be explained simply in macro trade and payments terms. The role of leading mesoeconomic firms, in key sectors, is crucial to the global market outcome.

The Quality Effect

There is no doubt that one of the main factors in the continued dynamism of West German and Japanese exports has been the quality effect. This included both the quality of management and reliability on their delivery times. As management naturally stress, reliable delivery dates can have a key effect on the overall cost schedule of the importing company for the simple reason that a delay in overall production, sales and revenue because of delay in an imported component can easily exceed by a significant margin the higher cost of importing components from countries with strong and revaluing countries. These are among the reasons why Japanese companies in the meso sector insist on daily and in some cases two-hourly delivery of components from their subsidiary, affiliate or contracting companies (Armstrong, Glyn and Harrison, 1984).

However, the 'quality effect' also includes the degree of innovation embodied in the product itself and the process by which it is produced. In this sense West German companies since the 1950s and Japanese companies since the 1960s have been close to what Perroux (1965) calls the 'innovation frontier' of a new product or process. They guarantee not only good delivery but also a better product in a modern market, with excellent quality control. Moreover, to achieve this, Japanese firms have not only introduced robotics and numerical control of the production process, but also committed major resources to upgrading the on-line skill and responsibility of the workforce.

Thus the 'quality effect' is not simply a matter of a good product delivered on time for which international customers are prepared to pay a higher price, along the lines of imperfect competition theory. It involves both the production and labour process, with a readiness to commit resources for investment, labour training and high wages rather than simply focus on reducing costs through wage restraint. US multinationals such as Ford have recently come to appreciate the significance of such differences in evaluating Japanese export success in their own markets (GLC, 1986).

Price Effects

Stressing the above factors, the offsetting of the conventional price, volume and trade effects of revaluation can be analysed by analogy with the modern modification of devaluation in the following terms.

Figure 5.5(a) shows the export price effect of revaluation for a West German export company if it maintains the pre-revaluation Deutschmark revenue for the product concerned. Maintaining the previous exchange rate of DM500 = £100, then a West German export company deciding to maintain its domestic export revenue will increase price in sterling terms to £120 following a revaluation of the Deutschmark in relation to the pound sterling of 20 per cent. Inversely, Figure 5.5(b) shows the domestic revenue effect of revaluation for a West German company which decides not to follow through such a 20 per cent revaluation of the Deutschmark by any increase of its export price in sterling terms on the British market. In this example the sterling export price remains at £100, but the export revenue to the West German company in Deutschmark terms falls from DM500 to DM400.

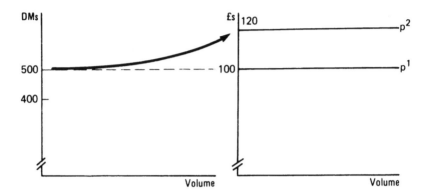

FIG. 5.5(a)   Export price effect of revaluation with constant domestic export revenue

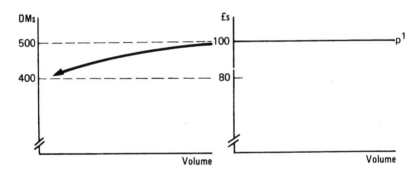

FIG. 5.5(b)   Export revenue effect of revaluation with constant export price

If there is a unitary price-elasticity of demand for exports following revaluation similar in effect to that illustrated for devaluation in Figure 5.2(a), and if the West German company was previously exporting 100 units of this product (per day, per week or per year) to the British market, then it could be expected that the UK demand for its exports would fall by 20 units, or 20 per cent, in the event of its raising the UK price from £100 to £120.

Structural Effects

In such a situation of falling export demand, and a corresponding fall in production in West Germany, there should be an increase in the West

German company's unit production costs, which in principle the company would seek to offset by shedding labour. There would also be further indirect effects through both the income and inter-industry or matrix demand multipliers, as the West German export company reduced its purchase of inputs from other West German companies. With one or more meso-economic companies, or a similar sequence for several microeconomic firms, this would result in a fall in the rate of growth or level of West German exports and a decrease in the macroeconomic export income, employment and matrix multipliers.

Such effects would reduce cash flow in the export sector, and also self-financing by export companies. Without offsetting state intervention, or the achievement of new export markets (either in other countries or through other products), the overall capacity of West German export companies to finance future rounds of investment would be hindered by this fall in export revenue and cash flow.

Thus, in principle, profits would fall, and with them the ability to finance the investment and launch costs for assault on new international markets. Or the development and introduction of new products would be diminished. Also, as profits fell in the export sector, it could be expected that fewer resources would be allocated to exports, i.e. a lower proportion of national income invested in export trade.

But in practice this conventional sequence has not happened in the West German case. Karl Georg Zinn has decisively shown the remarkable maintenance of a very high share of exports in West German national income throughout the period from the early 1960s when the Deutschmark was first significantly revalued after the war (Holland, 1978, chapter 5).

Specialisation

In addition to the 'quality effect' and government intervention, the very considerable specialisation which West German mesoeconomic companies have achieved in the export sector – reflected in the composition of West German exports – has been one of the factors explaining the successful maintenance of export share, and a persistent long-term increase in export growth in both value and volume terms.

For instance, 90 per cent of West German visible exports from the mid 1960s to mid 1970s was in either investment goods or machinery for industry. This meant real economies of scale in production, promoting self-reinforcing 'virtuous' supply-side effects, in turn making possible export growth in the sectors concerned. The major reconstruction of German industrial capital following the war, and the very fast and high rates of growth of capital accumulation in industry especially in the 1950s and earlier

1960s, resulted in a situation in which more capital was employed per worker in West German industry than in the UK or France, and in which in a real sense the long-run average cost curves of West German companies were lower than in similar industries in France or Britain (Zinn, ibid.).

It has already been allowed that the West German rate of inflation was very considerably lower than that of the UK during the post-1967 devaluation period. Without doubt, different degrees of wage pressure contributed to this overall difference in inflation rates, as is strongly argued by Armstrong, Glyn and Harrison (1984, chapter 17). Nonetheless, as argued by Godley and Cripps (1983, part IV) and as we will see in Chapter 8, the question whether wages were an active cause of inflationary pressure rather than a response to inflation is a separate methodological question.

Penetration Pricing

Assuming a Ricardian framework of trade between different companies in different countries but different long-run average costs in the same industry for competitors in those countries, it is possible to see how revaluation can in principle be offset by companies with price leadership in international markets, especially where quality and scale effects are taken into account.

In Figure 5.6(a), the long-run average cost curve of the West German company on its domestic market, LAC^1, is DM400, against an export price of DM500, which gives a profit rate of 20 per cent. On the right-hand side of the diagram, the long-run average cost, LAC^2, of a British domestic producer is higher in real terms, at £90, against a domestic price level of £100 at p^1, equivalent to the German domestic price level of DM500 and a UK profit rate of 10 per cent per unit of output.

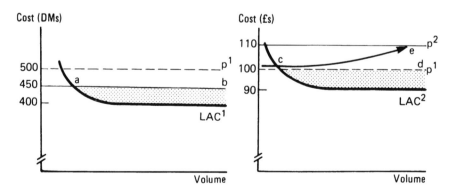

FIG. 5.6(a)   Unequal costs offsetting revaluation

Thus the British firm is assumed to be earning a unit rate of profit which is only half the percentage level of the West German company. If the German company is concerned to secure a sizeable long-run export penetration of the UK domestic market, it could well decide simply to reduce its profit rate on exports to the United Kingdom rather than increase the sterling price of those exports. If it were to maintain the UK sterling export price at £100, this would result in profits on its exports to the United Kingdom being halved in Deutschmark terms – from 20 per cent to 10 per cent – but its volume exports and market share in the UK being maintained.

On the left-hand side of the Figure 5.6(a), this is represented by the shaded area under the line ab and over the West German company's long-run average cost curve LAC^1. This in fact would give it a profit level equivalent in real terms to its UK competitor, i.e. the shaded area under the line cd and over the long-run average cost curve LAC^2. In such an example, the 'entry' price into the UK market would not be lower than that prevailing for UK competitors, with the additional 'quality factor' allowing the German company to increase its share of the UK domestic market. Thus unequal costs can offset the export effects of revaluation for unequally competitive firms.

Price Umbrellas

Besides, if the West German company is in a situation to exert what amounts to 'price leadership' in the UK market due to the combination of its own production cost advantage plus 'the quality factor', then it may be able to raise the price of its exports to the UK market with relative impunity.

Thus, in terms of Figure 5.6(a), the German company leads price on the UK domestic market with an increase from £100 at level p^1 to £110 at the level p^2. Because UK companies in the markets concerned are more weakly structured in their domestic production, there is reason to assume that the price lead given by the German export company will be followed through by British firms on the line of the rising price curve ce – i.e. the equivalent in international terms of what Edith Penrose has called the 'price umbrella' effect (Penrose, 1959).

In this sense, rather than having to take the post-revaluation price as given on the UK domestic market and lose export revenue in the manner assumed by conventional international trade theory, the German company would be able to offset the effects of revaluation while still giving itself a 'normal' profit level in Deutschmark terms on its exports to the UK. Such an effect is illustrated by the Greater London Council's report on Ford (GLC, 1986, p. 16). In the early 1980s, with a temporarily overvalued pound, Ford took advantage of high UK prices to make big profits by importing cars produced in dollars, pesetas or deutschmarks, and selling them in sterling.

Successive and Successful Investment

Such reasoning on the offsetting of revaluation through unequal cost structures becomes more realistic in a dynamic context in which account is taken of successive phases of investment, modernisation, and increased productivity reflected in lower average cost schedules. This situation is represented in Figure 5.6(b).

The Figure shows a situation in which the German exporting company which in period I had achieved a long-run average cost schedule, LAC^1, of DM400, by period II has achieved a lower cost schedule, LAC^2, at DM300. In reality such schedules may amount to abstractions for shorter-run cost curves over the long term. In this situation, the West German company could absorb the DM revaluation and maintain its price on the UK domestic market at level p^1, i.e. £100. Meanwhile, its British competitor, who has not reinvested or modernised over the two time-periods, retains a long-run average cost of £90 at level LAC^3, i.e. equivalent to LAC^2 in Figure 5.6(a). Therefore, the German company at LAC^2 in phase II – even post-revaluation – is earning double the profit of its UK competitor.

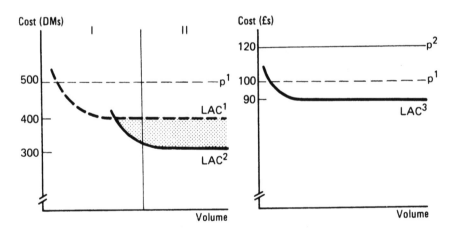

FIG. 5.6(b) · Dynamic cost reductions and revaluation offset

In principle this means that even a small cost advantage can be used in international trade to gain a big market advance. In practice, successive rounds of investment by West German (and Japanese) companies had by the late 1960s and early 1970s put them in a vastly superior position relative to their UK (and US) counterparts. Thus they were better placed to absorb the negative effects on export revenue from revaluation of the DM and the Yen on the lines of Figure 5.6(b) than UK companies were in responding to sterling devaluation, or US companies were in the period of dollar devaluation from 1971.

UK and US: Failure and Decline

For instance, despite dollar devaluation, the third major US car producer – Chrysler – was almost wiped out by 1979. Neither devaluation nor the OPEC oil rise gave the whole picture. The company lacked a strategy to restructure production. In the 1960s it had taken over the British Rootes company but failed to rationalise production between Rootes, its Simca subsidiary in France and operations in the US. A minority shareholding in Mazda in Japan had not managed to offset the main assault on US markets of Japanese producers who – despite persistent revaluation of the Yen – took the lion's share of an increase in US automobile imports of nearly 70 per cent between 1968 and 1978. Chrysler saw its home market share fall by nearly 38 per cent between 1968 and 1978, against a loss of less than 4 per cent for Ford and an increase of nearly 2 per cent for General Motors. By 1979 Chrysler was asking the US federal government for a $1 billion cash advance against future income – 'the biggest federal bailout in US history' (*Newsweek*, 13 August 1979).

In the UK, despite the intention of this author that Labour's National Enterprise Board should reinforce and promote 'offensive' export success rather than subsidise or support 'defensive' reactions to events (Holland, 1975), car producers such as Jaguar – with established international renown – were brought by the NEB within the umbrella framework of British Leyland and then left to their own devices. The result in the later 1970s was that Jaguar, producing excellent cars, did so with a paint shop which had been bought and installed in the 1940s and not since renewed. In the circumstances it was hardly surprising that a Japanese ambassador at that time publicised the fact that he was taking a Jaguar back with him to Japan, but was getting it painted at home, where modern techniques could achieve a better result.

Such illustrations of the low rate of investment and modernisation in the UK car industry are also reflected in the aggregate capital/labour ratios available for British domestic versus West German and Japanese cars in the 1970s. Against a capital/labour ratio of 1:1 for UK producers, German car companies had a ratio of 3:1 (i.e. each German worker was backed by three times as much capital as each British worker). For some Japanese companies the ratio was 7:1. British car manufacture at the time was literally assembly by hand at a time when not only the Japanese and West German but also the Italian industry was introducing robotics. Fiat for a time prided itself on the fact that it was 'designed by computer, welded by laser, and assembled by robot'.

Such massive disparities in capital/labour ratios imply both different feasible cost schedules and entirely different export strategies. British Leyland, at the time nominally under public ownership but in practice run like many British private companies on the basis of cost savings through labour wastage, could not absorb or offset the West German, and especially the Japanese, challenge through successive rounds of 'defensive' investment. The result was an ultimate indignity for the 'flag carrier' of the British vehicles industry. It first opted out of new product development and put the brand marks 'Rover' and 'Austin' on new Honda models (with interim British engines). It then suffered privatisation of some of its parts by the post 1979 Conservative government, who in February 1986 were trying to auction its main product divisions to Ford and General Motors.

Finance Capital

Such success for West German and Japanese export companies is not simply the result of market forces. In West Germany, Japan and also France, the state plays a key role in promoting and sustaining offensive investment and offensive exports. The West German and French institutions have already been cited in Chapter 2. In Japan the giant *keiretsu* are vast multiproduct, multisectoral and in many cases conglomerate enterprises actively backed and supported by the government through its Ministry of International Trade and Industry MITI.

Japan conforms very much to elements of Hilferding's analysis of finance capital (Hilferding, 1910), inasmuch as there is a very close liaison between state and private capital and the production and export decisions of these giant Japanese companies. Financial intervention and liaison in Japan includes not only investment credit but also export credit. For example, in the large-scale bulk carrier and tanker market in which the Japanese effectively gained a dominance of world trade within twenty years of the Second World War, the Japanese government provided credit equal to half of the purchase cost of the vessels to foreign buyers at a 5 per cent rate of interest, while special finance houses provided finance at a 4 per cent interest rate for 45 per cent of the remaining total purchase price. Thus 95 per cent of the cost of purchasing a vessel, to an accredited buyer, was covered through credit from the Japanese public and private sector (Holland, 1972). Without doubt, such credit policies contributed crucially to the export penetration which the Japanese were able to achieve in this and other markets at the time. Meanwhile British private shipbuilders, who had seen their share of world production fall from two-thirds to less than five per cent since 1900, were telling this author at the time of the introduction of Labour's Industry Bill in 1975 to get the state off their backs. By 1985 they had little to produce except warships for the Royal Navy, financed through public spending. With the oil-rig boom over, such firms were hard up or bankrupt.

'Offensive' Export Strategies

Specific institutions in postwar West Germany and Japan aided and abetted high levels of go-getting 'offensive' investment in key export industries. The process in Japan, as already described, operated essentially through the government department MITI. In West Germany, it operated through the Kreditanstalt für Wiederaufbau (KFW), or Reconstruction Loans Corporation, set up in 1948 in the first instance – as indicated in chapter 1 – to fulfil a role in allocating counterpart funds to Marshall Aid. The chairman of the Reconstruction Loans Corporation, Herman Abs, was also chairman of the Deutsche Bank, and the public funds concerned were channelled into industrial companies through the private banking system as a whole. By the early 1970s the role of the KFW had diminished, but mainly because by that time self-financing from successful West German exporters had reduced the need for it.

Again, Hilferding's analysis of finance capital, based on German experience before the First World War, is relevant to such channelling of savings into investment in individual companies undertaking 'offensive' foreign investment strategies. The mechanism operated through the 'supervisory boards' or Aufsichtsräte – i.e. the highest-level policy board of companies on which German banks as shareholders have historically been represented. Such supervision gave them an overview of both production bottlenecks within the country, and of the potential overall national and export performance (similar to Harrod's natural growth concept, but as applied to international export potential). This enabled West German bankers, using either private, public or state backed funds, to allocate savings for investment modernisation in export-promoting companies in such a manner as to reinforce and encourage success – in contrast with much of the investment in British industry in the postwar period, where a private stock market mainly washed its hands of relative decline or failure, financing less than a twentieth of the investment needs of UK industrial and commercial companies in the postwar period.

The Long-Term View

The overall results of this process were a ready availability of finance for investment for West German and Japanese companies where they could reveal a potential foreign export market. MITI could and did afford to take a very long-term view of export potential. In many cases – including steel and bulk carriers or tankers in the 1950s and 1960s, automobiles throughout the postwar period, and television, videos and other electrical goods through the 1960s to the 1980s – this credit-for-exports horizon could range up to ten or twenty years. Japanese managers have drawn attention to the fact that in new product markets, they frequently have anticipated that in the first 3–5 years of production they will be operating with spare capacity, but that thereafter for 10–15 years they could be running at full capacity when the rest of the world was wondering whether or not to invest. Microelectronics investment by Japan in the silicon chip and its derivative industries, several years ahead of the world, is a clear example of this (see Kojima, 1977, chapters 1, 6 and 7).

This is not to say that there is no difference of opinion within Japan on the most appropriate way in which to intervene in the structure of supply in such a way as to offset the effects of continuing Yen revaluation. In analysing what he calls the 'long-term path' of the Japanese economy, Kojima had contrasted the view of the Japanese employers' federation Keidanren that there should be a focus on applying the next generation's technology rather than simply winding down traditional industrial structures, and the view of the government's Industrial Structure Council that the pace of introducing tomorrow's technology should be matched by moving out of the heavy engineering and chemical industries. But such differences occur within a framework which accepts that structural change to adapt both to the world after OPEC and to Yen revaluation should be within the framework of a 'planned market economy' (Kojima, 1977, p. 141).

In Japan such planning occurs at company level within the mesoeconomic giants which dominate production and trade. The contrast with UK policy is very clear. In Britain during the 'Keynesian era', with only a few exceptions, it was almost impossible to gain acceptance from established economists for the case that successful devaluation would need to be accompanied by offensive go-getting intervention in the supply side of the economy *at the level of leading firms*, rather than at sectoral or industry working group level. The fact that the UK was losing world export market share with a devaluing currency from 1967, while Japan was gaining it with major revaluation, was a paradox to be explained by the orthodox Keynesians in terms of price 'stickyness', trades-union 'imperfections' in the labour market, or virtually any factor other than the evident success of the UK's main competitors in gaining results from public intervention at company level.

5.5 Multinational Trade and Revaluation

However, through the 1970s and early 1980s Japanese and West German exporters were finding that modernisation and cost lowering through new investment could not easily offset further revaluation. Japanese companies were increasingly locating subsidiaries in South East Asia, in lower-wage markets, while German companies had decided to locate production in newly industrialising economies such as Brazil.

From National to Multinational

This transitional phase from national to multinational production was not as simple as suggested by some of the exponents of 'stages of growth'. In practice, European big business has tended to go multinational in two broad stages: first to intermediate countries in the southern European periphery, and secondly to less developed countries in Latin America or South East Asia. Many multinational companies have also located direct production for re-export back to Europe and the USA on what Charles Levinson (1979) has called a 'vodka-cola' basis in Eastern Europe.

However, while factors other than exchange rates were clearly relevant to this multinational capital outflow from strong currency economies such as Germany and Japan, the multinational expansion of formerly national capital can enable it to offset revaluation of the currency of the 'home' country to the extent that components produced at lower cost in either intermediate or less developed countries are imported for assembly or incorporation into the product finally exported from the 'home' country itself.

Evidence that British big business has been aware for years of the gains from multinational location was revealed to the House of Commons Expenditure Committee in the early 1970s, where leading companies openly admitted that they could employ labour at a tenth or a twentieth of its UK cost in economies such as Hong Kong, Singapore, Taiwan or South Korea (House of Commons, 1972).

Offsetting Revaluation

Such advantages also became especially apparent to Japanese companies as the yen was revalued during the 1970s. For instance, Ohmae (1985, p. 154) reports that the Japanese Matsushita Electric Industrial company built an advanced world-class compressor plant in Singapore, comparable to their Japanese facility, with an annual throughput of 3 million units. This plant was aimed not only at the South East Asian market, but also at the Middle East, Europe and the United States. Since it had the advantages of (i) low-cost labour combined with (ii) advanced 'state of the art' production technology plus (iii) economies of scale, Ohmae comments that 'it was an easy victory for Matsushita to use this plant to penetrate the traditionally very difficult US market. Today Matsushita sells over 30 per cent of low-end compressors consumed in the United States for refrigerators.' He also cites another Matsushita success story based on a similar strategy for its air-conditioner plant in the Selangor district of Malaysia. Here again the company built a state-of-the-art production plant comparable to its main factory in Japan. But with access to labour at one tenth of the Japanese rate – despite a Malaysian productivity rate half that of Japan – the company was able to produce air conditioners at significantly lower cost in Malaysia.

Matsushita Electric Industrial is not exactly a household name in Europe or the United States. However, it is world famous for its brand name National in Japan, Asia and Europe, and Panasonic in the United States. Having taken over Motorola's television division in the United States, it now has a further brand name Quasar. On top of this, it has introduced the Technics brand at the top end of its audiophonic line. Without irony, the initials of Matsushita's other subsidiary company JVC stand for Japan Victor Company.

Certainly Matsushita combines both the old and the new in models of the firm and industry. Its product differentiation through different brand names (familiar in the theory of 'imperfect' competition since the 1930's) is now combined with a multinational scope and scale for exploiting precisely the combination of advanced technology, scale economies and low-cost labour which have recently confounded conventional models of trade and investment based on the Ricardian theory of international division of labour.

A stylised example of the production, location and export sequence of a hypothetical Japanese multinational, comparable to the sequence for Matsushita, is given in Figure 5.7. This indicates that from the newly industrialising country of Malaysia it exports to the intermediate countries of South East Asia (IMC^1) and the Middle East (IMC^2), as well as to the more developed countries of Europe (MDC^1) and the United States (MDC^2). Three points are worth noting from this production, location and export sequence. First, the location of the production plant is outside the home country of Japan. Second, the least developed countries of the global economy are excluded. Third, the scope and scale of such trade and transfers make possible a range of discriminating pricing procedures whose consequences are significant for the transfers of payments and technology within the global economy, as analysed in some detail in the following chapter. Certainly, the scale of the cost advantage open to a company such as Matsushita from its Malaysian location gives credence to the offsetting of revaluation through lower cost schedules illustrated in Figures 5.6(a) and (b) in the context of multinational trade, with the key difference that the lower long-run average cost schedules (LAC^2 in Figure 5.6(b)) are considerably more dramatic in the case of location by multinationals in developing countries.

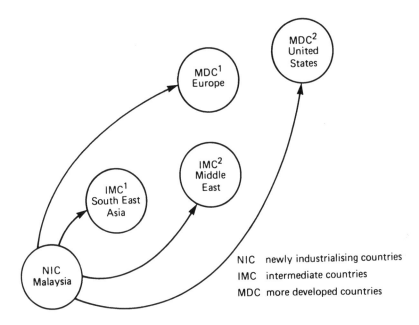

FIG. 5.7   Foreign production and export sequence: Japanese multinational company

Capacity Use

Besides the foregoing argument, there is evidence from empirical study and direct investigation that leading multinational companies discount exchange-rate changes on the basis that response to revaluation or devaluation in the countries where subsidiaries and their plant is located poses major problems for the optimal use of production capacity. Evidence on this has been cited by Christopher Tugendhat – at the time a journalist on the *Financial Times*, subsequently a Conservative MP and EEC Commissioner.

Tugendhat cites in particular the case of the Swedish ball-bearing company SKF (Tugendhat, 1971). He does so without formalisation of the argument, or generalisation in diagrammatic terms. Yet such representation further illustrates the qualification of exchange-rate changes by multinational companies.

For instance, in Figure 5.8 a hypothetical company called Scandinavska MNC, apart from producing in Sweden, produces through subsidiaries in

Germany and the United Kingdom respectively. The cost schedules of its plant in the two countries is assumed to be identical. It is also assumed that the plant in both countries are initially producing at full capacity, and that there is a unitary or 1:1 price elasticity of demand for exports (so that an increase or decrease of 20 per cent in export prices give rise to an identical increase or decrease in demand).

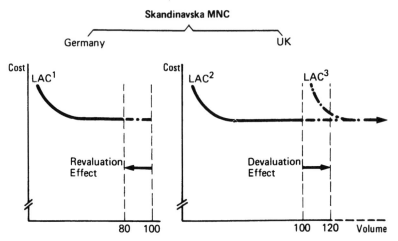

FIG. 5.8 Capacity utilisation versus exchange-rate response of a Scandinavian multinational company

In the case of the company's German subsidiary, a DM revaluation of 20 per cent, if followed through by an identical rise in the export price of the German subsidiary, would effectively wipe out its profits, granted a break-even point at 80 per cent of capacity use, and a 20 per cent fall in export demand. Conversely, if the exports of the UK subsidiary following a sterling devaluation of 20 per cent could be increased by a fifth, this would necessitate new investment in additional plant capacity in the United Kingdom.

Versus Exchange-Rate Changes

In other words, if Scandinavska MNC responded to the DM revaluation and sterling devaluation it would reduce production in Germany and increase it in the United Kingdom, thereby underemploying its German capacity while overemploying capacity in the UK.

If it were in fact to respond to the devaluation of the pound by increasing capacity in the UK, and even assuming that this addition to capacity was on the basis of the same technology and capital/labour ratios as previous investment, as represented in Figure 5.8 by the cost curve LAC^3, Scandinavska MNC would end with a spare capacity in the United Kingdom equivalent to 80 per cent of the new and additional plant. If it embodied later technology and productivity gains than those available when the initial plant were built in both Germany and Britain, it could thereby end with even greater spare capacity and proportionate loss due to the greater capital commitment implied by such technology and productivity increases.

Such representation gives force to the reasoning made by Tugendhat that a company such as SKF in reality ignores devaluations and revaluations in the short to medium term. A multinational company may well take account of the trend to revaluation and devaluation of a currency over the long term, and seek to discount this in its global location strategy.

Alternatively, a multinational company can operate most plant at full capacity for most of the time, while retaining a 'reserve plant' in one country to absorb spare capacity if international demand permits. It may also take advantage of short-term redundancy payments paid by the state in individual countries to run a given plant at full capacity, then shut it down entirely for several months in order to avoid the additional costs of spare capacity. This is illustrated by the case of Ford, which runs plants such as Genk in Belgium flat out for extended periods, thus achieving high levels of efficiency, followed by virtual shutdown during which the state pays the workforce a high proportion of its average earnings. Ford has also run its Dagenham plant in the UK below full capacity for long periods, playing the role of a 'buffer' plant, whose output is used to meet the fluctuating residual demand which is left after the output of the other plants has been absorbed (GLC, 1986, p. 13).

Certainly, as already observed in the context of domestic economic policy, mesoeconomic companies with an investment-planning schedule longer than the lifetimes of governments cannot be relied on to commit long-term investment in response to short-term fiscal and monetary changes by finance ministers. Multinational companies cannot afford to respond in their investment and production decisions to short- or medium-term exchange-rate changes if these impose losses which outweigh net benefits for their global operations in the long-run.

This argument obtains despite the fact that SKF, for example, is not only a dominant company on the Swedish domestic market, but is also a global major in the production of ball-bearings and related products. While monopoly or duopoly may be a game played for real by some multinational companies worldwide, even monopolists cannot escape the role of capacity utilisation in global profits.

5.6 Summary

(1) According to conventional exchange-rate theory (still formulated within the Ricardian paradigm of international trade between different firms in different countries), the appreciation, revaluation or rise in the value of a national currency should make the exports from that economy more expensive. Inversely the devaluation, depreciation or fall in the value of that currency should make possible lower prices for exports from that economy.

(2) Such conventional theory allows for different responses by firms to the appreciation and depreciation of domestic currencies whereby either (a) firms may offensively lower prices in foreign markets following depreciation with aggressive strategies aimed to increase foreign market share and export volume or (b) defensively absorb the higher profit possible following depreciation without lowering foreign prices or increasing export volume.

(3) Conventional exchange-rate theory rarely follows such export-led growth potential from depreciation or devaluation through to the dynamic implications for the costs of production and supply in the domestic market economy. In practice, as illustrated in Japan, today's successful exporters are tomorrow's dominant firms on both domestic and foreign markets.

(4) Multinational investment and production in different countries profoundly qualifies conventional international devaluation or depreciation theory. Thus a company producing in both the British and West German markets will not follow through a devaluation of sterling relative to the Deutschmark with lower export prices from its British subsidiary, since in so doing it would be 'competing against itself' by forcing a price reduction for its subsidiary on the West Germany market.

(5) Given the overwhelming share of multinational companies in US and UK visible export trade, such an 'own competitor' effect in large part explains the limited export volume response of US and UK manufacturers to the devaluation or depreciation of sterling and the dollar over the postwar period. This has had critical implications for global finance because of the role of sterling and the dollar as the second and first reserve currencies of the global financial system.

(6) While national microeconomic firms within the Ricardian paradigm could in principle follow depreciation or devaluation of a currency with lower export prices, such aggressive pricing is obstructed in the first place by 'no-entry' pricing by established business abroad or by

the more extreme 'elimination' pricing variant. Inversely, such micro firms tend classically to be 'price-takers' rather than 'price-makers' on import trade. As a result, in such economies, devaluation or depreciation may register insignificant effects on export prices and volume, while inflating imports and the domestic price level.

(7) In conventional theory the dynamic effects of revaluation or appreciation of a currency are assumed to be the reverse of those for devaluation. In other words, with a rise in value or price of the domestic currency, it is assumed that export revenue will fall overall as international competitiveness is lost through higher prices charged on foreign markets. In practice, however, this has not been the case for either West Germany or Japan following appreciation of the Deutschmark and Yen since the 1960s. Both countries have tended to generate major structural surpluses in international trade.

(8) One reason for such structural surpluses lies in the extent to which successive rounds of innovating investment 'warranted' by export success can reduce unit production costs and thereby offset the higher nominal export price implied by revaluation of the domestic currency. Such quantity effects in cost reduction from new rounds of investment are complemented by quality effects, as successful exporters advance the 'innovation frontier' for products, production processes or services in the global economy as a whole.

(9) The global division of investment and production by multinational companies implicit in product-cycle theory is now undertaken as part of a simultaneous production and export strategy by leading multinational companies, rather than the three-stage pattern of domestic production and export trade followed by direct investment, as assumed in the original Vernon product-cycle model.

(10) The imperative for multinational companies of optimal capacity use of different plant in different countries now offsets the effectiveness of both devaluation/depreciation and revaluation/appreciation as primary instruments of international trade adjustment in the global economy. Successful export trade in manufactures depends increasingly on effective intervention through industrial policy on the structure of export trade.

6 Transfers and Technologies

Conventional trade theory views international payments and transfers as essentially macroeconomic. Kindleberger allows that 'the view of international economics as relating to economic relations between national units ... should not altogether neglect the valuable insights afforded into the changing character of the individual units themselves' (Kindleberger, 1963, p. 11). But in his analysis of international transfers and payments, there is virtually no disaggregation down to the level of individual firms.

6.1 Transfer Payments and Pricing

Kindleberger distinguishes four major categories in the balance of payments: (1) the current account; (2) the capital account; (3) the gold account; and (4) errors and omissions.

A new fifth item should be added to these categories: i.e. (5) transfer payments on trade between the subsidiaries of multinational companies. Such payments are transacted through the transfer-pricing mechanism analysed extensively in this chapter. *Inter alia*, registration of such prices worldwide in published trade figures would illuminate Kindleberger's fourth category of 'errors and omissions', since these transfer payments are not fully represented in national accounts, nor do they necessarily 'come out in the wash' at the global economy level.

Unrecorded and Under-Recorded

This is indicated by the world's global accounting error. In 1983 the difference between registered exports and imports for all the world's economies totalled some $100 billion. This was equivalent to the gross domestic product of the thirty least developed countries in the world in the same year, excluding only India and China (World Bank, 1985). Such a global deficit is purely fictitious in the sense that the world does not yet trade with Mars or the Moon, and in principle all countries' exports should equal all their imports. In practice it arises from a combination of (i) unrecorded exports which have not been registered at all, and (ii) under-recorded or under-invoiced exports which have been stated at below their real market value or prevailing open-market equivalents.

The simple non-recording of exports is widespread partly because governments tax imports rather than exports and non-recording therefore carries few penalties. In the 1960s a major disparity was found by an Iranian customs official between published UK exports to Iran and actual Iranian imports from the UK. This led to a review of the degree of non-recording of exports by British firms, which in turn led to two revisions of the UK balance of payments. As already indicated in Chapter 5, this found that the UK balance of payments had been in surplus in 1964 when the incoming Labour government – working from official figures – reckoned that it was in major deficit. It also found that the UK had possibly been in a small surplus in 1967 when, under sustained pressure reflecting a major registered deficit, the government devalued the pound and thus in a real sense removed the last barrier against dollar devaluation in 1971.

Macroeconomic Effects

Thus such issues as the under-recording of exports (or inversely the over-recording of imports – as shown below) are not simply a technical accounting matter. They affect the fate of leading governments and the world's leading currencies. In turn, government failure to account for activities of multinationals means that transfer payments and pricing by the subsidiaries of multinational companies can seriously inhibit global spending and trade. Put simply, many governments think that 'their' firms are earning less in foreign markets than in fact they are, and therefore reduce public spending or domestic demand levels below their actual potential.

A schedule of the ways in which multinational companies and transfer pricing affect the macroeconomy should include the following:

(1) *under-recorded* exports in subsidiary trade through under-invoicing, reducing the registered value of exports in national accounts;
(2) *over-recording* or over-invoicing of imports in subsidiary trade, which inflates the value of registered imports in national accounts;
(3) *balance-of-payments* effects, which can be especially severe for less developed countries through understating exports and for developed countries through overstating imports;
(4) *inflation*, in the sense both of a direct inflation impact on the value of registered imports and also the indirect means this gives to multinationals to charge higher prices on the domestic market of the economy to which the good (or service) has been imported;

(5) *tax avoidance*, when multinational companies understate declared profits by overstating the import value of components, commodities or services;

(6) *public expenditure* effects, both directly through reducing tax revenue to national treasuries, and indirectly where deflationary polices are imposed through 'fictitious' balance-of-payments crises;

(7) *currency speculation*, through the leading and lagging of payments whereby, in order to profit from the anticipated devaluation or revaluation of a currency, multinational companies can speed up subsidiary imports (pre-devaluation) or hold them back (pre-revaluation) thus worsening or improving the country's balance of payments and in turn exerting self-fulfilling pressure for devaluation or revaluation;

(8) *exchange-control avoidance* through over-invoicing imports from subsidiaries abroad in such a way as to transfer funds out of the country on the trade rather than the capital account;

(9) *evading tariffs* by understating the real value of imports on inter-subsidiary trade (an effect countering the more normal trend to tax minimisation by overstating imports, but mainly relevant to less developed countries granted the low level of nominal tariffs in most developed countries);

(10) *social and political effects*, either in dramatic cases such as the destabilisation of the Allende government in Chile, or in more mundane cases such as those anticipated by Keynes, who warned of the effects on 'confidence' of the election of a Labour government in Britain or a New Deal Democratic administration in the United States.

National and Multinational

It should be noted that several of the above effects of transfer pricing can and do occur at national level between subsidiaries and production divisions or through a range of components *traded within the same company in one country*. In particular, through the same basic principle of under and over-invoicing for components or inputs traded within the circuits of a multi-product, multi-market or multi-divisional company, profits are understated or minimised for tax-reduction or tax-loss purposes. As with multinational transfers, this lowers government tax receipts and public expenditure potential, or prompts actual public-spending cuts. Nonetheless, it is in transactions between subsidiaries of multinational companies operating in different countries that transfer-pricing techniques achieve their full scope and scale.

It should also be stressed that there are several main ways for multi-subsidiary and multinational companies to transfer funds across accounts and across international exchanges. One method is through the price set on subsidiary trade (which is analysed in this part of this chapter). Another is to charge interest on borrowings between subsidiaries of the same bank or company which is operated in such a way as to qualify the classic function of shifting savings into investment. (This is described in part 6.2 of this chapter.) A third main means of transferring funds is through the direct or indirect charging of fees or royalties. Relating to the issue of patents, this especially concerns technology transfers (analysed in part 6.3 of this chapter).

As Brooke and Remmers put it, in one of the earlier pioneering monographs on transfer pricing (1970, p. 161):

> One might argue whether these means – royalties, interest and trade – should properly be considered a remittance of earnings for, in principle, they constitute payments for specific services or goods received by the subsidiary. But since many of these have no easily determined market value, companies have considerable latitude to charge the subsidiaries more (or less) than the fair arm's length value of the contribution. Indeed, since they are a before-tax charge against profits and often not subject to withholding tax, some companies have ample incentive to substitute these returns for dividends. Moreover, in some instances they may be easier to remit than dividends.

Familiar for decades in the seminars of business schools and to senior managers, such transfer payments are still unmentioned in many if not most of the basic introductory texts on international trade. It is more than time for the record to be redressed.

International Trade

Starting from the basics, transfer pricing can be analysed and understood as follows. Figure 6.1 gives an elementary representation of the conventional international trade model of the export and import process between different companies in the different countries. In the case cited, these countries are the United States and the United Kingdom respectively, with $200 being assumed equivalent to £100. The real cost of the American exporter is assumed to amount to $80. In most international trade theory and in trade accounting it is assumed that export goods are priced *fob* or 'free on board' the export vessel, or at least *fas*, i.e. 'free along side' the export vehicle whether this is a ship or plane. In our example it is assumed that the exporter includes a nominal mark-up or profit on the good. The cost of the good to the UK importer would be the sterling equivalent of $80, i.e. in our example £40. It is also assumed that the UK importer is bringing in an intermediate rather than a final good which will then be used as an input for a final product in the UK. Assuming further, for clarity of exposition, that the relative values which the

American and British companies add in production are identical, then the price of the final product as sold by the UK importer/producer amounts to £80.

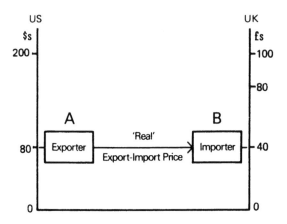

FIG. 6.1   'Real' export-import pricing in international trade

Normal or Cost-Plus Pricing

The normal cost-plus pricing schedules of different companies in their internationally traded prices are made more explicit in Figures 6.2(a) and (b). Figure 6.2(a) represents the long-run average cost curve of the US company at $60 per unit, and assumes that its profit is $20, giving both a final US domestic price and a 'real export price' of $80. In Figure 6.2(b), the obverse of this real export price is represented by the 'real import price', p^1, of the UK company, which translates into sterling terms at £40. Assuming that the cost price of the imported raw material or components is equivalent to two-thirds of the UK firm's long-run average costs (not unrealistic in terms of the previously cited evidence on the ratio of imported components by US automobile manufacturers in the UK to the value-price of their final product), the unit long-run average cost of the UK firm is £60. Again assuming the same relative profit and cost-plus price mark-up as for the US firm, the price on the UK market of the final product, represented by the line p^2, amounts to £80.

Transfer Pricing

In contrast with this example of transparent probity in international trade, Figure 6.3 represents a situation of transfer pricing between subsidiaries of the same multinational company in the United States and the United

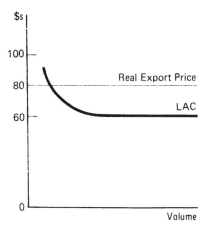

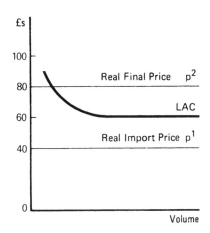

Fig 6.2(a) Real cost and export price: Fig 6.2(b) Real cost and import price:
US firm   UK firm

Kingdom. With a domestic cost in the US of $60 and a profit mark-up of $20 to a US domestic price of $80, the exporting subsidiary of the multinational company understates the value of the export by half in a transfer price which is registered in a tax-haven subsidiary of the company (such as the Bahamas). While the 'real' export-import price of the international transaction as represented by the broken horizontal line is equivalent to $80 and £40, the multinational company inflates the price of the transaction at the stage of its tax-haven subsidiary and re-exports the product to its subsidiary in the United Kingdom at the transfer price of £80. In other words the multinational company is now importing the good to the United Kingdom at a price

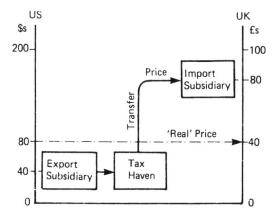

Fig 6.3 Basic transfer-pricing model

equivalent to double what would be charged for its import by an independent
UK company in international rather than multinational trade.

Nominal versus Real Prices

Such differences between international and multinational trade and payments may be clarified by the examples given in Figures 6.4(a) and (b). Figure
6.4(a) is identical to that for the international export model set out in Figure
6.2(a), with the crucial addition of the export transfer price at $40, on the line
tp^1, in contrast with the 'real export price' level of $80 given by the line p^1.
The counterpart transfer import cost comes in Figure 6.4(b). Here, in contrast
with the international trade and production assumptions in Figure 6.2(b),
where the product or raw material was imported into the United Kingdom at
the 'real import price' of £40, it is now imported by the UK subsidiary via the
tax-haven subsidiary at the import transfer price tp^2, which is £80.

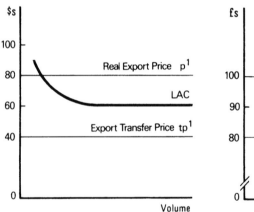 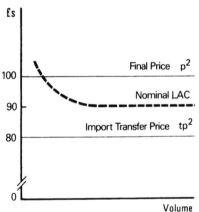

FIG. 6.4(a)   The export transfer price   FIG. 6.4(b)   The import transfer price

In turn this affects the nominal cost schedule of the UK subsidiary. While its
real cost level as shown in Figure 6.2(b) would give an LAC of £60, the
increase in the import cost of its components or raw materials through
transfer pricing from p^1 to p^2 makes it possible for the subsidiary to raise its
apparent or nominal LAC (or in practice its fictitious cost level for tax
purposes) from £60 to £90. As a result, the multinational company and its
British subsidiary can declare a lower rate of profit (11.1 per cent) than the
earlier example of an international British company importing from the
United States (33.3 per cent), while making higher real profits and charging a

price on the domestic UK market which is 25 per cent higher than would otherwise have been the case. *

Price-Makers and Price-Takers

Such transfer pricing is open to most major companies able to undertake direct operations in more than one country. Smaller multinational companies in the microeconomic sector will be less able to assure over-invoiced import prices or inflated final prices to the markets of individual economies than large multinationals in the mesoeconomic sector. This follows from factors analysed in detail in *The Market Economy* (Holland, 1987) and in previous chapters which examined the price-making power of large mesoeconomic enterprise dominant in individual markets, versus the price-taking response of smaller microeconomic enterprises which are not dominant. Where micro firms in the multinational sector are able to take advantage of transfer pricing on a major scale, this will tend to be because of the 'umbrella pricing' effect where the price level has been set by grace and favour of mesoeconomic leaders.

The relevance of the mesoeconomic concept in relation to transfer pricing by multinational companies becomes most explicit when we consider three key macroeconomic consequences. These include an increase in the registered value of imports, the tax-loss effect through the understatement of profits, and an inflation of the domestic price level.

Inflation, Trade and Tax

The effect of increasing the value of registered imports through transfer pricing, in this case as before in the UK economy, is illustrated in Figure 6.5. The mechanism, already implied in the earlier example, is essentially quite simple. Whereas under conditions of international trade between different US and UK companies, the registered import price reflecting a real import price would have amounted to £40, the value of the registered import through transfer pricing now amounts to £80.

This deterioration of the import bill – equivalent to a doubling of the real import price – is not unduly exaggerated. As shown later in this chapter, a series of studies on transfer pricing in Europe and Latin America, plus evidence revealed through government hearings and OECD and IMF enquiries, shows that such an increase in the registered value of imports may be moderate in comparison with reality.

---

* Multinational companies can transfer price between subsidiaries without recourse to tax havens. But such transfers reduce the opaque nature of profit and capital transfer, and increase the transparency of such operations to the tax authorities.

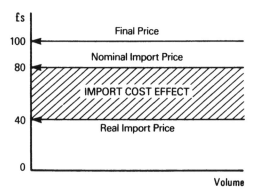

FIG. 6.5   The import-cost effects of transfer pricing

The tax-loss effects of transfer pricing through the under-invoicing of exports are illustrated in Figure 6.6(a). Maintaining the same values as previous examples, this shows a real long-run average cost curve of $60 per unit and a real price level, p^1, of $80. In this sense, following standard analysis, the real profit of the US company on the product concerned would be represented by the area between LAC^1 and p^1, or $20 per unit. Assuming a 50 per cent company or corporation tax, the US government on the basis of declared profits in international trade could expect to receive a tax revenue equivalent to the shaded area abc, or $10 per unit. However, the determination of a transfer price p^2 for the product, exported to the UK subsidiary of the company via a tax haven, effectively wipes out the declared profit on the

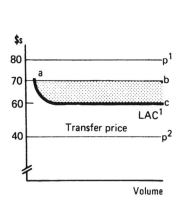

FIG. 6.6(a)   Tax loss through under-invoiced exports

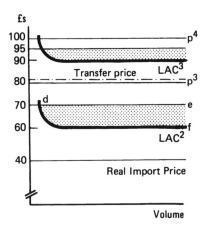

FIG. 6.6(b)   Tax loss through over-invoiced imports

transaction, and substitutes a nominal loss of 33.3 per cent. In practice, with the convention that losses can be offset against profits, the US company not only can avoid paying any tax at all on the profit it has made, but can write off the declared loss so as to further understate its overall tax liability.

Figure 6.6(b), again maintaining our earlier cost ratios, shows that the real import price of the component or raw material for final production in the UK would be £40, and the real long-run average cost (LAC^2) of the UK company would be £60. Allowing for the former cost-plus profit mark-up to a real final price level also at £80, and assuming again a corporation tax of 50 per cent on final profits, the UK government would be entitled to a tax revenue equivalent to the area *def*, or £10 per unit of production. However, with a transfer import price represented by the broken line p^3, the UK subsidiary of a multinational company can declare a nominal long-run average cost of £90 equivalent to LAC^3, and charge a final UK price of £100 at p^4. Thus the subsidiary of the multinational company in the United Kingdom is able to declare a profit of £10 per unit on a higher declared cost for the product. On the continued assumption of a 50 per cent corporation tax, it will pay a tax of only £5 per unit. In other words, through transfer pricing the UK subsidiary of the multinational is able to declare profits and pay tax at only half the real rate.

Avoidance versus Evasion

Such tax avoidance by multinational companies can be considerable. For instance, Mobil Oil paid only $1,900 in taxes over three years in the 1970s on sales in the State of Vermont which alone amounted to $27 million. After a court ruling, the State of Vermont picked up only an extra $76,000 in tax. Exxon paid no tax at all for four years in Wisconsin, and in a dispute with the State of Wisconsin claimed that it had lost around $4 million on sales of $60 million. Its final tax liability, even after an extended court case, amounted to only $316,000 (*The Economist*, 20 June 1981). Similarly, in part due to transfer pricing, but also due to the scale of tax rebates allowed by the UK government, Kay and King (1978, p. 199) show that against pre-tax profits of £4,323 million in 1976, the 20 leading UK industrial companies in the following year paid a combined total of only £145 million in tax. Twelve of the top 20 companies – including British Petroleum, Rio Tinto Zinc, Esso, Courtaulds, Grand Metropolitan, P & O, GKN, Dunlop, Reed International, Bowater, British Leyland and Ford – paid no tax at all. A major share of the tax under-payment by the UK companies was due directly to government write-offs made for other reasons (including tax relief on stock appreciation). But these companies also have major scope for the under-statement of initial tax liability through transfer pricing.

So far, such tax avoidance through transfer pricing is perfectly legal in many countries. It is also hard to challenge as long as national governments both give generous tax write-offs to multinational companies and continue to treat declared import values by multinational companies at face value in the same way as they treat those for national firms. For most governments, an import is still an import if priced, packaged and charged, whether it comes from a foreign national firm or from the subsidiary of a multinational. Even the implied or 'fictitious' cost schedule of the multinational company in the UK in Figure 6.6(b) can be justified on the present 'rules of the game' provided that the inflated transfer price for the import from the US subsidiary is recognised as legal.

Some tax authorities in some countries are beginning to catch up with bench-marks or profit and loss criteria drawn not only from concepts of a 'normal' profit, but also those available from the lowest prices charged on a least-cost basis by some companies in international trade (see further *The Economist*, 20 June 1981). But progress has been slow and dependent so far on bilateral rather than multilateral government co-operation.

Follow-the-Leader

When one or more multinational companies begin to transfer price on a major scale, a 'follow the leader' effect occurs. Neither major (meso) nor minor (micro) companies in the multinational sector can stand idly by and afford to see their competitors on a global scale increase retained earnings for a further round of investment and product innovation financed in large part through the mechanism of avoiding tax on real profits made. Subjective management preferences for 'doing one's bit for the nation' or 'pulling one's weight' on the tax burden quickly wilt before the pressure to follow suit with tax avoidance.

Thus once transfer pricing has been started by a particular 'market leader', the practice will tend to spread throughout the sector or market concerned. Aggregated through from this level to the national level, it can clearly be seen that such practices can register a very significant macroeconomic tax loss for the economy as a whole. Multiplied through to the global economy, as already indicated at the outset of this chapter, the effects can be astronomic.

Clearly companies can transfer price on certain products but not on others. Alternatively, they can transfer price on a range of products at certain staging posts in international foreign transactions. As illustrated in Figure 6.7, the transfer-pricing sequence in a product may well range between a couple of less developed countries (LDC^1 and LDC^2), an intermediate country (IMC) and a more developed country (MDC). The transfer pricing, employing tax havens TH^1 and TH^2, may occur only in the transactions between the first three countries. Therefore the final transfer between the intermediate country and the more developed country may well be 'clean'.

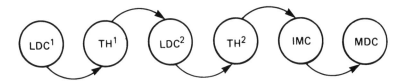

FIG. 6.7   Tax havens and transfer pricing

Complex Transfers

Such a sequence is still simple in relation to the range of products and countries in which multinational companies can transfer price with relative impunity under contemporary conditions of trade and payments accounting by governments. For example, Figure 6.8 shows a situation of nine countries and ten transfer stages in production and intra-company trade by a multinational company on a global scale.

The left-hand cluster of less developed countries (LDC^{1-4}) are each assumed to be producing a different component which is then traded by each subsidiary to the first major tax haven (TH^1). This tax-haven subsidiary of the multinational then registers the transfer prices for the products concerned direct to the more developed country (MDC). Simultaneously, four other components of the final product are being produced in intermediate countries (IMC^{1-4}), with the registered value of the transferred goods in trade declared in another tax haven (TH^2). The transactions from this are again sent through to the more developed country through transfer pricing. On the import side for the more developed country of destination, two tax havens will be registering eight declarations for the eight subsidiaries in the less developed and intermediate countries concerned in the respective stages of production. Clearly, for various components, the complexity of Figure 6.8 can be

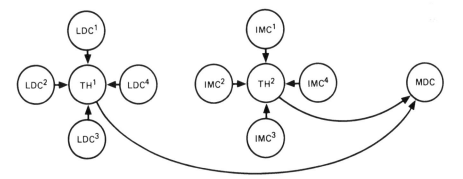

FIG. 6.8   Multinational location, production and transfer pricing

multiplied several times. This does not mean to say that the transfer-pricing phenomenon cannot be opened up and made transparent by governments. But at a minimum this would mean that governments would have to take measures to oblige multinational companies to break down their trade with subsidiaries on a systematic basis, comparable with conventional national income and expenditure categories (Holland, 1987, chapter 9).

The Inflation Effect

The inflation effects from transfer pricing are implicit in the previous examples. In terms of Figure 6.9, because of an inflation in the cost of the imported good from £40 to £80 through transfer pricing, the lower real price which could be achieved on the UK market of £80 is inflated to a final price of £100.

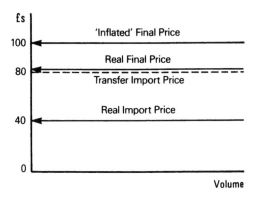

FIG. 6.9   Over-invoicing, imports and inflation

This qualifies one of the most basic principles of the division of labour in international trade theory, i.e. that imported goods can be cheaper than the least-cost domestic production. Such a qualification is represented in Figure 6.10, where on the left-hand side of the diagram the export/import price under international trade (p^1), reflecting normal profit on the exporter's long-run average cost curve, is lower than the domestic price (p^2) on the right-hand side of the diagram achievable by a domestic producer in the importing country for a comparable good, assuming a higher long-run average cost curve for the domestic producer and a similar normal profit.

If, however, under conditions of multinational trade, the transfer import price at a level p^3 is equivalent to the prevailing domestic price in the importing country, there is no net gain in price terms from the foreign import, while a negative impact is registered on the balance of payments. Moreover, if the multinational company through transfer pricing inflates the registered import price to the level of p^4, this will also have a net inflationary effect relative to substitutable domestic goods.

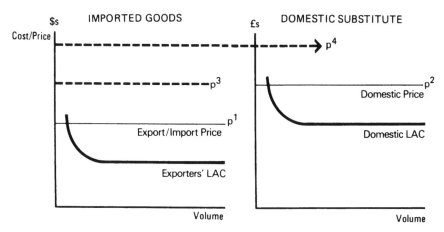

FIG. 6.10 Comparative costs, transfer prices and domestic inflation

Cumulative Effects

Neither the p^3 or p^4 price levels are entirely unrealistic under conditions of unequal competition between big and small business in the global economy. Whereas a microeconomic company in the multinational sector would not have the muscle or size to impose prices, nor be able to exert an upwards price leadership, a large multinational company typical of the mesoeconomic sector can do both. Therefore, provided that its market share is sizeable, there is no reason why it should not lead prices upwards to the p^4 level. As a consequence the inflated transfer price would not only damage the country's balance of payments but would also result in an upward shift in the macroeconomic price level.

Moreover, as illustrated in Figure 6.11, it is clear that a multinational company, taking advantage of the division of capital on a global scale in a plurality of subsidiary companies, can inflate the price of its product on a cumulative scale between several countries (illustrated by the respective differences between prices p^1 and p^2 in stages I to IV). None of this is familiar from textbook examples of microeconomic theory or the assumptions implicit in conventional models of international trade. Unfortunately it is all too common, on an increasing scale, in the pattern of multinational trade and payments in the world today.

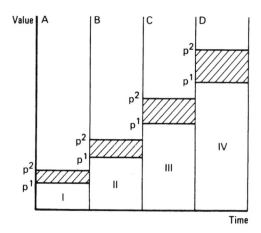

FIG. 6.11   Transfer pricing and cumulative inflation

6.2 Evidence and Evaluation

Such analysis does not mean that all multinational companies transfer price hand over fist on all products all of the time. To do so might attract the attention of tax authorities, government ministers, or – with some relevance for the issues of industrial democracy – trades unionists. During the North Sea oil bonanza of the 1970s, a trades unionist in the accounting division of a multinational construction company interrupted this author during a workshop on multinationals by stating that he now understood why the price of major components on oil rigs imported by his company from the United States but assembled in Scotland had increased by several hundred per cent within a few months. The company shortly thereafter told the Labour government that it was heading for a loss, and that the government either would have to subsidise it, or buy a rig off the shelf (despite no short-term demand for it) to keep its interest in assembling in Scotland.

Scope and Scale

However, extensive and less impressionistic evidence on the scale and scope of global transfer pricing by multinational companies is available from a range of sources. The literature on transfer pricing in specialist monographs and articles is now extensive.

Studies of transfer pricing by Lall (1973), Vaitsos (1974) and Roumeliotis (1977) found ranges of under and over-invoicing of up to 300 per cent on 'real' costs, with such costs determined *inter alia* by enquiry and research into the open-market prices of both final products and components.

Otherwise, indications have already been given of the scope for transfer pricing granted that up to 85 per cent of UK and US visible export trade has either been undertaken directly by multinational companies or by inter-subsidiary trade. Analysing US data, Helleiner (1977 and 1981) found that in the late 1970s nearly 50 per cent of all US imports originated with a subsidiary or party related by ownership to the buyer (in other words, a US firm or a subsidiary of a US firm). Of this share, just over half was intra-firm importing by US parent companies from majority-owned affiliates.

In analysing intra-firm or inter-subsidiary trade by multinationals, Little found that this accounted for over 60 per cent of US imports of industrial chemicals and synthetics, non-electrical equipment, and printing and publishing; half of US imports of electronic components and construction-related equipment; a third of US imports of medicines, soaps and cosmetics; and a quarter of fabricated metal products. Similarly, Little determined that from 50 to 80 per cent of US imports from newly industrialised countries such as Singapore and Hong Kong and the Caribbean countries was represented by intra-firm or inter-subsidiary imports by US multinational companies. Also, although such inter-subsidiary transfers have not played a major role in US multinationals' imports from Japan, Germany or the Netherlands, the inter-subsidiary trade of Japanese, German and Dutch affiliates of multi-national companies to the United States in 1977 represented between 40 and 60 per cent of US imports from these three countries (Little, 1986, p. 45). Similarly US Department of Commerce data shows that some 90 per cent of non-bank imports to the US from American multinational companies abroad were from subsidiary affiliates of multinational companies. Such figures amply demonstrate the qualification of Ricardian trade by multinationals.

The Ford Transit Truck

Indirect illustrations of the scope for price manipulation and transaction between subsidiary companies in the automobile sector have been given earlier in this volume. Direct evidence, however, is available from the comparison of different prices charged for identical components by the Ford Motor Company in Southampton and Amsterdam in 1981 (GLC, 1986). As shown in Table 6.1, the average 1981 price in Southampton of a Dagenham-produced engine was just over three-quarters of the average price charged in Amsterdam by the same company in the same year, while the actual price paid on 7 June 1981 in Southampton was just over-two thirds of the actual price paid in Amsterdam. Similar two-thirds ratios are evident on the prices charged on radiators and hubs/drums, and three-quarters for the Amsterdam price charged on front axles.

TABLE 6.1 Transit Diesel: Prices of Identical Components as Charged to Southampton and Amsterdam, 1981

Component	Source	Southampton		Amsterdam	
		Average price 1981	Actual price 7/6/81	Average price 1981	Actual price 7/6/81
Engine	Dagenham	644.35	644.35	785.07	879.58
Radiator	Basildon	19.54	19.54	27.10	32.32
Front Axle	Woolwich	20.71	20.71	24.90	26.74
Hubs R Drum	Leamington	10.74	10.74	15.70	14.95

Source: GLC (1986).

As the GLC Ford Report makes plain, such transfer pricing is not simply a matter of manipulation. Ford managed these transfer prices during a period in which it was pressuring trade unions in the Amsterdam plant to accept a closure, on the grounds that it could not, or would not, make a profit. Despite the claims for local management autonomy and decentralisation, it became evident to the local trade unions concerned that local management had little or no say in the closure decision. In this sense, the overcharging of components to the Amsterdam subsidiary not only understated profits, but imposed a nominal loss. In the words of Henk Voss of the Dutch Metal Workers' Union, to the GLC Ford Report (GLC, 1986, p. 43),

> Ford Netherlands tried to force a bankruptcy. At the end of October 1981 we were in a very bad position. It is very hard and almost impossible to fight against bankruptcy. We had to make the choice between two bad alternatives. The first alternative was to fight on until the bankruptcy with no jobs and no money for the people. Or to change the strategy – give up the fight for the continuation of production and fight for a good social agreement to guarantee the salaries, pensions and various other material rights for the workers.

In practice, after a struggle lasting nearly a year and a half, the Unions, Works Council and the workforce of the factory made the choice for a settlement. The irony was that the social agreement for the closure of the plant was more expensive than the most expensive alternative to continue production.

Pharmaceuticals

It was argued earlier, in illustration of the principles of transfer pricing in

Figure 6.5, that the example given of a transfer price amounting to 40 per cent of the final price was not necessarily exaggerated, but in some cases moderate in comparison with reality.

An illustration from pharmaceuticals should make the point. A UK Monopolies Commission investigation (1973) into the Swiss-based Hoffman La Roche company found that it had been overcharging by at least 40 per cent for Librium and at least 50 per cent for Valium (two of the most popular tranquillisers available through the National Health Service). Table 6.2 reproduces Roche's own submission of its costs and profits to the Monopolies Commission.

TABLE 6.2   Cost and Profit Claims for Librium and Valium by Hoffman La Roche

	Librium		Valium	
	£ per kilo	%	£ per kilo	%
Group cost:				
research*	115	16	308	15
other	214	29	444	23
Group profit	405	55	1,210	62
Average realised price	734	100	1,962	100

Source: Monopolies Commission (1973).
* Including 'research and development in the United Kingdom' (Librium £9 and Valium £24).

The table shows that group profits on Librium were more than half of average price, and on Valium nearly two-thirds. The bulk of this was registered by transfer pricing. With good reason the Monopolies Commission questioned even these figures, observing that 'they are based on allocations largely related to selling prices in 1970 and are therefore simply reflections of the Group's pricing decisions' (Monopolies Commission, 1973, p. 67).

Moreover, such pricing decisions reflected Hoffman La Roche's market dominance world wide. In a memorandum to the EEC Commission in February 1973 Stanley Adams, a manager of Roche, observed that Roche was the largest world producer of bulk vitamins and that:

> With its expanded production all over the world, and the consequent reduction of costs of production, Roche could see a price-fight coming some years ago. Thus Roche first embarked on persuading the smaller producers to close down their production facilities and purchase bulk vitamins from Roche at specially reduced prices. . . . These companies at the same time agreed to sell at the same price as

Roche at all costs. . . . It is clear that Roche has eliminated fair competition; and that where competition could not be eliminated, Roche . . . has distorted competition completely. [Adams, 1984, pp. 21–2.]

Implications

There are several implications from the Hoffman La Roche case. First, there is the issue of the power of the global corporation relative to the publicly responsible individual. Stanley Adams 'blew the whistle' on the company's practices to the Commission of the European Communities, under the provisions of the Rome Treaty concerning abuse of a dominant position. His reward was to be prosecuted under Swiss law and jailed, then faced with the personal tragedy of his wife's suicide as well as financial bankruptcy. It was only years later that the EEC Commission agreed in principle to pay him compensation – although, despite strenuous representations by a range of European politicians, at the time this goes to press such compensation had not been paid.

There also are implications for developing countries in their efforts to counter disease and promote generic drugs programmes. Citing Adams, again:

Multinational companies can act across national frontiers which means that the Third World may find not only that several of its drugs are suspect, or simply unnecessary, but that it may be paying much higher prices for them than it should. . . . Government economists in Colombia were puzzled to find in 1973 that the pharmaceutical companies were very keen to expand their operations, while at the same time they were reporting very low profits. An investigation revealed that the average over-pricing of ingredients by foreign-owned subsidiaries of the drug companies was 155 per cent. Librium, manufactured by Roche, was over-priced by a staggering 6,478 per cent.

With reasoning of a kind familiar to Adam Smith in his *Theory of Moral Sentiments* (1759), Stanley Adams commented that 'in moral terms, this amounts to exploitation . . .' (Adams, 1984, pp. 219–20).

Electronics

Even when governments are concerned to tackle the transfer-pricing problem, the range of goods transferred by multinationals on a global scale can render the registered accounts on trading activity opaque and difficult to penetrate by the civil servants or tax authorities concerned.

Several examples of this have been given in the electronics sector by Edmond Sciberras (1977). Thus, in the semiconductor industry, Plessey admitted that there was someone in corporate management whose job it was to monitor taxation levels internationally, and that it was corporate policy to shift prices between subsidiaries in such a way as to limit duties payable by the company. It was recognised that this could not be overdone without attracting the suspicion of Customs and Excise. However, within this limitation, the company's multinational transfer pricing was undertaken with a view to 'minimising total corporate costs' by minimising tax liability.

Similarly, in the case of a currency devaluation intended by government to offset national balance-of-payments difficulties (through lowering export prices in order to increase export volume), Plessey adopted a policy of international price standardisation amongst subsidiaries which in practice would prevent this. Thus, with inter-subsidiary trade in the semiconductor business in the early 1970s of the order of 40 per cent, a substantial share of sales was excluded from the price competitiveness that the 1967 devaluation was intended to induce. In the case of Ferranti, the policy decision whether to lower or maintain price following devaluation was taken administratively by the firm, depending on its own observation of the market. Thus the increased price competitiveness was not passed on to the market in the form of lower prices. In general, company policy was to maintain local price levels abroad and to reap the benefits of devaluation not in sales terms, but in terms of greater profit in the devaluing country. Similarly in Lucas, the government's intended effect through a currency devaluation was subject to internal company management decision-making rather than purely market forces (Sciberras, 1977, chapter 6). And this was only the smaller-league firms. Similar evidence, confirming the theoretical analysis of the early part of Chapter 5 of this volume, was found by Sciberras across the range of multinational electronics companies.

Global Control

It is implicit in the context of transfer pricing that the decision whether to over- or under-invoice, and whether or not to respond to a devaluation, is taken in terms of the global strategy of the corporation. Sciberras' findings again corroborate this argument for both major and minor firms in the electronics industry. Thus, for instance, Texas Instruments, Motorola and Fairchild entirely excluded their UK subsidiaries from the price decision-making process. Texas Instruments' policy was the most centralised, with multilateral 'fail safe' price ranges set at minima and maxima for each level of management in each national subsidiary, and determined globally from Dallas. The price levels were regularly updated by computer and available to the subsidiaries worldwide by satellite. In addition to this daily monitoring, regular three-monthly meetings of subsidiary management with the parent were designed to push or pull 'deviant' subsidiaries back into line with the global pricing strategy.

Fairchild also followed a centrally determined price-making policy, with every price having to be checked back through 'central marketing' for approval. For Motorola, pricing was a regional management responsibility in the first instance, with the marketing managers for regions in the global economy establishing average selling prices. However, the central semi-conductor divisional management in Phoenix had the final responsibility of ensuring that the overall coordination of worldwide prices was observed by regional management. For ITT, despite the mythology of arm's-length relationships, regional product-line European area management in Brussels ensured that inter-subsidiary price rivalry was prevented (Sciberras, 1977, chapter 7).

In commenting on this author's earlier claims (Holland, 1975) that multinational companies have acted to prevent a lowering of prices in foreign subsidiary markets following devaluation, Sciberras found in the semi-conductor industry that multinationals' competitive strategies do not yield positive effects in terms of export volume and may create a response by the firms of capital outflows which exacerbate the crisis which the government's policy was intended to allay (Sciberras, 1977, chapter 8). In other words, the findings confirm those of Hague, Oakeshott and Strain (1974) that, rather than affecting export volume *for the country*, devaluation mainly affected export profitability *for the company*.

On the wider effects of global corporate control, academic research confirms the brazen claim of Harold Geneen, cited by Anthony Sampson (1973), to the ITT stockholders in 1962, where he boasted that ITT has in its time:

> met and surmounted every device by governments to encourage their own industries and hamper those of foreigners, including taxes, tariffs, quotas, currency restrictions, subsidies, barter arrangements, guarantees, moratoriums, devaluations – yes, and nationalisations.

At almost the same time that Sampson was going to press, the ITT scandal had broken in Washington and revealed that the company had been accused of bribing the Nixon administration to drop an anti-trust suit, and of trying to persuade it to undermine the elections in Chile.

Commodity Trade

The limits to the data on transfer pricing and the changed postwar role of the IMF are both reflected in the fact that until 1965 it was possible to compare declared and adjusted values on transfer pricing because the IMF itself continued to publish accounts of adjustments in its annual *Balance of Payments Yearbook*. This showed that in the 1940s and early 1950s, the value of banana exports from the Central American countries was understated by some 40 per cent by the multinational companies which dominated the export trade of the region.

Transfer pricing by multinationals in copper has been notorious through a range of countries including Chile, Peru, Zaire and Zambia. The copper case also illustrates the relative imbalance in power between a national government and a multinational company. In August 1969 the Zambian government announced its intention of taking a majority interest in all the copper-mining operations in the country, and by January 1970 the government owned 51 per cent of all operating copper mines. But this gave it less than total control over the global distribution of sales, or the prices charged, on copper exports. Mainly because of the lack of local alternative management expertise (it has been estimated that when Zambia gained independence a few years earlier there were less than three dozen qualified graduates in any subject in the country), the government's takeover arrangements included management and marketing contracts to the private multinational companies which formerly owned and managed the mines.

Switching

Two marketing companies were established, based in the tax haven of Zug. While the government contracted to sell its entire planned production of copper, the process was managed by the multinationals through a so-called 'switching' process. As a result, the marketing companies were able to make a 'discount' of between $40 and $70 per tonne. Profits on this (i) were not shared with the nationalised copper company ZIMCO; (ii) were realised in a tax haven rather than paid Zambian tax; and (iii) avoided Zambian exchange controls. As Lamaswala (1980) has observed, the discount 'was pure profit transfer for the operating companies'.

In the case of aluminium, Roumeliotis (1977) found that the percentage of under-invoicing by multinational companies fluctuated between one per cent and nearly 20 per cent according to the different types of aluminium and their different destinations. The weighted average of under-invoicing (for a period between the mid-1960s and mid 1970s) was over 8 per cent. And this assumes that multinationals agree to buy the raw material for aluminium (bauxite) in the first place. In the 1970s the Manley government in Jamaica sought to gain a higher share of the value of the final world market price for aluminium by negotiating arrangements with multinational companies that the bauxite would be processed in Jamaica rather than simply exported for processing abroad. It met a 'blackmail' effect from the multinationals, who threatened to stop buying bauxite from Jamaica.

The Role of Tax Havens

As already indicated in the theoretical examples of the technique of transfer pricing, tax havens play a key role in enabling multinationals to extract profits from global transfer payments. Many such havens are known as 'offshore', following in particular their rise 'offshore' the United States in countries such as the Bahamas or the Cayman Islands. (Some of them in fact are landlocked – such as Switzerland, Lichtenstein or the almost anonymous Zug.)

Such so-called 'offshore' tax havens come in a variety of forms. First there are those such as the Bahamas, Bermuda, the Cayman Islands and New Hebrides, which have virtually no taxes and provide complete tax exemption. Second, there are those which impose taxes but do so at very low rates, such as Lichtenstein, Switzerland, the British Vrigin Islands, and Gibraltar. Third, there are havens which tax income from domestic sources but exempt income from foreign sources, such as Hong Kong, Liberia and Panama. Fourth, there are those which allow special tax incentives and privileges for certain types of holding companies, including Luxembourg and the Netherlands Antilles. Fifth and finally, there are those countries which within limited areas allow exemptions and privileges for certain types of activity, such as the free-trade airport zone at Shannon in Ireland (Murray, 1981, chapter 16).

Offshore Banking

The growth of offshore tax havens has been closely related to the growth of 'offshore' banks. This has resulted in some bizarre outcomes. For instance, by 1983 more than 300 of the top 500 US corporations had subsidiaries in the Bahamas (Clairmonte and Cavanagh, 1984). This was matched by nearly 300 subsidiaries of financial institutions or banks, or one bank for every 800 residents – some twenty times the ratio for the United States. The Bahamas is the archetype of tax havens, having no income tax, no corporation tax, no inheritance tax, no estate duty, and no capital gains tax or withholding tax.

Major companies can use such havens to avoid, if not evade, tax. As was well put by *The Economist* (20 June 1981): 'in one instance, according to the [US] internal revenue service, an American company bought domestic oil and sold it to a tax haven company, which the American company claimed was not an affiliate. The oil was sold through a number of different companies, and then the same oil was bought by a foreign subsidiary of the American parent and eventually got back into America through a string of third parties.

The initial sale by the American company to the tax haven operation was at a low (controlled) price. The oil was eventually sold back into America at the higher world price. The big mark-up was left offshore.'

A specific illustration of offshore lending in the debt crisis of three Latin American countries has been given in the case of Peru by Robert Devlin (1981). In the 1960s commercial banks were still restrictive lenders to Peru. However, the total number of commercial private lenders rose more than fivefold from under 30 to nearly 170 in the 1970s, although a few major lenders accounted for almost all the lending in absolute terms. Given the large volume of credit thereby extended to Peru at this time, most commercial banks sought offshore finance, in particular US banks which faced domestic capital controls. As Devlin puts it:

> While headquarters still remained the main source of loans (47% of all credit), London, the Bahamas, Luxembourg and other offshore centres became important points of funding and booking of loans. Another reason for sourcing loans abroad; especially in tax havens like the Bahamas, was to enhance income through foreign transactions.

Global Trends

Such offshore banking operations reflect the liberalisation of trade and payments which has been encouraged by many economists, and by the US administration, since the later 1950s. While no one factor can be singled out to explain the offshore market evolution, Sarah Bartlett (1981) has stressed a combination of the following factors:

(i) In the 1950s the Soviet bloc transferred most of its dollar accounts abroad,

(ii) Specific national legislation on credit-expansion interest levels hampered banking operations and led to a greater expansion of branches abroad;

(iii) Large US balance-of-payments deficits resulted in an increasing volume of dollars being held in other nations' central banks, which were re-lent elsewhere abroad;

(iv) With the growth of world trade and increasing internationalisation of production, multinational companies expanded their 'global reach' and multinational banks followed their corporate clients abroad, thereby providing a parallel structure of financial services for the foreign expansion of non-banking enterprise;

(v) The placing of OPEC petrodollar surpluses with US multinational banks led them to assume a recycling operation of mammoth proportions in the 1970s.

Transfer Booking

Despite their attraction for upwardly mobile executives, and the chance to spend some time on the beach, the branches of multinational banks in tax havens such as the Bahamas or the Cayman Islands tend to be 'shell' branches with a brass plate business address rather than substantial operations. They nonetheless offer extensive facilities to the global operations of both major and minor multinational companies.

One of the most basic schemes, known as 'booking', amounts to the following. A big or small bank can place the loans on its books in the Bahamas in order to minimise tax liabilities. In the US case this is because the government allows banks to earn tax credits from areas where they have had to pay a higher level of tax to a foreign government than they would to the US government. Such credits are wasted unless the banks can levy them against the normal level of US taxes on a low-tax area. In the UK case, when the British government in 1975 increased its tax on bank earnings to 52 per cent (in comparison with the standard 48 per cent in the United States), multinational banks could use the 4 per cent tax credit against their Nassau (Bahamas) branches' earnings, to increase the attractiveness of those earnings worldwide.

Bartlett (1981) cites the potential scale of this kind of booking operation from the case of Citibank, whose internal documents show that in the mid 1970s more than one third of Citibank's loans made in dollars outside the US were booked in the Bahamas. Inversely, Nassau was the main springboard for loans by Citibank to the Western hemisphere, and in particular Brazil and Mexico, which were two of the countries most heavily indebted to Citibank's Nassau branch (Bartlett, 1981, p. 101). As the Senate Foreign Relations Committee argued in 1977:

> These bank haven branches, which are rarely subject to local taxation, can be extremely useful in helping a bank to distribute or 'book' its transactions among various tax jurisdictions so as to minimise its global tax burden. Such 'selective siting' of loans and deposits serves much the same purpose for multinational banks as transfer pricing does for other multinational corporations.

It is worth observing at this stage that Citibank's freeloading indebtedness to Latin America via the Bahamas rendered it the most exposed of all US banks to the Latin American debt crisis in the 1980s.

Transfer Parking

'Transfer parking' is a practice whereby multinational banks transfer their foreign-exchange position (which they take, as a matter of course, in a range of different currencies) from one branch to another. As Bartlett (1981, pp.

103ff) stresses, the basic mechanisms of this procedure came to light in a court case involving a Texan named David Edwards and Citibank. Edwards became disturbed by what he construed as a misuse of Citibank's foreign-exchange dealings, collected evidence on it and sent it to senior management, believing that they would halt it. He was promptly fired and a long court case ensured for wrongful dismissal.

As Barlett (ibid., p. 103) has said, the Edwards case showed that Citibank 'in shifting its foreign exchange position around its global network, also adjusted the exchange rates at which transactions took place with others of its branches. The result was to make it seem as if the European branches of Citibank had taken losses on the transactions, thus lowering the level of income which was taxable in those jurisdictions, while the profits appeared to rise in the Bahamas branch'.

One clear outcome of the Citibank case was an illustration of the extent to which such multinational banking operations were essentially controlled from the head office. This belies the alleged complexity of unravelling transfer pricing by multinational banks – Citibank had nearly 2,000 offices in over 90 countries at the time.

Accounting and Accountability

As already indicated, a number of governments have been catching up with the transfer-pricing activities of some multinationals in recent years. There are four main respects in which they could increase accountability on such activities.

(1) Governments could introduce legislation to gain information on the subsidiary transactions of multinational companies, whether in agribusiness, industry, services or finance. For instance, this provision should be met in the case of the European Community by its insistence on 'transparency' in international operations within the EEC area. Such provisions are backed by articles 85 and 86 of the Rome Treaty. Nonetheless, in practice, the European Community has shown no collective will to remedy the transfer-pricing problem. To date, the studies undertaken by its Competition Division on the activities of big business have been restricted almost entirely to the national rather than multinational level.

(2) Governments could check the prevailing market price for final products against a so-called 'arms length' price and tax authorities could have the power to substitute the price which would have been charged in an open international transaction for the price actually charged by a multinational corporation in its transactions with its own subsidiaries. This is one of the techniques which has been used by the independent analysts of transfer pricing to identify the difference between the prices charged by multinational

companies and those which would include a normal cost-plus profit factor.

(3) A standard cost-plus profit mark-up criterion on the above lines provides a further potential basis for assessing the degree of under or over-invoicing by multinational companies and the degree of their tax avoidance or evasion. Nonetheless, such a cost-plus pricing bench-mark has two main problems. First, such costs are notoriously subjective. As indicated in the *Market Economy* (Holland, 1987, chapter 4), there is very considerable difficulty in identifying the share of overheads, advertising, research and development expenditure or asset depreciation in the specification of essential long-run average costs. Second, the sale price of a product can depend as much on what the market will bear as on what the product itself costs.

(4) Nonetheless, granted the overwhelming dominance in transfer-pricing techniques of the multinational companies which command a major share of global trade and the fact that the top 200 companies represent a third of global GDP, there is a strong case for the 'top countries' which constitute the home base of such 'top companies' introducing legislation which gains transparency and accountability from their own leader companies. If proposals for such accountability were agreed by the Group of Five (the US, the UK, France, West Germany and Japan), the feasibility of achieving a public national countervailance for private multinational transfer pricing would be greatly advanced. If individual countries within the Group of Five were not able to agree such procedures, then proposals standardised within regional areas such as the European Community could still make a major contribution to gaining a closer alignment between real costs, real profits and real prices in the global economy.

6.3 Innovation and Technology Transfers

The conventional theory of technology and innovation is still restricted in the main to the framework of the nation state. Thus Richard Lipsey (1975, pp. 720 and 721) contrasts what he calls 'growth in a world without learning' and 'growth with learning'. But 'the world' he considers is a national economy.

National and International

Richard Lipsey contrasts the view of the classical economists who saw the economic problem as one of fixed or limited land, a rising population and a gradual exhaustion of investment opportunities, with the evident possibilities for raising productivity through the embodiment of technical progress. As he stresses, productivity and economic growth can be promoted both by raising the quantity of capital per worker and through innovation in the form of embodied or disembodied technical change. The former means 'new knowledge and inventions [which] can contribute markedly to the growth of potential national income . . . [which] will be growing because of the growth of knowledge rather than because of the accumulation of more and more capital.' Disembodied technical change, in Lipsey's words (ibid., p. 723), 'concerns innovations in the organisation of production that are not embodied in the form of the capital goods or raw materials used. One example is improved techniques of managerial control.'

Lipsey admits the role of international trade in technology and innovation. Nonetheless, assuming still a conventional framework of trade between different countries rather than between the same companies in different countries, he argues (ibid., p. 726) that 'the most important advantage that the existence of international trade confers on a growing country is that it allows it to escape from its own resource limitations, both natural and human, and concentrate its growth effort in the areas in which it has a genuine advantage. . . . With an open economy a small country is free to grow rapidly in sectors in which it enjoys a comparative advantage and meet the rest of its requirements through foreign trade.'

In these respects, Lipsey is reflecting the orthodox treatment of technical progress and innovation in conventional macroeconomic theory. But as we will see in Chapter 8, in the analysis of Marx, Kondratieff, Schumpeter and others, the impact of technical progress and innovation on the macro-economy is in no sense necessarily balanced. Keynes, while focusing almost exclusively on the short-run activity of an economy without change from embodied technical progress, emphasised the disequilibriating tendencies of market forces. Likewise, the remaining part of this chapter makes plain that smaller or less developed countries are in no way guaranteed gains from trade by the diffusion of technology through international division of labour when multinational companies can combine low wages with advanced technology in their own global division of capital. Further, the example cited by Lipsey of 'improved techniques of managerial control' has worked through the circuits of multinational companies in such a way as to promote the interests of the technologically advanced versus the less advanced countries. Indeed, one of the techniques of management in multinational companies is precisely to ensure control by themselves of technology within the orbit of their own companies' worldwide operations.

Keynesian Technical Progress

Keynes himself paid little attention to technology and innovation for the simple reason that his main task was to counter the claims of 'monetarism' in his time and persuade economists and politicians of the case for demand management to offset slump. 'Keynesian' theorists such as Harrod and Kaldor have stressed the macroeconomic impact of technical progress – albeit in the framework of national economies.

Thus Harrod in 'Are Monetary and Fiscal Policies Enough?' (1964) restated his basic growth equation (which we analysed earlier in Chapter 3) and stressed that 'the natural rate of growth is one that can be achieved in consequence of population increase and technical progress'. Defining the required savings ratio for a given growth path as S^r, G^n as the natural growth rate and C^r as the required capital output ratio (and also as the accelerator), Harrod wrote that 'we have then a basic equation in which the determinant, put on the left-hand side, is not the growth rate itself, but the savings ratio, thus: $S^r = G^n \, C^r$. The equation concentrates attention on the amount of growth attainable through population increase and technical progress and on the "requirement" for saving as something consequent thereupon.'

In one sense Harrod's reformulation of his basic equation could be seen as a concern to stress that his own model of economic growth gives a central role to technology and innovation, in response to former criticism that it understated the importance of technical progress. Nonetheless, Harrod's analysis maintained the assumption of a 'representative entrepreneur', by which he means in effect an entrepreneur who 'on average' behaves like other entrepreneurs in the system. This standard macro-micro approach in no way meets the need to identify the main actors in technical progress and innovation at the level of individual firms, especially mesoeconomic and multinational enterprise.

Kaldor (1961) stressed the role of the entrepreneur. Thus he argued that 'the mere accrual of investment opportunities through technical progress will not alone ensure the continued growth in production. . . . It is necessary to postulate a certain minimum "buoyancy" in entrepreneurial behaviour to ensure that the investment necessary to generate the profits which will call for a further increase in investment . . . does take place.' He also argued that 'whereas the rate of technical improvement will depend on the rate of capital accumulation, any society has only a limited capacity to absorb technical change in a given period. . . . The more "dynamic" the people in control of production, the keener they are in search of improvement, and the readier they are to adopt new ideas and new ways of doing things, the faster production (per person) will rise and the higher is the rate of accumulation that can be profitably maintained' (Kaldor, 1961). He nonetheless admitted that his model, 'like other macroeconomic models, is based on simple aggregate concepts of income, capital, profits, etc.' It is also essentially national rather than international in character. As with Harrod, Kaldor makes no distinction in the role in technical progress and innovation of big rather than small firms, or multinational rather than national companies.

Top Companies and Top Countries

Yet, in reality, it is the multinational company which now dominates the process of innovation and technology transfers on a global scale. It is multinationals which determine the rate, pace and scale of technical change and innovation, and which societies shall absorb it, in what way, at what time. This is not to say that such companies are 'disembodied' from their countries of origin. As already indicated in the analysis from Clairmonte and Cavanagh (1984), over half of the top 200 companies now accounting for a third of global GDP are based in five countries. This is reflected in the OECD (1982) findings that 85 per cent of the world's research and development is undertaken in the same five countries (the US, the UK, West Germany, France and Japan).

Where this trend has been offset, it has been through state-owned or public enterprises. But many of these – especially in developing countries – are in practice dependent on multinational companies for their technology through licensing agreements. Certainly the above figures show the superficiality of arguments which became fashionable in the early 1980s, especially in the United States and the United Kingdom, about the contribution to innovation and employment made by small firms. Modern technical progress can still be made by very small enterprises. The growth of 'Silicon Valley' in California and the similar development of electronics companies in the vicinity of the Massachusets Institute of Technology in Boston are evidence that small groups of entrepreneurial innovators can and do succeed in achieving significant technical progress. Nonetheless, the vast bulk of actual innovation, i.e. the embodiment of technical progress in production, is undertaken by large companies dominant in the global economy as a whole. Small companies first stride, then struggle in the foothills of technical progress. The heights of innovation are commanded by a handful of multinational firms.

It is also crucial to recognise that in contrast with conventional theory which stresses the role of technical progress on the macroeconomy of a single nation state, new technologies are now transferred across national frontiers through multinational companies. The contrast between conventional theory and the new multinational reality may be illustrated as follows.

The Conventional Model

Figure 6.12 shows a simple sequence by which research leads to development and then to production undertaken within one country, with export of the goods embodying the technology. While the model appears simple (and is taken to be so by many policy-makers), the reality is more complex. For instance, as illustrated in Figure 6.13, the central sequence from research and development through production to export has various implications which provide an open door to the application of new technology for big rather than small business, and in developed rather than less developed countries.

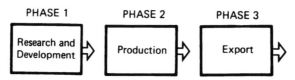

FIG. 6.12   Innovation and exports: a conventional sequence

In phase 1 of Figure 6.13, the research and development cycle implies less 'eureka' insights to technologists in their baths (or showers), than a sustained process by which public academic and private research, and directly sponsored government research programmes, facilitate technological break-throughs. The defence programmes of governments play a central role in this process, although it is now widely recognised that such defence expenditure in the US and the UK may well have been counter-productive for innovation in the civilian market. For instance, apart from their direct effects in lifting satellites useful to multinational companies in co-ordinating transfer pricing worldwide, there is little evidence that the National Aviation and Space Administration (NASA) research in the United States has done more than offer the civilian consumer the advantage of non-stick frying pans. At a stratospheric rather than astronomic altitude, the US Defense Department's support of the Boeing B47 bomber programme nonetheless covered the original research and development, and offset the initial production costs of the 707 passenger jet which paved the way for Boeing to break into the 'jumbo' 747 market.

In Japan, by contrast, government assistance to research and development has been directly related to the second phase in Figure 6.13, for instance in the application of robotics and numerical control to the innovation process in production itself. In turn this generates a range of indirect effects. In the first place the matrix multiplier operates not only in the sense of generating inter-firm and inter-industry demand, but also the requirements for the application of technology sufficient to reduce input costs for the production process. Japanese companies have been especially sensitive to this, and in one

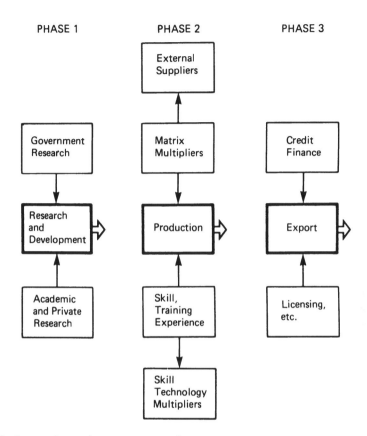

FIG. 6.13   Innovation and exports: a complex sequence

illustrative but significant case, requested that a UK supplier should raise its price to make more provision for research, development and innovation in future production. Moreover, the skill and training experience related to actual innovation, as illustrated in phase 2 of Figure 6.13, generates a skill and technology multiplier for those companies providing the inputs for multinationals' production.

In turn, in phase 3 of Figure 6.13, both the credit and finance for exports and the terms of licensing for foreign production are of crucial importance in the global domain and effective dominance of a few multinational companies based in a handful of leading countries. Reference has already been made in this context to the extent to which the Japanese Ministry of International Trade and Industry (MITI) has provided favourable credit and finance for Japanese exports on the global market.

Simple and Complex

Thus the simple sequence of Figure 6.12 from research and development to production and export is extensively qualified by the implications of Figure 6.13. This becomes especially important for those less developed countries which at a certain stage of development have considered that they can afford to import modern or advanced technology, but which in practice have lacked the social and economic infrastructure necessary to exploit it.

This point has been well put by Stephen Hymer (1972, p. 126):

> It is not technology which creates inequality; rather it is *organisation* [which] arbitrarily creates unequal capacities to initiate and terminate exchange, to store and retrieve information, and to determine the extent of that exchange and the terms of the discussion.

Such a complex of social and economic structures for the generation and diffusion of new technologies is not readily available to less developed countries. Castro, Ganiatsos and others (UNCTAD, 1984) have claimed that Algeria represents 'perhaps the most clear-cut example of direct foreign investment being supplanted by alternative channels of technology transfer. Almost all foreign firms were nationalised in 1966–71 and the acquisition of technology from abroad since then has given considerable emphasis to turnkey contracts supervised mainly by foreign engineering firms.'

Although Algeria gained substantially from the rise in oil and natural gas prices following the first OPEC price increases in October 1973, it could not replicate an indigenous process of transfer through from research and development to production and export on the lines of Figure 6.12 because it lacked the complex of social and industrial structures indicated in Figure 6.13. Thus effective transfer of technology cannot be achieved simply by a government seeking to 'buy in' know-how. A complex dynamic of research, development, education and public finance is involved which includes both the *social relations* of technology transfer, and the *sponsorship role* of the state.

Multinational Transfers

Multinational companies both benefit from such social and sponsorship relations in developed 'home' countries, and seek to prevent their replication in less developed 'host' countries. Thus, as shown in Figure 6.14, the transfer of their technology as developed in phase 1 in a more developed country (MDC) will be transferred worldwide through their own 'internalised' production in subsidiaries in other more developed (MDC), intermediate (IMC) or, to a much lesser extent, less developed countries (LDC).

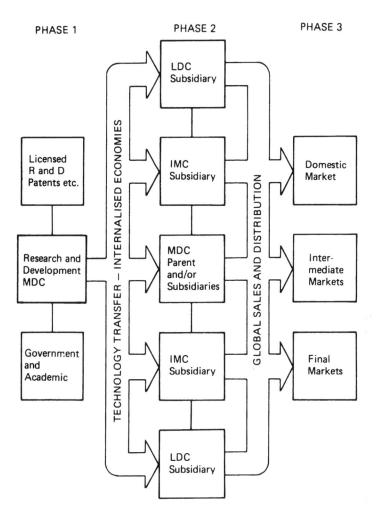

FIG. 6.14 Innovation and exports: a multinational sequence

Where this occurs, or where other companies or governments purchase patents and licences, what is transferred to intermediate or less developed countries is essentially a technique of production, not research and development capacity. This is well illustrated by Lahera (1985, p. 46), who demonstrates that the subsidiaries of US multinationals spend less than 0.5% of their research and development expenditure in Latin America. It is also typical of such technology transfer that it is partial rather than general. It can and does mean the export of the most modern production techniques available on a global scale, from developed countries to intermediate and less developed countries. But it is crucial that this process occurs within the subsidiaries of multinational companies, rather than between independent firms in different countries.

This does not mean to say that the multinationals export precisely the same technology or techniques of production to less developed countries which they would use in their more developed home base. For one thing, products frequently need to be adapted to suit special local needs in either an individual national market or several countries which constitute a region of the world economy (e.g. Latin America).

In other cases, the multinational company may well have penetrated the foreign market through the takeover of a domestic firm by elimination tactics of the kind described in previous chapters or by straight purchase. In this case it will inherit techniques of production which it may well adapt to the new products developed in more developed countries until such a time as replacements of the capital equipment become either more desirable or necessary. Third, and importantly, the very low wages which can be paid by multinational companies in less developed countries make it economic for the company concerned to employ less capital per worker than would be the case in a developed country.

The Modified Product Cycle

The Vernon product cycle is being modified within this global context, as is the conventional sequence of national export trade followed by multinational investment.

For instance, Figure 6.15 extends Ohlin's (1933) analysis of the manner in which foreign direct investment will tend to offset and substitute for visible

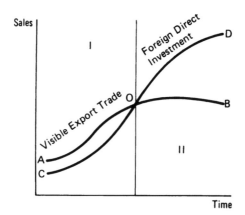

FIG. 6.15   The Ohlin trade and foreign investment model

export trade. Thus a successful visible export increase on the lines *AO* in phase I will be offset by the multinational trend of foreign direct investment on the line *COD*, which in turn may depress the visible export trend on the line *OB*.

This in turn is paralleled by the global product-cycle model. Thus as translated through to Figure 6.16, the foreign direct investment line in Figure 6.15 implies the 'new', 'growth' and 'mature' phases of the product cycle in the three main stages of the standard Vernon model.

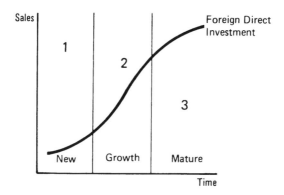

FIG. 6.16   The global Vernon product-cycle model

But with increasing globalisation, following the exposure of big business in one country to competition with such business in other countries, major companies can no longer afford the relative leisure of the Vernon product cycle from innovation and growth in home markets to export of goods (or investment) to other markets in phase 3 of the product cycle.

Translated through to actual economies, it is no longer the case – as was for some time part of the conventional wisdom – that 'what the Europeans create, the Americans commercialise and the Japanese copy'. In reality, the global corporation is increasingly pursuing the three phases of research and development, production, and export on an integrated basis, for the global market as a whole (Ohmae, 1985, chapter 9).

In Vernon product-cycle terms, this confirms the trend towards an elision of stages 1 and 2 of the product cycle as illustrated in Figure 6.17. But in this global innovation process, research and development is increasingly concentrated in more developed countries and production is undertaken directly in developed, intermediate or less developed countries according to criteria determined on its own terms – irrespective of government policies – by the multinational corporation.

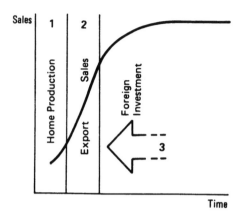

FIG. 6.17   Global innovation: elision of the Vernon product-cycle model

Technology Transfers and Payments

In the early 1970s Charles Cooper argued that the essence of technology transfer is the capacity of the parent multinational company to furnish a package of 'elements of technology' to subsidiaries. This technical assistance, as Cooper stressed, includes not only engineering but also sales and market-penetration techniques (Cooper, 1971). The vehicle for this transfer of know-how can operate both directly through the circuits of the multinational worldwide or through indirect payments of fees and licences. Thus trade and payments are complemented by technological trade and payments, with similar surpluses and deficits.

The vehicle for the transfer of this know-how is the range of patents and licenses which the multinational company makes available to its subsidiaries abroad, but excludes from local national firms or competitors. In this respect it could be said that the 'entry' of multinational companies through direct investment and technology transfer in less developed countries simult-aneously implies 'no entry' for other companies, and in particular, micro-economic companies in the less developed country which lack either the size or sophistication to be attractive as subsidiaries acquired through takeover. Thus technology transfer for mesoeconomic big business through multi-national operations is a crucial feature of the relations between subsidiaries and the parent company. Partial access to a technique of production on which the patent may already have expired for the parent company in its home country or abroad will not enable a local firm in the other country to compete effectively through imitation of the partial technique when the imitator lacks the overall technology package developed in the first instance by the innovating company.

Dunning (1985, p. 4) has expressed the point well when he says that the technology imperative provides a good reason for multinational companies to be linked to each other in the production process through hierachial 'galaxies', with a pivotal group of firms which control the key technologies being surrounded by satellite suppliers. As Dunning explains it:

> In such a [multinational] divison of labour, the structure of international production is determined by oligopolistic hierarchies competing among themselves rather than by independent buyers and suppliers at arms length prices. . . . In such conditions, industrial restructuring by multinational companies may link one economy to another in a way unacceptable to either or both. In such cases, the role of international hierarchies is less that of resource transferors, or tutors in resource usage, more as allocators of economic activity to meet their global goals.

Technologies and Technicians

In addition, unlike models of 'perfect information' in neoclassical economic theory, while technology may be available in principle through imports, the translation of a technique into innovation and production inevitably involves processes of adjustment and problems of application. As in the 'octopoid' example of Figure 6.14, the subsidiaries of multinational companies in other countries benefit from integrated technical, supervisory and managerial assistance from staff allocated by the parent company. An independent company in a less developed country would not benefit from this relationship between a subsidiary and the parent multinational company even if it were able to afford the purchase of the patent in the first place. Such benefits would be less likely the smaller the company concerned. In other words, a microeconomic enterprise in a less developed or intermediate country has little or no chance of importing the most advanced technology in its area from a multinational company in the mesoeconomic sector of the kind which dominates research and development in the more developed countries.

Global Standards

Standardisation of technology, and its use by subsidiaries, is central to the global strategy of most multinational companies. Sometimes it goes too far and yields bizarre results. Michalet cites, as an example of the absurd degree to which such standardisation can occur, the case of the factory built in Africa by a Swedish multinational group whose roof was capable of resisting the weight of a snowfall some ten metres deep (Michalet, 1976, p. 190). But such absurdity is not typical of the transfer of techniques of production and technology by multinational companies in their subsidiary operations abroad. On the product profile, it may take some multinationals time to catch up, as in the impact in Japan of the 'Barbie' doll, where the company concerned first failed to make any impression, and then realised the need to introduce a shorter, dark-haired and less 'all American' product, which took off like wildfire (Ohmae, 1985, chapter 8). There has also recently been evidence of increased flexibility in the sourcing of components 'bought in' by advanced-technology companies, due partly to the disincentive to undertake major investment projects 'in house' when these may result in long-term spare capacity caused by the slow rate of growth of world demand (Ergas, 1984 and Holland, 1987a).

Nevertheless, while allowing for both flexible component sourcing and product 'segmentation' suitable for local market needs, the standardisation imperative is very clear in the foreign operations of multinational companies. It includes not only installation, production and maintenance, but also techniques of distribution and market penetration. On the engineering side, the flow of skilled management personnel is not only one way, i.e. from the more developed country of the parent company to the less developed country of the subsidiary. The two-way flow of engineers and technicians is increasing between the home country of the parent company and the home country of the locally employed staff in the less developed country. Multinational companies not only tend to bring such local engineers and technicians to the parent company for direct instruction and management training, but also in general seek to integrate them into the economic environment of the 'global corporation'. This can include their access to management training courses organised by independent bodies or institutions, and in some cases their company-sponsored pursuit of higher educational qualifications in universities or business schools in the more developed country (Michalet, 1976, p. 191).

The most consistent form of standardisation by multinational companies in technology transfer is in the assembly of components produced either in the home country, or very possibly in an intermediate country, with the assembly process itself undertaken in a less developed country. Some production by the subsidiaries of multinationals in less developed countries will combine the assembly of some components with the production of others. The logic of the relationship between the parent and subsidiary companies of the multinational firm is towards global production techniques and conditions and terms of sale. In such a way, the sequence of transfer payments and pricing illustrated earlier in this chapter in Figures 6.10 and 6.11 imply the parallel transfer of technology between countries within the circuits of multinational companies rather than the conventional division of labour in international trade.

Global Sales Strategy

Global production increasingly is now matched by a global sales strategy within the multinational company. This has not only macroeconomic implications, but also implies a change in the conventional view of the structure of management and organisation in the theory of the firm. Thus in Chapter 5 of *The Market Economy* (Holland, 1987) a parallel was drawn between the organisation of the single-market, multi-market and multi-national company, and the vertical, multidivisional and area structures of management taught for decades on the model introduced by Sloan at General Motors (1965). Despite some recent claims that this strategy has become both more flexible and more decentralised, multinational companies still operate a global sales strategy which aims to achieve the standardisation of production techniques, and technology transfer.

For example, Ford and General Motors have modified their earlier concept of a single 'world car' to take account of different consumer tastes and varying government regulations in different countries (not least fuel emission standards). Nonetheless, the global aim of such companies remains a worldwide standardisation of components. The body or 'skin' of Ford and GM cars stays the same irrespective of the individual market. What differs is the trim, fittings and fixtures. The main object of global strategy is still enormous economies of scale.

Thus global big business still seeks to combine economies of scale with production differentiation. The leasing of products in sophisticated markets is a classic case in point. IBM is renowned for its control over the conditions and terms of the leasing of computers in different countries. But even in less expensive or complex products than main frame computers, the parent multinational company is likely to standardise not only the technology of production but also the techniques and conditions of sale.

Clearly a multinational company will find different market conditions in different countries. It will also find different pricing and profit opportunities at different stages of the product cycle and the penetration of new products in new markets. Thus it may be able to 'profit cream' in an individual national market where it is the first, or among the first, to introduce the sale of a new product, while obliged to reduce profit levels in other markets where the product is already established.

Nonetheless the standards by which such pricing policies are established tend to be determined by the parent company. The public relations personnel of multinational companies frequently argue that they need to replicate the conditions of the market in the operations of their subsidiaries, due to the complexity and scale of their multifarious operations. As indicated earlier in this chapter, however, Scibberas (1977) has shown the extent to which standard criteria and techniques for the sale of products embodying new technology are established by the parent company rather than the subsidiary.

A good example of this comes from the GLC (1986, p. 42) Report on Ford, where it was made plain by the Dutch Metal Workers Union that while Ford is always talking about the independence of local management, the spending authorisation of such management through the managing director of Ford Netherlands has a very low limit, which inhibits local management autonomy. As Henk Voss put it:

> This means the managing director of a plant employing about 2,000 people, if he wants to buy two IBM typewriters, cannot take the decision himself, but needs the O.K. from Ford-Europe. The authorisation of the President of Ford-Europe has a limit of $1.5 million. This man is responsible for the jobs of 100,000 people in Europe and cannot make a decision on investment above the sum of $1.5 million. That is the independence of the President of Ford-Europe.

In reality the terms on which goods are supplied, as well as the technology by which they are produced, are increasingly centralised by multinational corporations on a global scale.

6.4 Technology, Growth and Trade

It has already been stressed that the volume of production by multinational companies worldwide is already greater than the total volume of world trade. It has also been indicated that by the early 1970s the ratio of foreign production by multinational companies to visible US and UK export trade exceeded 4:1 and 2:1 respectively, while the multinationalisation of capital in countries such as Japan, West Germany and France has been proceeding apace.

This trend, accented on the transfer of production and technology abroad, has major implications for the global distribution of growth and trade. The contrast with both Keynesian models of national growth and the Ricardian model of international trade are very marked.

The Keynesian Model

The crucial stage of the research and development process in the conventional national model is production at home rather than abroad. This is the point at which production multiplier effects are supposed to engage in the classic Keynesian model. In other words, if the earlier sequence in Figure 6.13 is conceived in terms of Harrod's *Gn* or the technical potential of an economy, the production sequence and its multiplier effects are crucial to the Harrod/ Keynesian concept of Ga, i.e. actual growth. It is at this stage that the three main multiplier effects are supposed to promote a higher rate of growth in a given national economy. These include the spread effects of (1) the employment multiplier, (2) the income multiplier, and (3) the 'matrix' or inter-industry multiplier. Further, it is assumed that only a proportion of the goods concerned will be exported rather than distributed within the domestic economy. In other words, the distribution process involving both whole-saling and retailing of goods will generate further employment and income multiplier effects on the rest of the economy.

In turn, in terms of Figure 6.13 – and with cross-reference to the analysis of Chapter 3 – Keynesian theory assumes in Harrod terms that an increase in the Ga or actual growth, due to the embodiment of R & D (phase 1) into (phase 2) production, will raise Ga closer to Gn, i.e. will raise actual growth closer to the natural or potential growth rate of the economy. Similarly, whether the argument is expressed in straightforward accelerator or capital stock adjustment terms, it is assumed that the increase in investment and income promoted by the embodiment of savings in productivity-raising innovation will raise the confidence of entrepreneurs (or – in Keynes's own terms – the marginal efficiency of capital). In other words, the sequence between phase 1 and 2 of Figure 6.13 is supposed to raise both real profits and profit expectations, with the assumption that a 'virtuous circle' effect of expansion will be generated on the national economy as a whole. Added to this is the export gain represented in phase 3 of Figure 6.13, with the assumed export multiplier effects benefiting a national economy. Such a process will allegedly promote export-led growth to the extent that firms under price-competitive conditions are able to reduce their export prices as a consequence of the lower cost schedules available to them through the embodiment of the new technology, reinforced by further cost reductions through increased economies of scale in production.

Post-Keynesian Realities

There is a clear contrast between this assumed sequence of events and the reality of technology transfer in multinational companies. As already described in Figure 6.14, the process of research and development occurs in developed countries rather than in a single developed economy. But it takes place through the subsidiaries of a multinational company, rather than a single national economy. The links with government and academic research become indirect rather than direct, with the main gain for the multinational company accruing from the training of qualified specialists and graduate personnel at public expense before recruitment into its applied research and development division.

Such a multinational sequence of research, development and production qualifies the assumptions of embodied technical progress in standard Keynesian models. It explains the mechanism by which the conventional circularity of income and expenditure in Keynesian national models gives rise to the outflow of investment and innovation abroad, with the consequent 'export' of employment, income and matrix multiplier effects outlined in Chapter 2.

It is certainly possible that the more developed country where the main part of the production takes place will be the same as that or those in which the applied research and development within the multinational company has also occurred. But in contrast with the national model of Figure 6.13, there is no guarantee that this will occur. With the export of *production* embodying new technology, the standard multiplier effects assumed to occur in Keynesian macroeconomic theory may be lost to the individual national economy in which the applied research and development may have occurred in the first place.

Globalisation

At a minimum this will involve a multiplier 'leakage' even if the first and second ('new' and 'growth') stages of Vernon's product cycle are located in the more developed country or countries. In reality, as multinational companies themselves gain experience and maturity in their own foreign direct investment operations, both the second and third ('growth' and 'mature') stages of Vernon's product cycle tend to be located in other countries by multinational companies.

There are several implications. Not only are the external R & D multiplier effects of the development stage lost to any individual developed country, but the key linkage and spread effects of the employment, income and matrix or inter-industry multiplier are also lost to such countries. The superficial assumption that one country's loss should lead to another country's gain does not follow from the process of technology transfer by multinational companies. As already described, it is characteristic of the foreign production by multinationals that this should be divided between different operations in different countries, with either all or the main part of the production sequence concerned being 'internalised' within the firm, rather than 'externalised' to other firms.

In turn this qualifies the conventional national application of the multiplier. Instead of a multiplication of national 'spread effects' through the direct and indirect generation of employment, income and input demand, the global reach of the multinational corporation, and its internalisation of what otherwise could have been external economies, results in a division of production worldwide within one company rather than its multiplication within one country to several companies.

Global Multipliers – and Divisors

In this sense it is not far fetched to describe the new process as a 'divisor' rather than a 'multiplier' effect. Under contemporary conditions, such a 'divisor' is the counterpart of the new global division of capital and technology by multinational companies.

In the developed countries such as the United States and the United Kingdom, the process of technology and investment transfer has resulted in a highly uneven pattern of location and growth between more developed and less developed countries. Since the mid-1960s, as leading companies have typically located a higher share of their technology-embodying production in intermediate and less developed countries, a 'reverse backwash effect' has tended to occur between them and some of the more developed industrial countries.

Such an effect is not solely due to the process of technology and investment transfer abroad by companies in the mesoeconomic sector. It has also occurred through the penetration of the US and UK markets by multinational big business based in countries such as Japan, which itself has gone multinational in less developed and intermediate countries such as South Korea and Taiwan, from which the final product has been exported to the United States and the United Kingdom.

This global production, export and distribution sequence no longer registers employment and income multiplier effects within the economy in which the production has occurred. In other words, it takes the form and substance of Figure 6.14 rather than Figure 6.13. The multiplier process occurs within the global operations of multinational companies rather than the national economy of a particular country. Such companies in many cases have not only reduced but closed down their direct production operations in developed countries such as the United States and the United Kingdom in favour of production in intermediate and less developed countries.

Where there are recent exceptions to this trend, they reflect either a rising technical composition of production which reduces the overall labour content (analysed more extensively in Chapter 9) or a more effective supply of low-cost labour near to the more developed countries (as in the case of the growth of Mexican *maquiladora* development areas offering low-cost labour to US companies on their own back door).

Such a new 'divisor' versus 'multiplier' effect through technology and investment transfer by multinational companies qualifies not only the multiplier assumptions of standard macroeconomic growth theory but also its accelerator and capital stock adjustment assumptions.

Harrod Plus Multinationals

In this context it is meaningful to translate the macroeconomic terms of reference of growth models such as those of Harrod or Domar through to the mesoeconomic level and its multinational dimension. Therefore, instead of the standard Harrod equation $G = s/c$, the reality of the mesoeconomic company through its multinational operations in one country could be represented by contrast as:

$$G \text{ snc} = \frac{S \text{ meso}}{C \text{ mnc}}$$

where snc stands for the subsidiary national company of the multinational concerned, S meso represents the savings schedule by the parent company for investment in that country, and C mnc represents the capital-output ratio embodying the technology transferred by the mesoeconomic company through its multinational subsidiary.

The mesoeconomic modification of the Harrod macroeconomic equation makes even more sense of his later formulation of

$$s^r = Gn \ Cr$$

where in his own emphasis s^r stands for the required savings ratio, and Cr for the required capital-output ratio. Cr in Harrod's initial formulation refers both to the capital-output ratio and the accelerator, i.e. both to the proportion in which capital would be combined with labour and the reaction of management to the overall rate of growth of income in the economy.

Again, the reality of the multinational transfer of technology and investment by mesoeconomic companies worldwide clearly qualifies Harrod's equation. It could therefore be rewritten in the following form:

$$s^r \text{ (meso)} = G^{snc} \ C^{r(mnc)}$$

In this sense the savings required for investment in the foreign subsidiary of a mesoeconomic company are determined by it on a global scale (s^r(meso)), while the 'accelerator' mechanism, to the extent that it reflects the reaction of management to changes in the actual or potential rate of growth of sales and income, operates worldwide on a global scale through its distribution outlets (as indicated by phase 3 of Figure 6.14). Therefore the mesoeconomic company literally bridges the gap between the enterprise and the macro economy. But it does so not simply in Paolo Leon's terms (Leon, 1967), but between its own mesoeconomic reality and the macro economy of the world economy as a whole. Similarly Harrod's potential growth of a national economy (in his terms Gn) is transformed by the multinational operations of mesoeconomic companies into the potential growth of its product markets in the international economy worldwide.

Dependency and Dualism

Such qualifications of the main mechanisms of conventional macroeconomic growth theory through the transfer of technology and investment by multinational companies seriously undermine the programmes for economic development in less developed countries where these are still based on conventional macroeconomic reasoning.

The reasons relate to the character of large mesoeconomic firms rather than simply to their multinational operation. Such firms control the distribution of goods and services on global and regional markets. For instance, Marks and Spencer have computerised the design specification of clothes sold in their UK retail outlets through to various producers elsewhere in the world economy. The conventional wisdom of location by which it used to be assumed that small firms in the 'rag trade' needed to locate near to each other to assess changing market tastes and fashions has been superseded by the global telex and telecommunications reach of dominant buyers.

Multinational agribusiness exerts global market power as an oligopolistic buyer and seller rather than through sophisticated techniques for food processing. Thus the governments of countries such as Portugal and Greece could easily enough command the technology for the dehydration, powdering, canning, bottling, etc. of agricultural products for sale in the more developed economies in the rest of Europe or the United States. But they cannot as readily break into global distribution networks. Less developed countries face even greater difficulties.

Such global 'barriers to entry' arise not so much because the techniques of production in such processes are especially sophisticated, but because national governments, on their own, cannot match the link provided by the multinational company between the production and global distribution of food products. In principle, governments could match such links through multinational public-sector joint ventures or multinational public enterprise (Holland, 1975, and Brandt and Manley, 1985). But the vertical integration and the hold over buyers and suppliers open to multinational companies in the global economy is closed to many national companies, especially those in less developed countries. This makes sense of the fact that multinational companies dominate between two-thirds and 95 per cent of global commodity trade.

The result is a dualism between big and small, meso and micro, multinational and national companies, which now reinforces the classic dualism between the traditional and modern sectors of intermediate and less developed countries.

Relative Autonomy

Moreover, new investment and the embodiment of new technology in intermediate countries in no sense guarantees them an autonomous model of economic development. This is despite the fact that their labour or capital markets are not 'free' from state intervention in the manner assumed by Friedman and others.

Indeed, one of the striking features of the newly industrialised countries in the 1970s was the intervention of the state in the economy either through public ownership of key sectors of activity such as steel, chemicals and their derivatives, planning controls over the allocation of resources through financial institutions of the banking system, or in the South Korean case, through both price and import controls operated through the mechanism of a 100 per cent profits tax over scheduled price ceilings and import licensing through approved import companies. Thus where less developed countries in transition to intermediate development status have been able to avoid the full effects of the dependency syndrome, this has been mainly through state or public intervention rather than the workings of the 'free market' mechanism (Luedde Neurath, 1984).

In addition, through the circuits of multinational companies a dependency syndrome undermining the feasibility of autonomous development operates either through technology transfer or through overall control of the scheduling of savings into productive investment by the parent multinational company. As Michalet has stressed, the parent multinational company is generally the exclusive source of both product technology and techniques of production in intermediate or less developed countries. Even in the case where some research and development may be located in another developed country – as with some US multinationals in the UK – local researchers employed by the multinational company do not necessarily know the final context or embodiment of their own research. As Michalet puts it, 'decentralised laboratories are not functionally related to the activities of the units of production. ... The circuit of the production and circulation of knowledge is therefore disconnected from that of the production circulation of material goods' (Michalet, 1976, pp. 192ff).

In particular, because the work of research and development is related to the global needs of the multinational company, such research and development as may be undertaken in an intermediate country is not related directly to the needs of the local market. This relates to and reinforces the arguments already made on the division of various stages of production for a given final product by a multinational company in different subsidiaries in different countries. In other words, it reflects the 'divisor' rather than external multiplier effects of the multinational company.

Similarly, at the level of production itself, local management employed by multinational companies is not free or autonomous in determining the price or conditions of sale of those products which either may be available for the local market if the subsidiary is at the final stage of production sequence, or those products which are re-imported to the country concerned by the multinational company on completion of the production cycle. In some cases, the local management of the subsidiary may be able to establish conditions of 'relative autonomy' in relation to the parent multinational company. But as already illustrated in the case of the global electronics industry, for a variety of reasons which reflect the 'price-making' power of multinational companies on a global scale and which concern essentially the mechanism of their dominance over microeconomic companies in individual countries, the overall strategy of price determination and supply is typically retained, and guarded, by the parent company and its senior management.

6.5 Summary

(1) It has been established for some time that multinational companies can under-invoice exports and over-invoice imports on their trade between subsidiaries in different countries. However, such recognition of the technique of transfer pricing has not been effectively integrated into macroeconomic models of exchange and payments or into the macro-economic policies pursued by governments.

(2) Transfer pricing transforms the 'transparent' trade relationship between importers and exporters at visible and real prices into an 'opaque' relationship between the subsidiaries of multinational companies.

(3) For transfer pricing to occur (either between subsidiaries in the multinational economy or between subsidiaries within a major national company) it is not necessary for the transaction to pass through a tax haven. However, the phenomenal growth of tax havens in the last quarter century has greatly facilitated the multinational transfer pricing of products and thereby the shift of capital on a global scale through subsidiary trade transactions.

(4) On the trade account, under-invoicing reduces the registered export trade of a given national economy, while o· ·er-invoicing increases registered import values in the importing countr). Such transfer pricing

therefore can and does understate export values while overstating import values in the countries concerned, and thus damages their registered trade performance.

(5) Transfer pricing also permits tax avoidance by multinational companies. The under-invoicing of exports makes possible the registration of either low profits or no profits for the product or subsidiary concerned. Inversely, the over-invoicing of import costs can result in a similar low profit or no profit statement by the importing subsidiary. Given the major share of export and import trade now accounted for by multinational companies in total visible trade transactions (two-fifths or more of such trade for the US and UK), such tax loss through under-and over-invoicing can contribute sizeably to fiscal crisis in the states concerned.

(6) Transfer pricing also contributes to inflation to the extent that the over-invoicing of imports either contributes directly to a higher domestic price level, or indirectly reinforces price-making power and super-normal profits by oligopolistic firms typical of the mesoeconomic sector on the domestic market. Cumulative over-invoicing of imports between subsidiaries on a world scale can significantly contribute to global inflation.

(7) Multinational companies dominate modern technology in the global economy in a manner which has transformed the conventional sequence of research and development, innovation in production and successful export trade. Such companies dominate the terms and conditions of the transfer of technology between countries in the global economy.

(8) The multinational dominance of innovation and its complex sequence of technology transfer profoundly modifies Keynesian models of growth and technical progress within national economies. The global strategy for innovation and technology transfer by multinational companies divides national markets and qualifies the multiplier effects of growth innovation in individual countries.

(9) Technology transfer includes not only techniques of production and new products, but also sales and market-penetration techniques, whether 'standardised' or 'flexible'. Thus conventional trade and payments is complemented by technological trade and payments, with surpluses and deficits similar to that of orthodox trade theory, but operated through the subsidiary circuits of multinational companies worldwide.

7 Money and Monetarism

The rise of the mesoeconomy and global big business power has major implications for the conventional macroeconomic theory of money and the rate of interest, whether this is classical, neoclassical, monetarist or neo-Keynesian in character.

The most important challenges to the conventional theory of money and interest rates include:

(1) *unequal competition* for funds, so that bigger business can borrow at lower rates than smaller business;

(2) *price-making power*, and thus the ability of big business to pass on higher interest rates in the form of higher prices;

(3) *unequal costs*, or the offsetting of interest-rate changes through dynamic economies of scale;

(4) *self-financing*, or the extent to which big business can cover the major part of its investment needs without access to external finance;

(5) *multinational location* of production in countries whose lower labour costs can more than neutralise the cost of external borrowing;

(6) *transfer pricing* and techniques of tax avoidance by which global corporate gains can offset interest-rate charges on external finance;

(7) *transfer funding*, or techniques whereby the 'parking' of funds or foreign-exchange dealing can offset interest-rate charges or make interest gains;

(8) *investment of surplus funds* generated by the market power of multi-nationals, so that they become creditors as well as borrowers on global money markets (especially Eurodollar markets);

(9) *global demand* as the key determinant of the savings and investment process for multinational companies, rather than the monetary policy of any one country.

Keynes himself offered only some answers to the monetarism of his time in the case of the 'sound money' and 'balanced budget' theories of public finance. Naturally he could not be expected to anticipate the transformation of global markets after his time by multinational companies. But besides this, Keynes has not been well served by some so-called 'Keynesians', whose adaptations of his arguments hindered rather than helped the defence of his demand-management principles against the monetarist counter-revolution of the 1970s.

The first such modification was a stylised synthesis of a version of Keynes' arguments on monetary economics with the neoclassical monetary theory (confusingly called by him 'classical' theory) which he had sought to displace. The second and later modification by some Keynesians included the assumption that provided wage demand was restrained through incomes policies, or other means were found to reintroduce 'flexibility' in labour markets (a euphemism for wage restraint or cuts), Keynes' economics would again come into its own in a full-employment context. Third, and important to the neutering of some of Keynes' own arguments, was an almost patronising attitude towards him, illustrated by the argument of Alvin Hansen (1953) that 'not much would have been lost' if Chapters 16 and 17 of *The General Theory* 'had never been written', and reflecting the convention, criticised by Leijonhufvud, of Keynes 'as a brilliant man, and a great man, but a great man dabbling in economics' (Leijonhufvud, 1968, pp. 17 and 37). Economists of lesser stature, lifted by Keynes' vision, preferred their own more stylised and stigmatic view, and called it his own.

7.1 The Quantity Theory of Money

The monetarist 'counter revolution' to Keynes' economics, as Meghnad Desai (1981) has observed, 'is a notion at once two centuries old and ten years young'. Hayek also wrote in 1980 that 'the new-fangled word monetarism means of course no more than the good old name "quantity theory of money" as it was formulated in modern times by the late Professor Irving Fisher and reformulated by Professor Milton Friedman' (letter to *The Times*, 5 March 1980).

Fisher wrote his classic work on the quantity theory of money (1911 – revised edition 1922) before the First World War. But the quantity theory of money itself was developed in the eighteenth century by two men known today almost entirely for their philosophy – John Locke and David Hume.

Hume and After

Hume put the case for the quantity theory of money in a manner which a lay person today may easily understand: if the quantity of money were to double overnight, prices would eventually double:

It seems a maxim almost self-evident, that the prices of everything depend on the proportion between commodities and money, and that any considerable alteration on either has the same effect, either of heightening or lowering the price. Increase the commodities, they become cheaper; increase the money, they rise in their value [Hume, 1826].

Hume argued that an increase in money supply 'must first quicken the diligence of every individual before it increased the price of labour'. In other words, an influx of money will first increase employment at the prevailing wage; then, as labour becomes scarce, employers give higher wages while also demanding higher productivity. But while 'at first no alteration is perceived; by degrees the price rises, first of one commodity, then of another; till the whole at last reaches a just proportion with the new quantity of specie [money] which is in the kingdom.' Again, Hume's intuition is relevant to the contemporary debate. In other words, the initial effects may be positive but the longer-term effects can be negative and – crucially – the lag or delay is unspecified but taken to be long term.

Hume's arguments were opposed in his own time by James Stewart (1767), who queried the claims for proportionality between the quantity of money and prices. Stewart argued that if there were excess money it would be saved or 'hoarded up' – an anticipation of Keynes' later concern about the effects of hoarding – and that if gold and silver fell short of the demand for money there would be resort to 'symbolic money' or credit to fill the gap.

Ricardo versus Hume

When Ricardo joined the debate he not only restated Hume's theory but fundamentally changed it. In Hume's model, increased money supply had positive effects in the short run and negative effects in the long run. But for Ricardo, the positive short-run effects of increased money supply on demand and output were considered of secondary importance and stress was laid on the long-run determination of output by real factors such as labour supply, the capital stock and natural resources. For Ricardo, short-run fluctuations in money supply were temporary disturbances around this long-run level.

Thus with Ricardo, as Desai puts it, 'the classical dichotomy between real and monetary aspects of the economy is achieved . . . real factors determine real output and money becomes a veil'. The Hume-Ricardo divide persists today in various forms of monetarism. Some deny any short-term benefits from money-stock changes and others deny that such benefits can be permanent. The disagreement relates essentially to the 'transmission mechanism' and leads also to different views about the possible good or harm that a sensible or irresponsible monetary policy can effect (Desai, 1981, chapter 1).

In the Hume-Ricardo debate, Ricardo won hands down. His triumph was complete for over a century, not only on issues concerning money supply but on macroeconomic policy in general. His policy prescriptions subjected the British economy to successive periods of austerity, sanctioned by him and implemented by governments whose members it rarely touched. On its success Keynes (1936, p. 33) commented:

> That his teaching, translated into practice, was austere and often unpalatable, lent it virtue. That it was adapted to carry a vast and consistent logical superstructure, gave it beauty. That it could explain much social injustice and apparent cruelty as an inevitable incident in the scheme of progress, and the attempt to change such things was likely to do more harm than good, recommended it to authority. That it afforded a measure of justification for the free activities of the individual capitalist, attracted the support of the dominant social force behind authority.

Fisher's Assumptions

As already indicated, it was Irving Fisher who restated and reformalised the basic classical quantity theory of money. The essentials of Fisher's statement were expressed in his equation of exchange:

$$MV = PT$$

where M is the stock of money, V is velocity of circulation, P is the general price level, and T the index of the volume of transactions or traded goods. Fisher realised that in its basic form – like the Harrod-Domar formulation – his equation of exchange was an identity, i.e. true by definition. However, it became an equation implying causal relationships 'when we take into account conditions known quite apart from that equation' (Fisher, 1922, p. 156).

As he also put it (ibid., p. 155):

> the volume of trade, like the volocity of circulation of money, is independent of the quantity of money. An inflation of the currency cannot increase the product of farms and factories, nor the speed of freight trains or ships. The stream of business depends on natural resources and technical conditions, not on the quantity of money.

The crunch came in the following statement (ibid., p. 157) that

> We may now restate then in what causal sense the quantity theory is true. It is true in the sense that *one of the normal effects of an increase in the quantity of money is an exactly proportional increase in the general level of prices.*

Fisher not only assumed a constant velocity of circulation V or V^1 (where not only money M but also bank deposits M^1 are included in the equation), but also the independence of T and M, or of V and V^1, from M or M^1 and thus of the rate of inflation. In his book he derives estimates of M, M^1, V, V^1, T and P by comparing the actual movements with those predicted and he found a close correlation over long time-periods in Britain and the United States. But he did not test his assumed independence of T and M or V and V^1 from changes in the rate of money supply and prices, despite the fact that it is not the constancy of the velocity of circulation (V or V^1) in his formulation but its independence from M, P and T which is central to a causal interpretation of his equation of exchange. Thus, although Fisher restated the fundamental importance of the classical quantity theory approach, i.e. that money has no influence on real output but only on price levels, his case was still assumption rather than demonstration.

Competitive Assumptions

The quantity theory of money is the keystone of the classical and neoclassical theories of macroeconomics. Yet as some of the best exponents and critics of these theories have themselves made quite clear, such a theory depends crucially on price competition and price flexibility.

For instance, the Swedish economist Wicksell (1955) was one of the first to stress that economists in the first half of the twentieth century gave an explanation for *individual* prices which assumed a competitive process of supply and demand. He therefore argued logically that if they wanted to use the quantity theory of money to explain the *general* price level, i.e. the average of individual prices, then they had to show how money (M) entered into the determination of the supply or the demand of goods. In terms of his own analysis, with certain restrictive premises, and assuming in particular price competition at the microeconomic level, Wicksell demonstrated how the quantity of money would affect prices by affecting the demand for goods. In this respect he developed a theory of macroeconomic demand, incorporating money supply, which was integrated with a competitive microeconomic supply and demand structure at the level of price determination.

Similarly, Ackley (1961, p. 138, italics added) has argued 'that the simple quantity theory implies that *if only prices are flexible* the maximum level of output is automatically assured'. But a reduction in prices would create an incentive for employers to reduce their payrolls in order to reduce unit production costs in line with reduced cash flow. In turn this would reduce overall demand for output. Thus both the absolute level of prices and the structure of prices are involved in the maintenance of full employment. Nonetheless, in line with other Keynesian macroeconomic theorists, Ackley analysed the structure of prices mainly in terms of the wage-price ratio rather than in terms of the oligopolist pricing typical of the modern mesoeconomic sector.

Marshall, Keynes and Money

Marshall both reformulated the quantity theory and stated it in a form highly relevant to the contemporary debate on monetarism. While accepting the Fisher equation of exchange for the long term, he introduced the 'cash balance' approach for the short term, providing a microeconomic intuition (rather than a tested theory) as to why a certain quantity of money would be held in the economy. To some extent presaging Keynes' later observations on consumption and savings functions, Marshall related cash balances to what was held by the public in the form of income, wealth and property. Claiming that a stable or constant proportion of the nominal value of one or all three of these would be held in cash, he observed in passing that people held a tenth of annual income and one fiftieth of property in cash. In Keynesian terms he was talking of the transactions and precautionary motives for holding money.

But Marshall also had a wider view of the role of money supply, maintaining that the basic reasons for a long period of price fluctuation are 'changes in the methods of business and the amount of commodities' constituting the 'commercial environment'. In other words, Marshall maintained that both the holding of money and the rate of long-term price change were primarily related to the level of business activity and the habitual attitudes of businessmen rather than to the supply of precious metals or coins (Eshag, 1963, pp. 5–6).

Yet Marshall was certainly not a Keynesian before Keynes. In Chapter 17 of *The General Theory* (one of those of which Alvin Hansen claimed that not much would have been lost if it had never been written), Keynes challenged Marshall's endorsement of the concept that savings reflect deferred or forgone consumption by investors who are thereby assumed to be entitled to the interest gained on them by 'waiting' until they spend them. As Keynes bluntly put it:

> That the world after several millennia of steady individual savings, is so poor as it is in accumulated capital assets, is to be explained, in my opinion, neither by the improvident propensities of mankind, nor even by the destruction of war, but the high liquidity-premiums formerly attaching to the ownership of land and now attaching to money. I differ in this from the older view as expressed by Marshall with unusual dogmatic force in his *Priciples of Economics*.

Marshall's claims, challenged by Keynes, had been that:

> Everyone is aware that the accumulation of wealth is held in check, the rate of interest so far sustained, by the preference which the great mass of humanity have for present over deferred gratification, or, in other words, by their unwillingness to 'wait'. [Keynes, 1936, p. 242.]

7.2 Keynes and the Classics

Keynes himself argued that provided the state were to intervene on the demand side of the economy in such a way as to ensure a relative overall balance between existing supply capacity and aggregate demand, then the process of perfect and imperfect competition would take care of the supply of goods and services. In this respect, he assumed a competitive price structure on the supply side of the economy. Keynes might have questioned this microeconomic foundation for his macroeconomics had he been more aware of the greater monopoly concentration in continental European rather than British capital, analysed in detail earlier in the twentieth century by Hilferding and Bukharin. However, in his *General Theory* Keynes set himself a special task – to counter the theoretical basis of the economic orthodoxy which legitimated the slump syndrome of the early 1930s.

Thus, Keynes stressed the level of effective demand rather than the rate of growth of money supply as the prime determinant of output, income and employment in the macroeconomy. In terms of the quantity theory of money, his case amounted to a perception or *gestalt* shift. For most neoclassical economists the quantity theory had been used to emphasise a special relation between M and P in $MV = PT$. This stress could be perceived in the following way:

$$\widehat{M} V = \widehat{P} T$$

Inversely, Keynes maintained that the velocity of circulation was not constant, as assumed by classical monetarists, but would vary considerably in relation to both 'liquidity preference' and the rate of growth of effective demand or, in terms of the Fisher exchange equation:

$$M \underbrace{V} = P \underbrace{T}$$

Thus, while monetarists stress the role of M or money supply, Keynes stressed the role of T or the level of transactions demand in the economy. The monetarists of his generation placed a subsidiary emphasis on the relation between M and P (granted especially that prices were falling rather than rising in the early 1930s in Britain – in contrast with hyper-inflation on the continent of Europe in the early 1920s). Keynes downplayed the $M \rightarrow P$ relation and upgraded the role of T, i.e. the volume of transactions which could be taken as an index of effective demand.

Interest-Responsive Savings

Expressing the contrast between monetarism and Keynesianism in this way is simpler than Keynes' own exposition. One of the main targets which Keynes attacked in the monetarism of his time was the theory that there was an interest elasticity in the savings schedule. In other words, neoclassical theory assumes that savings are interest-responsive. According to the neoclassical argument, endorsed by Marshall but challenged by Keynes, the assumed elasticity of the savings schedule reflected savers' 'time preference', 'their impatience', the 'increasing marginal disutility of abstinence', etc. This case was a reflection of the value judgement of classical theory that savings were a reward for abstinence. The theory thereby claimed to legitimate inequalities in the distribution of wealth.

The basic principles of interest-elastic or responsive savings are illustrated in Figure 7.1. It assumes that on the diagonal line *SL*, savings and lending will increase with a higher rate of interest. Inversely, on the diagonal line *IB*, borrowing for investment is assumed to increase with a lower rate of interest.

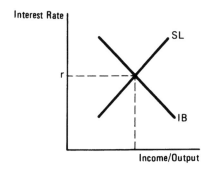

FIG. 7.1   The interest-elastic savings-lending and investment-borrowing model

The classical/neoclassical position represents a perception of the saving-investment process from the viewpoint of the individual lender and the individual borrower. But it is also crucial to the legitimation of classical and neoclassical macroeconomic theory that savings would be invested by borrowers, i.e. the same principles as argued essentially by Say.

By contrast, Keynes wanted to stress the extent to which such a view of the savings and investment process neglected whether or not there was a demand for the products which enterprise could produce at the end of the investment period. Similarly, he argued that when an economy was under-employed through insufficient demand and capacity, a low rate of interest would not be likely to result in an increase of borrowing since, without sufficient sales, new investment simply would not pay.

Keynes, Profits and Expectations

A key role in this context was played by Keynes' concept of 'the marginal efficiency of capital', which he defined in terms of 'the *expectation* of yield and of the *current* supply price of the capital asset'. In other words, the expected rate of return plays a crucial role in Keynes' analysis of the likelihood of savings being embodied in actual investment. In turn this depends on whether the use of savings and their investment currently yields a known rate of return (as for instance with government bonds) or whether the investment and its projected rate of return over and above a prevailing interest rate has yet to take place. As Keynes himself said, 'it depends on the rate of return expected to be obtainable of money if it were invested in a *newly* produced asset; not on the historical result of what an investment has yielded on its original cost if we look back on its record after its life is over' (Keynes, 1936, p. 136).

For neoclassical economists, expectations are assumed to be rational. For some monetarist economists in the 1970s and 1980s this has been embodied in the rational expectations or augmented expectations hypothesis, which argues that provided governments control the money supply, and – by implication – inflation, firms will be able to adjust their expectations in such a manner as to achieve a long-run equilibrium of their savings and investment schedules.

But Keynes himself was scathing on the role of expectations in a market economy. In Chapter 12 of *The General Theory* he stresses that there are not two separate factors affecting the rate of investment, namely the marginal efficiency of capital and the state of confidence, but rather that the state of confidence is one of the major factors determining the marginal efficiency of capital. On the other hand, he emphasises that 'there is, however, not much to be said about the state of confidence *a priori*. Our conclusions must mainly depend on the actual observation of markets and business psychology', and that 'if we speak frankly, we have to admit that our basis of knowledge for estimating the yield ten years hence of a railway, a copper mine, textile factory, the goodwill of a patent medicine, an Atlantic liner, [or] a building in the City of London amounts to little and sometimes to nothing' (Keynes, 1936, pp. 149–50).

Barometers, Stock Markets and Casinos

Keynes allowed that in principle the stock exchange is supposed to value and revalue investments in such a way as to help individual savers to revise their commitments. But apart from his well-known aphorism that the stock market was no more than a casino, he also observed that stock-market revaluations depend on the collective psychology of those in the market, which are as rational in terms of the real process of translating savings into investment as if 'a farmer, having tapped his barometer after breakfast, could decide to remove his capital from the farming business between 10 and 11 in the morning and reconsider whether he should return to it later in the week'. As he adds, 'thus the professional investor is forced to concern himself with the anticipation of impending changes, in the news or in the atmosphere, of the kind by which experience shows that the mass psychology of the market is most influenced' (ibid., pp. 151 and 155).

Keynes' Chapter 12 of *The General Theory* on the long-term state of expectations was not one of those which Alvin Hansen suggested might never have been written. But if it has been read and its lessons learned by many macroeconomists (whether neoclassical Keynesians or monetarists) it some-times is hard to tell the difference.

Liquidity Preference

The uncertainty which Keynes stressed in the process of translating savings into investment – at whatever interest-rate cost – in turn influenced his concept of 'liquidity preference'. This concept has played a key role in Keynesian and neo-Keynesian economics, but in a sanitised form which denies the force of Keynes' original concept. To some extent, Keynes himself may be responsible for this, inasmuch as liquidity preference – unlike the principle of effective demand, the propensity to consume, the marginal efficiency of capital or the state of long-term expectations – not only does not merit a separate chapter in *The General Theory* but fails to obtain even an index reference.

Nonetheless, liquidity preference is the essence of Keynes' Chapter 13 on the general theory of interest, where he argues that the preference for liquidity (or cash) may be defined as depending on three factors: (i) the *transactions* motive, or the need for cash to transact personal and business exchanges; (ii) the *precautionary* motive, i.e. the desire for security as to the future cash equivalent of a certain proportion of total resources; and (iii) the *speculative* motive, or the objective of securing profit from hoping to know better than the market what the future will bring forth.

Liquidity Preference and Disequilibrium

In conventional Keynesian or neo-Keynesian texts, the terms 'liquidity preference' and 'money demand' have come to be virtually synonymous. This is indicated in Figure 7.2, which implies that people or institutions will be prepared to hold more money (y versus x) the lower the rate of interest (r^1

rather than r^2) (Wall, 1985). But this is a stylised representation of Keynes' own concept, and misleading in its over-simplification. As Leijonhufvud (1968, pp. 175–6) has pointed out: 'Keynes' liquidity preference is not just a fanciful or flamboyant term for the demand for money. The latter usage reflects a very narrow interpretation of his theory of liquidity preference.' This has implications for the way in which the Keynesian neoclassical synthesis exorcised Keynes' analysis of destabilisation or disequilibrium in the market. In seeking to refine Keynes they thereby confined him inside an equilibrium framework.

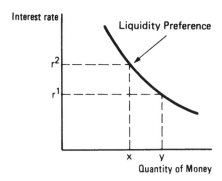

FIG. 7.2   Stylised and simplified 'liquidity preference' model

Keynes himself argued that private non-bank investors might well become net absorbers or releasers of cash and thus disturb the smooth functioning of the savings/investment assumptions of the classical model. He claimed that there was an inherent tendency for such speculative demand, or hoarding and dishoarding, to destabilise the market. Thus the demand for money would not simply be interest-elastic in the manner of the classical model.

His case did not depend on any particular range of interest rates. The point was that, at any time, wealth holders would have formed certain expectations concerning the rates of interest likely to obtain in the future or near future. Such expectations could prevent the rate of interest from operating in the manner of the classical model. The adjustment of the rate of interest would be limited by speculation. Thus shifts in saving or investment schedules would affect the aggregate demand for goods with the result that, if wages and prices were flexible, inflation or deflation would ensue. Alternatively, if they were rigid the result would be an increase or decrease in output and employment. Therefore, for Keynes, no particular rate of interest would attract funds for investment unless borrowers were persuaded that there would be a final demand for production that was sufficient to cover the borrowing costs.

Psychology, Saving and Spending

Apart from the fact that 'liquidity preference' and 'money demand' have become virtually synonymous in conventional macroeconomic theory since Keynes, his third main factor in the concept of liquidity preference, i.e. the 'precautionary' desire for security, has been dropped entirely or relegated to virtual footnote status by many of those claiming to understand Keynes, or calling themselves Keynesians.

Yet in Chapter 9 of *The General Theory* Keynes identified a range of motives concerning the saving and spending process which included not only (i) the *precautionary motive* which was part of his concept of liquidity preference, but also related motives such as (ii) *foresight* to provide for an anticipated need such as retirement or the maintenance of dependents; (iii) *calculation* that a larger real consumption at a later date is preferable to the smaller immediate consumption; (iv) *improvement* or the assessment that a later higher standard of living may be preferable to present consumption even though the capacity for its enjoyment may be diminishing with age; (v) *independence* and the power to do things without the constraint of debt, whether or not one has a clear idea of what one will do; (vi) *enterprise* or entrepreneurship sufficient to carry out speculative or business projects; (vii) *pride* either in the sense of anticipating conspicuous consumption or the power to bequeath a fortune; and (viii) *avarice* to satisfy pure miserliness, or the unreasonable but insistent inhibition against acts of expenditure as such.

Keynes draws up a corresponding list of eight motives for consumption such as enjoyment, short-sightedness, generosity, miscalculation, ostentation, extravagance, etc.

Hoarding versus Borrowing

In line with Leijonhufvud, it is worth observing that Keynes' identification of such motives for saving or spending (rarely, if ever, reproduced in conventional economic texts) was not just the fanciful expression of one of those rare economists who could also write, but reflects prevailing values and social psychology. In essence they are a short guide to the value system of the Protestant ethic, the value system of industrial capitalism analysed by Max Weber and Thorstein Veblen – whose theories also strongly influenced John Kenneth Galbraith. Such motives for saving or spending are less footnotes to theory than central to understanding the attitudes carried from small business practice or 'home economics' into government by those whose commitment to monetarism stems less from close analysis of Friedman's permanent-income hypothesis than a preference for low personal tax and a prejudice against public spending.

A classic example in the UK is the Conservative government since 1979. Indicting Keynesian economics, and extending the principles of 'home' or household economics to the national economy, Mrs Thatcher has advised the British nation that it cannot spend more than it earns, thereby totally denying the savings and investment function from which major financial institutions (whether banks, pension funds, insurance companies or the stock market) both make a living and generate future investment from current revenue. The propensity to thrift in Margaret Thatcher's preference for saving against spending (whether combining Keynes' precaution, foresight and calculation, or the inverse attributes of short-sightedness, pride and avarice) is reflected in her ardent desire to reduce the public-sector borrowing requirement (PSBR) at any cost, irrespective of the impact of such a reduction on public spending, investment, income, employment or output.

Totem and Taboo

Reducing the PSBR became a totem of the post-1979 Thatcher government. Keynesian deficit spending, fiscal policy or demand management became taboo. There is no particular subtlety about this phenomenon. In line with 'home' economics, reducing the PSBR becomes equivalent to taking money from current income and putting it in a tin under the bed. While high interest rates were wrapped round the necks of small business, the contraction of public spending collapsed demand.

For instance, in Chapter 1 we saw that some 95 per cent of the supply of public housing was provided by private contractors in Great Britain between the 1970s and the mid-1980s. To fulfil cuts in the public-sector borrowing requirement, the local authority or council housing expenditure budget was cut by the Thatcher government by over two-thirds between 1979 and 1984. As a result, private company liquidations in the construction industry doubled, from an annual rate of just over 1,000 in 1980 to nearly 2,000 in 1984 (Parliamentary Question, Department of Trade and Industry, 13 February 1986).

There is no evidence that Mrs Thatcher has ever opened *The General Theory*. Had she read it, Keynes could have warned her of the consequences of such monetarist policy in Chapter 9, where he wrote (ibid., p. 111) that 'the more virtuous we are, the more determinedly thrifty, the more obstinately orthodox in our national and personal finance, the more our incomes will have to fall when interest rises relative to the marginal efficiency of capital. Obstinacy can bring only a penalty and no reward.'

Neutral versus Natural

Keynes did not claim that interest rates exerted no influence over the savings and investment process. But he denied the concept of an equilibrium or *natural* rate of interest, beloved by both neo-Keynesian and monetarist economists. In Chapter 17 of *The General Theory* Keynes emphasised the difference between his own argument and that of the classical or neoclassical economists. He admitted that in his *Treatise on Money* (1930) he had defined what purported to be a unique rate of interest, which he then called the natural rate of interest and which, in the terminology of the *Treatise*, preserved equality between the rate of savings and the rate of investment.

However, in *The General Theory* Keynes stressed that he had overlooked the fact that in any given society there is, on this definition, a different natural rate of interest for each hypothetical level of employment and that he was no longer of the opinion that the concept of a 'natural' rate of interest had anything very useful or significant to contribute to the analysis of employment, interest and money. As he put it: 'it is merely the rate of interest which will preserve the *status quo*; and, in general, we have no predominant interest in the *status quo* as such.'

He added that if there is any rate of interest which is significant, 'it must be the rate which we might term the *neutral* rate of interest, namely, the natural rate in the above sense which is consistent with *full* employment, given the other parameters of the system,' although he adds that this rate might perhaps be better described as the *optimum* rate.

He also claimed that the neutral rate of interest supplies the answer to the question of what tacit assumption is required to make sense of the classical theory of the rate of interest. He admitted in passing that if the classical rate of interest is equal to that rate which will maintain employment at some specified constant level, 'there is little or nothing in its practical conclusions to which we need take exception'. He added that we thereby are 'safely ensconced in a Ricardian world'. (Keynes, 1936, pp. 242–4.)

In reality, Keynes was not as safe as he assumed. After his own demise, he would need to be defended not only against the 'born again' monetarists but also against those neo-Keynesians who neglected the disequilibrium and uncertainty implicit within his arguments, and arranged a posthumous marriage of his theory with those of the classical and neoclassical economists whose assumptions he was so concerned to contest.

Low Interest Rates

Before considering the arguments of the Keynesian neoclassical synthesis and its scope and limits, it is worth stressing that Keynes downplayed rather than dismissed the role of the rate of interest in the savings and investment process. While a higher rate of interest, he argued, could in principle attract higher savings, it would at the same time act as a disincentive to investment under either low or high growth conditions.

The argument is clear enough for conditions in which growth was low or where there was significant spare capacity. But Keynes also pushed the argument further, maintaining that profit expectations or the marginal efficiency of capital was at best, even under high growth conditions, a fragile commodity, depending in his own words on 'waves of irrationality'. In other words he claimed from past experience that depressed demand would depress profit expectations and cause management to reduce the rate of investment even if interest rates were low. A high or increasing rate of interest, even if it could attract increased savings, would act as a disincentive to actual investment and growth. Therefore Keynes argued that interest rates should be kept low during periods of both recession and growth. In practice, in the immediate postwar period in the United Kingdom a Keynesian Labour Chancellor of the Exchequer, Hugh Dalton, pursued a low-interest-rate policy of 3 per cent per annum.

7.3 The Keynesian-Neoclassical Synthesis: *LM/IS*

One of the main theoretical devices employed in the postwar period by so-called Keynesian economists was the product of a marriage between elements of Keynes' monetary theory and that of the classical/neoclassical theory of investment and savings. This is the *LM/IS* model. However, it is not strictly a model derived from Keynes. For one thing it fails to take account of the uncertainty which Keynes himself stressed in his analysis of liquidity preference and expectations. It also contradicts Keynes' economics in the sense that monetary policy played only a limited role in Keynes' own paradigm where (i) saving and investment determine income, rather than interest rates, and (ii) liquidity preference and the supply of money determine the interest rate, rather than money income. By contrast, through the *LM/IS* model, monetary policy strode to centre stage in a new 'Keynesian' neoclassical synthesis.

The *IS* Curve

The *IS* curve or line is associated with the notation of Alvin Hansen (1949), although the analytical technique which he employs stems directly from an article by Hicks (1937), while a similar analysis was undertaken by Oscar Lange (1938). Hansen's argument is illustrated in Figure 7.3(a). This graph describes combinations of income and the rate of interest on the horizontal and vertical axis respectively, which in turn relate to the level of investment and savings. It reflects the dependence of savings (S) on the rate of interest (r) and of investment (I) on income (y). It argues that if the rate of interest is high, investment will be low, since a high rate of interest discourages investment, and inversely that if investment is to be high, interest rates must be low. According to the argument, in order for investment to equal a high level of saving, the rate of interest must be low, and vice versa. The line combining the respective interest and income levels is labelled the *IS* curve, following Hansen's notation.

Apart from its constraints on Keynes' own exposition of the relations between savings and investment, Hansen's analysis also abstracts from (i) different profit rates in different enterprises, which in turn (ii) will reflect different self-financing schedules and tend to be related (iii) to the size and scale of enterprise (whether micro or meso), as well as (iv) the national or global markets in which they operate, and from which they schedule retained earnings for investment in individual economies. For instance, it is quite feasible that at income levels y^1 and y^2, companies may well be making such sizeable profits that they are prepared to pay higher interest rates than r^1 and r^2 respectively.

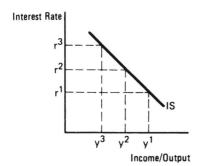 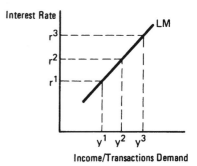

FIG. 7.3(a) Hansen's investment-savings schedule

FIG. 7.3(b) Liquidity, money supply and interest

Moreover, the model itself assumes a correlation between the income level, or the demand for funds, and the interest-rate level. But in practice it is not at all clear that this occurs. In the 1960s and the early 1970s, the interest rates on the Eurodollar market were especially high during a period of rapid growth in the European economy. Big business, typical of the mesoeconomic sector which was benefiting from such rapid income growth – both as a lender and borrower of funds – was prepared to pay high and fluctuating short-term interest rates to finance longer-term investment.

In other words it is not at all clear that if interest rates are high, investment will be low, because it is not clear that high rates of interest discourage investment if market demand is high. Nor, inversely, is it clear that if interest rates are low, investment will be high.

The issue is not simply a private language game played between economists. It has a momentous impact on policy assumptions, through the constantly re-stated claim that lower interest rates will 'stimulate' investment. Without effective demand there is no guarantee that they will do so. Overstating the case to gain impact, Keynes compared the investment promotion effect of lowered interest rates to 'pushing on a piece of string'.

The *LM* Schedule

Such qualifications of Hansen's *IS* curve also obtain from his *LM* or liquidity-money analysis. As illustrated in Figure 7.3(b), the *LM* line gives a correspondence between each interest rate and the matching level of money income. *M* is the total supply of money, while *L* allegedly represents Keynes' concept of liquidity preference, and *y* the transactions demand for money at a given level of income. If both prices and money are given, the *LM* line indicates the possible combinations of income and the rate of interest which will equate the supply and demand for money. In other words, the *LM* line shows the combinations of income and interest rates in which the market for money is assumed to be in equilibrium.

However, such an equilibrium requires that the speculative and transactions demands for real money add up to the total real money supply. This is not only a simpler version but a simplist reduction of the subtlety which Keynes himself ascribed to liquidity preference and the reasons why people (or institutions) would hold or demand money.

This point has been well put by Leijonhufvud (1968, pp. 201ff), who has emphasised that the differences between Keynes and later Keynesians on this issue lies in the way in which the aggregate money-demand function is specified. Textbook Keynesian models assume real money demand to be dependent upon real income and the interest rate. They also assume that this 'liquidity preference schedule' is stable in the long run. In Keynes' theory, however, the money-demand function depends not only upon income and the market rate of interest but also on the third variable, namely investor opinions or expectations with regard to the 'normal rate'. Or, as Keynes put it, 'what matters is not the *absolute* level of *r* but the degree of its divergence from what is considered a fairly *safe* level of *r*' (Keynes, 1936, p. 201). The *LM* model also abstracts from the extent to which expenditure is influenced by changes in returns to wealth (through stocks and shares) rather than simply changes in incomes from employment. The difference can be seen in

Keynes' own statement of the differences between himself and the 'Classics' on the theory of interest, where he wrote that: 'they would, presumably, not wish to deny that the level of income also has an important influence on the amount saved; whilst I, for my part, would not deny that the rate of interest may perhaps have an influence (though perhaps not of the kind which they supposed) on the amount saved *out of a given income*' (Keynes, 1936, p. 178).

LM Plus *IS*

The above constraints and qualifications on the *IS* and *LM* curves are compounded by their juxtaposition in Figure 7.4.

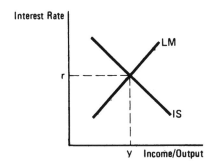

FIG. 7.4   The Hicks-Hansen *LM–IS* model

Again, the essence of such *LM–IS* analysis is simple. The *IS* curve shows the combinations of income (*y*) and the rate of interest (*r*) which reflect an equality between savings and investment. The *LM* curve shows the assumed combinations of *y* and *r* which, it is argued, express that stock of money which people or institutions are just willing to hold. At *r* and *y* both equilibrium conditions are satisfied. Savings equals investment, and money supply equals the demand for money. Any point on the line *IS* satisfies the first of these conditions; any point on the line *LM*, the second; but only their intersection satisfies both. Allegedly, this represents the 'solution' of the Keynesian and neoclassical systems.

But the model is too simple. It warps rather than weaves the pattern of reality. As Ackley (1961, p. 372) has shrewdly commented, 'the Hicks-Hansen diagram has elegant simplicity which appeals to many. It has the disadvantage, however, that most of the "works" are out of sight'. Any change in the data or functions which lie behind either curve affects their outcome.

The model is also highly dependent on its assumption of a given level of prices. Ackley admits this at various stages, yet nonetheless himself employs a 'wage and price level theory which ... is essentially that of the classical school'. He admits that such theory rests on the assumptions of (a) diminishing marginal returns in production as aggregate employment increases; (b) profit-maximising behaviour by employers; (c) *for convenience only* (our emphasis) pure and perfect competition in the sale of products; and when we allow money wages to vary freely, (d) perfect competition among workers for jobs' (Ackley, ibid., p. 377). Few of these assumptions obtain in the real world economy. Each of them has been extensively criticised as micro foundations for contemporary macroeconomics, not least because the multinational big business sector of the mesoeconomy has divorced key premises of the Keynesian and monetarist micro-macro synthesis.

Price-Making Power

The qualification of the interest elasticity of savings and investment represented by the price-making power of big business in the mesoeconomic sector is illustrated in Figure 7.5, in which both price and the rate of interest are measured on the vertical axis. For clarity of exposition the interest-rate levels r^1 and r^2 are equal to the price levels p^1 and p^3, and p^2 and p^4, respectively. If perfect competition obtains, in the sense that enterprises are price-takers rather than price-makers, then the Hansen conditions expressed in Figure 7.3(a) also obtain. In other words, higher rates of interest will deter investment.

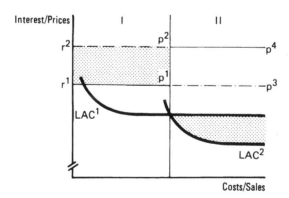

FIG. 7.5   Price and cost offset of interest-rate changes

However, as shown in Figure 7.5, if the enterprise is in a position to raise price from level p^1 to p^2 over the shaded area in phase I, then it can offset the interest-rate rise from r^1 to r^2 by its price-making power.

This is no more than we should expect from the theory of imperfect competition, analysed in some detail in *The Market Economy* (Holland, 1987a, chapter 4) and also indicated in outline earlier in this volume. In other words, imperfect competition can offset raised interest rates.

Lower Costs versus Higher Interest Rates

Similarly, lower long-run average costs made possible through new rounds of investment and dynamic economies of scale can offset interest-rate rises. This effect is indicated in the right-hand side or phase II of Figure 7.5, where the firm concerned embodies new technology and undertakes a new round of cost-lowering investment on the lines of the long-run average cost curve LAC^2.

Such dynamic effects are entirely ignored in most of the macroeconomic theory of the *LM-IS* variety, which tends to focus on very short-term or comparative static analysis, in which it is assumed that the only changing variable is the interest rate rather than price or cost.

Figure 7.5 does not suggest that firms can simply undertake major new investment projects in response to short-term interest-rate changes. Rather, the argument is that the successful innovating firm can offset what conventional *LM-IS* theory assumes to be the negative effects of interest-rate changes on saving and investment, by the lowering of its costs through a new round of investment. Thus a firm pursuing an 'offensive' investment strategy, with successive rounds of cost-lowering investment, will as a by-product be able to discount any medium-term trend to higher real interest rates irrespective of whether the government offsets such interest costs through concessional interest rates or investment subsidy.

Not least, bigger business may combine lower costs through new investment with oligopolistic price-making power. In other words, the firm undertaking investment and gaining cost savings equivalent to the shaded area above LAC^2 in phase II of Figure 7.5 may also be able to raise price from p^3 to p^4. Whether or not it does so is simply a bonus for the firm concerned, inasmuch as through cost lowering alone, the firm on LAC^2 would be offsetting the interest rise from r^1 to r^2. Rather, it shows the potential for the neutralising of interest-rate increases through a combination of price-making power and lower cost schedules.

Bigger Business – Lower Interest Rates

Figure 7.6 also indicates that mesoeconomic big business can obtain lower interest rates on its borrowing than smaller microeconomic firms. Thus the offsetting of interest-rate elasticity of the kind assumed in the *LM/IS* model does not simply arise from a combination of imperfect competition and cost saving from new rounds of investment. Evidence has already been cited in *The Market Economy* (Holland, 1987) and from Kumar (1984) and Shepherd (1979) that big business can and does gain lower interest rates in financial markets (whether through bank borrowing or in bond issues) because of its greater credit worthiness through greater market power.

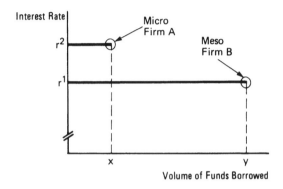

FIG. 7.6   Bigger business – lower interest rates

As Kumar (1984, p. 179) puts it: 'Since these institutions deal mainly in large blocks of shares, they have a preference for investing in large companies, which gives the latter favourable access to finance.' In international financial markets and especially the Eurodollar and Eurobond market, syndicates of 20, 30, 40 banks or more combine to reduce the risk of lending, which matches the attraction of secure and established global big business for borrowing at lower interest rates. Syndicated bank lending in global money markets has been reduced in recent years with the rising global crisis analysed in Chapter 9, but this does not affect the basic principle expressed in Figure 7.6 that micro firm A borrowing a volume of funds x will be charged an interest rate of r^2, whereas meso firm B (most frequently a multinational company) will be charged the lower interest rate of r^1 for the greater volume of funds at y.

Multinational Transfer Pricing

The transfer pricing analysed in Chapter 6 also makes possible the offsetting of interest-rate increases. Figure 7.7 simply applies the transfer-pricing sequence through four payments made by a multinational company in its global subsidiary trade against increased interest rates. The shaded areas below the price lines p^1 to p^4 represent the difference between the transfer prices charged by the multinational on its inter-subsidiary trade and the normal price which would obtain on a cost-plus or full-cost pricing basis in international trade. As the Figure illustrates, an interest-rate rise from r^1 to r^2 could easily be absorbed by the multinational company in stages II and III of the transfer-pricing process.

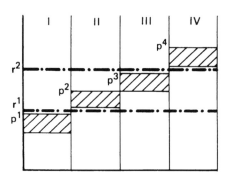

FIG. 7.7   Multinationals, transfer pricing and interest-rate offset

Chapter 6 has given several illustrations of the extent to which transfer pricing can overstate real costs and understate normal profit levels by 40 per cent. In reality, even with much lower levels of tranfer pricing, a multinational company could easily absorb the interest-rate increase from r^1 to r^2 within a fraction of the transfer price 'inflation' at one stage of such subsidiary trade worldwide.

Micro and Meso *IS* Schedules

The above qualification of standard *LM/IS* theory gains increasing force when attention is focused on the actual share of investment in total company costs, and therefore the proportion of costs which are sensitive to interest-rate changes. For instance, for most of the postwar period and for many companies, investment rarely exceeded 20 per cent of total costs. Thus even a 10 point rise in interest rates would amount to only 2 per cent of the company's total cost schedule. A far more realistic 2 point interest-rate increase would amount to only a 0.4 per cent increase on total costs, and a 1 per cent increase to 0.2 per cent.

Such fractions, if they are combined with evidence on business self-financing relative to external borrowing, indicate that an interest-rate rise of, for instance, 2 per cent will register not only a marginal but an insignificant influence on the translation of savings into investment by enterprise.

Moreover, less than a third to a fifth of such investment by big business needs to be externally financed. For instance, since the early 1970s total self-financing in UK and West German companies has ranged between two-thirds and 80 per cent of total investment needs (*Bank of England Quarterly Bulletin*, September 1984 and *The Economist*, July 1986).

Figure 7.8 illustrates the marginal nature of interest-rate changes to total investment funds in such a situation. Thus while the diagram includes standard *LM* and *IS* axes, the impact of a rise in the rate of interest from 10 to 12 per cent on the shaded area *abc* is on only 20 per cent of the investment of the enterprise in question (which is assumed to be self-financing 80 per cent of its investment needs). Therefore, translating through the arithmetic of the numerical examples given above on the minor share of investment in total company costs, an interest-rate increase of 2 per cent on only one-fifth of the investment needs of a company, which in turn was investing the equivalent of only one-fifth of its income, would amount to 0.008 per cent on total costs. If the self-financing ratio was only 60 per cent, the impact of the higher 2 per cent on interest rates would be 0.016 per cent, etc. In reality, such an inflation impact is less than the accounting error in even the best managed modern corporations.

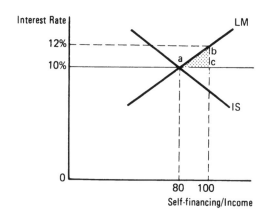

FIG. 7.8 Savings, interest rates and total corporate costs

Interest in Perspective

Such examples profoundly qualify assumptions of interest-rate sensitivity crucial to standard *LM/IS* models. Thus the model is undermined by five key factors:

(i) price-making power due to imperfect competition;

(ii)   lower costs available through new rounds of innovating investment;
(iii) the lower interest rates available to big versus small business;
(iv)   the transfer-pricing offset of interest rates available to multinational companies; and
(v)   the high share of self-financing versus interest-rate-sensitive external finance achieved by bigger business.

Certainly allowance should be made for the different degrees of price-making power open to meso and microeconomic enterprise. In other words, the bigger the business the greater its market power and potential self-financing, and its relative insensitivity to interest-rate changes. The smaller the business, the greater the negative impact of high interest rates. Higher interest rates as a macroeconomic policy tend to be punitive for the minor microeconomic enterprise, while insignificant for the mesoeconomic and multinational majors which dominate the global economy.

Figure 7.9 introduces such micro and meso dimensions to a macro analysis in which on the left-hand side of the diagram a micro investment and savings line for prevailing interest rates r^1 and r^2 still obtains. Corresponding to this, there is a macro *LM* line reflecting *inter alia* the readiness of financial institutions and other investors to put funds on the market at a prevailing rate of interest. However, the investment and savings schedule of the meso-economic enterprise is horizontal, rather than downward-sloping from left to right in the manner of the micro *IS* schedule. In reality, for big business, this obtains both for the five main reasons given above, and because such business decides to invest in terms of market growth, market share and sustaining innovation, rather than changed interest rates.

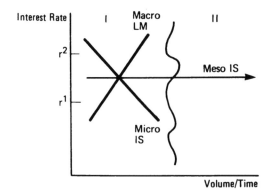

FIG. 7.9   Micro sensitivity and meso insensitivity to interest-rate changes

The Corporate Levy

The capacity of large and oligopolistic enterprise to generate a high proportion of its savings and investment through internally retained funds was stressed twenty-five years ago by Sylos-Labini (1962). In itself, this amounted to a major challenge to the interest-elastic savings and investment schedules assumed by the classical (and neoclassical) theory, with its emphasis on the dependence of enterprise on external finance for investment. Orthodox economics answered the challenge by ignoring it.

Likewise, Eichner (1976) stressed the significance of the supply of internally generated funds within enterprise. The reason, as he rightly observes, is that 'only a minor proportion of its investment expenditures will, in any case, need to be financed externally'. As he adds, stressing the planning period of big business, the large company can expect to arrange its financing in such a way that it will be able to tap the capital market for the marginal sums it may require during those phases of a cycle when the cost of borrowing will be at a minimum.

In terms of Figure 7.10, Eichner argues that the total supply of additional investment funds, *SI*, can be obtained simply by combining the supply curve for additional *internal* funds, SI^1, with the supply curve for *external* funds, based on a 'permanent' interest rate, *i* (ibid., p. 87). As he observes, since self-financed funds at the 'internal' interest rate *R* are available up to the point *Fa* in Figure 7.10 at less cost than the 'external' interest rate *i*, bigger business can be expected to obtain any additional investment funds internally through self-financing, or what he calls the 'corporate levy' (ibid., pp. 87–8).

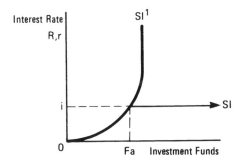

FIG. 7.10   Eichner's corporate levy and interest-rate insensitivity

Planning Supply and Demand

Developing his argument, Eichner argues that the price level in oligopolistic industry is set under ordinary circumstances so as to yield sufficient net revenue over the (Galbraithian) planning period to finance the level of desired investment. In other words, in Keynes' terms, the amount of planned savings likely to result from the prices that have been set is equal to the amount of 'planned investment' over the intermediate term. Thus he argues that there is good reason to assume that 'planned savings within the oligopolistic sector will be equal to planned investment'. This assumption implies an important modification of the savings-investment adjustment process formulated by Keynes in *The General Theory* (Eichner, 1976, pp. 196–200).

While this may well have appeared true of the conditions of savings, investment and growth in which Eichner developed his analysis, i.e. the late 1960s and early 1970s, it may have been less true of the crisis-ridden period of the late 1970s and early 1980s, as well as for some of the period post 1929. In other words, under conditions of major recession, depression or slump, even the big business corporation of the kind which Eichner characterises as 'the megacorp', or which Galbraith characterises as 'the planning system', may not be able to ensure that savings generated through internal funds equal investment needs. But, as with Sylos-Labini, conventional theorists did not answer Eichner's case. They simply ostracised it. Even 'progressive' texts such as those of Fischer and Dornbusch and (in its UK version) Begg, continued to assume that *LM/IS* models played a key role in the interpretation of the modern capitalist economy (Begg, Fischer and Dornbusch, 1984).

In practice, there is no doubt that the combination of a dominant market position and price-making power gives the mesoeconomic corporation a capacity to match internally generated savings and desired investment to an extent neglected by the standard micro theory with which the macro theory of both the neoclassical and Keynesian models has been wedded. The big business now dominant in the global economy is less sensitive to interest-rate changes in its savings and investment functions than the Keynesian neo-classical theory assumes, for the simple reason that its large scale gives it a major internal volume of funds generated through cash flow, and profits in excess of receipts, while the increased ratio of internal to external funds makes it less dependent on interest rates in its savings and investment decisions.

7.4 Friedman and Monetarism

We have seen in Chapter 2 how Friedman along with Duesenberry, Modigliani and Brumberg in different ways modified Keynes' consumption function by qualifying the primacy which he gave it in current income and demand. Instead, Friedman stressed relative, lifetime or permanent income. The significance of Friedman's permanent-income hypothesis was not purely theoretical. The emphasis on long-term permanent income meant less relevance for short-term government intervention through either monetary policy or demand management.

Despite these qualifications, the Keynesian paradigm remained essentially intact for a quarter of a century after the Second World War, reaching what Desai has called a *modus vivendi* or an 'accord' with the neoclassical paradigm that preceded it. The quantity theory of money in its original form had been in eclipse even before Keynes' *General Theory*, but the Keynesian revolution virtually obliterated it. Students were instructed that the quantity theory was no more than an identity and that by defining velocity circularly one could establish a Fisher or Marshall-type relationship. But this had no theoretical content. In *A Treatise on Money* (1930) Keynes had laid down full-employment conditions under which the quantity theory could come into its own, allowing that 'when the factors of production are fully employed . . . and when the volume of saving is equal both to the cost and value of new investment – there is a unique relationship between the quantity of money and the price level of consumption goods and of output as a whole, of such a character that if the quantity of money were to double the price levels would be doubled also.'

Nonetheless the Keynesian school thereafter ignored the quantity theory. Monetary policy in the Keynesian paradigm was an ineffective or insignificant influence on the level of employment or output. In *LM-IS* terms (despite our reservations on its application and use), the unresponsiveness or inelasticity of investment to interest-rate changes came to be expressed in terms of a horizontal *LM* line as in Figure 7.11(a), whether or not the investment and savings schedules moved from the lower level of IS^1 to the higher level of IS^2. Even when significant concessions were made on the

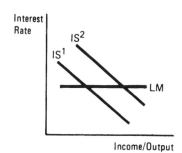

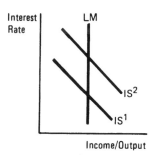

FIG. 7.11(a) 'Keynesian' interest-rate insensitivity

FIG. 7.11(b) Friedman's 'crowding-out' hypothesis

long-run nature of the consumption function or 'permanent income', and a more sophisticated multi-asset model of financial markets admitted in theory, 'the primacy of fiscal policy and the specificity of monetary policy were never questioned' (Desai, 1981, p. 60).

Friedman and the Demand for Money

Thus when in 1956 Milton Friedman claimed that 'the quantity theory of money is in the first instance a theory of the *demand* for money; it is not a theory of output, or of money income, or of the price level' (Friedman, 1969), he was making a statement which at the time was a key challenge to Keynesian monetary theory. In one sense Friedman was abandoning the Fisher version of the quantity theory of money in favour of Marshall's cash balances reformulation. But he did not accept any distinction between the transactions and the speculative demand for money which had played an important role in Keynes' concept of liquidity preference, nor between individual and business demand for money.

While both Keynes and Friedman admitted that the role of money supply was its ability to relate nominal incomes and price changes to changes in the aggregate stock of money, Keynesian macro theory had relegated money supply to being a passive agent in income determination. Friedman now made it an active ingredient. He did this in two ways. The first was to claim that the demand-for-money function was empirically stable, not in the sense of a constant income velocity of money but an econometric stability. The second innovation in using the demand for money and the theory of income determination was through claiming that the supply of money is *autonomously* determined, i.e. that it is a function of variable or changing factors which do not enter the demand-for-money function nor are determined by the demand for money (Desai, 1981, pp. 62–3).

The 'Crowding-Out' Hypothesis

In the Keynesian neoclassical model, exogenous money supply gave a relationship between the rate of interest and income on the *LM* curve which intersected with the *IS* curve. Implicit within this was the idea that the force of effective demand would determine real incomes as well as the assumption that prices were fixed. If price changes were related to the level of unemployment, as argued by Phillips (1958), it could still be said by Keynesians or neo-Keynesians that prices and incomes (with savings and investment) were still largely determined by the level of demand.

Friedman was aware of the incompatibility between his own case and that of Phillips (elaborated in Chapter 8). But he was also challenging the *LM-IS* version of the Keynesian neoclassical synthesis which accepted that M was exogenous. Essentially Friedman maintained that the level of income is determined by the level of autonomous demand irrespective of the interest rate (zero interest elasticity in terms of the IS curve). Thus the interest rate is determined by the position of the LM schedule rather than the investment-savings schedule (which in Friedman's terms depends upon M).

This situation, illustrated in Figure 7.11(b), gives the essentials of Friedman's 'crowding-out' condition. Thus in contrast with the 'Keynesian' assumptions of Figure 7.11(a) that a fiscal stimulus (or public spending) could raise investment and saving without influencing liquidity and money supply, Friedman maintained the reverse. In other words, in Friedman's paradigm, boosting money supply (for instance, through increasing public expenditure) will register no significant impact on investment and saving at full employment.

But herewith a paradox. For within Friedman's argument, the money supply only determines income if prices are stable. This means that the revised quantity theory claimed to *determine* a price level which it in fact *required* to be constant. Thus to obtain a theory of income determination from the quantity theory, Friedman had to choose one of the variables as determined and assume the rest as being fixed.

Lipsey simplifies the contrast between monetarists and Keynesians in the following form, claiming that: 'For monetarists, fluctuations in the money supply cause fluctuations in national income; the money supply is exogenous. . . . For neo-Keynesians, fluctuations in national income cause fluctuations in the money supply; the money supply is endogenous' (Lipsey, 1979, pp. 779 and 781).

Causation or Mirrors?

Friedman has been aware of the problem of demonstrating causality between changes in the money supply and changes in the level of demand or income. Indeed, in the 1960s he explicitly admitted that

> even under the most favorable conditions . . . the demand for money is quite inelastic with respect to the variables . . . which give at most a theory of money income: it then says that changes of money income *mirror* changes in the normal quantity of money. But *it tells us nothing about how much of any change in income is reflected in real output and how much in prices.* To infer this requires bringing in outside information as, for example, that real output is at its feasible maximum, in which case any increase in money would produce the same or a larger percentage increase in prices, and so on [Friedman, 1969, p. 62, italics added].

This is the essence of the modern monetarist claim to superior scientific status over the Keynesian paradigm on the macroeconomy. Friedman's use of the word 'mirror' in such a context is revealing. As Desai (1981, p. 64) comments: 'does "mirror" mean cause or can it be said to leave open the direction of causality between Y and M and assert only correlation?' Certainly the mirror image is striking not only in the sense of suggesting that it may 'all be done by mirrors' but in the more significant sense that philosophers have similarly found themselves resorting to 'mirror metaphors' when unable to demonstrate causality in their own arguments on facts and values. Mirror or 'picture' images played a key role in the early work of Ludwig Wittgenstein and his difficulty in demonstrating the applicability of his so-called 'atomic propositions', as did 'shadow' metaphors in Plato's celebrated failure to demonstrate the relation between transient temporal values and absolute or atemporal values. Mirrors are not only the last resort of metaphysicians. They are also the stock-in-trade of con-artists.

Stability in Question

Friedman claimed in 1956 that 'the quantity theorists accept the empirical hypothesis that the demand for money is highly stable – more stable than functions such as the consumption function that are offered as alternative key relations' (Friedman, 1956). But he was also aware that he needed more than mirror images to displace the Keynesian paradigm. His main counter-claim in this respect was his major work undertaken with Anna Schwartz, *A Monetary History of the United States, 1867–1960*, which alleged a strong correlation between changes in the money supply and changes in the level of business activity. Thus Friedman and Schwartz argued that there was a correlation between major recessions, associated with an absolute fall in the money supply, and minor recessions with a slowing down of its rate of increase below its long-term trend (Friedman and Schwartz, 1963). What this meant was the claim that monetary policy acted directly on income through changes in the money stock, rather than indirectly via the rate of interest through investment to income. The conclusion implied that money multipliers were larger in the short run than investment multipliers and that the 'transmission mechanism' of monetary policy was much simpler and by implication more effective than Keynes' preference for fiscal policy. In turn, this implied that Keynesian demand management was redundant.

Keynes versus Friedman

As already mentioned in Chapter 2, Friedman has claimed that he began his work on the consumption function as a Keynesian but that it was his empirical findings which prompted him to develop an alternative to the Keynesian theory of income determination. By contrast, critics of Friedman such as Andre Gundar Frank have claimed that during the period of alleged derivation of principles from practice in the 1950s, Friedman required his graduate and doctoral students to go back and 're-work' the data when they found evidence which conflicted with his own findings.

It certainly is clear that Friedman's revival of the quantity theory of money led to conclusions for macroeconomic policy which were totally opposed to those of Keynes. In short, Keynes is pro-intervention on the basis that – left to itself – the market mechanism cannot be guaranteed to 'clear' markets and restore long-term full employment and income equilibrium. Friedman's arguments imply that any government policy seeking to adapt money growth to variations of economic activity would destabilise the long-term equilibrium of the market. This led to the conclusion that political pressures to 'do something' should be resisted since yielding to them would do more harm than good (Friedman, 1969, p. 187).

Keynes Plus Friedman?

In contrast with this opposition of Keynes versus Friedman, Pennant-Rea, Cook and Begg (1985) have argued that Keynes and Friedman are compatible under different conditions. These are reproduced in Figure 7.12 within an *LM-IS* framework.

The argument stems from Keynes' claim that in a recession or slump the economy will be in the grip of a 'liquidity trap'. In other words, at very low interest rates, people or institutions do not care whether they hold money (cash) or bonds. Thus, because the *LM* curve at this level in phase I of Figure 7.12 is flat, changes in the money supply will have little effect on the output demanded. Certainly these are conditions in which Keynesian fiscal policy (or public expenditure) can be applied with impunity inasmuch as increasing savings and investment would simply shift the IS^1 curve to IS^2 and income from y^1 to y^2 without inflationary effects.

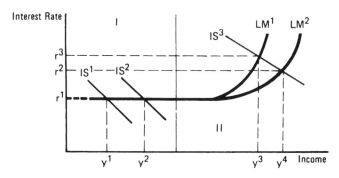

FIG. 7.12   Synthetic solution: Keynes plus Friedman

Friedman and the monetarists focus on a different case. Expressed in LM and IS terms, if interest rates are high (or very high), speculative demand for money is squeezed to almost zero so that the LM curve in phase II of Figure 7.12 is almost vertical. In such a situation, it is claimed that a shift in the IS curve to IS^3 through tax-cutting fiscal policy will have relatively little effect on aggregate demand, whereas a money-expanding shift from LM^1 to LM^2 would raise demand from y^3 to y^4.

Superficial Synthesis

Pennant-Rea, Cook and Begg (1985) argue that the only dispute between Keynesians and monetarists 'therefore seems to boil down to nothing more complicated than an argument over the slope of the LM curve. An obvious compromise was to admit that both theories made sense: use monetary policy to dampen demand if interest rates soar (e.g. in a boom) and fiscal policy to stimulate demand when interest rates are low (e.g. in a slump).' They then claim that the debate 'is dead'.

Now most so-called monetarists believe that demand management can affect output and employment only briefly, while Keynesians argue that the effects may last long enough to be worthwhile. So the focus of the argument is shifted to the supply side of the model. The central question is how the labour market reacts to changes in total demand (Pennant-Rea, Cook and Begg, 1985, p. 11).

However, while it might be attractive to many students to assume that LM and IS curves have been banished from their syllabus, the debate is far from dead. Certainly, an increase in investment and savings, either through fiscal policy or through public spending, will have less effect on interest rates or prices when demand is low or the economy is under-employed. Similarly, it will have more effect the closer the economy approaches to full employment. But a range of factors qualify the nature of the synthesis proposed by Pennant-Rea, Cook and Begg.

Qualified Full Employment

First, as already argued extensively in Chapter 3, the full-employment ceiling of the economy is relative. Raising the full-employment ceiling from FEC^1 to FEC^2, as elaborated in Chapter 3, depends not only on the elasticity of demand for migrant labour, but also on the extent to which increased labour demand in expanding sectors of the economy is countered by decreased demand for labour in other sectors. Evidence has been produced to show that in the so-called 'miracle' booms of postwar Germany, France, Italy and (most notably) Japan, structural and spatial shifts of labour from agriculture to industry and services and from less to more developed regions made possible sustained full employment without notable price inflation over a period of between a fifth and a quarter of a century. Such factors lie outside the constraints of a standard *LM/IS* framework.

Second, while Pennant-Rea, Cook and Begg argue that 'the central question is how the labour market reacts to changes in total demand', their own argument leads directly into issues of wage flexibility or inflexibility (wage cuts or defence of wage levels) and in turn to policies designed either to weaken the bargaining power of labour or – through incomes policies – to seek to restrain its impact on global demand and prices at full employment. (These arguments are developed in the next chapter.) However, at this stage, it is worth observing that while the main 'labour reserve' from agriculture has been reduced to a tenth or less of total labour supply in yesteryear's miracle economies, the application of technology and innovation in the global pace-making economies such as Japan already indicates the extent to which a new 'reserve' army of labour is being created by technical progress and accompanying technological unemployment.

Third, the synthesis of Keynes and Friedman under different employment and demand conditions, neglects the qualification of *LM-IS* arguments themselves by the rise of mesoeconomic power and multinational capital. Five such qualifications have already been illustrated in this chapter. They suggest not that the debate between Keynes and Friedman is dead, but that the argument has shifted to the structure of saving, investment and money supply in multinational markets, which is in turn transforming the demand implications of conventional *LM/IS* macroeconomic theory.

7.5 Monetarism in Question

For thirty years after the war, it was commonplace to claim that 'we're all Keynesians now'. President Nixon said so just before the decline of Keynesianism as the dominant macroeconomic orthodoxy, and his own demise from power. Over the last decade such claims are more hesitant or hardly heard. The influence of monetarism has been so pervasive that many commentators have come to talk of a 'new economics' of the new Right. Such a new orthodoxy has taken over not only treasuries and finance ministries, but also major international institutions such as the IMF.

Cherchez la Monnaie

However, as stressed at the outset of this chapter, monetarism is not new. It is one of the oldest forms of macroeconomics. Indeed, it was the 'old economics' of the 'old Right' which Keynes himself set out to criticise and demolish. For, while Friedman was not the first economist to reason that we should 'seek out money' to analyse inflation – or *'cherchez la monnaie'* – he was among the first to dress an old theory in new econometric clothes, and thereby reintroduce the assault on public spending and the mixed economy into the mainstream policy framework.

Ironically, in view of the confidence of his claims, Friedman himself has stated that he is not altogether satisfied with the term 'monetarism' and it is certainly clear that there is no agreement even among monetarists as to precisely what monetarism is. However, several of the key claims, as follows, have been identified.

Variable Quantity. For instance, although the quantity theory of money is nominally the basis of monetarist theory, it has several variations including the claims: (1) that the velocity of circulation is constant or at least stable (Fisher, 1911); (2) that the demand for money is interest-inelastic (Friedman, 1959, and Friedman and Meiselman, 1963); (3) that the demand for money has low interest-elasticity (Friedman, 1959, and Laidler, 1966); (4) that the demand for money is more stable than the consumption function (Friedman, 1959); (5) that the money stock and changes in the money supply are important determinants of aggregate macroeconomic activity as represented by nominal GNP (Friedman, 1956 and 1958, Friedman and Schwartz, 1963; and Sims, 1972, cit. Desai, 1981, chapter 4).

Self-Regulation. The monetarists' claim on the self-regulation of market forces is mainly implicit in econometric and academic statements of their theory. It nonetheless becomes explicit throughout Friedman's *Free to Choose* (1980). Self-regulation claims not only that the market mechanism (as in Keynes' analysis) could be relied upon at the microeconomic level to ensure sufficient supply of goods and services at a competitive price relative to demand, but also (unlike Keynes) that the macroeconomy – on assumptions of a regular rate of increase of the money supply – could be relied upon to adjust supply and demand in the microeconomy without government intervention.

By implication this meant that the Keynesian stress on involuntary unemployment or under-employment was arbitrary, and that high levels of unemployment were the result of the voluntary choice of workers to 'price themselves out of jobs'. With registered unemployment at over three million and real unemployment arguably over a million more in the UK in the mid 1980s, such an argument could well seem unattractive to workers themselves. Nonetheless, this was not the aspect of Friedman presented by Conservative politicians to the electorate. Rather, they pushed Friedman's other argument that incomes policies were irrelevant to inflation. Seeking with one bound to be free from wage restraint, several million workers thereby consigned themselves to the dole.

The Mixed Economy. The monetarist bias against public spending is part of the 'crowding-out' claim of monetarists, which amounts to the assertion (1) that public expenditure competes with private expenditure for a given level of savings; (2) that public expenditure diminishes private expenditure and that public expenditure 'drains' rather than 'sustains' the private sector of the economy (Friedman and Meiselman, 1963).

The argument of crowding-out in *LM* and *IS* terms has already been examined earlier in this chapter. However, it is notable that this monetarist case is expressed almost entirely in terms of competing demands for funds at full employment. The irony over the decade from the mid 1970s to the mid 1980s has been the lack of the full-employment condition against which the hypothesis can be tested.

Further, the monetarist crowding-out hypothesis simply does not consider the circularity of public income and expenditure outlined in Chapters 1 and 2 of this volume. In other words, no recognition is given to the extent to which public revenue taken through tax can be re-injected into demand through public spending, thereby generating income, employment and matrix multiplier effects (of the kinds analysed in Chapter 2).

Nor is any account taken of the arguments made in Chapter 3, and developed within a 'Hicksian' model of growth and cycles in the mixed economy. This partly derives from the unreadiness of monetarist economics to consider multiplier effects themselves (illustrated in the previously cited admission to this author by Chancellor of the Exchequer Nigel Lawson that the UK government in the early 1980s made no estimates of the private income generated by public expenditure). In turn, therefore, monetarism totally fails to analyse the direct or indirect effects of public spending on the private sector of the modern market economy.

Yet, such expenditure in fact 'sustains' rather than 'drains' the private sector. Illustrations abound not only from the widespread perception in the United States of the role of the military-industrial complex and the demand generated for private companies by the NASA and defence programme, but also in a more down-to-earth context, already cited, from the impact of public expenditure on the construction sector of the British economy.

The Natural Rate of Unemployment. Criticised by Keynes in *The General Theory*, as indicated earlier in this chapter, this is a consequence of the assumptions of the self-regulating market economy. As Desai has shown, the hypothesis claims in particular (1) that the equilibrium level of output and equilibrium unemployment are independent of the nominal price level. In turn this implies (2) that the trend of real economic variables such as output and employment is independent of the trend path of the nominal money supply (Lucas, 1972, and Sargent and Wallace, 1975); and (3) that only unanticipated changes in the money stock have any influence on economic activity (Barro, 1977), which has considerable implications for the 'augmented expectations' hypothesis of monetarists in relation to inflation (considered further in chapter 8).

The natural rate hypothesis was extensively attacked by Keynes not only on the grounds that such a rate itself could reflect widespread or mass unemployment, but also on the grounds that when the economy was in a 'liquidity trap', with insufficient incentive for investment due to depressed confidence or expectations (in Harrod terms, a low or declining rate of warranted growth), there is no guarantee that a recovery towards full employment would be achieved.

It is worth observing in this context that the 'natural rate' hypothesis runs the risk of the fallacy of 'naturalism' as expounded by G. E. Moore in *Principia Ethica* (1903). Put in simple terms, this amounts to claiming that empirical or so-called 'positive' phenomena are not simply specific particulars available from evidence at one time, but amount to 'principles of nature' and thereby assume not only *ex posteriori* but also a categorical *a priori* status.

Such concepts are charming when applied by Keats to the claim that 'Beauty is truth. Truth beauty.' But as economic propositions they are questionable. For instance, in the eighteenth century the philosopher Immanuel Kant tried to establish 'categorical imperatives', combining *a priori* and *synthetic* (or empirical) status at the same time. Kant held this to be the case with Newtonian physics. But such physics have since been profoundly qualified by Einstein and quantum physics. They become entirely negative when applied to either national economies or the global economy in the name of a monetarist metaphysics which, *inter alia*, has no proven empirical base on which to claim that most of the world 'naturally' should be unemployed, underemployed, or unable to gain the prospect of future employment.

Exogenous and Homogeneous. Exogenous money supply is a crucial supporting condition for the monetarist claim that changes in the money supply or the money stock are not demand determined but supply determined.

The argument becomes quixotic in relation to the monetary crisis in the decade since Friedman's works have become accepted by the world's policymakers, inasmuch as it is evident that the supply of petrodollars by OPEC surplus countries was matched by sustained demand from other countries, and in particular Latin America. The result was an outstripping of domestic translation of savings into investment through demand pull (in turn reflecting the readiness of governments to borrow to gain resources to meet development needs) rather than simply a supply-determined increase.

Exchange Rates

On exchange rates, 'the law of one price' is the international dimension of monetarism which claims (1) that through a transmission mechanism via stable demand functions, and the real balances in individual countries relative to the price levels of traded goods, exchange-rate movements will reflect the relative rates of domestic inflation. It implies (2) that exchange-rate changes are wholly determined by changes in relative price levels or purchasing-power parity theory (Frankel, 1979), and (3) that exchange rates reflect the international price of a country's money and thus that changes in the determinants of the demand for real money balances (incomes and prices) determine exchange-rate movements (Frankel, 1976, and Dornbusch, 1976, cit. Desai, 1981).

Such a 'law of one price' in the international transmission mechanism of monetarism has been challenged implicitly in Chapters 5 and 6, where it is argued that both Keynesian and monetarist terms of reference on international exchange rates, trade, pricing and payments have been transformed by the rise of multinational investment and trade on a global scale. The range of transfer-pricing or 'price-making' activities by multinational companies profoundly qualifies such basic assumptions of monetarist theory.

In principle, Friedman could argue that he need not concern himself with the activities of multinational companies or the way in which they qualify or undermine the effectiveness of exchange-rate changes for achieving greater export volume at a lower price, since by the monetarist's credo this amounts to unwarranted government intervention in the price mechanism. It was on this basis that the case for 'floating' rather than fixed (or supported) exchange rates gained ground.

But the monetarist case on exchange rates is fractured even on these grounds. For in reality a range of factors influence exchange-rate changes. These include (i) *competitiveness*, which is itself influenced, as in the UK case, by the scale of multinational foreign investment and production by companies which have thereby substantially reduced the strength of UK visible exports (conversely with West Germany or Japan, where predominantly national production and specialisation has assisted export performance, and revalued the Deutschmark and the Yen); (ii) the *balance of payments*, influenced both by export competitiveness and by the rate of growth of import-reducing domestic demand, which in turn is affected by the under-invoicing of exports and the over-invoicing of imports by multinational companies, on the lines analysed in Chapter 6; (iii) *speculation* on foreign-exchange markets, for or against particular exchange rates, including so-called 'pure' speculation (now accounting for some 85 per cent of foreign-exchange transactions following floating exchange rates, as against only

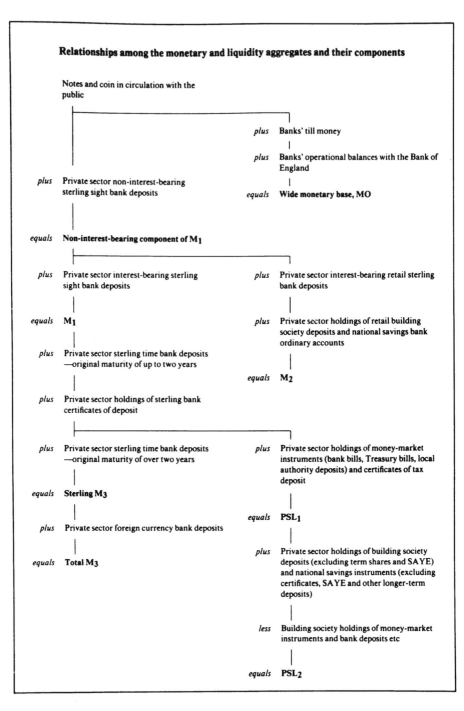

FIG. 7.13(a) The components of money supply
(Source: *Bank of England Quarterly Bulletin*, March 1984)

some 15 per cent fifteen years ago during the Keynesian era of 'fixed' rates), and also (iv) *leading* and *lagging* of payments by multinational companies whose slowing (or speeding) of export payments to subsidiaries in a given country can result in the actual devaluation (or revaluation) of its currency.

Which Money Supply?

Besides which, if the monetarist imperative is *'cherchez la monnaie'* monetarists themselves have been less than clear about which money to look for to explain their hypothesis. Some of the standard definitions in current usage are illustrated in Figures 7.13(a) and (b), with the latter drawn by *The Economist* for a sample period in the UK in 1983. M1 is currency plus 'sight' or demand deposits (i.e. deposits with commercial banks available on demand). M1 can be broken down between interest-bearing and non-interest-bearing money in private-sector sight deposits, as indicated clearly enough in Figure 7.13(b). M2 – not included in Figure 7.13(b) – covers savings accounts and time deposits (i.e. deposits which can only be withdrawn by giving notice), with the exception of large-denomination negotiable certificates of deposit or CDs. M3 includes, in addition, deposits held in thrift or savings institutions. These are the three main categories of money supply used by monetarists themselves. For purposes of exposition we should perhaps add to them M5 – not included in Figures 7.13(a) or (b) – which, in addition to M3, includes large-denomination negotiable certificates of deposit or CDs. M0 (or M nought) was a definition seized upon by Conservative Chancellor Nigel Lawson after the failure of correlations between M3 and price inflation, and, in contrast with the ambitious range of M3, it covers only notes and coins, till money, and bankers' deposits.

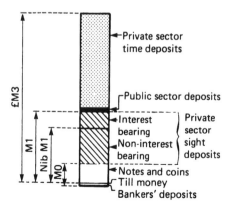

Fɪɢ. 7.13(b)   From M3 to M0

Hidden or Revealed?

There are also 'hidden' forms of money which are not included in conventional statistics. Among these, and important in countries such as the United Kingdom – although not in the United States – is the overdraft facilities granted by banks, enabling customers to make payments in excess of their actual credit balance. In addition there are notes and deposits in foreign currencies which can be converted into domestic money at the current rate of exchange, and which have very considerable influence in fluctuations in the money supply in the short term and assume considerable importance in view of the increased trade and payment of multinational companies between their own subsidiaries in different countries (Kaldor, 1982, p. 71).

Powers of Prediction?

Relative success may be achieved for one or other of the main definitions of money supply (in particular M1 and M3) for a given country in a given time-period, but not for both. Fellner has drawn attention to the way in which the empirical testing of money supply, meeting 'increasingly disappointing' results in the performance of models purporting to explain the behaviour of M1 (currency plus demand deposits), shifted increasingly to the behaviour of the broader M2 and M3 aggregates (Fellner, 1977, p. 91).

In the 1920s Irving Fisher recognised that interest-rate changes and expectations of changes in the price level would tend to produce variations in the velocity of circulation of money. The point at issue is that the quantity theorists, while recognising that the velocity of circulation may vary with changes in economic circumstances, insist that such variations are predictable in the form of the demand-for-money function. In other words, the monetarist in this respect claims that a stable velocity of circulation is a useful predictive device enabling policy-makers to forecast variations in key economic variables. The key alleged prediction is the claimed correlation between increases in money supply (Fisher's M) and increases in the rate of inflation (Fisher's P), as well as between the rate of growth of money supply (M) and the rate of growth of GDP, total output, or total transactions (T).

The alleged predictive power of monetarist theory for a correlation between inflation and the monetarists' most highly favoured index (M3) is assessed for the US and the UK from 1970 to 1985 in the following chapter. However, as Figure 7.14 (Desai, 1981, p. 166) shows, the ratio of £M3 to GNP in the UK over the period of a century exhibits massive variations for the postwar period alone, with a dramatic decline in the £M3 to GNP ratio after 1950/51 (except for the period of Conservative Chancellor Barber's 'boom' of 1973–4).

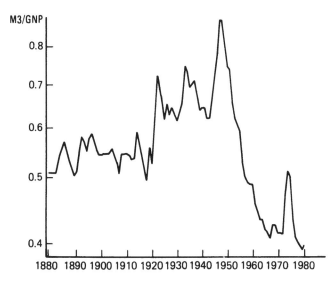

FIG. 7.14   Sterling M3 and GNP: secular instability (Source: Desai)

Monetary Targets

During the 'Keynesian' era, monetary targets were not given priority in government forecasting. Since Friedman, in some cases, they have been. For instance, from 1979 the Conservative Chancellors Sir Geoffrey Howe and Nigel Lawson tried to achieve precise targets for monetary growth in the UK economy. This exercise has been of more than local British significance. The leading government paying lip service to monetarism – that of the Reagan administration in the US – confounded the picture by combining monetary restraint with what amounted to a Keynesian policy of expanding demand. Thus the UK experience provides a 'testbed' for monetary targets like none other (even including the pragmatic monetarism of Chancellor Kohl in West Germany). The question whether heads of government or heads of state could tell the difference between either half of Fisher's equation at the time they put monetarism to the test – like the question whether they have ever opened Keynes' *General Theory* – is not relevant to the seriousness with which they sought to apply monetarist prescriptions in practice.

That seriousness was attested by Sir Geoffrey Howe before he became Chancellor of the Exchequer, in a speech made in the summer of 1978 when he stated that:

Proper monetary discipline is the key element in this battle [against inflation]. . . . This requires publicly stated monetary targets, for the rate of growth of the money supply. These targets must fall from year to year, so that inflation is steadily squeezed out of the economy. There must at the same time be a steady and determined reduction in the size of the Government's borrowing requirement. [Conservative Central Office Press Notice, 19 July 1978.]

This basic message was carried over into government. On coming into office, the Chancellor said in his budget statement:

It is crucially important to re-establish sound money. We intend to achieve this through firm monetary discipline and fiscal policies consistent with that, including strict control over public expenditure. . . . We are committed to the progressive reduction of the rate of growth of the money supply.

A key role was given to the M3 definition of money supply (cash and bank deposits) and to control of its sterling growth (£M3). In practice the government were to pursue this less through fiscal or taxation policies than through an attempt to control the Public Sector Borrowing Requirement (PSBR), which in practice meant efforts to cut public spending.

In its concern to affect confidence in monetarist policy, the government introduced the innovation of including a Medium-Term Financial Strategy (MTFS) in its financial statement and budget report to parliament. Its objectives were spelled out by the Chancellor in his 1980 budget statement. The MTFS set specific targets for a reduction of the money stock, measured in terms of £M3, of one per cent a year.

The Chancellor was emphatic – in 1979 – in describing the consequences of failure in meeting these objectives. As he put it, in a statement to the Commons Treasury Committee:

Any suggestion of a reversal would take us into horrendous areas of outer space so to speak. It seems to me that it is now pretty widely understood, and this is the strength of the analysis, that inflation is bad, that inflation can only be conquered if you have got effective control of monetary policy, and that has got a relationship with public borrowing and public spending, and that to achieve your results you have got to sustain that policy over a period of time [House of Commons, 1981].

Off Target – Off Course

In practice, for just over a year, it looked as if the incoming Conservative government of 1979 was more or less on line with its monetary targets. Sterling M3 until July 1980 was either within, or only just over, its upper target range. But from the latter half of 1980, as shown in Figure 7.15, it took off for the 'outer space' which Sir Geoffrey Howe had described as so horrendous. By December 1980, £M3 was growing at something like 25 per cent a year rather than the 7–11 per cent target range which the Chancellor had set himself.

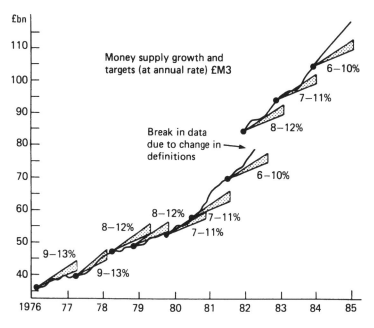

FIG. 7.15 'Off target': Sterling M3 outcomes 1976–85
(Source: *The Economist* and HM Treasury)

Abandonment of 'Minimum Lending'

Interest rates were also way off target. The government did not raise interest rates when £M3 'took off', preferring to seek to cut public spending. As shown in Table 7.1, the government's minimum lending rate first soared, then sank, then was abandoned altogether in August 1981.

TABLE 7.1   Minimum Lending Rate

Date of change	New rate (%)
1979	
April 5	12
June 12	14
November 15	17
1980	
July 3	16
November 24	14
1981	
March 10	12
August 20	Abandoned

Source: *UK Financial Statistics*, September 1981.

The real base rate of interest as determined by the big clearing banks (four of which command 85 per cent of UK deposit banking) showed that the Conservative government inherited a falling real rate which was actually negative at the time of the May 1979 election. It rose and rose again under their stewardship, with a peak in January 1981 and a still higher peak in the Autumn of 1981 – when the Chancellor responded by abandoning the minimum lending rate.

Meanwhile, the rise in interest rates had a dramatic effect on precisely the small and medium firms which the Tories had aimed to promote as their main vehicle for investment, jobs and exports. The rate of bankruptcies, particularly among the smaller firms which lacked the scope of bigger business to absorb or avoid higher interest rates through price-making power or transfer pricing, rose to unprecedented postwar levels. Sceptics and critics of monetarism in the corridors of the House of Commons at the time were heard to remark that when Labour's postwar Chancellor Hugh Dalton had set the postwar minimum lending rate at 3 per cent – less than a fifth of its level in November 1979 under the new 'monetarist' government – many Keynesians had reckoned that it was too high.

How did the professional monetarists react to this targetting fiasco? Several of them gave evidence to the Commons Treasury Committee (HOC, 1981) on the results of monetary policy. Broadly, they were divided between Purifiers, Purists and Pragmatists.*

The Purifiers

The 'Purifiers' are typified by Patrick Minford of the University of Liverpool. Minford's position is of interest not so much because of a direct influence on government as such, but because his rationale conformed so closely with the 'short, sharp shock' approach evident in the optimism of so many early Conservative government expectations of the anticipated effects of controlling money supply on both inflation and macroeconomic performance. The Purifiers expected parallel mechanisms to cleanse the system of inflation through monetarist policies of: (1) price flexibility, and (2) 'rational' expectations by firms and unions about the consequences of a given path of monetary policy. In turn this implies (3) a close and specific relation between the growth of money supply and inflation. According to Minford, with flexible prices, rational expectations and consistent growth of the money supply, the aims of monetarism could be realised in the UK in the near future.

The Minford 'purification' approach put much stress on the need for government not to confuse expectations by qualifying or modifying its

---

* The Committee itself chose a different categorisation of the New Classical School – the Gradualists and the Pragmatists.

policies over the short to medium term. If things get rough, the government should stick to its course and show evidence of a more determined commitment to bring money supply under control (i.e. cut public spending). The approach provided a theoretical background to the instinctive politics of 'the lady's not for turning', as Margaret Thatcher put it to the Conservative annual conference of 1980 during a period when it was evident that both money supply and inflation were soaring upwards.

The Purists

The key 'Purist' to give evidence on the government's record on monetary policy was Friedman himself. Yet what is notable about this evidence to the Commons committee is the extent to which he avoided the 'pure' approach proper for which he has become internationally famous (or infamous) and in fact qualified key aspects of his own previous position.

Friedman's role cannot be underestimated in influencing the Conservative Party after the two general election defeats of 1974. His attack on public spending and the public sector – as propagated by the Institute of Economic Affairs and drawn to Margaret Thatcher's attention by Sir Keith Joseph – had a major influence on those in the Conservative Party for whom his rationale nourished deeply felt presumptions against the welfare state consensus of previous Conservative and Labour governments. His simplisms that 'inflation starts in one place and one place only – national treasuries' was echoed time and again in Conservative front bench speeches before and after the general election of 1979. His claims to econometric and academic acclaim played an important part in the confidence of the 'high period' of Tory monetarism, i.e. those brave few months in which a new generation of politicians declared that they were, and were proud to be known as, monetarists.

Faced with the clear evidence that a government claiming to be monetarist, and inspired by him, was so seriously off course with his policies, Friedman was careful to qualify his argument to the Commons committee. He criticised the use of fiscal methods to control the money supply (endorsed by the government), and asserted that he saw no direct connection between the public-sector borrowing requirement (PSBR) and the money supply, in contrast with the government which had chosen this as one of the central planks of its policies.

Of more interest, Friedman profoundly qualified his former position on wage controls and argued in practice for that 'Keynesian' taboo of the Tory government, an incomes policy. In an Institute of Economic Affairs paper published in London (Friedman, 1974), he argued that there was a case for the indexing of wage contracts, i.e. linking wages to the retail price index as a means of reducing the unemployment costs of fighting inflation. He combined this with the judgement that on the basis of UK and other evidence, 'only a modest reduction in output and employment' would result from reducing inflation to single figures by 1982. In other words, Friedman was hedging his bets against the failure of the Thatcher government to deliver results from applying monetarism in Britain in the lifetime of one government. But to protect himself, he had modified the pure theory of monetarism. His political disciples would not thank him for the qualification. If they had entered the 1979 election offering yet another incomes policy they might well have lost it.

The Pragmatists

The chief pragmatist to give evidence to the Commons Treasury Committee on the government's monetary policy was self-styled. Professor Laidler distinguished himself from the instant monetarism school of Professor Minford. Formally, his position is not dissimilar from that of Friedman, though it lacks the authority of the oracle himself. As Laidler put it:

> The case for gradualism rests on the proposition that, ultimately, the main burden of adjustment will be borne by the price level. I stress the word ultimately, because in my view, the brunt of the impact of monetary policy falls not upon the price level at all, but rather upon interest rates and real income (and therefore employment). Only later do effects on the price level begin to come through. It is this belief above all which leads me to advocate a slow, rather than a rapid, reduction in the monetary expansion rate as the correct response to a deeply embedded inflation. . . .

In the short term, this was good news for the government. It supported the view that things would get worse before they got better. But it also encouraged the question of how long was 'later'.

Milton Friedman had encouraged the expectation that within two or three years of 'constant' money supply, a flourishing market economy based on freedom to choose would have generated sufficient initiative and entrepreneurship to revive the British economy. But any longer could outrun a general election.

'Monetarism is Dead: Official'

Shortly before the Falklands war the popularity of the Conservative government was at an all-time postwar low. Shortly thereafter it was at an all-time high. Thus the first electoral test of monetarist policies at the polls was postponed. Nigel Lawson succeeded Sir Geoffrey Howe as Chancellor in 1983 and continued the policy of 'there is no alternative', with frequent statements on the floor of the House of Commons that Keynesianism had been tried and failed, and that there could be no return to deficit spending and the inflation which it 'inevitably' caused.

Meanwhile, the collapse of manufacturing production (afflicted by the negative multiplier effects of cuts in public spending analysed in Chapter 3) continued apace and with a vengeance. By 1986 it had still not recovered to its 1979 level. The sterling exchange rate fell at one point to nearly £1 = $1, without the visible export boom anticipated by those who had previously argued (contrary to the case explored in Chapter 5) that nothing was wrong with British industry which could not be solved by a more competitive exchange rate.

Without North Sea Oil revenue, and without the electoral appeal of 'putting Britain back on the map' (of the South Atlantic) through the Falklands war, the monetarist experiment would probably have been over by 1983 or 1984. As it was, it took two or three more years before its official demise. It is reputed that a leading US monetary economist once argued that if Milton Friedman had been playing cards rather than shuffling definitions of money supply, he would long ago have been thrown out of any self-respecting casino. His disciple Chancellor Lawson shuffled alternative monetary targets to seek to distract attention from the government's failure to hit the favoured £M3 target in any year from 1979 through to the end of 1984 (as illustrated in Figure 7.15).

Having shrunk his targets from the broader M3 to the much narrower M0 of notes and coins, till money and bankers' deposits, which gained little credibility in the 'square mile' of the City of London, Nigel Lawson simply announced in October 1985 that the government would no longer be setting monetary targets. As a *Financial Times* leader commented that month: 'Monetarism is Dead: Official' (*Financial Times*, 19 October 1985). Thus the end of the pretension for monetarist targets came less with a bang than with an M nought whimper. Registered unemployment rose to over three million, despite several efforts by the government to stimulate jobs by massaging the statistics. At 13 per cent, this was some 10 per cent above the highest level of the allegedly 'failed' Keynesian era. Real unemployment, combining those taken off the figures by government statistical revision, plus Youth Training Schemes and married women, was over 4 million, and worse in absolute terms than the lowest depths of the slump of the 1930s.

By the autumn of 1986, Chancellor Lawson had reverted to demand expansion with a pre-election mini-boom, and his spring 1987 budget confirmed this by taking tuppence off income tax. If not 'back to Keynes', the Conservative commitment to fully-fledged monetarism was over.

7.6 Summary

(1) Monetarist theory focuses on the relation between money supply and prices in the basic Fisher equation, whereas Keynesian theory focuses on the relation between the velocity of the circulation of money and the level of transactions demand.

(2) There are important differences between Keynes' monetary economics and Keynesian neoclassical monetary theory, with the latter neglecting Keynes' stress on the subsidiary role of interest-rate changes in influencing investment, and his case on the irrationality of long-term expectations of the rate of profit on investment.

(3) The Hicks-Hansen *LM-IS* model overstates market rationality and understates the greater importance given by Hicks to the distinction between induced and autonomous investment (and its relation to expectations, or Harrod's warranted growth) in his original exposition of the dynamics of the trade cycle and economic growth in modern market economies.

(4) The influence of interest-rate changes assumed in the *IS* model can be offset either by (i) the price-making power of big business under conditions of imperfect or oligopolistic competition, or (ii) the cost savings made possible for bigger business by successive rounds of innovating investment, or both.

(5) Big business in the mesoeconomic sector can and does borrow funds at significantly lower interest rates than microeconomic enterprise, thereby further offsetting the impact of interest-rate changes on investment decision-making.

(6) Cumulative transfer pricing by multinational companies through their subsidiaries worldwide can more than offset major interest-rate changes in national or international money markets.

(7) Self-financing by bigger business accounts for between two-thirds and four-fifths of investment funds in given national economies (with lower shares in West Germany and Japan and higher shares in the US and UK). In practice this further reduces the significance of interest-rate changes on investment decision-making since big business can cover the major part of its investment needs without access to external finance. Multinational big business is more influenced by the imperatives of keeping abreast of the global technology frontier, and global market share, in its investment decision-making than by interest-rate changes, to which it is either insensitive, or markedly less sensitive than smaller national firms.

(8) While the basis of monetary economics is the role of money supply,

monetarists themselves, including Milton Friedman, have failed to establish consistent correlations between any given definition of money supply and the long-term performance of the market economies. Relative success may be achieved for one or other of the main definitions of money supply in a given country and a given time-period, but not for all countries or all time-periods. This in part reflects the differences in the structure of production (and not least multinational production and big business self-financing) in different economies.

(9) Monetarist theory claims that public spending drains the private sector of the economy through 'crowding out' the demand for private-sector funds. While in principle such a crowding-out effect may be relevant for some economies at full employment under specific circumstances, the crowding-out argument is vitiated by (i) the mass unemployment which has accompanied the monetarist experiment in economies such as Britain in the 1980s, and also by (ii) the availability of finance for investment through multinational money markets (the Eurodollar and Eurobond markets) on which multinational companies are both creditors through the placing of surplus funds as well as borrowers.

(10) The most transparent effort to pursue monetarist policies through monetary targets has been in the UK economy since 1979. Yet such targets were more consistently missed than hit by the government through to the mid-1980s, when it in practice abandoned the central priority which it had hitherto given in its Medium Term Financial Strategy to money supply, and reverted to a demand-led pre-election expansion.

8 Inflation and Deflation

It is well known that inflation redistributes resources – mainly from the weak and poor to the rich and strong in society. It is for this reason that several governments have claimed widespread popular support since the mid 1970s for giving priority to deflationary policies in the fight against inflation. But in many cases this has meant cuts in public spending on housing, health, education and social services and other forms of 'social income' policy paid indirectly through taxation rather than directly by cash. Justified by both some 'Keynesians' and monetarists, such cuts further redistribute resources away from the weak and poor who at the same time could also find themselves unemployed. Certainly, deflationary policies to 'fight inflation' entail costs and benefits which affect different social groups and classes within society. Neither inflation nor the policies to control it are socially neutral.

Theories of inflation have been subject to changing fashions among professional economists. It used to be assumed by the 'sound money' theorists that recession or deflation reduced real prices, as indeed it did in the 1920s and 1930s. Later, Keynesian economists claimed that in the 1950s and 1960s 'demand-pull' for labour reduced unemployment but increased trades-union bargaining power, causing 'cost-push' inflation. Through the 1960s and before the commodity and oil price increases of the early 1970s, some attention was paid by policy-makers – especially in continental Europe – to a different kind of cost-push caused by the increased price-making power of big business. But this was very much a minor theme in the literature. The 1970s were dominated both by external or exogenous inflation – especially oil and energy prices – and by the revival of monetarist theories of inflation. In the late 1970s and early 1980s, however, it became apparent that prices were not declining with the fall in the rate of economic growth or outright recession (as in the case of British manufacturing industry). Thus inflation combined with stagnation gave birth to 'stagflation'.

More often than not, economists favoured uni-causal explanations of inflation. After a survey of previous thought on the subject which gave the appearance of disinterestedness, theorists frequently proceeded to maintain one main cause of inflation at the sacrifice of others, with important implications for policy decisions.

Yet inflation is a complex rather than a simple phenomenon. Expressed in prices, it also reflects new power structures, including not only the power of trades unions or energy producers, but also the price-making power of the mesoeconomy and multinational big business. Not least, diametrically different conclusions can be drawn from apparently similar analyses of inflation itself.

8.1 Money Push and Demand Pull

As we have already seen in Chapter 7, monetarists have resurrected Fisher's identity $MV = PT$, where M is the money supply, V the velocity or speed of its circulation, P the price level and T the level of output or transactions. In recent years, monetarists have persuaded many governments that there is a unique relationship between the rate of inflation, P, and the rate of growth of the money supply, M, of which public borrowing and spending is a key component. Keynes had been critical of this supposed relationship, pointing out that the velocity of circulation of money, rather than its level or rate of increase, could have a crucial effect on demand and prices. As shown in Chapter 7 (p. 287), for Friedman the decisive relationship in the quantity theory of money is between M and P; for Keynes, the decisive relationship is between V and T.

Deflationary and Inflationary Gaps

The difference is critical. Nonetheless, in a key respect the arguments of Keynes and Friedman, and in a parallel sense those of the Keynesians and monetarists, appeared similar in their fundamental analysis of inflation. This was especially true of the so-called inflationary 'gap' between prices and output.

For instance, in a simplified form, the right-hand column in Figure 8.1(a) represents the level of demand and transactions within the economy. Keynes argued that if the supply of goods and services in a given economy fell off, from d^1 to d^2, this did not necessarily indicate that costs of production were too high or money supply too low, but rather that there was insufficient demand in the system. In Keynesian terms, the gap between full employment of capital and labour on the supply side of the system is called the 'deflationary gap'. Unlike the classical or neoclassical monetarists, who argue that insufficient supply will reflect inadequate competitiveness and therefore recommend reduced costs (including reduced wages), Keynes maintained that public intervention could assure a return to full employment by either direct spending or indirect inducements to spend (i.e. tax cuts or fiscal policy).

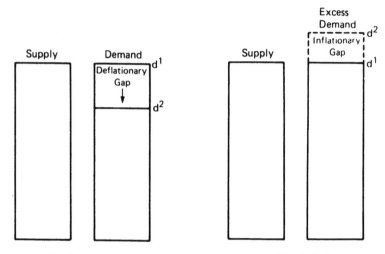

FIG. 8.1(a)   The deflationary gap   FIG. 8.1(b)   The inflationary gap

Inversely, as shown in Figure 8.1(b) Keynes argued that if there was too much demand in the economy relative to its supply capacity (either through a misjudgement of government policy or through some other reason), there would be an 'inflationary gap', equivalent to d^1d^2.

It was the apparent similarity in this respect between Keynes and monetarism, and the lack of an extensive alternative analysis of inflation in Keynes' *General Theory*, which proved the weak flank of the 'Keynesians' in government from the mid 1970s. It has already been seen that Keynes had discounted price-making power by big business as a factor in inflation. This made sense in his own time, and especially during the period when he was writing *The General Theory*, when – as shown in Figure 8.2 – prices in the United States (and also Britain) fell with the fall in output after 1931, and lagged behind output up to the end of the decade. But it made less sense from the 1970s, when increased inflation accompanied increased unemployment. Keynes also discounted the bargaining power of trade unions as an inflationary factor. Again, following the setback of the General Strike in 1926 and the weakened bargaining power of the unions thereafter in Britain during the post-1929 depression and slump, this conformed with the evidence of his time. Moreover, of course, Keynes did not live to see the rise of OPEC and the major increase in oil and commodity prices which was a marked feature of economic crisis in the 1970s.

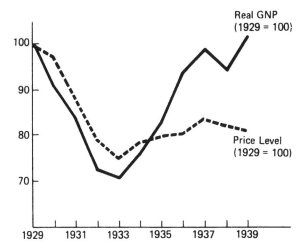

FIG. 8.2   Deflation and disinflation: the US economy in the 1930s
(Source: Dornbusch and Fischer, 1981)

Budgetary and Fiscal Policy

Nonetheless, despite its similarity in analysis of the inflationary gap, Keynes' own approach to inflation and deflation differed from monetarism in three main respects. First, it implied an active government budgetary or fiscal policy. Second, it maintained that lowering interest rates to reduce costs in a deflationary period, or increasing them under inflation, was of no major significance, since it was the level of demand and not the structure of costs which mattered. Third, since Keynes stressed a tendency to instability or disequilibrium in the system, rather than the equilibrium favoured by the monetarists, he reckoned that the state would need to assume a virtually permanent budgetary and fiscal policy – either 'disinflationary' to offset an inflationary gap, or 'reflationary' to make up insufficient demand.

According to Keynes, a 'neutral' budget by which the state simply balanced its books without either stimulating or restraining the system would be an exception; for the monetarists it should be the rule. (The concept of a neutral *budget* should be distinguished from Keynes' concept of a neutral *interest rate* which, as we have seen in Chapter 7, he defined as that rate which would promote or sustain full employment.)

But, again, by the mid 1970s, the combination of low growth with high inflation and mass unemployment posed problems for Keynes' analysis. In Britain, or the US in the 1930s, a reflationary package could increase employment without inflationary problems. How to reflate was a secondary issue, whether through fiscal stimulus by lowering taxes (the indirect approach) or by increasing public spending such as the New Deal programme under President Roosevelt (the direct approach). After the first OPEC oil price 'shock' of 1973, such a simple reflationary package seemed to be ruled out on both inflationary and balance-of-payments grounds. By the same token, however, a deflationary package designed to reduce inflation would – and did – increase unemployment.

Monetarist Claims

While these new problems for the Keynesian paradigm weakened the defences of those who, for a generation, had claimed to be Keynesian in their approach, the monetarist assault on Keynes' economics is more basic. Monetarists claim that Keynesian policies of demand stimulus tend to be inflationary whatever the initial level of unemployment. They argue that the very mechanism of the Keynesian 'unbalanced' budget, when seeking to stimulate the economy, directly causes inflation. They contend that the increase in the money supply entailed by a Keynesian reflationary budget (putting more money in people's pockets through tax cuts or through the wages and profits stimulated by direct public spending) will, by increasing M in Fisher's equation, necessarily increase P.

Monetarists such as Friedman have invoked the spectre of hyper-inflation in support of their policies. In this context, it is worth commenting that it was not hyper-inflation which arrested the economic miracle of a country such as Brazil, but the oil price shock of the early 1970s which restricted the purchasing power of the less developed countries to which, by that time, Brazil was selling the majority of its manufactured exports.

For half a century the developed countries have not suffered, nor are likely to suffer, from the sustained hyper-inflation such as gripped Germany in the 1920s or is typical of several Latin American economies today. Minor inflation accompanied the so-called 'miracle' growth of several leading economies in the 1950s. And moderate inflation was already apparent in the 1960s. But major inflation has been temporary and short-lived in most developed economies, even in the crisis years of the 1970s and 1980s.

Cautious and Brazen

Friedman's case is that inflation starts in one place only – national treasuries – through excessive money supply. The Friedman findings have been challenged on empirical grounds, on methodology and causation. Put simply, it is not clear that his findings demonstrate cause rather than effect between

Fisher's *M* and *P*, nor that they include other factors causing inflation in the twentieth-century economy.

On causality, Friedman himself (1969) has admitted that the evidence was less than clear-cut:

> The direction of influence between the money stock and income and prices is less clear-cut and is more complex for the business cycle than for longer movements . . . changes in money stock are a consequence as well as an independent cause of changes in incomes and prices. . . . This consideration blurs the relation between money and prices but does not reverse it . . . even during business cycles the money stock plays a largely independent role.

This academic statement of causal change is tentative and highly qualified (in contrast with Friedman's more brazen televised claims that 'inflation starts in one place and one place only – national treasuries'). Friedman also admits that the role of *lags* in the impact of changes in the money supply on incomes and prices is highly variable. Thus although he claims that 'the rate of change of the money supply shows well marked cycles that match closely those in economic activity in general and precede the latter by a long interval', he also admits that 'the timing varies considerably from cycle to cycle' and that 'the timing differences are disturbingly large'.

This nonetheless did not prevent Friedman from arguing, in a form readily adopted by governments (including the British Conservative administration from 1979), that the lag for the causal effect of changes in the money supply on income and prices would be 'around two years'. Nor did it prevent him from recommending that it was best to have a general rule for a fixed growth of the money supply and stick to it come what may.

Contested Claims: The US and the UK

Since millions of people have been thrown into unemployment on the basis of monetarist claims, it is worth recognising, as already stressed in Chapter 7, that monetarists themselves have difficulties in finding an adequate index of money supply against which to correlate inflation – allowing also for the fact that there are different indices of inflation itself, such as the retail price index or the GDP implicit price deflator (which is wider ranging and arguably a better index of inflation).

The important point is that monetarists have never been able to establish that a *given* increase in the money supply causes a *given* increase in prices. This is the case even with their favoured M3 definition of money supply (i.e. private and public-sector time deposits, private-sector sight deposits, bankers' deposits, and notes and coins in circulation). Figure 8.3 shows annual percentage changes in M3 money supply and inflation (GDP implicit price deflator) in the United States from 1970 to 1985. Such annual rates of change reveal the absence of a close link between the growth rate of money and the inflation rate in the short run. It is arguable that Friedman's claim that the rate of change in the money supply will precede inflation by 'around two years' gains some support from the US data in the 1970s. But such a lag effect breaks down in the first half of the 1980s, where the relationship between M3 money supply and inflation becomes asymmetric, even taking lags into account.

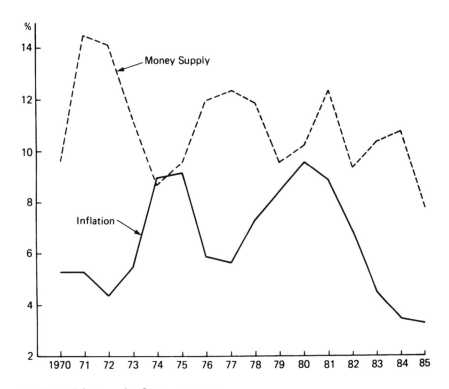

FIG. 8.3   US $M3 and inflation 1970–85

Similarly, Figure 8.4 for UK M3 money supply and inflation (on the same GDP deflator basis) shows similar results of an arguable lag effect up to the latter 1970s. But in 1979–80 there was no lag; instead there was an identical increase in M3 money supply and inflation (encouraging some newspaper editors at the time to conclude that an X per cent increase in the money supply equalled an X per cent inflation in the short term). From 1982 sterling M3 took off, while inflation continued to fall. Again, the data reveals the absence of a close link between the rate of growth of money supply and inflation, and suggests that other factors were also at work in determining the inflation rate. Ironically, a much better 'fit' can be gained for the much-maligned Phillips inflation/unemployment curve for the UK from 1980 to 1985 than for Friedman's claims of a correlation between M3 and inflation.

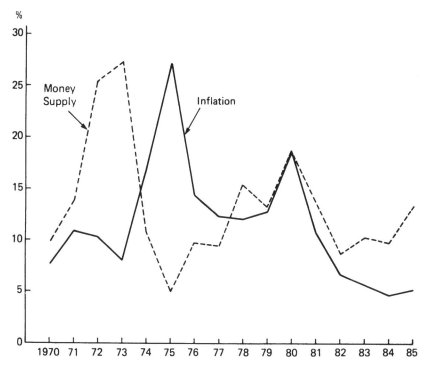

* Inflation = GDP deflator at factor cost

FIG. 8.4   UK £M3 and inflation 1970–85

Cost-Push and Demand-Pull

In one sense the monetarist analysis, though stressing money *supply-push*, amounts in effect to an analysis of *demand-pull* through the effects of the inflationary gap. In other words, increased money supply puts more money-demand in the economy, which thereby pulls up the rate of inflation. However, the main debate between demand-pull and cost-push theories of inflation has been between Keynesian economists and within the Keynesian paradigm prevailing until the mid 1970s.

One problem in analysing the role of cost-push and demand-pull in inflation – as with links between M3 and money supply – is determining a clear sequence of cause and effect. There are markets in which the suppliers may be so passive that price rises solely as a result of the competitive bidding of the buyers. In other markets, buyers may be passive and suppliers may raise prices as they see that they can sell their output at a higher price.

It is important to realise that neither form of inflation excludes the other: in practice the most common type of price changes may be those brought about both from pushing by the sellers and pulling by buyers. Empirical tests are generally inconclusive in trying to distinguish cost-push from demand-pull elements in such price changes. We simply cannot perform the controlled experiments necessary to make a good separation of demand and cost elements in inflation. Timing comparisons are not especially helpful. Causes in many cases are logically inseparable from effects. In a closely inter-dependent economy, effects can precede causes. Macroeconomic correlations alone cannot give the answers.

The cost-push theory maintains that it is increases in factor prices (the cost of capital or investment goods, labour or wages, etc) which cause increases in final goods prices, and that these changes in factor prices can occur independently of the state of excess demand. The demand-pull hypothesis reverses this order of causation, and says that it is increases in demand for final goods that causes increases in their prices. These price increases in turn cause a rise in the demand for factors of production, which, in turn, causes a rise in factor prices. Thus it is increases in the level of goods prices which cause increases in the level of factor prices. But the causal sequence is still less than clear.

Thus the competing cost-push and demand-pull theories of inflation may be closer to Doctor Doolittle's two-headed Push-Me-Pull-You creature, rather than to the proverbial conundrum of which came first, the chicken or the egg.

8.2 Cost-Push: Big Unions

The most common cost-push theory is that the rise in factor prices is caused exclusively by union power. It is this cost-push-through-union-power theory on which postwar Keynesian theory concentrated, and especially the claims of a trade-off between the rate of inflation and the level of unemployment argued in particular by Phillips (1958).

The Phillips Curve

In a study of UK data for almost a century, Phillips concluded that a high proportion of the variations in money wage rates could be associated with changes in unemployment, and hence demand for labour. The Phillips curve is represented in Figure 8.5. Essentially, it claims that the higher the level of employment, the higher will be the rate of inflation (or inflationary full employment, IFE), and that inversely the higher the level of unemployment, the lower the rate of inflation will be (or disinflationary unemployment, DIU).

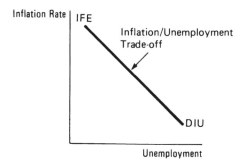

FIG. 8.5   The Phillips curve: inflationary full employment and disinflationary unemployment

Phillips argued that an equilibrium, in principle making possible zero inflation, could be achieved at five per cent unemployment. Low by today's standards, this nonetheless was double or two-thirds higher than the unemployment rate prevailing in the 1950s and 1960s during the height of the 'Keynesian era'.

There are several such wage-cost-push variants. The hypothesis (1) that the cost-push by unions is of a uniform pressure predicts that wages, and therefore the general price level, will show a steady upward trend (with random variations around this trend). In fact, however, the general price level shows no such steady trend. A second and slightly less crude version of the cost-push-by-unions hypothesis is that (2) the pushing is related to union strength. To make this testable we would need a measurable index of union strength (e.g. percentage of labour force unionised, or the size of union funds). The third of the possible labour cost-push hypotheses is that (3) the pushing is related to changes in the cost of living. A fourth version of the cost-push theory is that (4) the strength of the cost-push is related to the level of business activity. According to this theory, unions push strongly upwards on wages when business activity, cash flow and profits are high, and less strongly when they are low.

Proportionality?

Since movements in the price level of goods consumed by workers conform quite closely to movements in the general price level, the theory suggests that wage-push should vary with the price level. This variant gives rise to the wage-cost-push spiral: prices are determined by wages (e.g. price = cost + standard mark-up) and wages are proportionately determined by prices (a 1 per cent increase in prices causes a 1 per cent increase in wages). The economy could be at equilibrium at any price level, but as soon as some exogenous factor causes prices to rise, a situation will develop in which wages chase prices and prices chase wages in an upward spiral. Granted the assumptions of proportionality, a 10 per cent increase in wages not only would cause a similar increase in prices, but yet another increase in wages of the same percentage, etc, ad infinitum.

In itself, even allowing for 'knock on' or spread effects from initial wage increases, it is worth bearing in mind that while wages and salaries can be as high as 70 or 80 per cent of total costs in services, they are frequently around 30 or 40 per cent in manufacturing (and less than 10 per cent in some parts of the Japanese automobile industry). Thus at full employment, according to the Phillips curve theory, a 10 per cent wage increase would result, in its first-round effects, in a 7 or 8 per cent increase in services, a 3 or 4 per cent increase in manufacturing in economies such the US or the UK, but less than a 1 per cent increase in Japan.

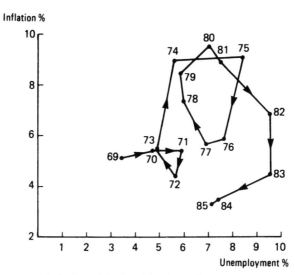

* Inflation = GDP implicit price deflator

FIG. 8.6   US evidence: the 'knotted' Phillips curve

US Evidence

How far does this get us? The measurement of the coefficient relating wages to prices does not provide a complete theory of inflation so long as the wage-price correlation is less than one to one.

Figure 8.6 shows the annual correlation between registered unemployment and inflation (GDP price deflator) in the United States from 1969 to 1985. As is immediately apparent, in contrast with the left-to-right downwards-sloping curve of the Phillips hypothesis, no linear correlation emerges. Indeed, on such US data, the Phillips curve has got itself 'knotted'.

Such recent data – albeit in more dramatic form – confirms earlier findings by Dornbusch and Fischer (1981) and by Samuelson and Solow (1960). Taking Phillips' main conclusions – that the money wage level would stabilise with some 5 per cent unemployment, and that the rate of increase of money wages would be held down to 2–3 per cent with about 2.5 per cent unemployment – Samuelson and Solow argued (1) that if there is any such relationship characterising the American labour market it had shifted in the previous 50 or 60 years, and (2) that it might take 8–10 per cent unemployment in the US to stabilise money wages.

UK Evidence

Testing of the Phillips curve against recent UK evidence is interesting in terms of Samuelson and Solow's hypothesis that it might take over 8 per cent unemployment to get a 'fit' with the data. As illustrated in Figure 8.7, the downward left-to-right slope of the Phillips curve for the UK from 1980 corresponds almost precisely with the standard Phillips curve as illustrated in Figure 8.5. This is despite the fact that in the first half of the 1970s, the UK evidence shows virtually no relationship at all between the rate of inflation and the rate of unemployment, with the inflation rate rising vertically from 1969 to 1974 (other than for the 'cul-de-sac' of 1971–72) and soaring to nearly 28 per cent in 1975, despite unemployment increasing from just under 3 per cent to around 4.5 per cent.

In this context, it is also worth observing (though for ideological reasons Phillips himself and others refrain from doing so) that the essential argument of the Phillips curve relates to Marx's theory of the role of the reserve army of labour. While Marx stressed the role of a reserve army of unemployed in facilitating capital accumulation as the 'reserves' were drawn into the 'active' labour force, the corollary of such labour reserves is the ability of firms to restrain wage increases as workers compete for jobs at lower wage rates when faced with the alternative of unemployment.

Nonetheless, while the Phillips curve may enjoy a 'second coming' from the

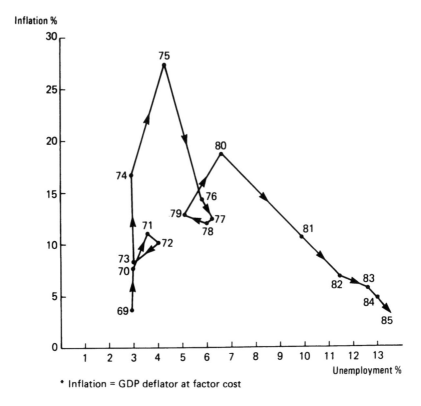

FIG. 8.7   UK evidence: the Phillips curve and mass unemployment

evidence of the UK data for 1980–85, it would be a mistake to extrapolate such findings to the role of unemployment in determining wage rates in the market economies as a whole. Figure 8.6 shows that no such 'fit' of the Phillips curve obtains for US inflation and unemployment in the same 1980–85 period. Thus, although the Phillips curve prima facie fits better than Friedman's claim for a correlation between money supply and inflation for the UK data for the 1980–85 period, we still need to look elsewhere for a more complete theory of the role of labour and wage demand in inflation.

Wage Costs and Labour Supply

In particular, we need to look at the structure of the labour market in relation to the structure of capital and especially the costs of multinational companies. For instance, a conventional model of wage costs and labour supply is given by Pennant-Rea, Cook and Begg (1985). Reproduced in Figure 8.8(a), this maintains that there is a straightforward labour demand schedule, LD, reflecting a ratio between the wages offered by enterprise and a labour supply schedule, LS, reflecting the willingness of workers to take employment at a given wage level. As represented in Figure 8.8(a), at wage level w^1 the labour supply will be at LS^1 and the fuller employment level E^1. Conversely, at the higher wage rate w^2 the labour supply schedule LS^2 will be at the lower employment level E^2.

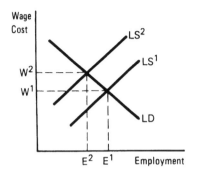 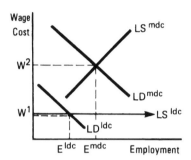

FIG. 8.8(a)   The conventional national labour supply and demand model

FIG. 8.8(b)   The dual multinational labour market

However, the Pennant-Rea, Cook and Begg argument both implicitly assumes that workers are prepared to price themselves into or out of jobs, and also assumes a national rather than multinational labour market. By contrast, Figure 8.8(b) illustrates the dual labour market structures available to enterprise which are both national and multinational in character. Thus while in more developed countries the labour demand line (LD^{mdc}) and the labour supply line (LS^{mdc}) corresponds in form with the model of Figure 8.8(a), with a wage cost at w^2, the employment level in the more developed country (E^{mdc}) is greater than that implied by the Pennant-Rea, Cook and Begg model. By contrast, the multinational company having access to labour at the lower wage cost w^1 on the labour demand schedule in less developed countries (LD^{ldc}) can achieve lower wage costs at employment level E^{ldc} in such less developed countries.

Global Labour Reserves

The argument is important both because it takes into account the access of multinational companies to lower-cost labour in less developed countries, but also for its dynamic implications. In other words, Figure 8.8(a) amounts to a comparative-static analysis between alternative wage levels in one country. While compatible with Phillips' analysis on the trade-off between unemployment, wages costs and inflation (or Marx's analysis of the reserve army of labour), it fails to take account of the extent to which multinational capital does seek and can gain access to labour at a dramatically lower cost in less developed (and especially intermediate) economies. In other words, the 'reserve army of labour' argument implicit in the Phillips hypothesis now obtains for multinational capital in the global economy as a whole, where it can draw on labour reserves at much lower cost in less developed countries, rather than simply within a single national economy. This in turn has implications for government policies which seek to restrain inflation by raising unemployment in the developed countries, since there is virtually no way in which any such government in the First World could achieve wage rates comparable with those in the Third World (i.e. from a half to a tenth lower wage costs) without both provoking social confrontation and collapsing internal demand in the more developed country.

Dynamic Effects

Further, the comparative-static analysis within the conventional wage costs and labour supply model of Figure 8.8(a) takes no account of the dynamic effects of lower production cost schedules available either to national capital through go-getting 'offensive' investment policies (such as those pursued with such success in recent years by big business in Japan) or the effect of 'global labour reserves' by which multinational companies can achieve the most appropriate combination of high-cost technology with low-cost wages wherever it best suits them in the world economy.

Figure 8.9 illustrates such comparative factor (i.e. capital and labour) costs for a multinational company. Thus whereas in phase I the long-run average cost of a company in a more developed country (LAC^{mdc}) makes possible a normal profit at price p^1, with a wage level W^{1mdc}, in phase II the cost curve of a multinational company in a less developed country (LAC^{ldc}) at wage cost W^{2ldc} makes possible either a normal profit at price level p^2 or a super-normal profit at price level p^1.

Such arguments and such relative profit rates attainable for multinational companies through location in less developed countries should by now be quite familiar from the previous argument of both this volume and *The Market Economy* (Holland, 1987). However, despite the fact that both Keynesian and monetarist theories of inflation choose for the main part to stay in the stratosphere of testing correlations between macroeconomic data, the significance of such lower cost and higher profit schedules attainable by multinational companies is in practice very considerable. This is especially so if account is also taken of the extent to which multinational companies can avoid tax through transfer pricing, which again enables them to offset the

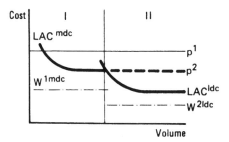

FIG. 8.9   Unequal wage costs: national versus multinational capital

impact of higher wage rates in more developed countries on their total global costs.

Over-Consumption and Union Power

An alternative Marxist theory of cost-push by trades unions is the argument of Glyn and Sutcliffe (1972) that the share of wages in national income has been rising and profits therefore falling. 'Over-consumption' will not only cause profits to decline. It will also tend to register 'inflationary gap' effects on the lines of Figure 8.1(b).

Glyn and Sutcliffe supported their case almost wholly from British evidence on wages and profit shares and rates, laying special emphasis on the marked decline in profits from the mid 1960s. They saw the rise of trade-union bargaining power as the underlying reason for a rise in wages and fall in profits in national income, and based a brief analysis of strategy for the Labour movement on this. Essentially, they argued that organised labour in the trade unions has the power to bring capitalism into crisis, through squeezing profits, and should do so as the basis for its socialist transformation.

There is no doubt that over the century since Marx finished the first volume of *Capital*, the share of wages in British national income has been rising. This long-term trend certainly offset a cataclysmic crisis of British capitalism through under-consumption. The rise of the trade unions and their power to protect or increase wages played a role in this wage trend, although it could be questioned whether union organisation alone in the late nineteenth century and early twentieth century actually caused it.

Moreover, when British capitalism hit serious trouble in the mid 1920s and mid 1980s the trade-union movement could not prevent a cut in real wages by the 1926 General Strike, nor mass unemployment by the miners' strike of 1984–85. Thus union power to squeeze profits appears to be associated with fuller rather than lower employment. This is not so surprising. When the Phillips curve 'got knotted' in empirical testing in the 1960s and early 1970s, it was argued by many theorists that wage-push inflation could be reduced by levels of unemployment higher than Phillips' prescribed 5 per cent, and the evidence already analysed in this chapter indicates that a close enough fit can be found for the Phillips curve association between lower inflation and higher unemployment above levels of 8 per cent.

Evidently, such a 'second coming' for the Phillips curve is bad news for the monetarists' claim that inflation is related solely to rates of growth of the money supply. Ironically, however, such a 'fit' for the Phillips curve on recent UK evidence corroborates rather than contradicts basic Marxist analysis, inasmuch as it was essential to the role which Marx himself ascribed to the reserve army of labour (or a permanent pool of unemployed) that this should exert a downward pressure on wage demands.

Qualifying Factors

However, there are further factors qualifying the 'over-consumption' case on trade-union bargaining power and its implications for profit squeeze.

First, as Lamfalussy (1961) stressed some time ago, low growth in economies such as Britain or Belgium tends to mean self-reinforcing 'vicious' effects for both investment and profits, in contrast to 'virtuous' effects of self-reinforcing high growth as in the West German or Japanese economies, where productivity growth may raise both profits and wages.

Second, while allowing for real profit decline in some traditional sectors of the economy, real profits have increased in modern and advanced technology sectors. Apart from the implications of state intervention to sustain innovation and profits in the defence sector, phenomenal rates of profit of 30–40 per cent have been achieved by conglomerates in the late 1970s and early 1980s in the United States in part through the extent to which such enterprise has been able to reduce its commitment in traditional areas and take advantage of the 'profit creaming' open to enterprise early in the product cycle of a new or advanced technology (Holland, 1987a, chapter 6).

The Mesoeconomy

Third, aggregate macro figures on profit decline neglect the power of multinational firms in the mesoeconomic sector to declare – within limits – what they choose to register as profit. In a high-tax country there is an incentive to understate profits relative to lower-tax countries or tax havens abroad. Since multinational companies for several years have accounted for 85 per cent of British visible trade, their capacity to understate real profits in the UK is considerable. As indicated earlier, the fact that the decline in declared profits since the 1960s coincides with the period in which Channon (1973) has shown multinational activity to be accelerating in a 'dramatic' manner among the mesoeconomic leaders of British capitalism, suggests that this factor alone could account for a considerable proportion of any profits squeeze. Nonetheless, from 1968 to 1976, the top 25 companies in the UK increased their share of total pre-tax industrial and commercial profits from one-fifth to two-fifths (Kay and King, 1978).

Fourth, Glyn and Sutcliffe put particular emphasis on the British figures on profits decline in the later 1960s. But this followed the deflationary cut-back on expenditure by the Labour government in July 1966, with the result that capital was under-employed and profits likely to decline in the short run whatever scope for understatement accompanied the spread of multinational capital during this period. With the reflation of the economy by the post-1970 Conservative government, declared profits rose again – in some cases dramatically. In effect, the Glyn-Sutcliffe argument overestimated a short-term downturn and underestimated the capacity of the government to influence the general profit level through demand management.

Fifth, the union power or over-consumption profits thesis argued by Glyn and Sutcliffe is weakened by the failure to stress the role of mesoeconomic firms as wage leaders in the economy, and the range of consequences which this entails for wages, costs and profits in the microeconomic sector. Big firms tend to be confronted by big unions. They are prime targets for pressure in the wage struggle, and the prime wage settlers. They can afford to make pace-setting settlements to the extent that their super-normal productivity and profits tend to lead the rest of the industry concerned. Moreover, even where unions are not strong, as in the Japanese big business sector, paternalist management counters the 'reserve army of labour' case for wage restraint by granting high real wage increases, while guaranteeing lifetime employment.

The Microeconomy

Also, as Sylos-Labini (1962) has shown, when such leading firms make a settlement, union pressure to match it can throw smaller firms into crisis. In other words, a major wage increase which firms in the mesoeconomic sector can afford can squeeze profits radically in smaller firms with lower productivity in the microeconomic sector. Thus, successful wage demands agreed by leading firms in the mesoeconomic sector can reinforce unequal competition between big and small firms, and accelerate the trend to monopoly domination by the big league.

This has considerable political implications. For instance, if unions push wage claims in the mesoeconomic sector where they can be afforded, this may well throw small firms in the microeconomic sector into crisis before critically low profit levels are reached in the mesoeconomic sector. This would be accompanied by pressure on the government to save employment in the small and medium-firm sector either by pumping in public money, or by extending long-term loans with deferred payment into the micro sector. Meanwhile, big firms in the meso sector would pick up viable 'squeezed' firms in the medium range in the micro sector virtually for the asking, at depressed valuation levels, further reinforcing the monopoly trend and thereby their profit share. This occurred in Britain on a major scale in the early and mid 1980s with a takeover and merger boom on a scale unprecedented since the late 1960s of which the mutual bids of Guinness and Distillers for each other, and the predations of the Hanson Trust, were typical.

8.3 Cost-Push: Big Business

The above argument should indicate the extent to which focusing exclusively on national money supply or national wage costs fails to provide a general theory of inflation in the era of the global corporation. The brightest and best of the Keynesians, such as Joan Robinson, were not immune from such a one-sided view of the world (illustrated, with reference inter alia to Wittgenstein's 'duck-rabbit' image, in *The Market Economy* (Holland, 1987, chapter 1)). For instance in her 'Economics of Hyperinflation' (1938 and 1960), Joan Robinson claims that it is 'essential to realise that without rising money wages inflation cannot occur, and that whatever starts a rise in money wages starts inflation; the *essence* of inflation is a rapid and continuous rise of money wages'.

Half a century after Joan Robinson first made this argument, it is evident that inflation can occur without a corresponding rise in money wages. It may occur due to a bad harvest in a commodity such as coffee, to a producers' cartel in oil or natural gas, and to pocketing of a share of the difference by multinational companies through techniques such as transfer pricing. Also, global big business may compensate for falling sales (or a fall in the rate of growth of expected sales as against committed investment) by raising prices during periods of recession, simply to maintain forecast revenue or cash flow and to protect anticipated profit rates.

Price-Making Power

Certainly, administered prices by big business are central to any wage-cost-push hypothesis. In other words, wage demands cannot result in inflation if firms are compelled to resist them by 'price-taking' through consumer sovereignty. Put differently, if the conventional textbook theory of consumer sovereignty (endorsed without qualification by Friedman) were to obtain in reality, no individual firm would be able to pass on a wage increase in higher prices without going out of business. Even allowing for the role of modern trades unions in industry wage bargaining (as in West Germany), wage settlements in economies such as the United Kingdom have consistently been negotiated at company rather than industry level by trades-union representatives. In many cases, such as Vickers in the UK in the 1970s, there was no overall company wage bargaining rather than individual bargaining at plant level.

Nonetheless, in contrast with the bias against big union power in Conservative politics, big business prefers to deal with big unions on the basis that a deal once struck is the more likely to stand, and thereby can facilitate the longer- term planning of investment, production and prices. Moreover, it is evident that firms make price increases for other reasons than wage-cost increases. For one thing, as argued extensively elsewhere (Holland, 1987), price-making firms look as much to the leadership of other firms on price increases as they do either to wage costs or the price elasticity (or responsiveness of sales to prices) established by allegedly sovereign cosumers. Such inter-firm price increases tend (i) to be set by mesoeconomic price leaders, with 'price-umbrella' or 'follow-the-leader' effects for micro followers, thereby affecting industry or sector inflation rates through price leadership rather than costs plus prices. Further (ii) the significant corollary is that if wages and prices are set by mark-ups, an inflation cannot be initiated exclusively in the short run by excess demand, as in the 'inflationary gap' hypothesis of Figure 8.1(a) – nor stopped by deficient demand, as assumed by the 'deflationary gap' hypothesis of Figure 8.1(b).

From Micro to Meso

As already stressed in earlier chapters, the rise of mesoeconomic and multinational power has increased the share of the economy within which big business can 'make' rather than 'take' prices. Again, we are not reasoning in terms of a single or sole factor in inflation. But the analysis of mesoeconomic power indicates a historically important and currently crucial factor in what has been called 'the new inflation'.

The textbook model of the competitive market, composed of many small firms and easy entry, meant that if a single producer raised price above the prevailing level which gave competitors a 'normal' profit, the price-raiser either would sell nothing, would sell less, or would attract new entrants to the market who would be happy to make a 'normal' profit and would thereby in due course bring prices down to the previous level. But under the new conditions of oligopoly and mesoeconomic power, the notable trend in price leadership has been upwards, rather than both up and down.

This should not really be surprising. Monopoly has always been the skeleton in the cupboard of conventional price theory. It is the orthodox advocates of free competition who are most explicit on the prerogative of the monopolist to raise prices against the public interest. If this power is true for the individual monopolist, it is also true for oligopolists, provided one of them does not try to steal a lead on the others through price restraint or price cutting. And in practice, price restraint or price cutting is very rare for the leaders in the mesoeconomic sector. When the financial press announces that a big-league firm has established a new and higher price level (or a leading bank or building society a higher interest rate), the correspondents usually predict that specified other firms (or banks, or building societies) in the big league will follow suit within a few days. Such predictions are usually correct.

One reason is the fear with which mesoeconomic leaders view price competition of the kind assumed in the old competitive model. Such competition tends to be highly unstable, and instability is anathema for leading firms under modern conditions, partly because the scale and cost of applying new technology have risen over time, and now involve forward company planning over a time-period of five to fifteen years – the Galbraithian 'planning system', analysed in chapter 2.

Mesoeconomic Power

Since the 1940s, there has been a marked trend to the domination by bigger business of industry, services and now – increasingly – agriculture in the European economies. The evidence on this has been elaborated in *The Market Economy* (Holland, 1987). Thus, while the top 100 manufacturing companies in Britain in the 1930s controlled less than a fifth of net output, by the mid 1970s they had doubled this output share. In contrast with some 350 independent commercial banks in Britain at the time when Ricardo wrote his *Principles*, four banks now have 85 per cent of commercial or high street banking in the United Kingdom. While their service charges and interest rates now need to reflect the entry into the banking sector of non-bank financial intermediaries such as the building societies which have begun to issue their own current-account and credit-card services, financial services in the UK economy are nonetheless dominated by a handful of giant firms.

The major restraints on monopolistic pricing in the industrial and financial sectors of an economy such as that of the UK have been exerted respectively by (i) foreign industrial competition, especially from West Germany and Japan, and (ii) the countervailance of price-making power in the industrial and agribusiness sectors of the economy by a handful of oligopsonistic retail companies. Despite the apparent evidence of cost-plus pricing in the retail sector, no government seriously concerned to ensure a price-competitive and disinflationary policy can afford to neglect the transformation of retail services which has occurred in the postwar British economy. As already indicated in *The Market Economy* (Holland, 1987), while half the retail sales in the UK were made by more than 4,500 firms in 1950, the number of firms accounting for this share of sales had been reduced by 1984 to just over 100 companies.

It is not necessary to be an unqualified devotee of Adam Smith to see the relevance of his observation that nothing is more certain, when two or three businessmen are gathered together, even for merriment or diversion, 'than that they will seek to conspire against the public interest by some contrivance to raise prices'. Even the Competition Directorate of the EEC Commission (whose series of concentration studies have been notable for their restriction to purely national analyses of concentration, thereby understating the multinational control of industry or services in the Community) found in the mid 1970s on the basis of four-firm concentration ratios (the share of markets commanded by the largest four firms) that there was a significant correlation between market dominance by big business and inflation. As they bluntly put it (EEC Commission, 1976), 'inflation is rife in the more concentrated sectors of industry'.

Pricing and the Product Cycle

There is considerable evidence that where prices are reduced over time in any given industry, this may reflect the dynamics of inter-firm competition as much as a reaction by firms to macroeconomic phenomena such as the money supply as favoured by the monetarists, or the level of unemployment as favoured by Phillips. For instance, in the electronics industry, the initial leaders in new technology tend to 'cream off' super-normal profits when they have a virtual monopoly during the first phase of the cycle, followed by dramatically lower pricing when new entrants muscle in on the market (Sciberras, 1977).

Ironically, this new entry and dramatic price reduction is not so much the consequence of equal or open competition on the lines of the conventional pricing model, as the consequence of asymmetric and accelerating technical progress in micro-circuitry, sustained in large part by defence contracts to leading firms by governments, with 'satellite' subcontracting to smaller league firms. In other words, the parcelling-out of defence contracts between mesoeconomic enterprise helps several of the leaders stay more or less in range of the technical frontier of an industry where component costs can fall from 10 to 1 in two to three years. The invisible hand of Adam Smith's spectator has been replaced by the backhand of the state as spender and underwriter of research in the defence sector.

In some cases in which dynamic small-league firms in the micro sector have attempted to break into the big time, such as Ferranti in Britain, defence contracts alone have not helped very much. Ferranti has a much better record for technical breakthrough than innovation, and has licensed more ideas than it has applied itself. Even this joint source of finance – from government and from the mesoeconomic leaders elsewhere – has not kept Ferranti in profit as a small firm in a big-league industry.

One of the reasons why competition remains so unequal in electronics is the kind of entry barrier stressed by Bain (1956), which can be lowered so hard and so fast by the giants that smaller firms are sometimes fortunate to be excluded rather than caught under it.

Prices and Unequal Competition

Bain has shown that entry barriers take the form of prices set temporarily by leading firms at a level which deny the would-be entrant achievement of a normal or necessary rate of return after entry. This is not the only way in which such barriers can operate. Economies of scale do not simply concern the gains from size in production stressed in the text books. They also concern hold through size over buyers and sellers, market hold through distributors and joint sales agreements, simple market sharing or carve-up between the big league (you take France and I'll take Germany and Italy), and the shallow learning curve in some industries where even proficient managers may learn too late.

Thus temporary price reductions – contributing to disinflation – are one of the most familiar and the most powerful forms of barriers to entry. In general it is a mesoeconomic firm which will be first in the field in volume, whether or not it has itself pioneered the process or product. It is on the second or mass-production phase of the product cycle that production economies of scale will enable it to earn a normal or even a super-normal profit at a price level which the would-be entrant will not be able to charge and make a normal return. There is no formal abuse of competition which would result in a judgment against the leader by anti-trust authorities or a Monopolies Commission. Similarly, once a dominant position has been gained on a particular market, there is no economic restraint on 'abuse of a dominant position' (to employ the terminology of the Rome Treaty) by which such a firm can raise prices over and above normal costs.

The same is true of the more extreme variant of 'elimination pricing' analysed by Sylos-Labini (1962 and 1969). In this game the big-league firm wants to push out or takeover a smaller-league firm already established in the market. It can do so very quickly by temporarily reducing prices below the level which the smaller firm must charge in order to meet its wage bill and variable costs. Again, such an elimination price does not necessarily mean that the more established firm has to make a loss. It may only need to reduce super-normal profits to normal levels for a period. The challenged firm would need to be able to demonstrate the real cost and profit structures of the challenger, and show that in practice it was making a loss on the product or product range, if it hoped to gain a sympathetic hearing from anti-trust or competition agencies. Since this ranges from the difficult to the impossible, it is easier to lie back and enjoy a golden handshake.

The Competitive Frontier

None of this means that new entry to markets and disinflation does not occur at the firm and industry level. But it does mean that any firm forcing an entry into a mesoeconomic market has to be either foolhardy, plain lucky, or itself a leader elsewhere in the national or international economy. Otherwise it will not be able to bear the kinds of pressures which the leaders will adopt to exclude its entry or eliminate it once entry has occurred, including if necessary the use of greater bank and other financial credit or ride out price competition, made possible by their more established position and their higher probability of success.

In practice most new entrants to markets are themselves dominant in other industries or services. The conglomerate boom in the United States exhibited these features, where the established base for the predatory firm was in other unrelated sectors rather than from within the sector itself. A relatively recent British example which shows an appropriate gentleman's agreement to join forces rather than fight was the merger in a new company of EMI electronics and the Hughes aircraft, property, mining, film and Playboy empire in the United States.

Put differently, price competition with its counter-inflationary benefits is still a marked feature of some areas of the modern capitalist economy. But this is either in the shrinking microeconomic sector of small national or regional firms, or on the frontier between the meso and microeconomic sectors. The competitive frontier is continually being shifted in their favour by mesoeconomic price-makers against microeconomic price-takers. Along the frontier, price is used as much as a weapon to increase mesoeconomic power as to maintain market share, or reduce inflation.

The only *buyers* capable of countering producer power are themselves producers and bulk buyers in the mesoeconomic league. It is they who get their orders at a fair price, at the right quality and at the right time. The micro firms must join the queue and pay at non-discount rates, or rates of discount which, like branded retail goods, reflect the super-normal profits going to brand-name firms, with normal profits going to retailers.

Accolades and Ironies

Sometimes the individual consumer or small firm is an unsuspecting beneficiary of a tactical struggle between meso and microeconomic firms. If so, they possibly attribute it to an unexpected bout of competition, proving in hard times that the old competitive maxims still obtain. But in many cases such entry-barring, entry-forcing or elimination-price tactics do not produce a drop in nominal price levels. Under inflationary conditions, big-league firms only have to hold nominal prices stable for a period of time to effect real price decreases. When general costs – and especially wages – are rising, this will squeeze the profit margin of the challenged firm and soften it up for takeover. For instance, the Minnesota Mining and Manufacturing Company penetrated the desk photocopier market by holding prices in Britain at £48 for several years through the 1960s and early 1970s. It then jumped the prices up by rapid stages to the region of £70.

Hence an irony. The entry-barring, entry-forcing or eliminating big-league firm may find itself receiving public accolade for price restraint while serving its own ends through defence or increase of its market share and long-term price-making power.

Moreover, nominal prices are rising rather than being held stable. This is not surprising. To the extent that prices are held stable for these reasons, they may be a tactic in the longer-term price and market strategy of the company. And as previously argued, it is not in the interests of mesoeconomic enterprise to adopt a strategy of pricing near cost when short-term changes in demand can cut cash flow and endanger the viability of the project.

However, there are other reasons why the long-term pricing strategy of mesoeconomic leaders appears to favour regular and constant increase. One of the most important and far-reaching in its consequences is the prevailing policy framework on profits and pricing.

Limits to Competition Policy

Put simply, governments and international institutions in the capitalist economies are still caught in the paradigm of the sovereign consumer and price-competitive model. They admit that monopolistic competition can occur. But they see this as peripheral rather than central to the system. They have not caught up with the fact that joint monopoly, oligopoly and mesoeconomic power now commands the system and dominates price-making on the periphery. Averitt warned against this in his *Dual Economy* (1968).

Ever since the break-up of Standard Oil, no one has denied that the anti-trust, anti-monopoly or competition agencies have teeth. Their main trouble has been the lockjaw imposed by the big firms' contol of information on their own real cost and profit structures. As is well illustrated by the fact that virtually no big-league firm has been broken up since Standard Oil – until ATT in the early 1980s – professional management in the mesoeconomic sector may turn its talents to concealment. Like the liquor sellers during Prohibition, it may respond to new competition laws by going underground – or nowadays also overseas. For instance, Texas Instruments uses computer-linked satellites over the Indian Ocean for the simultaneous trading of prices on 17,000 products in its various multinational subsidiaries. In its recent pursuit of IBM, the US government secured an order to search the company's files. But the information they wanted was not there when they arrived, and may not have been there in the first place despite grounds for thinking the case well-founded in principle.

However, while governments and competition directorates can be regarded with equanimity most of the time, big-league firms in the mesoeconomic sector can be more respectful of the microeconomic firms in their own industries when these trade products which are plausibly comparable in cost with their own. At worst, such a firm might be able to demonstrate that the mesoeconomic leader's costs are not significantly different from its own, and win an action with the support of the Anti-Trust Division, the Monopolies Commission, or in the European Court of Justice. At best, the noise made by such a firm or a small-league producers' association could be bad public relations and dent the image of the 'soulful' corporation.

Inflation and the 'Price Umbrella'

For these reasons, as already indicated in *The Market Economy* (Holland, 1987, chapter 6), mesoeconomic leaders tend to shelter microeconomic firms, over the long run, under a price umbrella. This 'umbrella effect' was noted some time ago by Edith Penrose (1959), who observed that prices will tend to be set by leading firms at that level which permits the least efficient firm to survive which leading firms choose to allow to survive.

In short, it is increasingly clear that prices under contemporary capitalism, as in the microeconomic model, are still set by the *most* efficient firms. But the basis and direction of such pricing has been reversed by the attempt of liberal capitalist agencies to impose microeconomic conditions on mesoeconomic leaders. To the extent that costs are taken into account, they may be the cost of the *least* efficient firms in the system, in which case the macroeconomic effect is inflationary.

This is one of the reasons for the unequal incidence and stop-go nature of state price policies. A selective price policy distinguishing between meso and microeconomic firms would make considerable sense. As already noted, the mesoeconomic firms are all national or multinational in operation, and operating mainly in markets of different quality from the microeconomic regional and local firms. Different criteria, with different degrees of restraint between the two main sectors, would prove difficult in some cases, but less difficult than the kind of general price policies which have been tried with notable lack of success by many Western governments.

In effect, general policies of price restraint tend to prompt exactly the sort of vocal protest from less efficient firms in the small-league sector that could be expected on a wider scale if mesoeconomic leaders priced nearer to costs. This was illustrated by the contradictions of the nonetheless relatively successful campaign launched by the Confederation of British Industry during and immediately after the October 1974 general election. Meso-economic leaders were in the process of publishing profits results which were up to 100 per cent better than the previous year or half year, while the CBI was maintaining that British industry was caught in a cash-flow crisis which would destroy the economy unless tax cuts and public subsidies were allocated to the private sector as a whole. They did not need to provide widows and orphans to support their case. It was massively supported by small- and medium-sized firms in the microeconomic sector which had been very seriously hit by the Conservative government's price restraint policies.

Multinational Pricing and Inflation

The association of big business 'price-making' power with the extended scope and scale of multinational companies in the global economy has already been stressed in earlier chapters. A variety of techniques has been elaborated by which multinational companies can and do inflate prices through trade transactions between their subsidiaries in different countries. One of the striking features of the examples already given is the extent to which theoretical models derived from multinational practice in fact simplify a highly complex reality. Thus the examples devised in Chapters 6 and 7 are simply the 'tip of the iceberg' for companies, many of which simultaneously price and transfer price up to a thousand or two thousand products through an information exchange which involves the permanent booking of satellite time to maximise corporate cash flow and minimise declared profits in the global economy.

Nonetheless, such practices, with a very few exceptions, take the basic form of under-invoicing or understating the value of exports in subsidiary trade, and inversely over-invoicing or thereby inflating the declared value of imports. The sequence, as already stressed in earlier chapters, classically takes the form of understatement of exports from low-tax countries and the overstatement of imports (with both direct and indirect inflationary effects) in high-tax countries.

If the share of national and multinational capital in the global economy were reversed, with multinational business representing only a minor or marginal proportion of visible world trade, the impact of such transfer pricing by multinational companies on national or global inflation might indeed be a fit subject for monographs and specialist articles rather than mainstream economics and priority attention by policy-makers.

But the issue is not simply transfer pricing alone. It is the link between their concentration and command of trade and their multinational pricing which gives mesoeconomic big business such a key role in global price determination. For instance, it has already been stressed that multinational trade accounts for about 80 per cent of US and UK trade. In the early 1980s less than one per cent of Spain's exporting companies were responsible for nearly 40 per cent of all Spanish exports, and for almost 60 per cent of all imports. Indeed, 100 companies, equivalent to 0.3 per cent of total exporting firms, accounted for nearly 40 per cent of exports; the leading 25 companies for 25 per cent, and the leading 10 companies for nearly 10 per cent (Ministerio de Economia y Comercio, 1982).

At the global level, the share of multinational companies and scope for inflationary effects through transfer pricing has already been illustrated by evidence from the European Community, which itself accounts for about half of global trade and over 60 per cent of manufactured trade (despite the export penetration of Japanese companies in individual sectors), and where, as Locksley (1981) has pointed out, 140 companies now account for one-third of the gross domestic product of the Community. In the world economy as a whole, Clairmonte and Cavanagh (1984) reveal that 200 multinational companies represent one-third of the total volume of non-communist world trade.

Both national anti-trust agencies and international bodies such as the UN, OECD and EEC should confront such price-making power of multinational big business as a matter of priority. A methodology for gaining such increased 'transparency' over sector and price leaders has already been outlined in Chapter 9 of *The Market Economy* (Holland, 1987).

8.4 Stagflation and Deflation

Most macroeconomists, whether Keynesian or monetarist, focus on so-called 'inflexibilities' to explain the paradox of combined stagnation and inflation in the developed market economies since the mid 1970s. Their analysis has tended to concentrate in particular on the inflexibility of labour markets, with the consequent argument that wage rates have to be reduced to reasonable levels either through raised unemployment (the Phillips curve effect) or prices and incomes policies.

However, in line with the almost total neglect by either Keynesian or monetarist economists of the implications of price-making power for the theory of inflation, little or no attention has been paid to the consequences for leading firms of a decline in the rate of growth of their sales with deflationary policies. In turn, this reflects a compartmentalisation (or failure to relate different aspects of macroeconomic theory) whereby macroeconomists think in terms of trade-cycle theory when considering macro fluctuations in the market economy, and in terms of cost-push or money-push theories when interpreting inflation, without relating the premises of these two areas of analysis.

Certainly, one of the main functions of the trade cycle in the development of the market economy has been falling prices during recession, or at least a restraint of price increases. During the interwar slump, as already indicated in Figure 8.2 for the United States, real prices fell dramatically. But with their enlarged postwar market share, and an increase in their dominant market position, the big-league firms typical of the mesoeconomic sector have frequently been able to increase prices during a recession in sales. They may do so less in Adam Smith's terms as a conspiracy against the public interest, than simply to offset falling sales and maintain the volume of cash flow necessary to meet fixed-interest external borrowing and/or maintain the flow of self-finance necessary for future investment. This tendency of prices to be sustained or raised by oligopolistic leaders was noted by Sylos-Labini in the second edition of his *Oligopoly and Technical Progress* (1969).

The 'stagflation' effect of price-making power is illustrated in Figure 8.10(a). The firm's fall in sales, if unaccompanied by an increase in prices, would reduce cash flow, reinvestable surplus, and potential market share. It is therefore fully understandable in terms of maintaining market share that the enterprise with price-making power should seek to compensate for its falling sales by raised prices in order to maintain cash flow.

If the recession is temporary, such firms may restrain the rate of price increase thereafter. But if it is both pronounced and apparently deepening, they may increase prices the deeper it gets. An example of this was the price

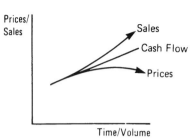

FIG. 8.10(a)   The stagflation
syndrome

FIG. 8.10(b)   Increased sales revenue
and decreased prices

increase on a range of models which General Motors announced when sales
slumped following the OPEC oil price increases in 1973.

Put differently, the rise of mesoeconomic power has accompanied a
reversal of the main price sequence in the trade cycle. The cycle used to show
rising prices during expansion and falling prices during recession. Now it
shows rising prices during *both* expansion and recession.

This is not necessarily a conspiracy in the boardrooms of big business. It is
an imperative dictated by change in the sources of finance for big-league
firms, and the fact that the pay-off period for investment is longer than the
short-term cycle, unless recession grinds into depression and curtails future
investment spending.

Disinflation and Cash Flow

By contrast, Figure 8.10(b) shows that with an increase in sales and a fall in
prices, business will be able to maintain its cash flow, and therefore its
standard profit mark-up on unit costs. Such an analysis, well known to firms
themselves, rarely if ever appears in the textbook treatment of the inflationary
process; yet it has major implications for the feasibility of reversing the
assumptions of both Keynesian and monetarist macroeconomic theory
through reducing inflation by reflating demand in the economy.

This process is further illustrated within the context of the contemporary
mixed economy in Figure 8.11(a), which combines the assumption of falling
sales during recession with rising prices designed to preserve corporate cash
flow. Figure 8.11(a) extends the analysis of Figure 8.10(b) to the context of a
downturn in the trade cycle and adds the fall in public expenditure frequently
employed by policy-makers under the influence of both the conventional
'Keynesian' and the orthodox monetarist policies of contemporary governments. The paradox implicit in such policies is that the further public
spending and aggregate demand is reduced, the greater the inflationary trend

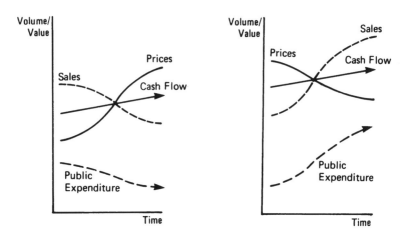

FIG. 8.11(a)   Deflation and inflation   FIG. 8.11(b)   Reflation and
disinflation

through the compensation by price-making firms for lower sales and loss of
cash flow.

Reflation and Disinflation

By contrast, Figure 8.11(b) illustrates the potential for disinflation through a
recovery of public spending, an increase of sales and thereby a preservation of
the cash-flow trend of price-taking firms through increased output rather
than increased prices. However, there is a caveat in the argument. Such a
reflation assumes a price-competitive framework at the firm or enterprise
level. In other words, if consumer sovereignty obtained in terms of the
microeconomic premises of both Keynesian and monetarist macroeconomic
theory, a reflation of public expenditure (in contrast with the monetarist
hypothesis, though consistent with the Keynesian paradigm) would promote
a fall in the macroeconomic price level – or, translated into rates of growth, a
fall in the rate of inflation.

Granted the scale of price-making power under the mesoeconomic and
multinational dominance of the global economy, there is no guarantee that
such disinflation, through reflation of demand, can be achieved in practice.
Either Japanese-type conditions will obtain under which the relevant public
authorities (including MITI) choose to exercise leverage to ensure that firms
do not abuse price-making power, and thereby maximise long-term global
market penetration through price competitiveness. Or, alternatively,
public intervention through policies for price control or price restraint (as

implemented at various times by French policy-makers since the mid 1960s, or by some developing economies such as Brazil in the mid 1980s) will be necessary to provide the conditions within which a combination of reflation and disinflation could occur.

For developed economies (such as France and Japan) with an extensive control over their own enterprise, both within the domestic economy and the international arena, such an exercise in price restraint and reflation is feasible if difficult. In developing countries, with their high dependence on multinational companies and limited control over their price-making power, such policies are considerably more difficult to achieve without international co-operation (whether bilateral or multilateral) on the price-making and transfer pricing by multinational companies. Such issues have recently been addressed in the Manley-Brandt report on global development issues from the Socialist International (Brandt and Manley, 1985).

Circular and Cumulative Causation

Many macroeconomic analyses of deflation assume a 'short sharp shock' treatment restraining demand in the short term as the premise to a medium-term recovery. It has already been seen in Chapter 5 that this is the basis of the 'Keynesian theory' of combining devaluation with a deflation sufficient to release further resources for export, in which case it is assumed that the export multiplier for the national economy will re-engage, with increased exports, achieved at lower prices in foreign markets, generating further indirect pull effects on investment modernisation and growth in the domestic economy. The qualifications for economies with a highly multinational structure of trade and payments have already been analysed in the same chapter.

However, whether or not devaluation engages 'virtuous' circle effects within the export sector of a national economy (and in this respect some economies are still more national in their export structure than others), the cumulative effects of deflation tend to be both circular and self-reinforcing over the medium term, if not offset by government policies. Expressed in Keynesian terms of the circularity of income and expenditure, Figure 8.12 shows that reflation or deflation through the public sector (higher or lower public expenditure) will promote increased or decreased public and private income. In turn this will further increase or decrease public and private savings, and raise or lower total investment and employment. In turn, higher or lower corporation or profits tax, and taxes from income will raise or lower the feasibility of public expenditure as a stimulus to the expansion of the system.

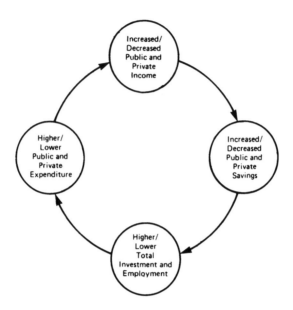

FIG. 8.12   Virtuous and vicious circles: the role of public spending

Virtuous and Vicious Circles

After Keynes, the arguments on 'virtuous' and 'vicious' circles were developed by Ragnar Nurkse (1952) in terms of a lower or higher level disequilibrium in the economy which perpetuates itself and results in either economic growth or stagnation.

Analysing in particular the problem of underdevelopment, Nurkse argued that the concept implies: 'A circular constellation of forces tending to act and react upon one another in such a way as to keep a poor country in a state of poverty.' As examples he cited the case in which 'a poor man may be weak; being physically weak, his working capacity may be low which means that he is poor, which in turn means that he will not have enough to eat; and so on. The situation of this sort, relating to a country as a whole, can be summed up in the trite proposition: "a country is poor because it is poor"' (Nurkse, 1952).

However, Nurkse stresses that the process can in principle be reversed into a 'virtuous' circle. The sequence then would be that if a poor man is given more to eat, his health improves; since he is physically strong his working capacity is greater, which in turn means that he gets more to eat, and so on. In this way, the downward disequilibrium of decline could be reversed by a cumulative upward movement, improving consumption, productivity and therefore output. In turn, Nurkse's proposition then would read that 'a country is becoming richer because it is less poor and therefore becoming richer' (Myrdal, 1968, vol. 3, p. 1846).

Deflation and Cumulative Decline

Gunnar Myrdal (1957 and 1968) developed the theory of circular and cumulative causation in three main contexts. The first (which independently suggested the concept to him) was the analysis which he made of the problem of black people in the United States, and the extent to which their social and economic conditions reflected a vicious circle of cumulative causation by which black people become poorer because they were poor in the first place (Myrdal, 1944).

The second context was that of spatial analysis and regional development, in which Myrdal argued that 'the play of forces in the market normally tends to increase rather than decrease the inequalities between regions'. It does so because capital and labour will be attracted to those areas in which growth originally began. This attraction will tend to be cumulative, and reinforced by increasing internal and external economies in the faster-growing area. In turn this process will register positive 'spread' effects, by which expansion is distributed centrifugally on other areas. But it will also have 'backwash' effects inasmuch as factors of production are attracted away from other areas and regions, leaving them 'more or less in a backwater' (Myrdal, 1957, pp. 26–7).

The third area is the international economy, where Myrdal outlined his analysis in his earlier work (1957) but later developed a major and extensive analysis, with a range of other authors, of the problems of development and underdevelopment in the Asian economies (Myrdal, 1968). In terms of the dynamics of deflation and reflation, the implications of relative 'vicious' and 'virtuous' circles have been well expressed by Paul Streeten (1964) in a manner more directly relevant to the circularity of income and expenditure in a 'Keynesian' model of the kind outlined in Figure 8.11. Thus, as Streeten (1964, p. 56) says:

> Typical examples of such cumulative processes are the following: capital supply; increased productivity; higher real income; higher capital supply etc. Higher demand; higher incentive to invest; higher productivity; higher demand etc.

Inversely, the negative cumulative circle of decline with deflation sustained over the medium term would include spare capacity; reduced productivity; lower real income; lower inducement to invest, etc. Lower demand; lower investment; lower productivity; lower income, and thus yet lower demand.

Social Income and Expenditure

Myrdal and Streeten are prepared to consider not only the social conditions of labour, but also the relation between economic, sociological and political analysis important to evaluating policy alternatives of a kind which may offset cumulative decline and promote cumulative recovery. Such imagination is notably lacking from monetarist economists of the Friedman school, whose vision of the world appears closer to that of the medieval Manicheans than to modern social and political reality. The Manicheans were a sect of the Christian church who for their own reasons (on which twentieth-century psychology might well speculate) chose to divide the world into 'good' and 'evil', thereby presaging the more fanatical sects of Calvinism in the Renaissance period and the later association in the Protestant ethic of spending with self-indulgence and debt with guilt. It is notable in this context, and also that of the prejudice against borrowing on the part of Mrs Thatcher and others, that the German and Dutch word for debt and guilt are synonymous (*Schuld*).

The irony of monetarist arguments for maintaining a constant rate of growth in the money supply over the medium term, in order to secure derivative 'virtuous' effects, is that Friedman himself does not allow for the feasibility of cumulative deflation being promoted by a contraction of public spending through restraint in growth in the money supply.

This is partly the result of Friedman's own prejudice (certainly in the sense of pre-judgement) against public spending in practice, derived from the 'crowding-out' analysis of competition for funds between the public and private sectors of the economy. It also in part derives from the rejection by monetarists of the Keynesian multiplier which (as seen in Chapter 2) was derived indirectly from Keynes' analysis of the consumption and savings function in the modern market economy.

Friedman's followers in government have followed his prejudice/pre-judgement to the extent of deleting (and thereby suppressing) explanatory figures and arguments on the circularity of income and expenditure in the modern capitalist economy from the government publications of the Central Statistical Office.

Thus, for example, before the incoming Conservative government of 1979 had had time to revise the Keynesian framework of the public presentation of statistics, the 1980 edition of *Social Trends* included an explanation of the circularity of income, tax revenue and expenditure as set out in Figure 8.13. The different components of household income follow a flow in which individuals receive income from many sources, but the most important are earnings from employment and social security benefits. Tax is paid on both earned and unearned income, and the individuals also pay national insurance

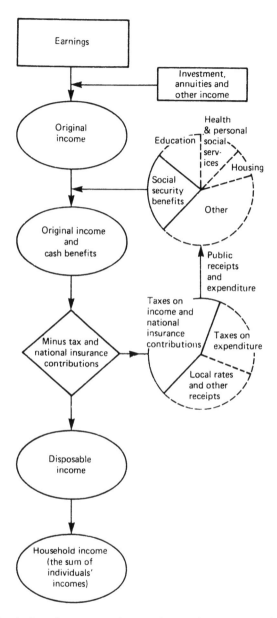

FIG. 8.13 Circularity of income and expenditure: the 'suppressed' official picture (Source: CSO, *Social Trends*, 1980, p. 133)

contributions. Once these taxes have been paid, the income that is left is 'disposable income', and it is this which constitutes household income. The explanatory text of *Social Trends* allows that not all of the money that is paid out as income tax and national insurance contributions goes back to individuals in the form of cash benefits. In the later 1970s, income tax and national insurance contributions made up just over 40 per cent of public revenue, and cash benefits accounted for about 25 per cent of expenditure. The difference was explained by other items of government expenditure. However, individuals and households also received 'benefits in kind' in the form of education and health services, which were not paid for directly through private expenditure but indirectly, via taxation, through public funds (*Social Trends*, 1980).

This was the last edition of *Social Trends* in which this diagram, and such Keynesian heresy, was to appear in a government publication under the Thatcher Conservative government. Thereafter, the Kahn-Keynesian multiplier was consigned to the status of a footnote in economic history. Yet this failure to admit, far less understand, the dynamic effects of public expenditure and the multiplier in reinforcing deflation and decline, has contributed in large part to the contrast between the 1930s and the 1980s in the British economy. In other words, while unemployment in both decades was high (although higher in the 1980s), deflation and recession of spending and demand in the 1980s has been accompanied by continuing inflation, in contrast with the 1930s when real prices fell as fast as the fall in output and (as in the United States) thereafter lagged behind the recovery of output.

8.5 Prices and Incomes

It has been stressed several times that Keynes himself was not especially concerned with the problem of inflation because deflation and mass unemployment were the outstanding issues of his time. The trouble with subsequent 'Keynesian' and monetarist analyses of inflation has been their simplism. The monetarist case has already been analysed. Reduced to essentials, it amounts to the assertion of Milton Friedman that 'inflation starts in one place and one place only – national treasuries'. In other words, too much (public) money chasing too few (private) goods and services. It may well be that, in a short time, monetarism itself will be relegated to the footnote status to which Mrs Thatcher was concerned to consign Keynesian analysis of the circularity of income and expenditure. Certainly, there is some evidence in the mid 1980s from public opinion surveys that the British public see little reason to thank Mrs Thatcher for reducing inflation when, in the process, she has decimated production and increased unemployment in the UK economy.

Yet if an alternative is to be achieved to the more extreme forms of monetarism attempted by the Thatcher government since 1979, it cannot be on the basis of Keynesian 'prices and incomes' policies.

Wage and Price Controls

One of the remarkable aspects of Friedman's monetarism is that by stressing money supply as virtually the unique determinant of inflation, he writes off 'combinations' of either capital or labour (producers or workers) in the distribution and inflation process. This has led him at times to bizarre conclusions. Thus shortly after the first major increases in the price of oil by the OPEC cartel in 1973, Friedman predicted that the forces of the market would prevail and OPEC collapse within a few months. It was not seriously under strain for ten years. On the labour and trade-union side, he has argued that combinations of labour can exert only negligible influence on the distribution of income over the short run, and virtually none over the longer term.

Some governments for some of the time have sought to follow the Friedman prescription. Thus the Conservative Party in Britain before its election to government in 1979 maintained that it was in favour of free collective bargaining and would not pursue an incomes policy. After election it maintained the same formal position, but imposed cash limits on the public sector (including central and local government, education, health and social services) in a manner which in effect entailed wage restraint on those employed in that sector.

Similarly, the Labour government from 1975 to 1979 had followed some of the main precepts of monetarism in terms of public expenditure restraints, but combined this with efforts to impose an incomes policy. In the three years between 1975 and 1978 real incomes, as a result, declined by some 10 per cent. Thus prescriptions based on an extreme form of neoclassical theory were adapted in practice in such a way as to reduce the living standards of labour at a time when (from late 1974) corporation tax or mainstream profits tax was virtually abolished in Britain (Kay and King, 1978).

Proto and Neo Keynesians

The neglect of the price-making power of big business and its influence on the distribution of income was challenged in the postwar period by two of the most notable neo-Keynesians, Nicholas Kaldor and Joan Robinson. Also, before Keynes, but in a more developed form after him, Michael Kalecki had sought to incorporate oligopoly and price-making power into the division of income between capital and labour.

Kalecki was relatively circumspect on the policy conclusions which might be drawn from his analysis. Kaldor was less so. As economic adviser to the Treasury in the 1964–70 government (and twinned by Thomas Balogh who at the same time was economic adviser to the Prime Minister), he contributed substantially to policies which were a logical consequence of his theoretical analysis: i.e. prices and incomes policies, rather than incomes policies alone. This was institutionalised in a Prices and Incomes Board whose task was intended to be the restraint of prices and incomes in such a way as to achieve both price stability and a defence of the real wage level.

In reality, however, in the 1960s, the prices and incomes policies rarely managed to restrain or reduce price increases by big business in the mesoeconomic sector, i.e. the oligopolistic price-makers within the system. By contrast, it was relatively effective in achieving a restraint of wages.

Meanwhile, other expectations of the government's management of the economy in the late 1960s were not fulfilled. One of the key commitments of the incoming Labour government in 1964 had been to the establishment of a National Plan, and a planning process which in particular would raise productivity and incomes through harnessing the 'white heat of technological progress'. The phrase was Prime Minister Harold Wilson's but the concept was compatible with the emphasis on technical progress in Keynesian growth models to which Kaldor himself had contributed, and whose failure to disaggregate to the level of the firm and enterprise has already been stressed in Chapter 6.

The National Plan failed within just over a year of its publication and within four months of the government attaining a majority of nearly a hundred seats in Parliament. In July 1966 a major deflationary package was introduced, which doubled the level of unemployment within four years and restrained the rate of growth of investment and modernisation necessary to increase international competitiveness. Within three years the government had clearly switched its emphasis from restraining both prices and incomes to restraining labour within the economy. Thus the Labour government in 1969 sought to introduce a bill in Parliament, based on the policy document entitled *In Place of Strife*, which would have imposed legal penalties (despite offsetting nominal benefits) on trades unions.

The Need for Disaggregation

The case for disaggregation of macro phenomena has been argued at various stages throughout this work. Attention has been drawn to differences in the behaviour of micro and mesoeconomic enterprise, and differences in the sectoral structure and the spatial distribution of activity. But the case for disaggregation is also important within the macro categories of capital and labour, or in the social distribution of income and wealth between different economic classes in society.

The irony about disaggregation is that few people deny its desirability. Many of the theorists of the economics of income distribution stress the importance of proceeding further with disaggregated models. But it is rare for them to do so.

This is doubly remarkable since the main conclusion emerging from the application of Keynesian theory to income policies is that they have failed in large part because of their over-aggregation. No one recognising the high share of wages in national income or output would be taken seriously if they sought to deny the importance in principle of the cost of labour in total costs and thus on the distribution of income between capital and labour.

But there is a difference between the arithmetic share of labour in total income (including profits) and the meaning of its share in terms of the real economy. Similarly, there is a difference between the simplified cost-push theories of wage inflation stressed by Keynesians in the 1960s and 1970s, and the more complex reality of the inflationary process in the modern capitalist system.

Stagflation and Capacity Use

We have examined earlier in this chapter the extent to which deflation may promote inflation under conditions of 'price-making' power. Without reiterating the main points of this analysis, it is worth drawing attention to the relation of such deflation to devaluation in the context of capacity use by big business worldwide. Thus, in Chapter 5 it was stressed that a Scandinavian multinational company such as SKF planned its global corporate trade and payments on the basis of maximised capacity use in different countries. In Chapter 5, this was used to illustrate the extent to which a multinational such as SKF would not necessarily follow through a devaluation in any individual country, since this could necessitate the undertaking of entirely new plant in such a country while underemploying capacity in plant in other countries.

Inversely, however, where deflation in one or more countries reduces capacity use for mesoeconomic or multinational companies with 'price-making' power, this will tend to increase pressures for them to compensate for forgone sales by increasing prices. This 'stagflation' phenomenon does not necessarily fulfil Adam Smith's expectation that when two or three producers are gathered together they will seek to conspire against the public interest by raising prices. Rather, it may reflect 'responsible' pricing policy by the management of the multinational corporation which – rather than seeking to raise cash flow through inflationary pricing – is simply seeking to preserve cash flow by raising prices to compensate for falling sales.

Devaluation and Inflation

Further, while considering the perverse effects of *de*flation on *in*flation through companies with 'price-making' power, the inflationary effects of devaluation itself should not be discounted. Indeed, it is a classic premise of devaluation in conventional trade and payments theory that while this may in principle increase the international price competitiveness of 'national' firms, it will inversely inflate the price of imports to the economy of the devaluing country. The insensitivity of multinational companies to devaluation in terms of lower pricing of exports is therefore twofold. In the first instance, import prices in the devaluing country certainly will be increased, since there is no incentive under the market mechanism for firms to resist higher import costs, other than undertaking new rounds of cost-reducing investment. In practice this is more expensive and more demanding in terms of managerial and financial resources than 'lying back' and adding a price-bonus to the import-led inflation.

Second, and of major significance for the global economy of a kind almost wholly neglected in conventional theory, the failure of multinational companies to follow through devaluation with lower prices on foreign markets, results in an asymmetric upwards drift in prices in the global economy as a whole. In other words, while in our previous example in Chapter 5, Halivaux under independent national ownership may have had an incentive to lower prices on the German market in order to compete with Lepo, through the global corporate pricing strategy of General Automobiles, there is no way in which a multinational company will follow through a devaluation with lower prices in foreign markets in such a way as to compete against itself.

Banks, Bonds and Borrowing

This is apart from a further key factor in the new inflation – one which concerns less the public money supply through government spending monotonised by Friedman in his concern to correlate M and P in Fisher's equation, than the private money supply through banking systems which increasingly are multinational in the global economy. There are various dimensions to this contribution of private banks to the global inflation syndrome.

One is the extent to which private enterprise itself has increasingly sought bank or bond borrowing rather than extended equity or share ownership as the basis of its external financing for investment needs. In the nineteenth and early twentieth centuries, companies financed such needs mainly through share or equity issues made on the stock market. Since the Second World War, an increasing share of such external finance by major companies in the leading market economies has come from the Eurodollar and Eurobond markets. As we will see in Chapter 9, the scale of this borrowing is now running at more than $2 trillion, or three to four times the national income and expenditure of the leading European economies.

Inflation and Fixed Interest

However, whereas dividend payments on equity or share issues could be neglected or 'passed' in times of recession or low return by companies seeking recourse to the stock market for their main funding and external finance, bank and bond borrowing is different. In other words, bank and bond borrowing is set at a particular rate which has to be met – year in and year out – irrespective of sales, cash flow and profit achievements. With a fall in sales and volume profits, the result of this private bank and bond borrowing market is that big business in the mesoeconomic and multinational sector with 'price-making' power is under pressure to increase prices in order not only to preserve cash flow but also to ensure the financing of its debt. Small business in the microeconomic or national sector hesitates to commit itself to fixed-interest borrowing on Eurobond markets, but nonetheless may fall victim to the Protestant ethic of the local bank manager. Thus, as indicated earlier, faced with a fall in sales and volume profits – if not profit rates – those small firms which are not 'dropped' out of the market may well find themselves strangled by high interest rates. This reflects the distinction made between micro and mesoeconomic interest-rate sensitivity in the qualification of LM and IS curve analysis earlier in this chapter.

Commodities and Inflation

Furthermore, big business has not been immune from simple and straight-forward speculation on commodity markets during periods of high inflation. During the period of dramatic commodity-price inflation in the early 1970s, it was estimated by some City sources that as much as half of the increase in commodity prices was caused by speculative buying, with large banks and wealthy private investors seeking investments to beat the increase in the cost of living.

It is in such a context that the impact of OPEC price increases and those of other commodities should be evaluated in the dramatic trend to price inflation in the developed market economies in the early 1970s, and the renewed price inflation following from the further major round of OPEC oil price increases from 1979. In other words, inflation in the mid-1970s was neither due exclusively to oil prices alone, nor to the wage demands of 'inflexible' labour in the developed capitalist countries. Indeed, in terms of the oil price inflation itself, it is notable that the widely unlamented Shah of Persia asked publicly early in 1974 where at least a dollar per barrel of the new increase had gone. He claimed that the producers, such as Iran, had not got it, while the consumer paid the increase. In other words, the difference of a dollar per barrel had quietly disappeared through the transfer pricing of the major oil companies into their tax havens offshore, onshore, or outside the remit of the tax authorities in the developed countries.

Deficit Financing and Tax Push

Within such a wider analysis of the nature of inflationary pricing in the modern capitalist economy, it is both reasonable and realistic to admit the context within which deficit financing and tax-push may contribute to inflation. In other words, reflecting the analysis made earlier in this volume, and elaborated in Chapter 9, it is evident that some of the simpler solutions to rising unemployment undertaken within the paradigm of the 'Keynesian' revolution encouraged demand without a corresponding increase in supply. This certainly was the case with the boom promoted by the Conservative Chancellor of the Exchequer Christopher Barber in 1973–74. This has some interest for academics in the sense that it was virtually the only period in the postwar British economy in which demand arguably outstripped supply. It has nonetheless become established as a classic case of the failure of 'Keynesian' demand management in the eyes of the Thatcher government, which has repudiated both the Heath-Barber boom and the subsequent efforts made by the Labour government between 1974 and 1979 to offset the trend to increasing unemployment through a variety of measures designed to remedy and alleviate the costs of poverty rather than promote employment itself.

Similarly, 'tax-push' inflation may be significant in some economies. But in contrast with the simplistic arguments of Laffer and his back-of-a-napkin sketch of the disincentive effects of taxation, it should be recognised that if governments have taxed big business less and personal incomes and consumption more, a structure has emerged within which big business pays either low tax or next to no tax at all, while individuals are pushed to the limit of their tolerance by revenue increases demanded by the tax authorities. In the UK in the mid 1980s, the Inland Revenue has not even managed to computerise its service to citizens, with the result that any individual – as a working constituency Member of Parliament will realise very well – may receive three or four tax demands from different Inland Revenue authorities, thereby alienating the individual away from the modern capitalist state.

Moreover, when taxes on income and consumption rise, people naturally fight for income increases to protect their real standard of living. This concerns not simply the big trade-union battalions of the income-earning population, but also those professional salary earners and pensioners who, in terms of the postwar Keynesian consensus, should have been able to count upon sufficient increases in their real standard of living and pensions to avoid confrontation with the political system. Put more simply, after a critical level, which clearly has already been passed, classic Keynesian deflation through raised consumer taxes tends to increase inflation itself. The pressure results more from the perversity of government indirect policies on taxation than from mindless sectional bargaining by trade unions in individual countries.

Inflexibility and Inflation

Such arguments are especially relevant to the claim of Keynesian and monetarist economists alike that one of the reasons for the alleged postwar failure of the British economy has been the 'inflexibility' of its wage structure. Translated into simpler terms, this amounts to saying that trades unions were too strong and the management was too weak.

There are, however, several flaws in the argument on 'wage inflexibility'. First, while rising wage demands may squeeze profit rates in individual enterprise, such enterprise needs to be individualised in order to determine whether it is price-making rather than price-taking, and whether the fundamental problems posed for such firms arise essentially because of wage bargaining power or because of the dynamics of unequal competition in the national and international arena.

Not least, both the Keynesian and monetarist theories of excess labour power and labour market 'inflexibility' need to take account of the extent to which multinational companies are able to secure lower cost labour in less developed countries, combining such costs with more advanced techniques of production, distribution and exchange. The Japanese in the postwar period have been past masters of this process; European and American countries, by contrast, have allowed their companies to seek lower-cost labour in global markets without recognising the implications for domestic policies on wage restraint. Put more simply, there is little point in the Thatcher government in Britain seeking to reduce wages by 5 per cent, 10 per cent, or 15 per cent, when the cost of labour as already available for some 20 years to UK multinational capital in intermediate countries has been as little as a tenth of UK labour costs. The fact that, in recent years, wage levels have risen in the 'city state' newly industrialising economies such as Singapore and

Hong Kong does not invalidate the main analysis. A reduction of labour costs in developed countries to the level obtaining in the lesser or least developed countries would result in a reduction of purchasing power and the promotion of a consumption crisis in the developed countries of a kind which big business in the multinational sector is not at all anxious to see happen. In other words, in contrast with the small microeconomic and national enterprise which Mrs Thatcher has bankrupted on a major scale through cuts in public spending, big business has realised for a long time that while it can exploit labour in Third World countries on a major scale, it needs to keep profits and also prices at a high or sustained level in the developed market economies in order to fulfil its profit objectives and survive in the global market economy.

Prices and Incomes in Context

Thus, in contrast with Joan Robinson's claim that inflation cannot occur without wage inflation, it is evident from the scale of multinational companies in the production, profits and pricing sequence in individual economies that it can and does do so. The mechanisms include Joan Robinson's 'imperfect competition' of higher prices and profits and also an inflationary pricing sequence (either compensating for falling sales by raising prices, or through multinational transfer pricing) by 'price leaders' in the market economy.

Advancing beyond both Joan Robinson's analysis, and that of Keynesian and monetarist economists, it is evident from the complexity of the profit and pricing process in a global economy dominated by multinational enterprise that the fight against inflation cannot simply be reduced to a single macroeconomic target for all prices and all incomes in the economy. Certainly, it can be recognised that profit rates in individual economies are affected by the ratio between costs and prices. But the extension of the realm of 'price-making' power by major mesoeconomic and multinational companies means that any prices policy should be selective between both meso and microeconomic firms and different sectors of the economy.

In effect, any policy aiming to secure a relative balance of prices and incomes in the modern capitalist economy should in turn ensure that transparency is introduced to the process of transfer pricing by multinational companies, and also that the need to secure 'national champions' (Vernon, 1974) in international trade is matched by an accountability of the price-making power of big business within any individual national economy.

Quantity and Quality

Besides which there is the practical consequence of incomes policies in terms of their social class impact when wages, but not profits, are restrained. While the economic intent behind such policies (if at all coherent) may be to increase the share of profits in total income and thus provide the means for further rounds of accumulation and investment, deflationary conditions such as tend to accompany periods of wage restraint militate against an expansion of output and thus of investment. Thus economies pursuing macroeconomic policies of deflation may provoke the resistance of labour as a class, not so much because no trades-union leader can grasp the importance of wages in total incomes but because trades unionists have intuited (and very probably also been advised on) the self-defeating consequences of pursuing deflationary polices with the aim of re-structuring capital and investment.

There is also a skill dimension of incomes policies. Even with a prevailing structure of income differentials within the working class, rather than a conscious policy of redistributing income within it, there are significant differences between the wages of skilled and unskilled workers and often younger and older workers and men and women within the same enterprise and certainly within the same sector of activity. It is sometimes assumed that opposition to an incomes policy implies no policy for incomes. But this is hardly the case. An incomes policy derived directly or indirectly from macro theories of distribution implies an aggregate and normally a percentage norm for incomes which is respected or imposed throughout the system.

Such a policy of a maximum annual percentage increase quickly runs up against the rigidity which it imposes within the labour market itself. A successful enterprise may wish to reward all its employees by more than this percentage, as was the case with the Ford Motor Company of Great Britain which between 1977 and 1978 more than doubled its profits, yet was recommended by the government only to increase wages on average by 5 per cent. Managers wanted to pay more and workers wanted to earn more. The breakdown of the recommended settlement at Fords breached the 1974–79 Labour government's 'social contract' wages policy, opening the gates to successive wage claims in excess of the norm.

Social Justice

A macroeconomic incomes policy based on absolute rather than percentage norms will have a redistributive effect. This was the case with the £6 wage increase negotiated by the trade unions and agreed by the Labour government in July 1975. Thus a £6 a week increase is worth proportionately more to a semi-skilled or unskilled worker than to a skilled worker or technician who has higher earnings. Such a policy is not necessarily unacceptable to those in the higher earnings or skill categories. But its acceptability, again, will depend in large part on what happens in the meantime to prices, and thus to real earnings. If prices are relatively stable, or lower than the increase in wages, the policy has some chance of success. If they are not, then the real incomes of those gaining less than they otherwise would have gained through 'free collective bargaining', or the free working of the market, will decline.

In addition, the prices concerned cannot simply be considered as those of purchased goods, or in particular consumer goods. The rents and purchase terms of housing (either of the initial purchase or, for those countries where they obtain, the mortgage terms), the price of public utilities (gas, electricity, water supply, public transport, etc) and the cost of local taxation (rates in the UK and local taxes in the US) all enter into the cost-and-benefit calculus consciously or intuitively evaluated by wage and salary earners faced with the prospect of an incomes policy. Again, if governments focus simply on the wages element in income distribution but neglect other factors in costs (some of which fall directly in their own domain), they should not be surprised by negative reactions to macroeconomic incomes policies.

Not least, there is the key question of wealth and its distribution. Reactions to disparities of wealth are complex and we should admit as much. There are considerable grounds for maintaining that most people are concerned to achieve a relative increase in what they have, rather than to leap from the lower-paid working class to the ranks of the rich or super-rich. This does not imply that there is some kind of golden mean of characteristic social behaviour, but rather a more realistic appreciation by most people of what may be within their grasp in the society in which we live.

8.6 Summary

(1) Both Keynesian and monetarist theory share an analysis of inflation as essentially too much money chasing too few goods and services. This overlap was the crucial bridgehead by which monetarist theory attacked and, from the mid 1970s, for a time successfully dethroned the Keynesian paradigm in the treasuries and chancelleries of the developed economies.

(2) The paradox and crisis for Keynesian theory lay in the combination of high inflation with high unemployment. Yet in theoretical terms monetarism has never proved a correlation between a given increase in money supply and a given increase in prices. Even with lag effects, there is no clear association (far less a causal link) between any given measure of the money supply and inflation.

(3) Monetarist theory challenged the cost-push and demand-pull theories

of inflation developed by neo-Keynesian economists. But such neo-Keynesians paid far more attention to wage cost-push on the supply side of the economy than to other supply-side factors in inflation.

(4) The Phillips curve claimed a correlation or trade-off between inflation and levels of employment, with the general conclusion that the money wage level would stabilise with unemployment at some 3.5 to 5 per cent. But the Phillips curve is 'knotted' for the US even at unemployment levels higher than 5 per cent. In the UK economy, a correlation of the Phillips type has only been achieved since 1980 as unemployment doubled from just under 7 per cent.

(5) The Phillips curve did not therefore provide policy-makers with a viable trade-off between slightly lower employment and lower inflation. With high unemployment, the Phillips effect is more similar to the depressive effect on wage rates of Marx's concept of 'a reserve army of labour'.

(6) Both neo-Keynesian and neo-Marxist economists (such as Glyn and Sutcliffe) have argued that union power can give rise to inflation through over-consumption. But the feasibility of high real wages depends on productivity. In the Japanese big business sector, where unions are not strong, management counters the 'reserve army of labour' case for wage restraint by granting high real wage increases and guaranteeing lifetime employment to core workers.

(7) Price-making power in the multinational big business sector now plays a key role in global inflation. Big business typical of the mesoeconomic sector can absorb or pass on cost increases of a kind which throw the profit levels of smaller microeconomic enterprise into crisis. Where prices are reduced over time, this tends to reflect as much the dynamics of big business competition as a reaction by all firms to macroeconomic phenomena such as the money supply, as favoured by the monetarists, or the level of unemployment, as favoured by neo-Keynesians.

(8) The range of pricing techniques open to and used by multinational companies on a global scale, and especially transfer pricing, can and do exert an inflationary effect by over-invoicing and inflating nominal costs and the final price level.

(9) Deflation can cause inflation under mesoeconomic conditions whereby oligopoly price-making registers a major impact on the price level, as leading firms compensate for a fall in their rate of growth of sales by raising their rate of increase in prices, often simply to preserve cash flow.

(10) Inversely, reflation or expansion of demand (either in competitive markets, or through public policies to restrain price increase in the mesoeconomic sector) can reduce inflation as firms achieve a fuller use

of existing capacity and thereby reduce their unit costs in production.

(11) Market inflexibility as a factor in inflation therefore includes not only wage inflexibility under some circumstances, but also the more pervasive structural inflexibility of mesoeconomic price-making power. This tends to be aggravated by the extent to which such big business may pass on the higher costs of external borrowing under inflationary conditions in higher prices.

(12) Both deflation and reflation register cumulative effects on the economy. Reflation makes it possible to regenerate, reconstruct and renew production and productivity. Deflation in general not only destroys less efficient production but also depresses profit expectations and degenerates productive potential.

(13) Social income and social justice are critical factors in the feasibility of any negotiated incomes policy. Policies such as social contracts or social accords (as applied in some of the OECD economies in recent years) have proved less than their full potential, as governments either have failed to defend the social wage or social income to households, or have restrained wages without likewise restraining higher incomes or prices.

(14) Government prices policies cannot succed for more than a short time simply by setting macroeconomic norms for all enterprise irrespective of its size, scale, global reach or market dominance. An effective prices policy needs to get alongside individual price-makers and determine norms which reflect their real cost and profit structures. It needs to be selective and disaggregated rather than general and unspecific, using a scalpel rather than an axe.

(15) Price policies affecting the minority of firms in the mesoeconomic sector mean that the state need not intervene directly in the pricing of the majority of firms in the micro sector, although such firms will need safeguarding against profits squeeze if they lose the shelter of the meso price 'umbrella'. The practical application of selective price agreements with meso enterprise is analysed in *The Political Economy* (Holland, forthcoming).

9 Accumulation and Crisis

It is clear that the current economic crisis is not simply cyclical or short term. It reflects more fundamental changes in the structure of production, trade and payments in the global economy and the balance of private and public power.

Originally, crisis meant 'decision'. In medical terms it often refers to a turning point, as in the course of an illness (Evans and Kaplinski, 1985). In economic terms, crisis generally refers to a 'breakdown' of the system, including what Attali (1978) has referred to as the contrast between 'implosive' and 'explosive' relations between the main factors in the growth or decline of the economy. Or as Gunnar Myrdal (1957 and 1968) has put it, the convergent process of self-reinforcing 'virtuous' circles of cumulative causation give place to divergent 'vicious' circles of cumulative disequilibrium. More recently, the international banking community and the world financial press have used the term 'crisis' in the context of international debt, and the breakdown of the postwar Bretton Woods global trade and payments system.

Such general observations on economic crisis can be analysed more rigorously by distinguishing (1) disproportion or imbalance between the supply and demand sides of the economy, including the problems of under-consumption and over-production; (2) the relation between short- and long-term cycles and the role played by innovation; (3) compound crisis, combining a range of asymmetric and self-reinforcing factors in the structure of supply and demand; and (4) the globalisation of crisis in the 1970s and 1980s, including international debt.

9.1 Marx Plus – Keynes Plus

Conventional economic theory polarises Marx and Keynes. But in key respects this convention is misplaced – not least in their mutual analysis of crisis. For instance, both Marx and Keynes stressed the cumulative nature of under-consumption in market economies, and instability or disequilibrium in the working of market forces. Both Marxists and Keynesians have been concerned about unequal, unbalanced or disproportionate growth on the supply side of the economy, which the market itself could not remedy. This was especially the case in development economics with an extensive debate throughout the 1950s and 1960s, following pioneering work by Rosenstein-Rodan (1943) and Nurkse (1952).

Moreover, although Keynesian analysis was primarily concerned (and in Keynes' own economics, almost exclusively concerned) with short-term problems of under-consumption, there is no Keynesian principle which excludes extension of his argument to long-term under-consumption or stagnation in the economy. Many economists broadly accepting a Keynesian short-term *gestalt* have also concerned themselves with the longer-term issue of unevenly distributed innovation and especially the decline in demand when an innovation wave has spent its main momentum. Nor need there be any analytic inhibition from combining neo-Keynesian with neo-Marxian components in the analysis of crisis in a compound crisis framework.

From Marx to Keynes

Marxist explanations of profits crisis stress general factors at work in the capitalist system, rather than specific factors such as state intervention. They also emphasise the difference between long- and short-term factors in profitability, or secular trends versus cyclical swings.

One of Marx's main points on disproportion was that crisis can occur precisely because of the unrestrained freedom of the market. Where investment decisions are made by independent entrepreneurs, some industries become over-extended in the course of an upswing because the output of complementary goods has not kept pace with them. A second emphasis in Marx is closer to Keynes, and stresses the under-consumption which would follow from disproportion – essentially increasing profits for capitalists and diminishing wages for workers. Thus profits will encourage a boom, but demand for products will be less than in the previous period. A third emphasis in Marxist theory assumes that an upswing does create full employment and raise wages, at least temporarily. But because the same shift to profits does not occur, investment is insufficient to sustain demand and depression ensues.

The under-consumption argument in Marx parallels Keynes' later emphasis on insufficient 'effective' demand in the capitalist system. Basically, this reflected a contradiction between the concern of individual producers to minimise their own wage costs and their desire for high demand – implying high aggregate wages – in the economy as a whole. When there was a downturn in demand in the system, profits would fall. Capitalists could not cut back on their constant or fixed capital (plant, equipment and buildings) unless they could find buyers for it, which would be less likely in a downturn of trade than when trade was high. Therefore they would try to cut back on variable capital or costs, either cutting wages or sacking part of the labour force, or both. But this would further reduce demand for goods and services as workers were unemployed, or wages lowered, and would further reinforce the downward trend in incomes and employment (cf., *inter alia*, Marx, 1887, pp. 84 and 120).

Keynes After Marx

Marx also expresses the under-consumption argument in terms of hoarding, i.e. the unwillingness or inability of the capitalist to translate his savings into actual investment. This is an 'anticipation' of Keynes which might have helped him escape more rapidly from Say's law (the assumption that all savings will find profitable investment), had Keynes made his way through Marx with any application.

This is not to claim that Keynes derived his own analysis from Marx. In fact he found Marx difficult. George Bernard Shaw encouraged him to read Marx, but in a letter to Shaw on 1 January 1935 Keynes wrote: 'I've had another shot at old K. M. last week . . . without making much progress. I prefer Engels of the two. I can see that they invented a certain method of carrying on and a vile manner of writing, both of which their successors have maintained with fidelity. But if you tell me that they discovered a clue to the economic riddle I am still beaten – I can discover nothing but out-of-date controversializing.' This is perhaps the more remarkable granted Keynes' passing but notable credit to Marx on under-consumption in *The General Theory* (Harrod, 1963, p. 462).

Keynes countered the tendency to under-consumption in successive business cycles with his theory of state control of general expenditure in the economy through fiscal and monetary policies. For nearly a third of a century after the war, Keynesian economists reckoned that this policy of demand management had succeeded in the sense that governments could raise demand through cutting taxes and interest rates. They tended to neglect the key role played by rising long-term public spending in offsetting under-consumption. They were also notably less successful in calling forth a sustained flow of investment equal to the technical potential of economies such as those of Britain and the United States without resorting to military expenditure.

Under-Consumption and Deflation

The compatibility between Marx's and Keynes' analysis of under-consumption or deflation can be illustrated in terms of Figure 9.1(a), in which a fall in demand gives rise to a deflationary gap. This assumes that demand falls below the equilibrium of s^1 and d^1 to a deflated level of d^2. In modern Keynesian terms, such a deflationary gap may occur because of (i) public expenditure cuts, (ii) cuts in wage expenditure or (iii) cuts in real expenditure through increases in indirect taxation, or (iv) the same effect through rises in public service charges on gas, electricity or transport, as has been the case in the 1980s in Britain under the Thatcher government.

The supply and demand side columns of Figure 9.1(a) correspond with an extension of Marx's distinction between what he called the Two Departments of production and consumption, i.e. (i) the Means of Production, or 'commodities having a form in which they must, or at least may, pass into production consumption' and (ii) the Articles of Consumption or 'commodities having a form in which they pass into the individual consumption of the capitalists and the working class'. Although some Marxist economists have tended to focus on the production or supply side of Marx's two departments, Marx himself was highly conscious of the dual nature of production and consumption, thus rejecting Say and anticipating Keynes (Marx, 1887, Vol. II, pp. 395–421 and Vol. I, part vii).

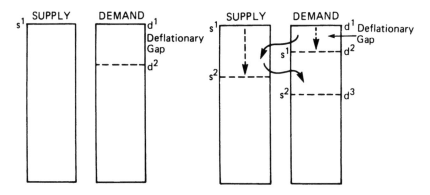

FIG. 9.1(a)   The deflationary gap

FIG. 9.1(b)   The cumulative deflationary gap

In *Capital* (Vol. I, pp. 439–40), in direct anticipation of Keynes' analysis of declining effective demand, Marx wrote that the subsitution of machinery for labour not only unemploys workers, 'but, at the same time . . . withdraws from their consumption. . . . The circumstances that they were "freed" by the machinery from the means of purchase changed them from buyers into nonbuyers. Hence a lessened demand for those commodities – *voilà tout*. . . . If this be not compensated from some other quarter, the market price of the commodity falls. If this state of things lasts for some time, and extends, there follows a discharge of workmen employed in the production of these commodities. . . .' (cf. further *Capital*, Vol. I, part vii).

Multiplier Effects

However, while Marx stressed the dynamic effects of lower demand on under-production, it was Keynes' application of the multiplier (not anticipated in a formal sense by Marx) which opened the way in the twentieth century to a fuller understanding of instability and crisis in the market economy.

Thus it is important to the Keynesian analysis that if an initial deflation is registered on the demand side of the economy, its impact on the supply side will be multiplied and exceed the initial demand deflation. Therefore, extending the multiplier analysis of Chapter 2 in Figure 9.1(b), a deflation from d^1 to d^2 will be accompanied by a contraction of supply from s^1 to s^2, in practice through a combination of the income multiplier and the intersectoral or matrix multiplier.

The income multiplier effect means that just as an expansion of income within the market system generates a multiplied expansion of other incomes, a contraction of income similarly results in a higher cumulative contraction over time, with its specific incidence depending on the prevailing social expenditure patterns and the prevailing structures of class and income distribution. Relating Keynes' concept of the deflationary gap to the supply side of the economy, the negative multiplier from income contraction means that consumers buy less and thereby demand less from a range of firms and enterprises.

In turn, through the matrix or inter-industry multiplier, firms buy less from other firms, whether components for production or raw materials and supplies. In addition, the firms with falling sales will tend either (a) to restrain wage increases, (b) to cut real wages or (c) to lay off workers, thereby failing to offset the deflationary gap on the demand side of the economy or aggravating it through further cuts in consumption and demand. This results in a feedback effect from the supply to the demand side of the economy, with a further contraction of demand.

Cumulative Crisis

Such a deflationary gap can be caused by internal or external factors. For instance, the export sector of a given economy may contract through loss of export competitiveness. This may include both price and quality effects in a low-growth economy in which relatively high inflation is not offset by successive rounds of cost-lowering and quality-raising investment. Or the international economy as a whole may suffer from under-consumption and a reduction in mutual demand between countries for their respective imports and exports. In either event (while allowing for the qualification of such macro assumptions by the multinational sourcing of components in the meso sector), the contraction of export sales will tend to result through the matrix multiplier in lower demand from other branches of the domestic economy, wage cuts, lay-offs or all three. Thus, like deflation in Figure 9.1(b), the initial contraction of export sales may result in an indirect contraction of domestic demand in the economy which begins a downward spiral in the system as a whole.

These are the dynamics of under-consumption which Keynes addressed in non-Marxist terms. Yet they directly complement Marx's analysis of under-consumption and his claim that there is nothing in the free working of the market which can be counted on to redress such a downward spiral through a lowering of wages aiming to restore profitability.

In such respects Marx and Keynes were confronting the same issues of disequilibrium or asymmetry in the market mechanism. Indeed the question posed by Harrod on instability and of what was to stop a market system, once in a downward spiral, from 'hitting the floor', is precisely the kind of question which Marx posed in terms of cumulative crisis. Since the 1970s, with the increased interdependence of trade and payments which followed postwar liberalisation, it has become a burning issue for the global economy as a whole.

Capital Intensity and Over-Investment

Under-consumption is the main feature of crisis in Keynes' economics. Marx, however, also stressed the role of rising capital intensity with the increased investment necessary for mass production (in his terms, a rising organic composition of capital). Without elaborating Marx's exposition at this stage, his essential point was simple, i.e. that rising capital intensity can result in over-investment which in turn contributes to crisis. *

Over-investment should not be conceived simply as the inverse of falling demand. It can occur independently of deflation or under-consumption in the economy. For instance, putting the case in non-Marxist terms, Figure 9.2(a) shows that the trend rate of growth of investment and supply $s^1 s^2$ (either for an industry or for the economy as a whole) may well exceed the trend rate of growth of demand $d^1 d^2$. In this case, firms with excess stocks on the line $s^1 s^2$ relative to demand and sales on the line $d^1 d^2$ are likely to reduce their stock inventories as they adjust supply to demand. This stock or inventory phenomenon plays an important part in the analysis of conventional trade-cycle theory, and is one respect in which markets may clear or adjust supply and demand over the medium term.

* Marx's labour theory of value and the counter case of neo-Ricardian value theory are analysed in some detail in *The Political Economy* (Holland, forthcoming).

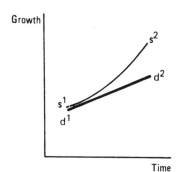
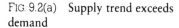

FIG. 9.2(a)   Supply trend exceeds demand

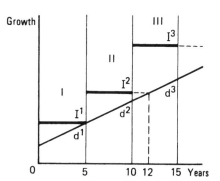

FIG. 9.2(b)   Minimum efficient investment exceeds constant demand growth

However, there is a more basic underlying phenomenon of over-supply in a modern capitalist economy, which is represented in Figure 9.2(b). This represents three investment phases for an enterprise, which for purposes of exposition are of equal length. In practice, a lengthening investment cycle or pay-off period for amortization tends to occur with larger-scale plant which embodies both technical economies of scale and the most modern technology available.

In investment period 1 in Figure 9.2(b), it is assumed that firms in year 1 correctly anticipate the rise in the trend rate of growth of demand over a five-year period. They therefore, in year 1, commit that investment which adequately matches demand over a five-year period. Supply thus matches demand with a coincidence between I^1 and d^1. Reflecting the Harrod's distinction (analysed in Chapter 3) between actual and warranted rates of growth, a matching of actual demand trends with the level of investment judged to be warranted by firms in year 1 can be expected to encourage firms in Phase 2 to proceed with a further round of investment.

The Innovation Frontier

However, the technical feasibility or innovation frontier moves over time. The result is that the plant considered adequate for investment in Phase 1 may no longer yield the technical economies of scale (or embodied technology) being employed by competitors. Since technical economies tend to be associated with economies of scale or larger size, firms therefore will need to invest on a larger scale in Phase 2 of their investment cycle than in Phase 1. But, over a five-year period, this would not match supply with the actual trend rate of growth of demand and would leave an over-supply gap – the difference between I^2 and d^2 at the end of Phase 2.

In principle, cautious or pessimistic firms therefore might delay their introduction of Phase 3 of new investment until demand matched supply at the juncture of the broken lines in Figure 9.2(b), coinciding with the twelfth year of the overall investment cycle, in which case the rate of investment in the economy will fall. However, reflecting the analysis of the lower cost curves from further rounds of investment embodying new cost-lowering technology, competitive pressures may force firms to bring forward the further round of new investment (Phase 3 in Figure 9.2(b)) and commit it in year 10. The result, reflecting the trend to larger scale plant, would be a major over-supply of investment capacity relative to the growth demand, with substantial spare capacity by year 15. In terms of Figure 9.2(b), demand at point d^3 would represent some 75 per cent of supply available at I^3, which would not allow the firm (in terms of our previous analysis of cost schedules in the market economy) to break even, far less register a significant profit.

Excess Capacity

The essentials of Figure 9.2(b) should be plain. Over-supply does not necessarily represent a short-term mismatch of output to the trend rate of growth of demand. Even with a constant rate of growth of demand on the lines d^1, d^2 and d^3 in Figure 9.2(b), the imperatives of larger scale, innovation-embodying new plant may result in over-supply and potentially chronic over-capacity in the industry concerned.

This is precisely what was occurring in the steel and petrochemical industries in the advanced capitalist countries from the mid-1960s to the mid-1970s, before the impact of the oil crisis and over-reaction by government deflationary policies depressed demand way below the 75–80 per cent break-even level which was critical for steel plant to be commercially profitable.

In effect, there has been a trend to greater capital intensity in production in modern capitalism, which corroborates part of Marx's thesis and illustrates the depth of his perception a century ago. On the other hand, the trend to excess capacity throughout the economy was offset until the mid 1970s by the upwards trend of public spending, analysed in the context of growth and cycles in the mixed economy in chapter 3.

Rising Technical Composition

The trend to productivity-raising innovation has further major implications for imbalance in the modern capitalist economy. Figure 9.2(c) again assumes a constant trend rate of growth of demand on the intermediate line D. However, over time, whether five, ten or fifteen years, the rise in productivity represented by technical progress and innovation will enable enterprise to produce more while employing less labour. Therefore, the productivity increase of PTY^1 to PTY^2 is offset by an employment decrease of E^1 to E^2.

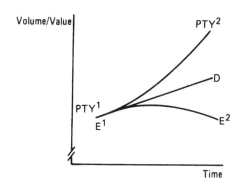

FIG. 9.2(c)   Constant demand growth, increased productivity and decreased employment

For the enterprise, considering simply the economies of cost, rate of return and profit, this registers as an internal saving. If the workers are unemployed through natural wastage, there also might be no significant external social cost or demand effect on unemployment. If, however, the trend line E^1 to E^2 reflects redundancies and a reduction of the labour force of working age, this in turn will have aggregate demand effects comparable to those in the analysis of the deflationary gap in Figures 9.1(a) and 9.1(b). In other words, the displacement of labour because of productivity-raising innovation may tend to impose an external diseconomy through reducing overall demand.

In practice, if the firms concerned generate significant export earnings through their higher productivity and technically more progressive investment in foreign markets, this could offset the effect of domestic underconsumption. If, however, the effect of higher productivity is globalised throughout the world economy for a range of sectors, there is no automatic compensating effect available through higher exports since global demand would be reduced. Such a point is not insignificant in relation to the major labour displacements which have occurred in manufacturing industry over the last 15 to 20 years, and which are now being registered on a major scale in the services sector (as analysed more extensively in *The Political Economy* (Holland, forthcoming).

Disproportion and Imbalance

Such analysis substantially corroborates a further element in Marxist theory of profits and crisis – the 'disproportion' factor. As indicated earlier, in Marx's terms, this means a disproportion between the investment goods sector of industry and the consumption goods sector (Marx, 1887, vol. II, pp. 395ff). But in more general terms it can be expressed as the inherent imbalance in a process of unplanned development. More simply, it means that now too much, and now too little, is produced relative to demand and sales (cf. Paul Sweezy, 1968, pp. 156ff).

Such a thesis does not depend exclusively on the imbalanced or disproportional impact of innovations in a capitalist economy. It also arises to the extent that no firm by itself is big enough to plan both its own market *and* the size and structure of national and international demand. Each firm plans its own production on incomplete knowledge of what final sales will be, whatever the extent of its hold over consumers through advertising, or its hold over other firms through market dominance.

Thus, big firms in the mesoeconomic sector stand between the competitive aspirations of government policy and supply by small firms of the conventional model. But they are still dependent on factors outside their control, including imbalanced development of different branches and sectors of the economy as a result of technical progress and innovation. In the advanced-technology area of computers, aircraft and nuclear power, government purchasing can partly substitute for a disproportion between the massive initial costs of research, equipment and development.

In this sense, government defence spending can create a market which partly overcomes the three main elements in crisis theory expressed so far: under-consumption, rising organic compositions of capital and disproportion. Long-term and high-volume government contracts for the defence industries can sustain demand, guarantee a profit on capital-intensive ventures, and iron out some of the disproportion which otherwise would occur through the free working of the market. This role of armaments spending in post-war capitalist intervention has been stressed since the early 1950s by several commentators, such as John Strachey in his *Contemporary Capitalism* (1956). But in general, Marxists were taken aback by the sustained expansion of the western capitalist system because of an under-estimation of the extent to which capitalist expansion, once started, would tend to be self-reinforcing as a result of the factors analysed in Chapter 3. For instance, the 1946 Manifesto of the 4th International asserted that: 'there is no reason whatever to assume that we are facing a new epoch of capitalist stabilisation and development'. This contrasts with Lenin's assertion that there was no crisis from which capitalism could not recover (Report to the Second Congress of the Communist International).

9.2 Cycles and Crisis

For understandable reasons, political interest has focused on Marx's long-term predictions for the future of the capitalist market economy. The popular assumptions of what could be termed 'vulgar' Marxism is that crises of over-production and maladjustment between supply and demand will result in explosive fluctuations of increasing force, to the discomfiture both of the proletariat and bankrupted capitalists who could face a political breakdown of the system.

Crisis and Restructuring

In simple terms, such a cumulative downswing of the system is illustrated in Figure 9.3(a), whereby successively widening and deepening cycles would intensify a long-term and cumulative crisis within the capitalist system. Higher peaks are associated with lower troughs. Such cumulative cycles involve both the over-production and under-consumption dimensions of crisis analysed earlier in this chapter. They fulfil certain objective functions within the long-term development of the capitalist system, including (1) the elimination through bankruptcy of inefficient firms and branches of production in the trough of the cycle; (2) increased centralisation of production in the hands of fewer, larger and more efficient firms during the downturn of the cycle; (3) reinforced dynamism of production on 'a cyclopean scale' by bigger business during the upswing of recovery; and (4) a restructuring of labour – complementing such reconstructed capital – as its bargaining power is weakened in the downturn or trough of economic activity, lowering wages and raising potential profit rate for a further upswing of activity.

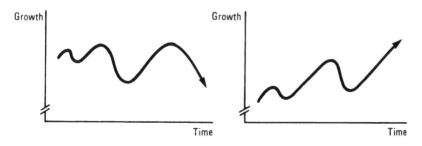

FIG 9.3(a)   Marxian cumulative decline

FIG 9.3(b)   Schumpeterian cumulative upswing

Marx himself has been criticised for determinism or the assumption that cumulative crises of bigger and deeper cycles would result in a final crisis of the capitalist system. In fact, Marx is ambiguous rather than explicit about any such final crisis of the system. He certainly did not claim that there would be a 'permanent crisis', but stressed that cycles and crisis would tend to restructure profits and create the conditions for further recovery. Marx's theory in this respect is the subject of an immense theoretical literature. But historical analysis is presented with a fairly simple final case for judgement. Beset by cycles though it has been, the capitalist system as yet has not broken up.

Innovations and Public Spending

For one thing, in the nineteenth century, most technical innovations involved both better ways of making or doing the same things, and technical breakthroughs which made possible entirely new products, industries and services. In other words, they were both process innovations and product innovations. For instance, capitalists were engaged in cheaper ways of making existing goods such as furniture, stoves, carpets, clothes, mechanical equipment, and so on. The steam, coal, iron and steel, gas and transport 'revolutions' were either at their peak or coming to a head during the mid nineteenth century. But entirely new industries based on new products and services were either in their infancy, unborn, or unconceived. In the late nineteenth and twentieth centuries these have included the industrial and household use of electricity; the telephone, telecommunications, radio-television and electronics; the automobile and petro-chemical industries; plastics, pharmaceuticals, aircraft, nuclear power, and so on. These new industries and services were to create vast new areas for profits which were to qualify the Marxist thesis of a declining rate of profit through the rising organic composition of capital. Much of the labour displaced by rising capital intensity in some branches of industry would be absorbed into new jobs in entirely new industries and services.

Moreover, Marx wrote before the role of the modern capitalist state as spender or allocator of goods and services had occurred. It was only shortly before his death that Bismarck in Germany introduced a social security framework for German workers, and only in the early twentieth century that Lloyd George did the same for Britain. Public spending programmes were pursued especially on infrastructure projects and public works, but still represented an insignificant share of total spending. The role of the state in the nineteenth century was limited mainly to law, order and defence through the courts, the police and the military. Factors offsetting a long-term cumulative downturn in economic activity such as the rising share of Hicks' long-term investment – fulfilled in practice (as illustrated in Chapter 3) by a significant rise in public expenditure – was to occur in some European countries in the 1930s, in the United 'States at the same time through the New Deal programmes, but mainly through armaments programmes before the First and Second World Wars, and armaments plus welfare programmes from the mid twentieth century.

Schumpeter: 'Creative Destruction'

Avoiding 'vulgar Marxism', Schumpeter (1934) was influenced by both Marx and Kondratieff (see later). In particular, Schumpeter realised that major product innovations not only could offset tendencies to crisis and decline but also sustain a cumulative and successive expansion of the system on the lines of Figure 9.3(b).

Thus for Schumpeter, innovation was not only the essential function of the 'creative entrepreneur' but also the basic dynamic of capitalist production itself. Also, as each wave of innovation spent its force, the markets for its clustered range of goods became saturated. This analysis, consistent with the stress on the role of product cycles analysed both in this volume and *The Market Economy* (Holland, 1987), provided Schumpeter with an explanation of the downturn in economic activity which ranges beyond the short-term 'overheating' analysis of either Harrod or Glyn and Sutcliffe (1972). In other words, paralleling the declining rate of growth for firms in individual markets with products at saturation in the mature phase of a product cycle, profits fall, lay-offs occur, unemployment rises, and income demand declines.

Schumpeter's term 'creative destruction' was a conscious paradox illustrating the 'phoenix'-like potential of the capitalist system to recover from crisis. This concept is similar to Marx's analysis that downturns in the economic cycle are not so much 'failures of the system' but – with their associated elimination of inefficient capital – a precondition for a new creative upswing in activity. But while Marx's concept of the rising technical composition of capital in new upswings of activity clarifies part of the process by which innovation occurs, Schumpeter stressed that technical progress applied in embodied investment through innovation was a *prime reason* for reversals in the downswing of economic cycles and in the dynamism of the upswing. In other words, in contrast with the monetarists, who tended to assume that lower wage costs alone would increase profits and thereby investment in the transition from downswings to upswings of activity, Schumpeter downgraded monetary factors of the kind later highlighted by Friedman, and stressed instead the role of technical progress and innovation in the real economy.

'Bunched' Innovation

Certainly Schumpeter's theory complements the more theoretical exposition of accelerator or capital-stock adjustment principles of the kind analysed in Chapter 2.

For Schumpeter, therefore, development or recovery is not simply a matter of creating sufficient conditions for profitability. Nor do innovations come sporadically, springing fully armed from the inventor's head. Rather innovations tend to be 'bunched', creating a series of further spiralling innovations, in which innovation in one branch of activity will itself promote others. Examples are readily available from the period in which he wrote his own main work in the 1930s. Thus the revolution in electrical engineering before the First World War promoted the suburbanisation of cities through electric tramway networks, with new house building and new consumer durable goods of the kind now commonplace in the developed economies – such as electric irons and vacuum cleaners, electric ovens and toasters, refrigerators etc – while the electrical revolution later made possible the electronic revolution which transformed the radio industry of the interwar period into the television, record player and taperecorder revolutions after the Second World War.

Small Firms and Big Firms

Schumpeter stressed that innovation may work in one of three different ways. First, it may speed up the replacement of existing plant and make it obsolete. Second, it may create an expectation of high profits for the first firms in the field of innovation. Third, it may raise the propensity to consume by offering a product so attractive that consumers are willing to cut into their savings to buy it. Schumpeter himself stressed the second type of expansion.

Christopher Freeman (1982) has claimed that there are two distinct versions of Schumpeter's innovation theory. The mark 1 version is that developed by the young Schumpeter before the First World War and expounded in his *Theory of Economic Development* (first published in 1912). The second, mark 2, is that of Schumpeter's later book, *Capitalism, Socialism and Democracy* (1943). With considerable relevance to our own analysis of differences between meso and microeconomic enterprise, Freeman comments that: 'the main differences between Schumpeter mark 2 and Schumpeter mark 1 are in the incorporation of endogenous scientific and technical activities conducted by large firms' (our emphasis). There is a strong positive feedback from successful innovation to increased R&D activities setting up a 'virtuous' self-reinforcing circle leading to renewed impulses to increase market concentration.

This mark 2 version contrasts with Schumpeter's earlier mark 1 model of small-firm innovation. As Freeman comments, both big and small business innovation play an ongoing role in the contemporary capitalist economy. Despite their high rate of infant or adolescent mortality, small firms do play a significant role in innovation in new-technology areas such as electronics and scientific instruments. Nonetheless, by 1942 Schumpeter saw inventive activities as increasingly under the control of large firms and reinforcing their competitive position. The 'coupling' between science, technology, innovative investment and the market, once loose and subject to long time delays, is now much more intimate and continuous (Freeman, 1982, p. 214). Such a judgement confirms our own analysis of the internalisation of innovation and technology transfer on a global scale, within the circuits of the multinational company, as analysed in some detail in Chapter 6.

Four Phases

Four main phases of Schumpeter's model of innovation and cycles of economic activity are illustrated in Figure 9.4. Thus an upswing during a period of prosperity in phase 1 will be followed by a downturn or recession in phase 2, followed in turn by both depression (phase 3) and recovery (phase 4). Nonetheless, according to Schumpeter (1939, chapter 2), a distinction should be made between the four-phase form of business cycles and their specific innovations. For Schumpeter, each business cycle was unique because of the range, scale, scope and spread of its specific technical innovations, as well as a variety of external or exogenous events such as wars, gold discoveries, or harvest failures. Anticipating, and indeed influencing, the product-cycle model of Vernon, Schumpeter had argued that there will be a strong 'band-wagon' effect whereby the entry of many new firms into rapidly expanding innovation sectors would attract new entrants through initially high profits from innovation. However, this in turn will be followed by a period of 'competing away' profits as new industries matured. This played an important role in the second and third phases of recession and depression in the Schumpeterian business cycle. As Freeman has commented (1982, p. 209): 'such an explanation appears to fit the facts of the post-war boom. It had been remarked already in the 1960s that the general rate of profit was beginning to fall in several OECD countries and this tendency was aggravated by more severe international competition. This became still more marked in the 1970s, especially in some of the erstwhile rapid growth sectors such as synthetic materials and consumer durables.'

There can be no doubt that Schumpeter's analysis of the role of innovation illuminates understanding of cycles and crises. Certainly Schumpeter's analysis challenges market equilibrium theory by stressing that the very

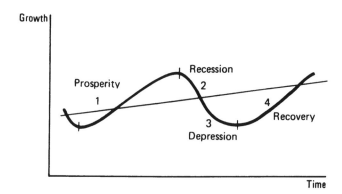

FIG. 9.4   Four phases in the Schumpeter cycle

freedom to innovate which was characteristic of capitalism would also tend to mean a staggered, uneven or bunched rate of innovation. It also counters the subjective misjudgement theory of cycles – reflected especially in the monetarist or neo-monetarist theory of 'augmented expectations', (Schumpeter, 1934 and 1939). Through his disciple François Perroux, it influenced the postwar French government in its efforts to promote 'entirely new' sectors and branches of economic activity, with a higher advanced-technology strategy for intervention in the supply side of the economy (Perroux, 1965).

Scope and Limits

Nevertheless, there are a number of qualifications to Schumpeter's 'creative destruction' analysis which cannot be ignored. It would be an exaggeration to maintain that innovation alone is responsible for the upswings in longer-term cycles in modern capitalism. For one thing, there was the role of the state in promoting capital accumulation and innovation in the nineteenth and twentieth centuries. Two simple examples illustrate the point. As stressed in Chapter 3 of *The Market Economy* (Holland, 1987), it was investment by both local States and the federal government, with an associated range of concessions and incentives, which made possible the establishment of a national railway network in the United States. And in Germany in the nineteenth century, under Bismarck, railways were publicly owned or nationalised from the start, on the not unreasonable assumption that leaving the development of the national infrastructure to private capital would at best be uncertain and at worst long delayed.

Similarly, to take a more recent example of the transport revolution, the development of jet-engine technology was pioneered in both Britain and

Germany by the state rather than private enterprise during the Second World War, and massively promoted by the federal government in the United States, where the B-47 bomber programme prefaced and in large part underwrote the development costs of the later Boeing 707 passenger aircraft, which in turn presaged the now familiar 727 and 747 Jumbo jets and other civilian derivatives from military prototypes.

A second respect in which the global diffusion of innovation depended primarily on state intervention rather than on Schumpeter's 'creative entrepreneurs' alone, lay in the role of extensive protection in the United States, Germany, France and Japan at successive stages throughout the nineteenth century. This reality, again contradicting claims for market innovation unsullied by state interference, has also been analysed in Chapter 3. Upswings as well as peaks in activity since the Second World War have not been unrelated to war expenditure and the armaments economy, as becomes more apparent from consideration of the Russian 'grand master' of long-cycle theory, Kondratieff.

Kondratieff: Long Cycles

Marx influenced Kondratieff in his assessment that there was a periodicity of ten years or so in the re-investment of fixed capital. But Kondratieff modified Marx's idea, introducing a graduation in durability, in the production period and in the amount of investment corresponding to different kinds of capital goods. On its basis, Kondratieff developed the concept of a longer cycle, some fifty to sixty years in length. As he put it: 'the material basis of the long cycles is the wear and tear, the replacement and the increase of the fund of basic capital goods, the production of which requires tremendous energy and is a long process.' The basic goods are 'big plants, important railways, canals, large land improvement projects [plus] the training of skilled labour' (Kondratieff, 1925).

Kondratieff stressed that: 'The wave-like fluctuations are processes of alternating disturbances of the equilibrium of the capitalist system; they are increasing or decreasing deviations from equilibrium levels'. He did not believe in a strict periodicity. As he put it: 'A strict periodicity in social and economic phenomena does not exist at all – neither in the long nor the intermediate waves. The length of the latter fluctuates at least between 7 and 11 years. . . . The length of the long cycles fluctuates between 48 and 60 years.'

He suggested the following dating of 'long waves': (1) from the end of the 1780s to 1844–51, with a peak in 1810–17; (2) from 1844–51 to 1890–96, with a peak in 1870–75; (3) a rise from 1890–96 to 1914–20, when he believed that a decline 'probably began'.

Stylisation and Simplification

Kondratieff's suggestions have provoked more than passing interest. Figure 9.5 represents a 'stylised' construction of four long cycles from 1780 to the year 2000 devised by Robert Beckman (1983). Bearing in mind that any construction of periodicity in long-term cycles is subject both to Kondratieff's own caveat against strict periodicity and to overstatement of symmetry, Figure 9.5 nonetheless reflects Kondratieff's own analysis for the upswings and peaks of the first three cycles to the 1920s, and also his concept of an intermediate wave – or a partial recovery after the long-cycle peak, which in his own words, 'fluctuates at least between seven and eleven years' (Kondratieff, 1925).

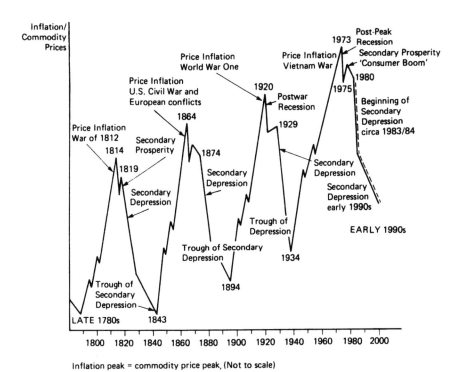

FIG. 9.5 'Stylised' Kondratieff cycles (Source: Beckman, 1983)

Such a distinction between primary and secondary phases of long-term upswings and depression is in notable contrast with Friedman's monotonic emphasis on the association of the money supply and prices (M and P in the Fisher $MV = PT$ equation). It also contrasts with the emphasis on the short-term relationship between employment and prices in the Phillips curve. In contrast with conventional theory of either the monetarist or neo-Keynesian varieties, the Kondratieff cycle implies that major periods of price inflation are associated with the end of long periods of sustained expansion in investment and output, rather than short or medium-term changes in specific macroeconomic variables.

Presaging the stress on cumulative cycles of innovation for which Schumpeter later credited him, Kondratieff identified the first three long cycles in economic activity with a series of related innovations. With some reason, these read like a textbook series of the innovations taught to many students as the primary causes of 'the industrial revolution'. Thus the upswing of cycle 1 from the later 1780s to the period at the end of the Napoleonic Wars was based on cotton and wrought iron; the upswing of the second main Kondratieff cycle, from the mid-1840s, was based on railways and steel, and that of the third main Kondratieff cycle from the 1890s on electricity, chemicals and related products.

Mensch: Towards a Fifth Cycle?

Beckman's diagram and its implications for the fourth main Kondratieff cycle from the mid-1930s to the early 1970s derives in part from the analysis of Gerhard Mensch (1975 and 1979), which is an exercise in both explanation and vindication of the Kondratieff analysis. Mensch claims that throughout the last 200 years the pace of technological innovation has systematically varied and he traces this process in detail for hundreds of innovations (Hall, 1981). According to Mensch, the fourth Kondratieff cycle from the trough of the 1930s was based essentially on automobiles, aircraft, aerospace and electronics. According to Mensch, by the mid-1970s about half of all the innovations of the fourth Kondratieff cycle had already reached the stage of commercial feasibility and innovation. On this basis, Mensch boldly announced that the decade of maximum innovation for new micro-technology, bio-engineering and other products will start in 1984, but that 1989 will be the year of 'peak innovation'.

Further questions have been asked about Mensch's extrapolation of the Kondratieff cycle. Reflecting our earlier analysis of differences in the international and multinational location of innovative investment, Peter Hall (1981) has commented that 'the fact [is] that evidently the locus of innovation shifts'. As he puts it, in the first Kondratieff of cotton and iron it was unambiguously located in Britain. But in the second Kondratieff of steam and steel, Britain was starting to share pride of place with Germany and the United States. In the third Kondratieff of chemicals and cars, the lead passed to the United States, although Germany still played an important role. In the fourth Kondratieff – in particular the post-1945 cycle focused on aircraft, weaponry and computers, as well as a range of new service industries – the centre of innovation undoubtedly was in the United States, but with Japan playing a progressively greater part. As Hall puts it, 'the question everyone must ask is the locus of the fifth Kondratieff cluster of innovations. For, as each major nation becomes the innovation leader, so does it become the world's economic leader' (Peter Hall, ibid.).

9.3 Compound Crisis

As both Kondratieff and Schumpeter were well aware, 'long-wave' theories of expansion and recession are compatible with Marx's analysis of cyclical crisis in the capitalist market economy.

Four Theses

But how consistent are the main theses in Marxist crisis theory? In part they are self-exclusive and in part mutually consistent. For instance, there is a clear enough difference between the stress on under-consumption in economists such as Sweezy, and what has been called the over-consumption argument of Glyn and Sutcliffe. The four main hypotheses – (1) under-consumption; (2) over-consumption; (3) over-supply, through (a) a rising organic and (b) a technical composition of capital; and (4) disproportion – can be consistent and indeed may compound general crisis on specific assumptions. Thus the rising scale of capital combined with higher technical progress can aggravate profits squeeze if combined with general under-consumption in the downturn of a trade or business cycle.

This problem in turn can be aggravated by general disproportion at the level of individual economies, such as insufficient domestic supply relative to demand in the investment goods sector, or to final demand, and a disproportionate share of long-term imports over exports – promoting debt, deflation, devaluation and inflation. Alternatively, taking the perspective over the long term, and the factors in different combination, an over-consumption or profits squeeze on Glyn-Sutcliffe lines could prompt a loss of national export performance, a cutback in domestic consumption and imports as incomes fall in the export sector, and domestic under-consumption. This could coincide with problems of profit realisation through a rising organic composition of capital, and disproportion in capital-intensive advanced-technology industries.

The combination of all such factors – in sequence – cannot be generalised. This is especially true of disproportion, on which Sweezy has commented that 'disproportionalities arising from the planlessness of capitalism are by nature not amenable to explanation in terms of general laws' (Sweezy, 1968, pp. 157–8).

'Fordism', Expansion and Crisis

Certainly it is widely enough recognised, as in Figure 9.3(a), that Marx expected booms and slumps of increasing size because of a combination of the rising organic composition of capital and under-consumption, and he thought these would lead to a general crisis of capitalism. Inversely, as illustrated in Figure 9.3(b), Schumpeter anticipated that cycles in economic activity promoted by innovation would regenerate the capitalist market economy despite intermediate periods of recession and depression.

Some of the factors which postponed the earlier onset of crisis in the period following the Second World War have already been elaborated. In other words, in contrast with the prediction of some Marxist economists in the immediate postwar period that capitalism was unlikely to recover from the ashes of slump and war, the rise of long-term public spending and increased wages in national income generated demand, which in turn promoted and sustained successive rounds of Schumpeterian innovation.

In the theses of Aglietta (1976) and Lipietz (1982 and 1984), the combination of innovation, production economies of scale and the wage demand made possible through mass production promoted the phenomenon of 'Fordism'. This variant of Marxist theory claimed that a disproportion between Marx's Department I (investment goods) and Department II (consumer goods) was offset by the rise of mass consumption generated through high wages which could be afforded through gains from economies of scale in mass production by big business. Deriving its title from the classic example of Ford's mass production of the Model T, the 'Fordism' thesis as expounded by Aglietta contests the relevance of neoclassical equilibrium theories of economic growth and stresses the relations between structural factors and complex social relations in the nature of economic crises. Aglietta's interpretation of accumulation in the United States parallels the main form of the Kondratieff/Mensch long-term cycle, with a fifth era of structural crisis emerging from the mid 1960s.

In a manner very similar to our own analysis of the changing nature of US economic growth in the nineteenth century (Holland, 1976b, chapter 6), Aglietta's thesis contrasts the 'extensive' regime of accumulation in which the United States expanded to its natural frontiers, with an 'intensive' period in which further expansion became possible through mass-production economies of scale in the modern corporation. Contrasting the mythology of 'the new frontier' and its equation of free enterprise with freedom to acquire and accumulate land, Aglietta stresses that 'Fordism' assumes intensive exploitation of not only industry but also of mining, agriculture and the service sectors, with the derivative income multiplier meaning that extension of the 'Fordist' principle implied the generation of a mass-consumption market through increased wage demand.

Fordism in Question

Aglietta's application of the 'Fordist' thesis has significant implications for the social distribution of demand and the role of different social classes in the process of accumulation and crisis, which are analysed in more detail in *The Political Economy* (Holland, forthcoming). Davis (1978) has offered extensive criticism of Aglietta's basic thesis on the grounds that it fails to take account of: (1) the role of the state in promoting demand, and in turn the role of public spending and especially military expenditure in the postwar expansion of the modern market economy; (2) the fiscal crisis of the state, as governments have sought to offset declining rates of accumulation and profit by rebating tax or granting subsidies to private-sector enterprise; (3) neglect of the changing role of the firm and enterprise on the supply side of the economy, including oligopoly and the rise of multinational companies; and (4) the 'uneven development' or unequal spatial distribution of gains and benefits from mass-production economies of scale, which in turn relates to the multinational trend of economic activity.

Lipietz (1984) has sought to offset such criticisms of Aglietta's basic model by distinguishing (i) a period of erosion of 'Fordist' growth from 1967 to 1974; (ii) an ensuing period of 'Keynesian' management of economic crisis folllowing the initial OPEC price increases, from 1974 to 1980; and (iii) the period of 'monetarist shock' from 1980, whose effects have not as yet been countervailed.

Lipietz specifically addresses the issue of the slowing down of productivity in the 1970s and 1980s in terms of Kondratieff-type 'long wave innovations'. He also recognises the implications for the economics of global mass production of the location by multinational companies of investment in a handful of newly industrialised countries such as Mexico, Brazil, Korea, Taiwan, etc.

As Lipietz stresses, the reduction of labour costs implicit in such multinational location provided what amounted to a 'second-wind' for those companies which were encountering increasing wage demand in the developed countries in the 1960s and 1970s, with the result that the newly industrialised countries at the time were able to obtain rates of growth of up to 10 per cent per annum. However, the monetarist counter-revolution deprived multinational capital on a global scale of the opportunity to realise profits gained through exploitation of low-cost labour in the NICs in some developed market economies. At the same time, the process innovations open to indigenous producers (and in particular state-assisted producers) in the newly industrialised countries lowered the market-entry threshold to mass-production techniques of the kind already stressed by Dan Jones (1985). In other words, computerised technology has meant that instead of three, four or five production assembly lines for different models, a single production line at a third, a fourth, or a fifth of the investment cost of the US meant that a reverse challenge to Fordism from the United States was possible from newly industrialised countries as well as from Japan.

This is separate from the power of state intervention since Marx or Kondratieff to alleviate, offset or delay specific features of profits crisis resulting from under-consumption, rising organic composition of capital and disproportionality.

The degree to which this lesson has been learnt by the developing economies of South East Asia has been extensively illustrated by Gordon White, Robert Wade and others (1984). In effect, various combinations of Keynes' demand-management policies can offset under-consumption, or impose deflation in such a way as to cut back wages and demand. Rising organic composition of capital, and its profits problems, can be partly offset by the state underwriting profits and risk in the two extremes of the economy – the basic industries and the advanced-technology industries. To some extent, the state can also offset disproportion in the system by planned intervention.

Short and Long Term

It is clear that consistency in Marxist theories of compound crisis depends on a particular combination of short- *and* long-term factors. For instance, in a long secular boom, wages may rise relative to profits. In a short-term upswing of the economy within a secular trend, profits may rise relative to wages. The Marxist emphasis on the way in which short-term recessions destroy small-scale capital or wipe out firms in the microeconomic sector is an important element in understanding the way in which the longer-term trend shows a centralisation and concentration of capital of the kind which promotes the interests of multinational companies in the mesoeconomic sector.

It is over the long term that the Marxist stress on compound crisis through a combination of rising organic composition of capital (relative capital intensity), technological unemployment, under-consumption and dis-proportion becomes increasingly relevant to understanding the nature of the crisis in the global economy. As illustrated extensively in this text, with sustained expansion in the period since the Second World War, there has been a considerable increase in the intensity and technical composition of capital in the advanced capitalist economies. Thus Keynesian demand management can cope with the under-consumption problem in short-term recessions. But it is inadequate to cope with the increased concentration of capital in relatively advanced technology sectors producing goods which ordinary consumers do not or cannot buy because they are unemployed or under-employed, unpaid or under-paid. Put differently, productivity may be raised substantially by the computer, data-processing and other labour-saving innovations made possible through technical progress in electronics. But this displaces labour and reduces incomes and demand.

The Role of the State

Long-term government contracts in advanced-technology and capital-intensive industries such as defence can offset low profits and under-consumption. The state guarantees a mark-up of profit on the project and also ensures that highly skilled labour is employed. But there is a dis-proportion in the pattern of state intervention in industry, and an unequal mix in the public and private sectors of the economy. The state intervenes to assure long-term investment in the basic and advanced-technology sectors, but largely leaves the pace-setting intermediate sectors of manufacturing and services in private control. Overall, postwar state expenditure rose, partly in response to political pressure for social spending on housing, health and education. Such state expenditure directly sustained social consumption and investment in housing, health and education. But, lacking a coherent macro framework, sustained demand and an effective profits tax, such expenditure could not be maintained.

The Keynesian Case

In these respects, Marxist analysis of economic crisis complements the Keynesian analysis presented by economists such as King and Fullerton (1984) and Stephen Marris (1985). As shown in Figure 9.6(a), and confirming the analysis of the trend to fiscal crisis, the marginal rates of company taxation in leading economies have been reduced – in the case of the UK, dramatically – since the 1960s.

In turn, as illustrated in Figure 9.6(b), with a decline in growth, since key developed economies in the OECD reduced their public spending following the first OPEC price increases in the autumn of 1973, OECD private-sector savings have persistently exceeded private investment, while in turn the

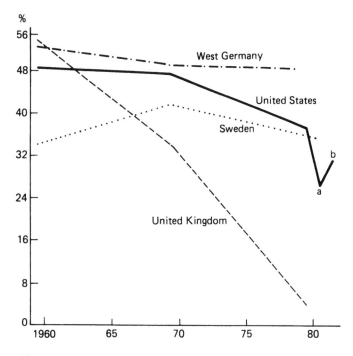

a. After the 1981 Economic Recovery Tax Act.
b. After the 1982 Tax Equity and Fiscal Responsibility Act.

FIG. 9.6(a)   Marginal rates of company taxation in four countries, 1960–82 (Source: King and Fullerton, 1984 and Marris, 1985)

surplus of private savings has been symmetrically offset by public dis-savings (reflecting in part the reduction of effective taxation as governments vainly sought to promote private-sector investment by tax cuts).

With crucial relevance to the role of the public sector in sustaining rather than draining private-sector expenditure (as outlined in particular in Chapters 3 and 7 of this volume), Figure 9.6(b) shows the degree to which the rising budget deficit of the OECD countries until the impact of the OPEC price increases in 1973 has thereafter been offset by a reduction of the deficit in all of the OECD countries other than the United States. In other words, while the United States since 1981 has pursued a policy of monetary restraint with fiscal deficit (in practice military Keynesianism or demand expansion promoted in large part through the defence programme), the rest of OECD (ROECD) has restrained its budget deficit and in 1975 achieved an overall budget surplus.

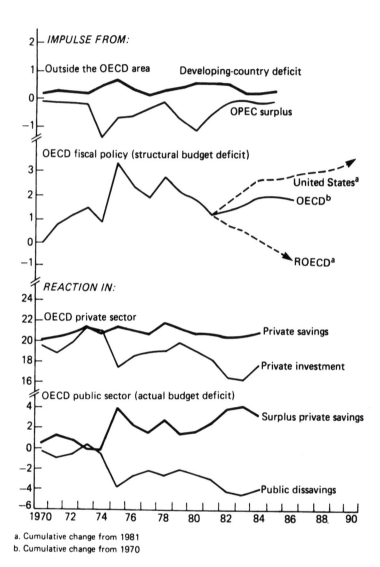

FIG. 9.6(b) Major shocks to world's investment-savings balance, 1970–90 (percentage of OECD GNP) (Source: Marris, 1985).

Fiscal Crisis and Social Spending

The result has been a restraint and relative decline of public and social spending in most OECD economies other than the United States (and Japan) which in turn has had profoundly deflationary effects on the global economy.

In terms of the Hicksian analysis as adapted in Chapter 3, the falling ROECD line in Figure 9.6(b) is equivalent to a reduction of the lower equilibrium line *LEL* in Hicks' basic model of the trade cycle. It will be recalled that, in Hicks' analysis, it was the rise of this long-term expenditure and lower equilibrium line which ensured that the economy did not 'hit the floor' in the manner which Harrod had anticipated in his model of instability with cumulative downswing effects (reinforced by negative multipliers). With cuts in public expenditure, introduced under the prevailing monetarist paradigm or prevailing ideology, there is little in the global economy to offset a cumulative 'vicious circle' of decline unless countervailing intervention is undertaken by the governments of the developed market economies.

Increasingly, governments have resorted to greater subsidy to the private sector via investment grants and allowances, tax concessions against amortisation, regional grants and subsidies, export rebates and so on. But these major incentives are based on a price-competitive model of liberal capitalism. They make no distinction between big and small, or national and multinational business. They also make little allowance for the fact that small-league firms in many cases lack the professional management resources necessary to make effective use of the available incentives.

Such a tax gap for government, or the fiscal crisis of the state, includes (i) the extent to which such tax concessions, grants, allowances and rebates have offset the 'tax take' of governments, as well as (ii) the tax avoidance by multinationals through extensive transfer pricing in the global economy on the lines already analysed in Chapter 6. O'Connor's (1973) analysis of an emerging fiscal crisis focuses especially on the United States and the crisis in funding of metropolitan areas by state governments such as those of New York. But this crisis is now not only local and national but multinational in its range and scale.

Moreover, fiscal incentives to enterprise may offset declining rates of profit during periods of falling demand or slowing rates of growth of output and profits. But they no more promote investment during such periods of slowing growth than do lower interest rates. This is the context in which the difference between Keynes' analysis of expectations and the 'Keynesians' sanitised version of *The General Theory* assumes a special importance. It was stressed in Chapter 3 that the difference stemmed in part from the elision of the different theories of Harrod and Domar into a stylised Harrod-Domar theory. In other words, Domar's capacity model not only focused attention on the importance both of higher savings and investment and lower capital-output ratios, but also implied equilibrium conditions for sustained economic growth. By contrast, Harrod's model included a behavioural theory of economic growth (his *Gw* or warranted growth) and analysed the way in which expectations would be depressed by falling rates of growth or output.

Thus many Western governments are trying to stimulate investment and jobs through subsidies and tax cuts, but their efforts are contradicted by the force of declining long-term profit expectations. Meanwhile, they thereby undermine their fiscal base through a failure to tax effectively. Nominal tax from industrial enterprise was offset by a range of subsidies which meant that in a country such as Britain, the industrial sector was by the mid 1970s, paying virtually no mainstream tax at all. Without effective taxation, governments cannot continue to finance public expenditure or welfare programmes.

State Intervention and Crisis

The result is that the current crisis in private investment accumulation has been paralleled by a crisis in state intervention itself. This reflects (i) a rising capital intensity and disproportion between overall supply and demand; and (ii) an imbalance between national public demand management and predominantly multinational private management of supply. The dictates of technology and the pressures to keep ahead in a capitalist world economy also mean continual pressures on the state to intervene in sectors which are of questionable use to society as a whole. Social expenditure itself becomes secondary to the primary imperative to invest on the frontiers of technology, without serious questioning of the sense of such investment. The private criteria of profit and exchange value (in Marxist terms) predominate over the public criteria of social need or use value.

In Marxist theory, this problem is expressed as a contradiction between an increasing socialisation of production and the failure of a system based on private profit to serve the needs of society. In simpler non-Marxist terms, it is expressed by Galbraith as the contradiction between private affluence and public squalor (Galbraith, 1957).

The rise of state intervention in capitalism on a scale unprecedented in Marx's time, and not anticipated by him, renders it possible in principle to offset some of the cyclical impact of short-term crises on (i) the *structure* of output and production, and (ii) private investment and *social* consumption, and (iii) *spatial* distribution between regions and countries. But these problems are posed in more acute form the greater the expansion of a capitalist system. In other words, structural, social and spatial inequality are heightened the greater the development and dominance of private modes of capital accumulation, profit and expansion. The system works through inequality and causes further inequality.

State Capitalism

In this sense, state intervention to overcome crisis in the system is itself often disproportioned, unequal and imbalanced.

It is also strikingly disproportionate in other ways. Nuclear defence spending has a questionable exchange or use value. In other words, its exchange value (both commercially and militarily) assumes a deterrent capacity which is either questionable in theory (after mega-kill delivery reaches a certain state) or negative in practice if actually used (when everyone is annihilated).

Cataclysm apart, defence spending means the allocation of massive resources into sectors of industry which bring no direct return or use to those not employed in the firms and industries concerned. Defence spending does little or nothing to offset the major disproportions in capitalism between social expenditure and private expenditure. It can also aggravate the imbalance between declining and advanced-technology industries. With some exceptions, state money to sustain new armaments tends to mean less state aid for the modernisation and diversification of declining sectors of industry in problem regions and areas. But there are other general ways in which disproportion in the allocation of capital and employment of labour can imbalance a capitalist system, and result in a declining rate of profit for enterprise in both industry and services.

In the 1960s it was a common thesis, put forward in particular by Nicholas Kaldor, that the British economy suffered from an excessive expansion of employment in services relative to manufacturing industry (Kaldor, 1966). Basically, the argument was that too much capital and labour had drifted into the expansion of services, and too little had been invested and employed in productive activity. In other words, the profit perspective of the individual firms and investors who had diversified or expanded into services has been short-sighted. It has meant the under-development of the manufacturing industry on which high profits and productivity in services ultimately depend.

According to this theory, the expansion of profits and jobs in services was more than Britain as a trading nation, highly dependent on manufacturing exports, could afford. And what is true of services in general has also recently been true on a large scale for property development and speculation. The City of London has been more concerned to invest in office blocks than in manufacturing companies. For the big firms in the mesoeconomic sector, this is no particular handicap, since little or next to nothing of their finance for investment now comes from the City. But for the small firms in the microeconomic sector, such disproportionate investment outside manu-facturing means the difference between expansion and relative or absolute decline. Without new investment financed from outside the company, their profits will collapse.

Questions on Late Capitalism

From a Marxist viewpoint, Ernest Mandel (1975) has underlined the importance from the late 1960s and early 1970s both of inflation and the debt crisis. Stressing that credit expansion had always facilitated an upswing in long cycles, Mandel with reason drew attention to the expansion of Eurodollar and Eurobond borrowing in the later stages of the upswing of the fourth Kondratieff cycle in the 1960s and 1970s. Arguing that such borrowing would not be compensated or covered by sustaining profits, Mandel confidently predicted a further phase of depression and crisis in global capitalism.

However, in a volume which in its English translation amounts to nearly 600 pages, Mandel devotes only three pages to the analysis of actual public spending, drawing his evidence exclusively from the German and American economies. In this he describes the rise of federal spending alone, which thereby understates the real rise of public spending in the postwar market economies. In reality, expenditure in the European economies was transformed after the Second World War, with public spending increasing its share from an earlier level of between a fifth and a third to a later level, by the mid-1970s, of up to half or more of total spending.

While cause and effect in such factors is difficult to isolate with precision, it is clear that the rise in public spending played a crucial role in what can be described as the fourth Kondratieff cycle. No analysis of the factors associated with the 'long boom' from the mid-1930s to the mid-1970s merits scientific pretension which focuses only on Schumpeterian innovations or market forces without regard to public sponsorship and the role of public spending (especially when, in Mensch's analysis, these especially concern state-promoted sectors of activity such as aircraft, aerospace, electronics and, with them, armaments).

This is not to say that public spending programmes alone can avoid the downturn of economic activity predicted for a fifth Kondratieff cycle. Certainly, with prevailing levels of income distribution both between social groups and classes and different regions and countries of the world economy, it is not clear that the consumer spending in the civil economy which, for example, has sustained the postwar expansion of the automobile and electronics industries, can be sustained indefinitely when demand saturation has already been achieved for those who can afford to purchase their second car, second or third television, deep-freeze or digital quadrophonic hifi.

Social Distribution

But social distribution is not irrelevant either to earlier phases of the so-called

Kondratieff cycle or to the issue whether a long term downturn in the 'fifth' Kondratieff cycle is inevitable. In the upswing of activity from the 1930s through to the 1970s, major waves of innovation such as in automobiles and consumer durable goods only in part created 'their own markets'. Automobiles and electrical consumer durables had been pioneered and innovated before the First World War. But it was their wider social distribution from upper to middle and then skilled working classes within society which provided the sustained effective demand necessary for their large-scale mass production in the manner associated with the boom upswing of the 1950s and 1960s. In such a context neither public spending nor social distribution are irrelevant to recent long-term cycles in economic activity. If in the short term a monetarist counter-revolution to Keynesian orthodoxies has resulted in retrenchment through cuts in public expenditure, consequent rise in unemployment, and resultant weakening of trade-union bargaining power, this does not mean that strict periodicity or inevitability should be assumed in the case of a 'fifth' Kondratieff cycle, any more than it should be assumed in Marx's earlier analysis of longer-term accumulative crisis in the capitalist system.

This is especially relevant in view of the extent to which many of the innovations occurring at the current phase of the 'fifth' Kondratieff cycle tend to be in process rather than product innovation. In other words, the electronic and robotic revolutions accompanying the peak of the long-term cycle in the 1970s and 1980s have resulted in precisely that displacement of labour by a rising organic and technical composition of capital which Marx himself had analysed in mid-nineteenth-century Britain. With it, the series of compound crisis effects analysed earlier in this chapter tend to come into play. With the compound effects of both cuts in public expenditure and under-consumption through displacement of labour, both the first and second lines of defence of a downswing in activity, as analysed in Chapter 3, are broken within the public and the private sectors of the economy. As argued in detail in *The Political Economy* (Holland, forthcoming), rather than questioning the viability of public spending and social redistribution, the current economic crisis of the 1980s may instead suggest a wider socialisation as a precondition of further long-term development of the global economy.

9.4 Global Crisis

Not so long ago the monetarists offered simple prescriptions for economic crisis: float exchange rates, liberalise international trade, stabilise money supply and privatise the public sector. More than a decade later, the global economy is deep into slump, with no light at the end of the tunnel, no sustained upturn in sight, and a financial crisis without precedent for fifty years. In reality, such prescriptions were simplist rather than simple. Monetarism – with much of mainstream Keynesian economics – has neglected the power of Keynes' own insights into the workings of a mixed economy, while ignoring the dominance of global trade, payments and banking by a handful of multinational companies.

Further, the very success of the postwar boom in part entailed its own later failure. Competition in expanding markets rewarded the strong rather than the weak, the big rather than the small, and multinational rather than national enterprise. Innovation and the extension of interwar élite products to mass-consumption markets promoted first boom, then recession as markets became saturated. Technical progress first raised productivity, then technological unemployment. Trying to step back from Keynes' economics and the mixed economy through cuts in public spending only restrained growth or deepened slump. Monetarist myths could not restore Friedman's alleged 'golden age' of market forces from Waterloo to the First World War in part because the monetarists failed to analyse twentieth-century realities, and in part because their interpretation of the nineteenth century was itself a fantasy (Holland, 1987, chapter 2).

Past, Present and Future

Such a romanticised model of the past has no future other than sweat, toil, tears and slump. Osvaldo Sunkel (1984) has stressed this futility of going back to an unreal past by identifying key features of the liberalisation of the world economy which in turn have helped promote the crisis today.

First, Sunkel identifies the role of privatised financial markets. He stresses that during the Bretton Woods period and for much of the postwar boom, international financial markets were predominantly public rather than private. This was not simply a matter of governments seeking to maintain relatively fixed exchange rates. For instance, in the early 1960s nearly two-thirds of the resource inflow to Latin America was public or governmental in origin. By the late 1970s this had shrunk to less than 7 per cent. The banking sector dominated this new market. In the early 1960s only 2 per cent of foreign private capital inflows into Latin America were through banks. By the late 1970s, private bank finance was approaching 60 per cent of such inflows. Such private bank finance was highly oligopolistic, organised by some thirty big multinational banks (Sunkel, ibid.).

The result by the 1980s was plain to see. Repayment of private-sector debt by Latin America had assumed horrendous proportions. While Latin America included most of the big debtors (notably Mexico, Brazil and

Argentina), a similar problem confronted the South of the global economy as a whole. For the first time since the war, the less developed countries became net creditors of the more developed, and especially the most advanced country in the world – the United States. Development sustained through the 1970s through the recycling of petrodollars has now been blocked for most countries by a combination of global deflation and crippling debt. The drain of resources from the South has been compounded by adverse terms of trade (or declining prices for their key commodity exports), only offset in part by the decline of OPEC oil prices in the early 1980s. Now, perversely, dollar devaluation further aggravates the crisis for commodity exports from developing countries by increasing their import price to the United States. Of at least equal importance, a major reduction of the US budget deficit reducing US imports to their 1980/81 level could take as much as $100 billion out of world demand. Such deflation would be a formula for global slump.

The Debt Crisis

If deflation of global spending and trade (other than in the US and Japan) is one of the fundamental causes of the current global crisis, debt is its outstanding and dramatic symptom. As illustrated in Figure 9.7, global debt by the end of 1985 amounted to some $3 trillion ($3,000 billion), of which four-fifths was in the form of so-called Eurocurrency loans.

The debt of the developing countries was some $1 trillion, or a third of total global debt. This was concentrated in Latin America but there was also significant indebtedness by South Korea, the Philippines, Indonesia, Nigeria and Yugoslavia.

But it is not the scale of debt alone which counts. The key problems derive from the increased share of export earnings from less developed countries absorbed annually by interest payments. According to the World Bank (1985), debt service payments in the early and mid 1980s accounted for between a quarter and third of the export earnings of many developing countries. For Latin America the debt crisis is particularly severe. As the ministers of the countries of the Cartagena Group said, referring to the 1976–84 period: 'The total value of Latin America's external debt is more than half its GNP and three times the value of its annual exports. Debt payments have risen to almost double the value of exports'.

The 'Eurocurrency' Markets

As already indicated in Figure 9.7, some four-fifths of total global debt has been funded by the so-called Eurocurrency markets. In essence these are multinational money markets in which commercial banks accept interest-bearing deposits denominated in currencies other than the currency of the country in which they operate, which then in turn are re-lent elsewhere in the global economy. Because of the dominant position of the US dollar in international finance since the Second World War, and despite dollar devaluation in 1971, these multinational money markets have been dominated by the Eurodollar or Eurobond finance, although the so-called Eurocurrencies include not only sterling and the deutschmark but also the yen.

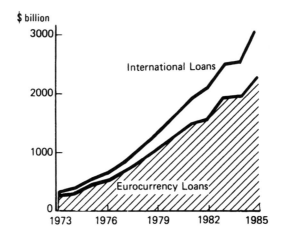

FIG. 9.7   Global debt (Source: BIS and Bank of England)

These postwar multinational money markets started on a small scale in the mid 1950s when European banks, with UK 'merchant' banks playing a leading role, began the practice of accepting US dollar deposits and relending them to other European banks or their own customers to finance either foreign trade or domestic economic activity, rather than returning the funds to the US money market. The initial growth of the market reflected the controls imposed in the US by the federal reserve system under Regulation Q, which prohibited American banks from paying interest on demand deposits. A further impetus was given by the liberalisation of exchange markets and a return to external convertibility in the Western European currencies from 1958.

However, it was two further factors which really gave the boost to Eurocurrency lending on a global scale. The first was the major dollar deficit on global markets or the fact that – especially in the 1960s – the US was buying more abroad than other countries were buying from the United States. The second major boost to the Eurocurrency markets was the OPEC price increases from September 1973 and the resulting major 'petrodollar' surplus in the early to mid 1970s.

Lenders and Borrowers

Figure 9.8 illustrates in simple form the overall lending and borrowing pattern in the global money market dominated by Eurodollar and other Eurocurrency issues. It indicates that the lenders are also borrowers, with the difference that lending has been concentrated among the oil-exporting countries during their periods of surplus, while the borrowers have been mainly the 'big debtor' developing countries, especially Latin America. The main institutions which act as suppliers of Eurodollar deposits include (i) official institutions such as governments and their central banks, and international organisations; (ii) commercial banks, including increasingly the 'offshore' banks already analysed in Chapter 6; and (iii) business corporations, especially major multinational companies.

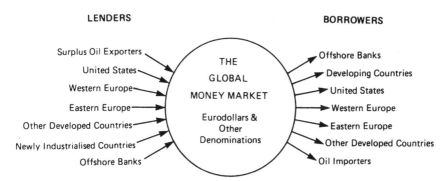

FIG. 9.8   Circular global lending and borrowing: the 'Eurocurrency' market

A range of factors affect the demand for Eurodollars. These include: (i) the availability of national versus multinational credit; (ii) the differential between Eurocurrency loans and those of domestic bank loans; (iii) the expectations concerning exchange-rate movements and especially the difference between the current 'spot' rate and the forward rates at which international currencies can be bought and exchanged against anticipated further use; (iv) the demand for funds in countries whose rates of economic growth exceed internally generated savings.

National and Multinational Interest Rates

In a significant study which predated the major growth of the Eurocurrency markets, Clendenning (1970) analysed the rise of the Eurocurrency markets in relation to four of the main factors claimed to determine interest rates (as already analysed in chapter 7), i.e. the investment demand for money, the availability of savings or the savings function, liquidity preference, and the quantity of money.

In the Eurocurrency market the structure of interest rates should in principle be determined by the same basic factors as in the national interest-rate structure. However, as Clendenning (1970, p. 80) stresses, because of the international nature of the Eurocurrency market, 'the investment-demand, savings and liquidity preference functions must be defined in an international sense and not in terms of the national functions of any particular country. In addition there is no central monetary authority in the market which can control the quantity of Eurodollars and, hence, the overall level of liquidity.'

Speculation versus Precaution

It is certainly clear that the new Eurocurrency markets fulfil the three main elements of Keynes' concept of 'liquidity preference'. In other words, (i) access to multinational money fulfils the *transactions* motive, or the need for cash to transact business on a global scale. Such markets also fulfil (ii) the *precautionary* motive, or the desire for security as to the future cash equivalent of current money. Yet it is (iii) the *speculative* motive, or the aim of gaining profit from hoping to know better than the market what the future will bring forth, which (with the notable failure to translate borrowed savings or debt into actual investment) has been the most destabilising feature of the new multinational money markets on a global scale in the 1970s and 1980s.

Keynes' precautionary motive for liquidity is met in part through the technique of 'arbitrage' and 'hedging'. In multinational money markets, both depend on the short-term interest rates in different countries and the spot and forward exchange rates. The essence of both techniques is similar. Covered arbitrage includes 'an international transfer of spot funds for short-term investment purposes covered by a simultaneous forward transaction of the same amount in the opposite direction'. Hedging can be defined as 'a sale or purchase of foreign exchange calculated to reduce the pre-existing exchange risk of the operator – i.e. it covers or reduces [the] original open position' (Tsiang, 1959).

Despite the arcane nature of the definitions, it should immediately be apparent that such precautionary moves to cover in advance against potential loss amount in practice to speculation on the future level of interest rates and exchange rates prevailing between different countries. Thus the boundary between arbitrage, hedging and speculation is relative.

The rise of the Eurocurrency markets has increased the supply and mobility of arbitrage funds for the kinds of reasons already analysed in some detail in Chapter 6. Multinational companies (or banks) can exploit interest-rate differentials in different national capital markets over a period of a few days, or even a few hours within a given day, and thereby make substantial gains on minor interest-rate changes for substantial volumes of funds traded in the global money market. Similarly, hedgers and speculators can use the Eurocurrency markets as an alternative to forward exchange markets. In other words, they can finance their activities either in the currencies of individual countries, or in the Eurocurrency markets themselves.

With the floating of national currencies following dollar devaluation, foreign exchange or FOREX dealers have come to the fore in international currency transactions. The Keynesian precautionary motive of avoiding loss through hedging has given way to speculation on a full-time basis. Serviced by satellite telex services, the local speculation which Keynes derided on the London stock market has become a global casino, in which money is made from speculation on short-term changes in the value of currencies rather than any long-term relation between savings and investment.

Expectations and Instability

Under fixed or managed exchange rates, such as obtained in the 'Keynesian era' before the devaluation of the dollar, the scope for arbitrage, hedging and pure speculation was relatively limited. Some 85 per cent of the foreign-exchange transactions in world markets were concerned with the more serious business of obtaining finance to cover actual trade, or savings to finance actual investment. Since the floating exchange rates from the early 1970s, some 85 per cent of such foreign-exchange transactions in the mid 1980s are now the result of purely speculative anticipation of exchange-rate changes in global markets. One result has been a dramatic increase in the instability of international exchange rates, since exchange rates themselves tend to be determined by the expectations of short-term changes as anticipated by speculators. This does not mean to say that speculation is rational or accurate. Figure 9.9 illustrates the evidence of adaptive (and wrong) expectations in exchange markets for the Deutschmark and the dollar as forecast by 13 international banks in the early 1980s (Marris, 1985, p. 121). As Marris comments: 'the majority of operators in exchange markets are concentrating on what is likely to happen in the next few hours or days rather than over the next months or years'. Or as Harold Lever has put it: 'nobody will sell the dollar on Monday in the opinion that it will be lower next year if he thinks he can sell at a higher price in the next hour, next day, next week or next month. Any experienced currency trader will tell you that speculators who take a long term view usually end up in bankruptcy well before their "long term view" has been proved true or false' (Lever, 1985).

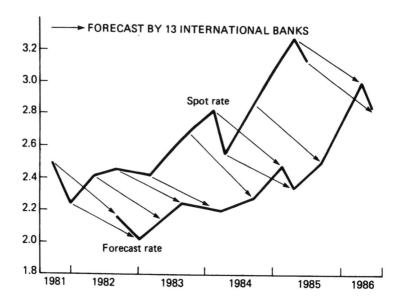

FIG. 9.9   False expectations in exchange markets 1981–86 (DM per dollar) (Source: Marris, 1985)

The result tends to be an increasing divorce between expectations of real rates of return on actual investment (at whatever exchange rate) and expectations of what exchange rates themselves may in the short term prove to be. Such instability was anticipated by Keynes when he wrote that: 'even apart from the instability due to speculation, there is the instability due to the characteristic of human nature that a large proportion of our positive activities depend on spontaneous optimism [and] can only be taken as a result of animal spirits – of a spontaneous urge to action rather than inaction, and not as the outcome of a weighted average of quantitative benefits multiplied by quantitative probabilities'. It was in reaction to such speculative transactions that Keynes proposed a substantial government tax on all such transfers, and was moved to argue that 'to make the purchase of an investment permanent and dissoluble, like marriage, except by reason of death or other grave cause, might be a useful remedy for our contemporary evils' (Keynes, 1936, pp. 160–1).

Real and Pretend

Such arguments are not facile. As already illustrated in Figure 9.6(b), and confirming the trend to excess savings in chapter 2, savings in the OECD private sector since the OPEC price increases in 1973 have persistently exceeded private investment. Inversely, as illustrated in Figure 9.6(b), the developing countries have registered an overall budget deficit reflecting the fact that both investment and consumption has tended to exceed domestic savings and income. Thus 'real' private investment is not matching private savings in the developed economies, while such investment has exceeded private savings in the developing countries. The result of the difference constitutes a major component of the global debt crisis.

Meanwhile, as foreign-exchange dealers shuffle their packs and deal swops, making nominal interest-rate gains within hours or minutes on global money markets, bankers and the advocates of 'sound money' in the developed countries still publicly maintain that the global debt problem is 'manageable'. This is despite the fact that at least the top ten banks in the United States and two of the big four banks in the United Kingdom are owed more by Latin America alone than their total reserve-asset ratios.

This situation has been graphically described in the *Global Challenge* report from the Socialist International committee on economic policy (Brandt and Manley, 1985, pp. 100–1):

> The result is a global game of 'pretend', not dissimilar to that which children play with less resources. Mexico illustrates the new rule. It has indicated that it will pay interest for 14 years but no principal. Like children playing 'pretend', international bankers 'pretend' that these debts are 'performing assets' versus the 'non-performing assets' which under normal conditions would be called in or written off. . . . The problem will not go away through wishful thinking. . . . The present optimism of leading governments and international institutions is not justified. [They] cannot afford a 'wait and see' solution, in the hope that if they do little or nothing, the global debt crisis will simply go away.

Beggar-my-Neighbour

In the real economy of actual savings and investment, income and trade, this global pretence on the debt crisis and their rationality of money markets is compounded by 'beggar-my-neighbour' policies sanctioned by leading world governments and implemented by the International Monetary Fund. Such a 'beggar-my-neighbour' response to the global economic crisis has been embodied in the IMF's conditions for lending to deficit and debtor countries. In simple terms this amounts to the three-point package of (i) devalue the currency, (ii) deflate public spending to release resources for export, and (iii) deny public spending on housing, health education and social services as the precondition for monetary restraint.

The limits of the IMF 'conditionality' package have been itemised in the *Global Challenge* report (Brandt and Manley, 1985). These limits include the fact that (i) the package imposes an asymmetric adjustment process on less developed countries, while imposing no such conditions on the world's major debtor, the United States; (ii) the period of adjustment allowed in IMF stabilisation is usually one to three years, which is far too short to make the structural adjustment needed to correct the original deficits; (iii) the package treats symptoms rather than causes, focusing on internal monetary and managerial problems, but failing to allow that deflation and disinflation may bankrupt the enterprises necessary for any recovery of global competitiveness; (iv) the package relies to much on currency devaluation, and the assumption that this will result in lower foreign prices and increased receipts, ignoring the extent to which multinational companies fail to follow through lower potential export prices due to the extent to which this would mean 'competition against themselves' in foreign markets.

Not least, the deflation/devaluation package pursued by the IMF is contradictory for the global economy as a whole. The point can be simply made by comparing the conventional consensus that beggar-my-neighbour protection is damaging for international trade with the assumption that deflation pursued in a range of economies has no significant effects on macroeconomic demand in the global economy as a whole. Figure 9.10(a) illustrates the standard assumptions of the negative effects on global trade and payments of protection. In other words, an increase from x to y in the tariff of country A reduces import demand on the lines ab, which in turn reduces export demand in other countries on the lines cd. By the same token, illustrated in Figure 9.10(b), deflation of domestic demand on the lines xy in country A reduces import demand on the lines ab, which in turn reduces export demand in other countries on the lines cd. Thus the IMF, following the conventional (and misguided) reasoning of the developed countries which dominate its board of governors and its policies, has now imposed beggar-my-neighbour deflation on so many of the world economies that it has substantially contributed to global slump.

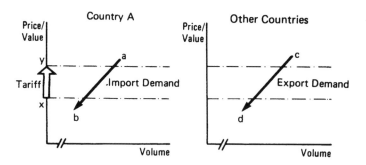

FIG. 9.10(a) Beggar-my-neighbour protection

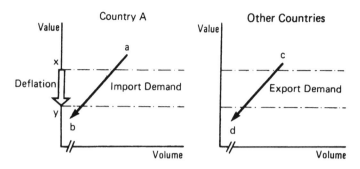

FIG. 9.10(b) Beggar-my-neighbour deflation

Beggar-my-neighbour deflation therefore deepens and intensifies the vicious circle of global contraction of trade and payments with cumulative effects.

– Several countries reduce domestic demand to restrain imports and achieve a positive balance in their payments. Reducing demand reduces the rate of growth of exports between the countries concerned.

– Failure to remedy the initial payments problem, through reducing demand, results in pressure on the currency, a loss of reserves and a loss of 'confidence'.

– Governments take measures to reduce demand directly, through cuts in public spending, rather than relying on indirect measures of demand restraint.

– The crisis deepens as reduced demand affects domestic sales and production and raises unemployment.

– Interest rates are raised to strengthen the currency, but thereby raise the cost of borrowing for firms, act as a disincentive to investment modernisation and promote bankruptcies.

– Devaluation, designed to increase export competitiveness, is undermined by the fall in global trade (as well as offset by multinational companies), increasing import prices and further inflationary pressures.

– Tax revenue falls as unemployment increases, raising government borrowing and debt servicing, and reinforcing a fiscal crisis of the state.

Better-my-Neighbour

By contrast, better-my-neighbour recovery implies that:

– Several countries simultaneously increase domestic demand, thereby increasing imports from other countries. This increases other countries' exports and results in mutual increase in trade.

- Mutual trade expansion registers positive effects by providing inputs for export trade as well as the spread of earnings in the exporting country through 'export multiplier' effects.
- Mutual trade also increases exports in other sectors in other countries in the world economy, not least commodity exports from Third World countries.
- The growth of trade stimulates flows of foreign direct investment which can gain real rather than nominal rates of return through the expansion of the domestic economies concerned.
- International crisis is offset as the demand-pull effect from the expansion of mutual trade reduces foreign-exchange constraints. This not only concerns those countries able to increase their exports and raise living standards and those countries increasing their imports, but registers beneficial effects in those countries both exporting and importing more goods overall.
- Increased use of productive capacity can reduce the 'unit costs' of enterprises or the cost per unit of output, thereby decreasing inflationary pressure on the lines analysed in Chapter 8, provided either the market mechanism or public policy ensures that such lower costs are reflected in lower prices.
- Restructuring becomes more feasible as unit costs are lowered through a fuller utilisation of productive capacity, and a higher rate of return on investment.
- Tax revenue increases and unemployment (with social security payments in the developed countries) falls, reducing government borrowing and offsetting fiscal crisis in those countries benefiting from recovery.

Global Challenge

Such an analytic argument does not underestimate the practical constraints on recovery in either the developing or developed economies imposed by current financial orthodoxies and speculative movements of capital against the currencies of those countries sustaining significant deficits. Certainly, recovery alone will not be adequate to offset pressure on individual currencies through speculation, or loss of reserves as they seek to sustain expansion. But a key question in recovery is where it starts and where it will spread. If recovery is sporadic and attempted in only some countries rather than in a group of major economies, it will have little chance of affecting the global distribution of trade, payments, employment and income. This is one of the reasons why both the *Out of Crisis* (Holland, 1983) report and the *Global Challenge* (Brandt and Manley, 1985) report stressed that there was little prospect of the less developed countries contributing to global recovery and development unless the developed countries themselves began the process of resolving their own economic crisis.

Further, both the *Out of Crisis* and *Global Challenge* reports stressed the importance of matching (i) a *recovery* of global spending and trade with (ii) a *restructuring* of both production and power relations and (iii) a *redistribution* of resources designed to offset global underconsumption and restore a 'virtuous circle' of effective demand. Such reasoning is Keynesian both in the sense that it stresses the importance of restoring effective demand in the global economy, and also in the sense that it recommends international agencies to counter global crisis on the lines which Keynes himself argued at Bretton Woods in 1944. However, it is 'Keynes plus' in the sense of arguing that a restructuring of production and trade should achieve new forms of accounting and accountability over the mesoeconomic and multinational structures of production, distribution and exchange which now dominate the global economy as a whole. It also goes beyond Keynes in its focus on the redistribution of world demand as a means of restoring 'better-my-neighbour' mutual demand, trade and payments between the developed and less developed countries.

At one level, such a contrast between 'better-my-neighbour' reflation and 'beggar-my-neighbour' deflation is simple and easy to grasp. At another, it challenges prevailing orthodoxies of monetarism and market forces. Not least, redistribution as a means of recovery may well mean long-term 'development deficits' registered by what should be developing countries in their trade with so-called developed countries. And in turn, within individual economies, such redistribution may imply a shift of resources from big to small business, from industry to services, and from the private to the public sector, as well as redistribution between different social groups and classes, and different regions and areas of the national or international economy.

Such a global challenge thereby implies not only a change in the balance of power between public and private institutions, but also a fundamental shift in both resources and decision-making towards the less developed and least strong social groups and classes within global society. It not only means denying Friedman and advancing on Keynes, but also challenging and transforming the fatalism implicit in Kondratieff's theory of long cycles. The arguments supporting such a case for recovery, restructuring and redistribution of power and resources are developed in the third volume of this trilogy, *The Political Economy* (Holland, forthcoming).

9.5 Summary

(1) Crisis in the modern market economy represents a combination of several factors, including (i) over-consumption or under-consumption, (ii) over-production or under-production, (iii) a disproportion between investment supply and consumption demand, compounded by (iv) fiscal crisis as governments vainly try to subsidise multinational capital to invest and produce in individual markets, and (v) a trade and payments crisis aggravated by falling international demand and the weak assumption that devaluation will result in export-led growth.

(2) Over-production is not simply the inverse of under-consumption. The rising scale of investment fully embodying modern technology (in Marx's terms the rise of the organic and technical composition of capital) may mean spare capacity and over-supply even with a constant rate of growth of consumption demand.

(3) Technical progress and innovation is not simply a residual or minor factor in the model assumed by Keynesian models of economic growth (including the Harrod-Domar model) but a primary factor (as stressed by Schumpeter) in the long-term upswing and downswing of the market economy. Such 'bunching' of innovation needs to be taken into account in understanding long-term cycles in economic activity.

(4) The Kondratieff model of long waves in the capitalist economies neglects the extent to which the rise of the mixed economy and public spending sustained economic growth in the period since the Second World War. Nonetheless, although overstated by some of its advocates, the stress on long-term cycles in Kondratieff's theory significantly qualifies both Keynesian and monetarist assumptions that markets will clear and balance at relatively full employment in the short to medium term provided that governments either (i) (in a Keynesian sense) intervene effectively in the level of demand or (ii) (on monetarist lines) ensure a relatively constant rate of increase in the money supply.

(5) If electorates and governments are not simply to be victims of compound crisis in the market economy, they need to respond to it by new forms of public intervention. Social expenditure and the redistribution of income can play a crucial role in offsetting crisis and sustaining longer-term demand. Neither the Keynesian nor the monetarist paradigms provide a framework for admitting such redistribution of social income and expenditure as a primary means of achieving recovery and development in the mixed economy.

(6) With the liberalisation of capital markets since the late 1950s, the rise of Eurocurrency lending and short-term currency speculation has imposed

profound instability on the global economy. In terms of currency speculation, liberalisation has transformed Keynes' 'casino' economy from individual stock markets to global financial markets as a whole.

(7) Accentuated by IMF market and monetarist policies, payments deficits and debt are now imposing 'beggar-my-neighbour' policies on the global economy as a whole. The IMF formula of deflate, devalue and deregulate the domestic economy lessens global demand as countries mutually reduce their imports. Devaluation increases domestic price inflation without ensuring export-led growth. Deregulation mainly opens individual countries' markets to multinational capital worldwide.

(8) Policies for 'better-my-neighbour' reflation could increase global trade and payments as countries increase mutual exports by expanding mutual import trade. But such a recovery of global spending and trade needs to be accompanied by a restructuring of financial institutions and the public and private sectors, as well as a redistribution of effective demand between different social groups and classes, and different regions and areas of the global economy.

(9) A genuinely new international economic order must be based not only on (i) the principles of recovery, restructuring and redistribution of spending and resources, but also on a new economic paradigm which admits (ii) the crucial role of the mesoeconomy in relation to microeconomic firms and macroeconomic performance and (iii) the interdependence of structural change on the social and spatial redistribution of resources in the national and international economy.

Bibliography

ACKLEY, G. (1961) *Macroeconomic Theory*, Macmillan, New York.

ADAMS, S. (1984) *Roche versus Adams*, Jonathan Cape, London.

AGLIETTA, M. (1976) *Régulation et Crises*, Calman-Levy, Brussels.

ARMSTRONG, P., with GLYN, A. and HARRISON, J. (1984) *Capitalism Since World War II*, Fontana, London.

ARTUS, J. (1974) 'The Behaviour of Export Prices for Manufactures', *IMF Staff Papers*, November.

—— (1975) 'The 1967 Devaluation of the Pound Sterling', *IMF Staff Papers*, November.

ASHWORTH, M. H., KAY, J. A. and SHARPE, T. A. E. (1982) *Differentials Between Car Prices in the United Kingdom and Belgium*, Institute for Fiscal Studies, London.

ASIMAKOPOULOS, A. (1977) 'Profits and Investment: A Kaleckian Approach', in G. C. Harcourt (ed.), *The Microeconomic Foundation of Macroeconomics*, International Economic Association, Macmillan, London.

ATTALI, J. (1978) 'Towards Socialist Planning', in S. Holland (ed.), *Beyond Capitalist Planning*, Basil Blackwell, Oxford.

AVERRIT, R. (1968) *The Dual Economy*, Norton, New York.

BAIN, J. S. (1956) *Barriers to New Competition*, Harvard University Press, Cambridge, Mass.

BAIROCH, P. (1975) *The Economic Development of the Third World Since 1900*, Methuen, London.

BARKER, B. L. (1986) 'US Merchandise Trade Associated with US Multinational Companies', *US Survey of Current Business*, May.

BARRATT BROWN, M. (1970) *What Economics is About*, Weidenfeld and Nicolson, London.

BARRO, R. J. (1977) 'Unanticipated Money Growth and Unemployment in the United States', *American Economic Review*, March.

BARTLETT, S. (1981) 'Transnational Banking: A Case of Transfer Parking With Money', in R. Murray (ed.), *Multinationals Beyond the Market*, Harvester Press, Brighton.

BECKMAN, R. (1983) *The Downwave: Surviving the Second Great Depression*, Milestone Publications and Pan Books, London.

BEGG, D., FISCHER, S. and DORNBUSCH, R. (1984) *Economics*, McGraw-Hill (UK), London.

BERLE, A. and MEANS, G. (1932) *The Modern Corporation and Private Property*, Macmillan, London.

BERNSTEIN, E. (1906) *Die Heutige Sozialdemokratie in Theorie und Praxis*, Birk, Munich.

BETRO TRUST COMMITTEE and ROYAL SOCIETY OF ARTS (1975) *Concentration on Key Markets*, London.

BRANDT, W. and MANLEY, M. (1985) *Global Challenge: From Crisis to Cooperation*, Pan, London-Sydney.

BRANSON, W. (1980) 'Trends in United States International Trade and Payments Since World War II', in M. Feldstein (ed.), *The American Economy in Transition*, University of Chicago Press.

BRETT, E. A. (1985) *The World Economy Since the War*, Macmillan, London.

BROOKE, M. Z. and REMMERS, H. L. (1970) *The Strategy of the Multinational Enterprise*, Longmans, London.

BRUMBERG, R. and MODIGLIANI, F. (1954) 'Utility Analysis and the Consumption Function', in K. Kurihara (ed.), *Post-Keynesian Economics*, Rutgers University Press.

CHAMBERLIN, E. (1933) *The Theory of Monopolistic Competition*, Harvard University Press, Cambridge, Mass.

CHANNON, D. (1973) *The Strategy and Structure of British Enterprise*, Macmillan, London.

CHENERY, H. (1952) 'Overcapacity and the Acceleration Principle', *Econometrica*, February.

CLAIRMONTE, Frederick F. and CAVANAGH, John E. (1984) 'Transnational Corporations and Services: the Final Frontier', UNCTAD, *Trade and Development*, no. 5, Geneva.

CLARK, J. B. (1917) 'Business Acceleration and the Law of Demand', *Journal of Political Economy*, March.

CLARK, J. M. (1961) *Competition as a Dynamic Process*, Brookings Institution, Washington DC.

CLENDENNING, E. W. (1970) *The Eurodollar Market*, Oxford University Press.

COOPER, C. (1971) 'The Channels and Mechanisms for the Transfer of Technology from Developed to Developing Countries, UNCTAD, Geneva.

COWLING, K. and SUGDEN, R. (1984) 'Exchange Rate Adjustment and Oligopoly Pricing Behaviour', OECD, Paris, September.

CROSLAND, C. A. R. (1956) *The Future of Socialism*, Jonathan Cape, London.

DAVIS, M. (1978) 'Fordism in Crisis', *New Left Review*, London.

DELORS, J. (1978) 'The Decline of French Planning', in S. Holland (ed.), *Beyond Capitalist Planning*, Basil Blackwell, Oxford.

DENISON, E. F. (1967) *Why Growth Rates Differ*, Brookings Institution, Washington DC.

DESAI, M. (1981) *Testing Monetarism*, Frances Pinter, London.

DEVLIN, R. (1981) 'Transnational Banks External Debt and Peru', United Nations Economic Commission for Latin America and the Caribbean, *CEPAL Review*, no. 14, August.

DOMAR, E. (1946) 'Capital Expansion, Rate of Growth and Employment', *Econometrica*, April.

DORNBUSCH, R. (1976) 'Expectations and Exchange Rate Dynamics', *Journal of Political Economy*, December.

DORNBUSCH, R. and FISCHER, S. (1981) *Macroeconomics*, McGraw-Hill, Kogashuka.

DUESENBERRY, J. (1949) *Income, Saving and the Theory of Consumer Spending*, Harvard University Press, Cambridge, Mass.

DUNNING, J. H. (ed.) (1971) *The Multinational Enterprise*, Allen & Unwin, London.

—— (1985) 'Multinational Enterprises and Industrial Restructuring in the UK', *Lloyds Bank Review*, October.

ECKSTEIN, O. (ed.) (1972) *The Econometrics of Price Determination*, for the Governors of the Federal Reserve System, Washington DC.

EEC COMMISSION (1976) *Report of the Study Group on Problems of Inflation* (mimeo), Brussels, March.

EICHNER, A. S. (1976), *The Megacorp and Oligopoly*, Cambridge University Press.

EISNER, R. (1960) 'A Distributed Lag Investment Function', *Econometrica*, January.

—— (1963) 'Investment: Fact and Fancy', *American Economic Review*, May.

—— and PIEPER, P. J. (1984) 'A New View of the Federal Debt and Budget Deficits', *American Economic Review*, March.

—— (1986) *How Real is the Federal Deficit?*, Collier Macmillan, London and the Free Press, New York.

ELLIS, F. (1978) 'Export Valuation and Intra-Firm Transfers in the Banana Export Industry in Central America', University of Sussex, D.Phil. thesis.

ERGAS, H. (1984) 'Corporate Strategies in Transition', in A. Jacquemin (ed.), *European Industry: Public Policy and Corporate Strategy*, Oxford University Press.

ESHAG, E. (1963) *From Marshall to Keynes: an Essay on the Monetary Theory of the Cambridge School*, Basil Blackwell, Oxford.

EVANS, D. and KAPLINSKI, R. (1985) 'Slowdown or Crisis?', *Bulletin of the Institute of Development Studies*, Sussex University, January 1985.

FELLNER, W. (1949) *Competition Among the Few*, Knopf, New York.

—— (ed.) (1977) *Contemporary Economic Problems*, American Enterprise Institute for Public Policy Research, Washington DC.

FISHER, I. (1911) *The Purchasing Power of Money*, Macmillan, New York, revised edition 1922.

FISHER, I. (1930) *Theory of Interest*, Macmillan, New York.

FORTE, F. (1965) *La Congiuntura in Italia*, Einaudi, Milan.

FRANKEL, J. (1976) 'A Monetary Approach to the Exchange Rate', *Scandinavian Journal of Economics*, May.

—— (1979) 'On the Mark: a Theory of Floating Exchange Rates Based on Real Interest Rate Differentials', *American Economic Review*, September.

FREEMAN, C. J. (1982) *The Economics of Industrial Innovation*, 2nd edition, Frances Pinter, London.

FREEMAN, C., CLARK, J. and SOETE, L. (1982) *Unemployment and Technical Innovation: a Study of Long Waves and Economic Development*, Frances Pinter, London.

FRIEDMAN, M. (1956) 'The Quantity Theory of Money: a Restatement', reprinted in Friedman (1969).

—— (1957) *The Theory of the Consumption Function*, Princeton University Press.

—— (1958) 'The Supply of Money and Changes in Prices and Output', reprinted in Friedman (1969).

—— (1959) 'The Demand for Money: Some Theoretical and Empirical Results', *Journal of Political Economy*, August.

—— (1962) *Price Theory*, Aldine, Chicago.

—— (1969) *The Optimum Quantity of Money and Other Essays*, Macmillan, London.

—— (1974) 'Monetary Correction: A Proposal for Escalator Clauses to Reduce the Costs of Ending Inflation', Occasional Paper no. 41, Institute of Economic Affairs, London.

—— and SCHWARTZ, A. (1963) *A Monetary History of the United States, 1867–1960*, Princeton University Press, New Jersey.

—— and MEISELMAN, D. (1963) 'The Relative Stability of Monetary Velocity and the Investment Multiplier in the United States 1897–1959', in *Commission on Money and Credit Stabilisation Policies*, Englewood Cliffs, New Jersey.

—— and FRIEDMAN, R. (1980) *Free to Choose*, Harcourt Brace Jovanovitch, and also Pelican Books and Secker & Warburg, London.

FRIEND, I. and KRAVIS, J. B. (1957) 'Consumption Patterns and Permanent Income', *American Economic Review*, May.

GALBRAITH, J. K. (1957) *The Affluent Society*, André Deutsch, London.

—— (1974) *Economics and the Public Purpose*, André Deutsch, London.

GAY, P. (1952) *The Dilemma of Democratic Socialism: Eduard Bernstein's Challenge to Marx*, Columbia University Press, New York.

GLC (1986) *The Ford Report*, Greater London Council, London.

GLYN, A., and SUTCLIFFE, B. (1972) *British Capitalism, Workers, and the Profits Squeeze*, Penguin Books, Harmondsworth.

GODLEY, W. and CRIPPS, F. (1983) *Macroeconomics*, Oxford University Press and Fontana.

GUILLAIN, R. (1970) *The Japanese Challenge*, Hamish Hamilton, London.

HAGUE, D. C., OAKESHOTT, W. E. and STRAIN, A. A. (1974) *Devaluation and Pricing Decisions, a Case Study Approach*, Allen & Unwin, London.

HALL, P. (1981) 'The Geography of the Fifth Kondratieff Cycle', *New Society*, 26 March.

HANSEN, A. (1949) *Monetary Theory and Fiscal Policy*, McGraw-Hill, New York.

—— with CLEMENCE, R. (1953) *Readings in Business Cycles and National Income*, Allen and Unwin, London.

HARCOURT, G. C. (ed.) (1977) *The Microeconomic Foundations of Macro-economics*, Macmillan.

HARROD, R. F. (1939) 'An Essay in Dynamic Theory', *Economic Journal*, March.

—— (1948) *Towards a Dynamic Economics*, Macmillan, London and New York.

—— (1963) *The Life of John Maynard Keynes*, Macmillan, London.

—— (1964) 'Are Monetary and Fiscal Policies Enough?' *Economic Journal*, December.

HECKSHER, E. (1958) 'The Effect of Foreign Trade on the Distribution of Income', in S. Mookejee (ed.), *Factor Endowment in International Trade: A Statement and Appraisal of the Hecksher–Ohlin Theory*, Asia Publishing House, Bombay.

HELLEINER, G. K. (1977) 'Transnational Enterprises and the New Political Economy of US Trade Policy', *Oxford Economic Papers 29*.

—— (1981) 'Intra-Firm Trade and the Developing Countries: an Assessment of the Data', in R. Murray (ed.), *Multinationals Beyond the Market*, Institute of Development Studies and Harvester Press, Brighton.

HICKS, J. R. (1937) 'Mr Keynes and the Classics', *Econometrica.*

—— (1949) 'Mr Harrod's Dynamic Theory', *Economica*, May.

—— (1950) *A Contribution to the Theory of the Trade Cycle*, Oxford University Press.

HILFERDING, R. (1910) *Das Finanzkapital*, trans. *Finance Capital*, Routledge & Kegan Paul, London, 1981.

HMSO (1985) *Economic Trends*, July.

HOBSON, J. A. (1902) *Imperialism: A Study*, Allen and Unwin, London.

HOLLAND, S. (ed.) (1972) *The State as Entrepreneur*, Weidenfeld and Nicolson, London.

—— (1975) *The Socialist Challenge*, Quartet Books, London.

—— (1976a) *Capital versus the Regions*, Macmillan, London and New York.

—— (1976b) *The Regional Problem*, Macmillan, London.

—— (1978) *Beyond Capitalist Planning*, Basil Blackwell, Oxford.

—— (1983) (ed.) *Out of Crisis*, Spokesman Books, Nottingham.

—— (1987) *The Market Economy* (vol. 1 of *Towards A New Political Economy*), Weidenfeld and Nicolson, London.

—— (forthcoming) *The Political Economy* (vol. 3 of *Towards A New Political Economy*), Weidenfeld and Nicolson, London.

HOLMES, P. M. (1978) *Industrial Pricing Behaviour and Devaluation*, Macmillan, London.

HOUSE OF COMMONS (1972) *Public Money in the Private Sector*, 6th Report from the Expenditure Committee, HMSO, London.

HOUSE OF COMMONS (1981) Third Report from the Treasury and Civil Service Committee, *Monetary Policy*, vol. I (Report) and vol. II (Minutes of Proceedings and Evidence) HMSO, February.

HOVELL, P. J. (1968) 'Export Pricing Policies', *District Bank Review*, September.

HUME, D. (1777) *Enquiries Concerning the Human Understanding*, ed. I. A. Selby-Bigge, Oxford University Press, 1902.

—— (1826) 'Of Money' and 'Of the Balance of Trade' in *Philosophical Works*, vol. III, reprinted in E. Rotwein (ed.), *Writings on Economics*, Nelson, Edinburgh, 1955.

HYMER, S. (1972) 'The Multinational Corporation and the Law of Uneven Development' in J. Bhagwati (ed.), *Economics and the World Order*, Macmillan, New York.

JONES, D. T. (1985) *The Import Threat to the UK Car Industry*, Science Policy Research Unit (SPRU), Sussex University.

KAHN, R. F. (1931) 'The Relation of Investment to Unemployment', *Economic Journal*, June.

KALDOR, N. (1961) 'Capital Accumulation and Growth', International Economic Association, *The Theory of Capital*, Allen & Unwin, London.

—— (1966) *Causes of the Slow Rate of Growth of the United Kingdom*, Cambridge University Press.

—— (1982) *The Scourge of Monetarism*, Oxford University Press.

—— (1983) *The Economic Consequences of Mrs Thatcher*, Duckworth, London.

KALECKI, M. (1954) *Theory of Economic Dynamics: An Essay on Cyclical and Long-run Changes in Capitalist Economy*, Reinhart, New York and Allen & Unwin, London.

KANT, Immanuel (1781 and 1787) *Kritik der Reinen Vernunft*, Felix Meiner Verlag, Hamburg, 1956.

KAY, J. A. and KING, M. A. (1978) *The British Tax System*, Oxford University Press.

KEYNES, J. M. (1930) *A Treatise on Money*, Macmillan, London (2 vols).

—— (1936) *The General Theory of Employment, Interest and Money*, Macmillan, London.

KINDLEBERGER, C. P. (1963) *International Economics*, Richard D. Irwin Inc., Homewood, Illinois.

—— (1967) *Europe's Postwar Growth: The Role of Labour Supply*, Oxford University Press.

KING, M. A. and FULLERTON, D. (1984) *The Taxation of Income from Capital*, University of Chicago Press.

KLEIN, L. R. (1951) 'The Life of John Maynard Keynes', *Journal of Political Economy*, October.

—— with GOLDBERGER, A. S. (1955) *An Econometric Model of the United States*, North-Holland Publishing Company.

KOJIMA, K. (1977) *Japan and a New World Economic Order*, Croom Helm, London.

KONDRATIEFF, N. D. (1925) 'The Long Wave of Economic Life', *Review of Economic Statistics*, vol. 17, no. 6, November. Originally published in *Voprosy Conjunktury*, 1925, and in German as 'Die Langen Wellender Konjunktur', *Archiv fur Sozialwissenschaft und Sozialpolitik*, 1926).

KONO, T. (1984) *Strategy and Structure of Japanese Enterprises*, Macmillan, London.

KRAVIS, J. B. and FRIEND, I. (1957) 'Consumption Patterns and Permanent Income', *American Economic Review*, May.

KUMAR, Manmohan S. (1984) *Growth, Acquisition and Investment*, University of Cambridge Department of Applied Economics, Occasional Paper no. 56, Cambridge University Press.

KURAIHARA, K. (ed.) (1954) *Post-Keynesian Economics*, Rutgers University Press.

KUZNETS, A. (1946a) *National Income: a Summary of Findings*, National Bureau of Economic Research, Washington DC.

—— (1946b) *National Product Since 1869*, National Bureau of Economic Research, Washington DC.

—— (1966) *Modern Economic Growth: Rate, Structure and Spread*, Yale University Press.

LAHERA, E. (1985) 'The Transnational Corporation and Latin America's International Trade', in CEPAL (United Nations Commission for Latin America and the Caribbean) *Review*, no. 25, Santiago, Chile.

LAIDLER, D. E. W. (1966) 'Some Evidence on the Demand for Money', *Journal of Political Economy*, February.

LALL, S. (1973) 'Transfer Pricing by Multinational Manufacturing Firms', *Oxford Bulletin of Economics and Statistics*, 35, August.

LAMASWALA, K. H. (1981) 'The Pricing of Unwrought Copper in Relation to Transfer Pricing', in R. Murray (ed.), *Multinationals Beyond the Market*, Harvester Press, Brighton.

LAMFALUSSY, A. (1961) *Investment and Growth in Mature Economies*, Macmillan, London.

LANGE, O. (1938) 'The Rate of Interest and the Optimum Propensity to Consume', *Economica*, February.

LEE, R. and OGDEN, P. E. (1976) *Economy and Society in the EEC*, Saxon House, Farnborough.

LEIJONHUFVUD, A. (1968) *On Keynesian Economics and the Economics of Keynes*, Oxford University Press.

LEON, P. (1967) *Structural Change and Growth in Capitalism*, Johns Hopkins University Press.

LEONTIEF, W. (1951) *The Structure of the American Economy 1919–1939*, 2nd edn, Oxford University Press.

LEVER, H. (1985) 'The Dollar and the World Economy: the Case for Concerted Management', *Lloyds Bank Review*, no. 157, July.

LEVINSON, C. (1979) *Vodka-Cola*, Gordon and Cremonsi, London.

LEWIS, W. A. (1954) 'Economic Development with Unlimited Supplies of Labour', *The Manchester School*, May.

—— (1984) 'The State of Development Theory', *American Economic Review*, March.

LIPIETZ, A. (1982) *De La Nouvelle Division Internationale du Travail*, Cepremap, Paris.

—— (1984) *The Globalisation of the General Crisis of Fordism*, Cepremap, Paris.

LIPSEY, Richard G. (1975) *An Introduction to Positive Economics*, 4th edn., Weidenfeld and Nicolson, London. 5th edn, 1979. 6th edn, 1983.

LIPSEY, Robert and KRAVIS, Irving (1985) 'The Competitive Position of US Manufacturing Firms', National Bureau of Economic Research Working Paper no. 1557.

LIST, F. (1885) *The National System of Political Economy*, Augustus Kelley, New York, 1966.

LITTLE, J. S. (1986) 'Intra-Firm trade and US Protectionism', *New England Economic Review*, January/February.

LOCKSLEY, Gareth (1981) 'A Study of the Evolution of Concentration in the Data Processing Industry', Commission of the European Communities, Brussels (mimeo).

LUCAS, R. E. (1972) 'Econometric Testing of the Natural Rate Hypothesis', in O. Eckstein (ed.), *The Econometrics of Price Determination*, for the Governors of the Federal Reserve System, Washington DC.

LUEDDE NEURATH, R. (1984) 'State Intervention in Forcing Direct Investment in South Korea', in *Development States in East Asia*, Bulletin of the Institute of Development Studies, April, vol. 15, no. 2, University of Sussex.

MACFIE, A. I. (1967) *The Individual in Society: Papers on Adam Smith*, Allen & Unwin, London.

MACHLUP, F. (1946) 'Marginal Analysis and Empirical Research', *American Economic Review*, September.

MADDISON, A. (1982) *Phases of Capitalist Development*, Oxford University Press.

MANDEL, E. (1975) *Late Capitalism*, New Left Books, London (first published as *Der Spatkapitalismus*, Surkamp Verlag, 1972).

MARRIS, S. (1985) *Deficits and the Dollar: The World Economy at Risk*, Institute for International Economics, Washington DC, December.

MARX, K. (1887) *Capital*, 3 vols, 1st English translation from 3rd German edition, and edited in English by Friedrich Engels. All references in this text to 1961 Foreign Languages Publishing House edition, Moscow.

MATTHEWS, R. C. O. (1959) *The Trade Cycle*, Oxford University Press.

MENSCH, G. (1975) *Das Technologische Patt*, Umschau Verlag.

—— (1979) *Stalemate in Technology*, Ballinger.

MICHALET, C. A. (1976) *Le Capitalisme Mondial*, Presses Universitaires de France.

MINFORD, P. and PEEL, D. (1980) 'The Natural Rate Hypothesis and Rational Expectations', *Oxford Economic Papers*, March.

MINISTERIO DE ECONOMIA Y COMERCIO (1982), 'Informacion Comercial Espanola', *Revista de Economia y Comercio*, no. 588/589, Madrid, August-September.

MODIGLIANI, F. and BRUMBERG, R. (1954) 'Utility Analysis and the Consumption Function', in K. Kurihara (ed.), *Post-Keynesian Economics*, Rutgers University Press.

MONOPOLIES COMMISSION (1973) *Chloriazepoxide and Diazepam*, HMSO, London.

MOORE, G. E. (1903) *Principia Ethica*, Cambridge University Press.

MURRAY, R. (ed.) (1981) *Multinationals Beyond the Market*, Harvester Press, Brighton.

MYRDAL, G. (1944) *An American Dilemma*, McGraw-Hill, New York.

—— (1957) *Economic Theory and Underdeveloped Regions*, Duckworth, London.

—— (1968) *Asian Drama: An Enquiry into the Poverty of Nations*, Allen Lane & Penguin, London.

NURKSE, R. (1952) 'Some International Aspects of the Problem of Economic Development', *American Economic Review*, May.

O'CONNOR, J. (1973) *The Fiscal Crisis of the State*, St Martin's Press, New York.

OECD (1982) 'Resources Devoted to Research and Development', *Science and Technology Indicators*, vol. 2, Paris.

OHLIN, B. (1933) *International and Inter-Regional Trade*, Harvard University Press.

OHMAE, K. (1985) *Triad Power: The Coming Shape of Global Competition*, The Free Press, New York, and Collier Macmillan, London.

PAVITT, K. (1971) 'The Multinational Enterprise and the Transfer of Technology', in J. H. Dunning (ed.), *The Multinational Enterprise*, Allen and Unwin, London.

PEARCE, J. (1981) *Under the Eagle: US Intervention in Central America and the Caribbean*, Latin American Bureau, London.

PENNANT-REA, R., with COOK, C. and BEGG, D. (1985) *Economics: Ancient and Modern*, The Economist, London.

PENROSE, E. (1959) *The Theory of Growth of the Firm*, Basil Blackwell, Oxford.

PERROUX, F. (1955) 'La Notion de Pôle de Croissance', *Economie Appliquee*, nos 1–2.
—— (1964) *L'Economie du XXe Siècle*, Presses Universitaires de France, Paris.
—— (1965) *Les Techniques Quantitatives de la Planification*, Presses Universitaires de France, Paris.
PETERS, H. R. (1981) *Grundlagen der Mesoekonomie und Strukturpolitik*, Haupt, Berne.
PHILLIPS, A. W. H. (1958) 'The Relationship Between Unemployment and the Rate of Change of Money Wage Rates in the United Kingdom 1861–1957', *Economica*, August.
—— (1962) 'Employment, Inflation and Growth', *Economica*, February.
POPPER, K. (1934) *The Logic of Scientific Discovery*, Hutchinson, London.
—— (1944) *The Poverty of Historicism*, Routledge and Kegan Paul, London.
POSTAN, M. M. (1967) *An Economic History of Western Europe 1945–1964*, Methuen, London.
PRESTON, Lee E. (1983) 'Mesoeconomics: Concepts, Analysis and Policy', Paper presented to the AFEE annual meeting, San Francisco, December.
RICARDO, D. (1816) *On the Principles of Political Economy and Taxation*, ed. P. Straffa (1951), Cambridge University Press.
ROBERTSON, D. H. (1950) *Some Recent Writings on the Theory of Pricing*, Economic Commentaries.
ROBINSON, Joan (1933) *The Economics of Imperfect Competition*, Basil Blackwell, Oxford.
—— (1949) 'Harrod's Dynamics', *Economic Journal*, March.
—— (1960) 'The Economics of Hyperinflation', in *Collected Economic Papers*, Blackwell, Oxford (originally published as 'The Economics of Inflation', *Economic Journal*, September 1938).
—— (1962) *Essays in the Theory of Growth*, Macmillan, London.
—— (1972) 'The Second Crisis of Economic Theory', *American Economic Review*, May.
ROSENSTEIN-RODAN, P. (1943) 'Problems of Industrialisation and South Eastern Europe', *The Economic Journal*, June-September.
ROUMELIOTIS, P. (1977) 'La Politique des Prix d'Importation et d'Exportation des Entreprises Multinationales en Grece', *Revue du Tiers Monde*, no. 70, April-June.
SAMPSON, A. (1973) *The Sovereign State of ITT*, Fawcett Crest and Stein & Day, New York.
SAMUELSON, P. (1939) 'Interaction Between the Multiplier Analysis and the Principle of Acceleration', *Review of Economic Statistics*, May.
—— (1976) *Economics*, 10th edition, McGraw-Hill, Kogakusha.
—— with SOLOW, R. M. (1960) *American Economic Review, Proceedings*.
SARACENO, P. (1983) 'Trenti 'Anni di Intervento Straordinario (1951–1980)', in *Studi SVIMEZ*, March-April.
SARGENT, T. J. and WALLACE, N. (1975) 'Rational Expectations, the Optimal Monetary Instrument and the Optimal Money Supply Rules', *Journal of Political Economy*, April.
SCHUMPETER, J. A. (1934) *The Theory of Economic Development*, Harvard University Press, Cambridge, Mass.

—— (1939) *Business Cycles*, Harvard University Press, Cambridge, Mass.

—— (1943) *Capitalism, Socialism and Democracy*, Allen & Unwin, London.

SCHWARTZ, A. and FRIEDMAN, M. (1963) *A Monetary History of the United States, 1867–1960*, Princeton University Press, New Jersey.

SCIBERRAS, E. (1977) *Multinational Electronics Companies and National Economic Policies*, JAI Press, Greenwich, Connecticut.

SCITOVSKY, T. (1952) *Welfare and Competition*, Allen & Unwin, London.

—— (1954) 'Two Concepts of External Economies', *Journal of Political Economy*, April.

SHEPHERD, W. G. (1979) *The Economics of Industrial Organisation*, Prentice Hall International, London.

SHONFIELD, Andrew (1965) *Modern Capitalism: The Changing Balance of Public and Private Power*, Royal Institute of International Affairs and Oxford University Press.

SILBERSTON, Z. A. (1970) 'Price Behaviour of Firms', *Economic Journal*, September.

SIMS, C. A. (1972) 'Money and Income and Causality', *American Economic Review*, September.

SLOAN, A. P. (1965) *My Years With General Motors*, Sidgwick and Jackson, London.

SMITH, A. (1759) *The Theory of Moral Sentiments*, London.

—— (1776) *The Wealth of Nations*, London.

SMITHIES, A. (1945) 'Forecasting Postwar Demand', *Econometrica*, January.

STEINDL, J. (1952) *Maturity and Stagnation in American Capitalism*, Basil Blackwell, Oxford.

STEWART, J. (1767) *An Enquiry Into the Principles of Political Economy*, ed. A. S. Skinner, University of Chicago Press, 1966.

STONIER, A. W. and HAGUE, D. C. (1957) *A Textbook of Economic Theory*, 2nd edition, Longmans, London.

SRAFFA, P. (1926) 'Laws of Returns under Competitive Conditions', *Economic Journal*.

—— (1960) *Production of Commodities by Means of Commodities*, Cambridge University Press.

STRACHEY, J. (1956) *Contemporary Capitalism*, Gollancz, London.

STREETEN, P. (1964) *The Economics of Integration*, Sythoff, Leiden.

SUNKEL, O. (1984) 'Transnational Enterprises in Latin America', mimeo, UN Economic Commission for Latin America and the Caribbean, Santiago.

SWEEZY, P. (1968) *The Theory of Capitalist Development*, Modern Reader Paperbacks, New York and London (first edition 1942).

SYLOS-LABINI, P. (1962) *Oligopoly and Technical Progress*, Harvard University Press (second edition 1969).

THIRLWALL, A. F. (1978) *Growth and Development*, Macmillan, London.

TINBERGEN, J. (1938) 'Statistical Evidence on the Acceleration Principle', *Economica*, May.

TREVITHICK, J. A. and MULVEY, C. (1975) *The Economics of Inflation*, Martin Robertson, Oxford.

TSIANG, S. C. (1959) 'The Theory of Forward Exchange and Effects of Government Intervention in the Foreign Exchange Market', *IMF Staff Papers* VII.

TUGENDHAT, C. (1971) *The Multinationals*, Eyre & Spottiswoode, Andover.

UNCTAD (1984) CASTRO, J. de, GANIATSOS, T., OLECHOWSKI, A. and QOQAYA, H., 'Changes in International Economic Relations in the Last Two Decades', in *Trade and Development*, Geneva.

UNITED NATIONS (1973) *Multinational Corporations in World Development*, New York.

VAITSOS, C. V. (1974) *Intercountry Income Distribution and Transnational Enterprise*, Clarendon Press, Oxford.

VERDOORN, (1949) 'Fattori che regolano lo sviluppo della produttivita del lavoro', *L'Industria*.

VERNON, R. (1974) *Big Business and the State*, Macmillan, London and Harvard University Press, Cambridge, Mass.

WALL, N. (1985) 'Money and Banking', Economic Briefs, *The Economist*, London.

WHITE, G. and others (1984) 'Development States in East Asia: Capitalist and Socialist', *Bulletin of the Institute of Development Studies*, Sussex University, April.

WICKSELL, K. (1955) *Lectures on Political Economy*, 2 vols (trans. L. Robbins), Routledge and Kegan Paul, London.

WITTGENSTEIN, Ludwig (1922) *Tractatus Logico-Philosophicus*, Routledge and Kegan Paul, London.

WORLD BANK (International Bank for Reconstruction and Development) (1985) *World Development Report*, Washington DC.

WRIGHT, D. M. (1949) 'Mr Harrod and Growth Economics', *Review of Economics and Statistics*, November.

ZINN, Karl-Georg (1978) 'The Social Market in Crisis', in S. Holland (ed.), *Beyond Capitalist Planning*, Basil Blackwell, Oxford.

Index

Abs, Herman, 223
absolute advantage, 147
  and multinationals, 162–3
accelerator principle, 85–92, 104–5,
  185–6
Ackley, G., 86–7, 285, 298–9
Adams, Stanley, 249–50
Africa, 8
Aglietta, M., 399–400
Algeria, 264
aluminium
  transfer pricing, 253
Amnesty International, 165
arbitrage, 414–15
armaments expenditure, see military
  spending
Armstrong, P., 218
Asimakopoulos, A., 37
Attali, J., 379
automobile industry, 221–2
  accelerator principle, 88–9

Bahamas, 254
Bain, J. S., 352
Bairoch, P., 3
Balogh, Thomas, 68, 205, 368
Bancor, 17
bank borrowing, 370–1
banking
  offshore, 254–5
Barber, Christopher, 372
Barker, B. L., 144
Barratt Brown, Michael, 75
Bartlett, Sarah, 255, 256
Beckman, Robert, 396–7
Begg, D., 311–13, 342–3
Berle, A., 61
Bismarck, 169
bond borrowing, 370–1
brand attachment, 59

brand names, 226
Brandt, W., 417, 420–1
Brazil, 8–9
Bretton Woods conference, 15–17
British Leyland, 221
Brooke, M. Z., 235
Brumberg, R., 53
budget, 92–3
business cycles, see trade cycles

capacity
  effect, 181
  excess, 386
  use, 227–9, 369
capital-labour ratio, 150, 153–4, 221–2
capital-output ratio, 100–2
capital stock adjustment, 87, 105,
  185–6
capitalism, 5, 406–8
car industry, see automobile industry
Carvel, John, 161
cash flow, 359–60
Chamberlin, Edward, 59
Chrysler, 221
Citibank, 256–7
Clark, J. B., 85
Clendenning, E. W., 414
Cobb-Douglas production function,
  150
Committee of Twenty, 20
commodities
  inflation, 371–2
  less developed countries, 8–9
  transfer pricing, 252–3
Common Agricultural Fund, 41
comparative advantage, 146–8, 163
competition, 66–8, 350–5; *see also*
  imperfect competition; unequal
  competition
  price, 352–4

Conservative Party, 325–7
consumption, 48–52, 292–3; see also
    over-consumption; under-
    consumption
consumption function, 49–56
Cook, C., 311–13, 342–3
Cooper, Charles, 268
copper
    transfer pricing, 253
corporation tax, 29
cost advantage, 163
cost and supply, 201–2, 204
cost-push, 337–57
Cowling, K., 196, 209–10
Cripps, F., 218
Crosland, Anthony, 5
crowding-out hypothesis, 308–9, 315
currencies, 191–3
currency transactions, 415
cycles, 389–98

Dalton, Hugh, 295
debt crisis, 11, 411
defence expenditure, see military
    spending
deflation, 10–11, 19, 330–78
    devaluation, 204–5
    IMF, 417–19
deflationary gap, 381–3
deflationary policy, 38
Delors, Jacques, 12
demand and redistribution, 55–7
demand and supply, 30–2, 48–96,
    305–6
    disjointed, 92
demand-pull, 337–8
Desai, Meghnad, 282–3, 314–15
Deutschmark, 13, 191
    revaluation, 213, 215–17
devaluation 19, 197–202, 204–12, 361,
    370; see also dollar devaluation;
    sterling devaluation
    IMF, 417–19
    multinationals, 206–12
Devlin, Robert, 255
disequilibrium, 85, 102–3, 107

liquidity preference, 290–1
disinflation, 359–61
disproportion, 380, 388, 398, 407
diversification, 65–7
dollar, 17–18
dollar devaluation, 18, 145, 190–3
Domar, Evesey, 98–9
Domar model, 99–103
Duesenberry, James, 51–2
Dunning, J. H., 163, 269

economic growth, see growth
Eichner, Alfred, 36, 58, 63–5, 88,
    305–6
Eisner, Robert, 34–5, 87–8
electronics industry
    pricing, 351–2
    transfer pricing, 250–1
elimination pricing, 210, 353
employment 97; see also full
    employment; unemployment
    women, 118
entrepreneurs, 68, 260
    consumption by, 54
entry barriers, 352–3
equilibrium, 102–3, 107
equity ownership, see share ownership
Eurobond markets, 371
Eurocurrency markets, 411–14
Eurodollar markets, 7, 18, 371
European Economic Community (EEC)
    Common Agricultural Fund, 41
    tariffs, 169
excess capacity, 286
exchange controls, 83
    abolition, 82
exchange rates, 15, 190–231
    devaluation, 197–202
    fixed, 190
    floating, 190, 317
    monetarism, 317–19
    survey of effect of changes in, 193–5
exogenous money supply, 316
expectations theory, 94, 137, 289
exports, 9–11
    effect of revaluation, 215–16

less developed countries, 8–9
  pricing, 236
  relative to imports, 133
  unrecorded, 232–3
  visible, 142–5, 160–2

Fairchild, 251–2
Fellner, W., 320
Ferranti, 352
finance, 60–3, 222–3
firms
  ownership, 61
  savings and investment, 57–65
fiscal incentives, 405
fiscal policy, 333–4
  Keynes' view, 22, 29
  mesoeconomic companies, 38
Fisher, Irving, 282, 284–5, 320
Ford Motor Company (of Britain), 79,
  89
  training and education, 166–7
  transfer pricing, 247–8
'Fordism', 399–401
foreign-exchange dealers, 415, 417
foreign investment, 82–3
France
  labour, 123
  Marshall Aid assistance, 12–13
  postwar planning, 102
  protection, 184
  state intervention, 69
  tariffs, 169
Frank, Andre Gundar, 311
free collective bargaining, 367
free competition, 350
Friedman, Milton, 1
  consumption function, 52–3
  inflation, 334–5, 366–7
  monetarism, 306–13
  state intervention, 24–5
  vs. Keynes, 27–9, 310–11
Friend, I., 53–4
full employment, 19, 24, 115–21, 312
  trade constraint, 115–16

Galbraith, J. K., 90, 186, 350

Geneen, Harold, 252
General Agreement on Trade and
  Tariffs (GATT), 13–15
General Arrangements to Borrow
  (GAB), 20
Glyn, A., 218, 345
Godley, W., 218
gold price, 190
government aid, see state intervention
government spending, see public
  spending
Group of Ten, 20
growth, 97–141
  history, 3–4
  labour, 122–4
  Marx, 106–7
  mixed economy, 137–40
  wages, 124
  warranted, 103–4, 186–7

Hague, D. C., 85, 161, 195, 205–6,
  252
Hall, Peter, 397
Hansen, Alvin, 86, 282, 295–7
Harrison, J., 218
Harrod model, 98–103, 108–10, 126,
  276–7
Harrod, Sir Roy, 16
Hecksher, Eli, 150
Hecksher-Ohlin model, 150–1
hedging, 414–15
Helleiner, G. K., 247
Hicks model, 111–15, 131–2, 133
Hicks, J. R., 108, 129, 295
Hilferding, R., 61, 110, 174, 222
Hobson, J. A., 110
Hoffman La Roche, 249–50
Holmes, Peter, 161, 195–7, 205–6
Honda, 68, 77, 222
Hong Kong, 164, 165–6
Hovell, P. J., 195
Howe, Geoffrey, 321, 326
Hume, David, 282–3
  vs. Ricardo, 283–4
Hymer, Stephen, 264

imperfect competition, 59, 208–10,
  300, 354
imports, 10–11
  less developed countries, 9
  relative to exports, 133
  tariffs, 167–75
income, 366–76
  consumption and, 49–54, 56
  distribution, 52–7, 367, 369
  expenditure and, 38–9, 363–6
  savings and, 49, 53–4, 56
income tax, 366
income policy, 282, 325, 367–8, 374–5
Industrial Reorganisation Corporation,
  68
industrialisation
  Japan, 183
  tariffs and, 168–9
infant industries, 174
inflation, 6–7, 19–20, 191–2, 330–78
  indices, 335
  Keynes vs. monetarism, 333–4
  monetarism, 334–5, 366–7
  multinational pricing, 356–7
  public spending, 133
  transfer pricing, 243–5
innovation, 215, 258–72, 385–6, 390–
  3
Institute of Economic Affairs, 325
interest rates
  Eurocurrency markets, 413–14
  Keynes, 22–3, 29, 293–5
  low, 294–5
  monetary policy, 63–4
  sensitivity, 302–4
intermediate economies (IMCs)
  foreign investment, 157–9
International Bank for Reconstruction
  and Development, see World Bank
International Monetary Fund (IMF), 2,
  15–17, 19–20, 41, 417–18
International Telephone and Telegraph
  Company (ITT), 252
international trade
  theory of, 39, 44–6, 142–67
International Trade Organisation, 14

investment, 142–89
  corporate, 57–63
  foreign, 82–3
  grants, 405
  induced, 104–5, 111
  long-term, 112–14, 134
  planning, 135–6, 186–7
  savings and, 48–9, 57–65
  supply, 57–8, 83–94
IS curve, 295–8; see also LM/IS model
Italy
  labour, 122–3
  Marshall Aid assistance, 13

Japan
  corporate finance, 62, 68
  exports, 133, 203–4, 213–14
  investment planning, 186–7, 223–4
  keiretsu, 177, 187, 222
  labour, 123, 166–7
  labour costs, 130, 133, 214
  Ministry of International Trade and
    Industry (MITI), 78, 183, 222–3,
    263
  multinational companies, 20–1
  protection, 182–4
  public spending, 139
  quality effect, 214–15
  research and development, 262–3
  state intervention, 62, 68–9, 222–3
  tariffs, 169, 171, 177
  training and education, 166–7
  zaibatsu, 177, 183
Jenkins, Roy, 32
Jones, Dan, 79, 208, 401
Joseph, Sir Keith, 325

Kahn, Richard, 69
Kaldor, Nicholas, 126–8, 205, 260,
  367–8, 407
Kalecki, Michael, 36–7, 87, 97, 103,
  367–8
Kant, Immanuel, 316
Kawasaki, 68
Kay, J. A., 241, 347
Keynes, John Maynard, 1, 22–9

consumption function, 49–51, 56
employment, 97
inflation, 331–3
liquidity preference, 290
marginal efficiency of capital, 84, 289
monetarism, 281–2, 287
on Marx, 381
rate of interest, 293–5
savings and investment, 48–9, 57–8,
288–9, 291
stock markets, 289–90
state intervention, 24–5
vs. Friedman, 27–9, 310–11
vs. the Keynesians, 25–7
Keynesians, 25–7
Keynesianism, 11
Kindleberger, Charles, 21, 122–3, 128,
175
King, M. A., 241, 347
Klein, Lawrence, 36
Kojima, K., 159, 162, 224
Kondratieff, N. D., 395–7
Kravis, Irving, 145, 160
Kravis, J. B., 53–4
Kumar, Manmohan S., 301
Kuznets, Simon, 50, 101

labour, 116–18; see also capital/labour
ratio
costs, 129–30, 163–5, 342–4, 373–4
Europe, 122–3
Japan, 123, 166–7
low-cost, 163–4, 343–4
supply, 126–8, 342–3
Lahera, E., 159, 265
Laidler, D. E. W., 326
Lall, S., 247
Lamaswala, K. H., 253
Lange, Oscar, 295
Lawson, Nigel, 70, 315, 321, 326–7
Leijonhufvud, Axel, 25, 102, 282, 291,
297
Lenin, 110
Leon, Paolo, 36
Leontief, Wassily, 151
less developed countries

capital and labour, 156–7
low-cost labour, 163–5, 343–4
oil prices, effect of increase in, 7–9
tariffs, 173
see also Third World countries
Lever, Harold, 415
Levinson, Charles, 225
Lewis, Arthur, 122
licenses, 268
Lipietz, A., 399–400
Lipsey, Richard, 21, 29, 309
accelerator principle, 85–6
international trade, on, 44–5
technology and innovation, 258–9
Lipsey, Robert, 145, 160
liquidity preference, 290–2
liquidity trap, 311
List, Friedrich, 172–4
Little, Jane Sneddon, 145, 168, 193–6,
247
LM curves, 297–8
LM/IS model, 295, 298–300
Locke, John, 282
long-term investment, 112–14
public spending, 134–5
Luedde Neurath, R., 178

Machlup, F., 195
macroeconomic policy
vs. microeconomic policy, 41–3
Maddison, Angus, 3, 5
Mandel, Ernest, 408
Manley, M., 417, 420–1
manufacturing industry, 407
marginal efficiency of capital, 84, 185–
6
Marris, Stephen, 402, 415
Marshall Aid Programme, 11–13
Marx, K., 37, 61
disproportion, 380–4
economic growth, 106–7, 125–6
labour, 117, 118–19, 341
Matsushita Electric Company, 225–6
Means, G., 61
Mensch, Gerhard, 397
mesoeconomic enterprise, 45–6

accelerator principle, 88–9
expansion, 65–7
investment planning, 135–6
Japanese, 68, 76–7
power, 350–1
profits, 60
role of, 37–9
supply, 43
mesoeconomy, 2, 36
definition, 40–1
Michalet, C. A., 278
microeconomic policy
vs. macroeconomic policy, 41–3
microcomputers, 187
military spending, 28, 407
Minford, Patrick, 137, 324
minimum lending rate, 63, 323–4
mixed economy, 29–34
growth, 137–40
long-term investment, 113–14
Modigliani, F., 53
monetarism, 2, 11, 22, 27–9, 281–329
Friedman, 306–13
inflation, 334–5, 366–7
state intervention, 24–5
monetary policy, 29
mesoeconomic companies, 37–8
money demand, 290
money supply, 283, 308, 309, 319–20, 325, 367
exogenous, 316
public spending, 133
monopolistic competition, see imperfect competition
monopolistic pricing, 350
monopoly, 174, 350
Moore, G. E., 316
motor industry, see automobile industry
Motorola, 251–2
multinational companies, 2, 39–40, 44; see also mesoeconomic enterprise
absolute advantage, 162–3
devaluation, 206–12
low-cost labour, 163–5, 343–4
pricing, 356–7
protection, 180–2

revaluation, 225–9
sales strategy, 271–2
tariffs, 171, 177–8, 180–2
transfer pricing, 301–2
visible exports, 142–5
multiplier, 69–83
export, 78–9
mesoeconomic, 76
microeconomic, 75–6
multinational, 79–82
Myrdal, Gunnar, 75, 155, 363–4, 379

National Enterprise Board, 68, 221
national insurance contributions, 366
Neo-Keynesians, 27
neoclassical economists, 111
New International Economic Order (NIEO), 2
new products, 215, 390–1; see also innovation
newly industrialised countries; see also less developed countries
foreign investmnt, 157–9
Nixon, President, 313
no-entry pricing, 210
nuclear defence spending, 407
Nurske, Ragnar, 362–3, 380

Oakeshott, W. E., 161, 195, 205–6, 252
offshore banking, 254–5
offshore tax havens, 254
Ohlin, Bertil, 36, 150, 155–6, 159, 266
Ohmae, K., 77, 203, 213, 225
oil price, 6–9, 145, 372
oligopoly, 41–2, 60, 196, 209–10
opportunity cost, 148–50
Organisation for Economic Cooperation and Development (OECD), 2
Organisation for European Economic Cooperation (OEEC), 12
Organisation of Petroleum Exporting Countries (OPEC), 6–7, 18, 145
over-consumption, 398
overdrafts, 320

over-investment, 384
over-supply, 386, 398

patents, 268
Peel, D., 137
Pennant-Rea, R., 311–13, 342–3
Penrose, Edith, 219, 355
permanent income hypothesis, 53, 57, 307
Perroux, François, 36, 102, 104, 117, 394
Peru, 255
Peters, H. R., 36
petroleum, 6–7
pharmaceutical industry
    transfer pricing, 248–50
Phillips, A. W. H., 308
Phillips curve, 337, 339–42
Pieper, P. J., 35
planning, 90–1
    investment, 135–6, 186–7
Plessey, 250–1
Postan, M. M., 127
press freedom, 165
Preston, Lee E., 36
price competition, 352–4
price controls, 26, 360, 367
price cutting, 350
price-making power, 176–7, 299–300, 348–9
price restraint, 350, 360–1, 368
price umbrellas, 219, 355–6
prices, 366–76
    effect of revaluation, 215–16, 218–19
Prices and Incomes Board, 368
pricing, 348–57
    elimination, 210, 353
    multinationals, 356–7
privatisation, 31
product cycles, 266–7, 274
productivity, 4, 6
profits, 124–6
property development, 407
protection, 168–84
    France, 184

Germany, 184
Japan, 182–3
multinationals, 180–2
public-sector borrowing requirement (PSBR), 293, 322, 325
public spending, 29–34, 133–40, 366
    Keynes vs. monetarists, 24–5
    long-term investment, 134–5

quality effect, 214–15
quantity theory of money, 282–6, 307–8

rational expectations, 94, 137, 289
recession, 5–6
    less developed countries, 8–9
reflation, 360–1
reflationary policy
    mesoeconomic companies, 38
regional grants, 405
Remmers, H. L., 235
research and development, 261–4, 272–3, 278
revaluation
    international trade, 212–24
    multinationals, 225–9
Ricardo, D., 48, 146–8
    vs. Hume, 283–4
Robinson, Joan, 37, 59, 65, 110–11, 348
robotics, 187, 215
Roosevelt, President, 151, 334
Rosenstein-Rodan, P., 380
Roumeliotis, P., 247, 253

sales
    global strategy, 271–2
Sampson, Anthony, 252
Samuelson, P., 21
    accelerator principle, 86
savings, 292–3
    consumption and, 49–52
    income and, 49, 53–4, 56
    interest-responsive, 288
    investment and, 48–9, 57–65
    outflow, 83

Say, George Baptiste, 48
Schumpeter, J. A., 68, 391–4
Schwartz, Anna, 310
Sciberras, Edmond, 250–1, 271
Scitovsky, Tibor, 148
SDRs, 17, 20
Selective Employment Tax (SET), 126, 128
services industry, 407
share ownership, 370
Shaw, George Bernard, 381
Shepherd, W. G., 301
shipbuilders, 222–3
Shonfield, Andrew, 5, 69
Silberston, Z. A., 195
Singapore, 164, 165–6
SKF, 227, 229, 369
Smith, Adam, 14
   free trade, 172
Smithies, Arthur, 51, 54
social distribution, 408–9
social groups
   consumption, 51, 54–5
South Korea, 164
Special Drawing Rights (SDRs), 17, 20
speculation, 414–15
spending, see consumption
stagflation, 330, 358–66, 369–70
Standard Oil, 355
state intervention, 68–9, 402–6
   finance capital, 222–3
   France, 69
   Germany, 222–3
   Japan, 62, 68–9, 222–3
   Keynes vs. monetarists, 24–5
   less developed countries, 164
   subsidies, 405
sterling devaluation, 128, 145, 191–3, 195, 205–6
Stewart, James, 283
stock markets, 61, 289–90
Stonier, A. W., 85
Strachey, John, 388
Strain, A. A., 161, 195, 205–6, 252
Streeten, Paul, 363–4
subsidies, 405; see also state
   intervention

Sugden, R., 196, 209–10
Sunkel, Osvaldo, 410
supply, 42; see also demand and supply
   cost and, 201–2, 204
   investment, 57–8, 83–94
Sutcliffe, B., 345
Suzuki, 68
Sylos-Labini, Paolo, 36, 305, 347

Taiwan, 164
takeovers and mergers, 348
tariffs, 167–80
tax avoidance, 241–2
tax havens, 243, 254
tax incentives, 405
tax policy, see fiscal policy
'tax-push' inflation, 372
taxation, 29–30, 406
technology transfer, 258–75
Texas Instruments, 251
Thatcher, Margaret, 83, 293, 325, 364
theory of the firm, 36
Third World countries; see also less
   developed countries
   foreign investment, 157–9
Thirlwall, A. F., 100
thrift, 293
Toyota, 76–7
   training and education, 166–7
trade, 142–89
trade constraint
   full employment, 115–16
trade cycles, 389–98
trade unions, 338–48, 373
   less developed countries, 164–5
   training and education, 166–7
transfer booking, 256
transfer parking, 256–7
transfer pricing, 15, 180–1, 232–80
   accounting, 257–8
   inflation effect, 243–5
   multinationals, 301–2
   tax avoidance, 241–2
   tax havens, 243, 254
Tugendhat, Christopher, 227, 229

under-consumption, 380–4, 398
unemployment, 4–6, 130–1, 315, 327
unequal competition, 210, 352–3
United Nations Conference on Trade
    and Development (UNCTAD), 2
United States
    agricultural exports, 151
    deficit, 34–5
    dollar, 17–18
    dollar devaluation, 18
    economy, 151–2
    exports, 160, 161–2
    Marshall Aid Programme, 11–14
    multinational companies, 20–1
    New Deal, 151, 334
    tariffs, 169

Vaitsos, C. V., 247
Verdoorn, 126
Vernon product cycle, 266–7, 274
Vernon, Ray, 183
Voss, Henk, 248, 282

Wade, Robert, 401
wage restraint, 282
wages, 131–2
    controls, 325, 367
    costs, 129–30, 163–5, 342–3, 373–4
    growth, 124

indexing of, 325
warranted growth, 103–4
    planning, 186–7
West Germany
    labour, 122
    Marshal Aid assistance, 13
    protection, 184
    quality effect, 214–15
    specialisation, 217–18
    state intervention, 222–3
    tariffs, 169, 172
White, Gordon, 401
White, Harry, 16
Wicksell, K., 285
Wilson, Harold, 368
Wittgenstein, Ludwig, 42, 310
women
    employment, 118
working class
    consumer needs, 51
World Bank, 15–16, 41
world debt, 11
Wright, David McCord, 98, 102

Yamaha, 68
Yen, 191
    revaluation, 213, 225–6

Zambia, 8
Zinn, Karl Georg, 217, 218

Printed in Great Britain
by Amazon